Westminster Daily Devotional

Gordon Kenworthy Reed

Fortress Book Service & Publishers
800-241-4016
www.fortressbookservice.com
fortressbk@aol.com

Grateful acknowledgment is made to:

Fortress Book Service & Publishers for use of *The
Fortress Edition of the Shorter Catechism*; Christy
Rodriguez for use of her picture of the Rose
Window of the North Transept of Westminster.

Scripture taken from the New King James Version®.
Copyright 1982 by Thomas Nelson, Inc. Used by per-
mission. All rights reserved.

Quotation on back cover from Warfield, B. B.
Selected Shorter Writings, Vol. 1, Phillipsburg, NJ:
P & R Publishing, 1970. pp. 381–384.

ISBN-13: 978-0-9793718-3-7
ISBN-10: 0-9793718-3-X

Printed in the United States of America

Book design, layout, and production by Martha Nichols/aMuse Productions

Question #1: What is the chief end of man?

Answer: Man's chief end is to glorify God, and to enjoy Him forever.

Scripture Reading: 1 Corinthians 10:31; Colossians 3:12-17

It has been said, and it is probably true, that few people ever ask the really important questions in life. The three most frequently asked questions in America are (1) How can I lose weight? (2) Where can I park my car? (3) Who won the ball game? Here in the first question of the Catechism, we are faced with life's most important question, *What is the chief end of man?* Another way of asking the same question might be, *Who am I?* or *Why am I here?* or *What is the meaning of my life?*

This question in the Catechism speaks to such things as reality and purpose. Are these things important for you? How long has it been since you gave serious thought to the meaning and purpose of your life?

Notice that the Catechism asks "what is the *chief* end of man?" By this word, recognition is given to those many lesser purposes which may occupy our thoughts and efforts. These things may be of greater or lesser importance in relation to each other, and some are of considerable importance indeed. Where we live and what career we pursue are important matters to consider. The choice of one's life-mate is far more important than career or location. However, the Catechism (and the Bible) recognize that there is one great purpose which overshadows all others, and for which we have been created and redeemed. Just to know that there is ultimate purpose and meaning to life is both exciting and comforting. To have one great purpose also gives added significance to all other purposes and goals. This means that all we do—working, planning, education, recreation, family life, and even eating and sleeping, have meaning which flows from the one great purpose. That purpose centers in God and our relationship to Him. The meaning of our existence depends upon this, and our greatest joy flows from it.

Prayer: Great and Gracious God, our Father in heaven, help us this day to glorify You by loving You with all our heart, mind and strength, and by obeying Your commands in thought, word and deed, that we may also enjoy You forever. Through Jesus Christ our Lord, to Whom, with You and the Holy Spirit be all praise, honor and glory forever. Amen.

Hymn for the day:
The Gloria Patri

PRAYERS & REMINDERS

Question #1: What is the chief end of man?

Answer: Man's chief end is to glorify God, and to enjoy Him forever.

Scripture Reading: John 16:19-24; Philippians 4:4-7

Our chief end above all lesser ones is to glorify God and to enjoy Him forever. This means that we must first know Him as He reveals Himself to us. It means to acknowledge His existence and His sovereignty. We are His people and the sheep of His pasture. To glorify God is to reflect His image and character, which may only be done by those who have been drawn to Him by irresistible grace and saving love in Christ Jesus. To glorify God is to honor Him by faith and obedience.

But to fulfill our purpose we must also enjoy Him. In fact, it would be impossible to glorify Him unless we do enjoy Him. This is a warm and glowing word. It is a word to gladden our hearts, for it is a love word. Joy and love walk hand in hand, and loving Him who first loved us is pure and holy joy. It is for this we were created and redeemed. It is for this we live, for unless we know, glorify, enjoy and love Him, we do not really live at all; we merely exist.

The final word in this formula for true living is *forever.* The answer is incomplete without it. It is the *foreverness* of our relationship to God that brings the greatest joy and enables us to truly glorify Him. Forever means heaven. It means a new heaven and a new earth, a restored and perfected creation. The last two chapters in the Bible, Revelation 20 and 21, give us a glimpse of what *forever* really means. Just a glimpse is more glorious than our minds can comprehend. But to know that we shall one day live in the midst of that wonder is truly glory and joy forever.

Prayer: Dear Father, may our greatest joy always be to bring honor and glory to You. Lead us in paths of righteousness for Your name's sake. Thank You for that blessed forever You have promised to Your people; that forever with You and with all Your people in heaven, through our Lord Jesus Christ. Amen.

Hymn for the day:
Rejoice, the Lord is King!

PRAYERS & REMINDERS

Question #2: What rule has God given to direct us how we may glorify and enjoy Him?

Answer: The Word of God which is contained in the Scriptures of the Old and New Testaments is the only rule to direct us how we may glorify and enjoy Him.

Scripture Reading: Psalm 119:1-8

The obvious truth that life centers in and derives its meaning from our relationship to God has led mankind on a frantic search for God from the earliest days until now. Tragically, that quest has never succeeded and is always doomed to failure. In fact, this quest has led mankind further and further away from God and has left us frustrated at every turn. Does this mean we may never know the true God? Does this mean we will never know our true meaning nor achieve our destiny? No, there is a way—God's way—by which we may know how to glorify and enjoy our Creator–Father. God has come in search of us that we might learn of Him and that in His search for us, we may find Him.

How and where do we learn to know, glorify, and enjoy Him forever? There are many attempted answers to this question, but there is only one that is true and right: *In the Bible alone.* The ability to know God depends directly upon this truth. All other avenues lead to error, darkness, and in the end, they lead to death and separation from God forever. The latter part of the first chapter of Romans comments on the futility of fallen creatures' search for the true creator. It is a depressing catalog of failure and futility.

However, God has revealed Himself. He has made it possible even for little children to know Him and to find salvation and life by that true knowledge. Do you know Him? Have you found His salvation?

Prayer: Father, thank You for Your Holy Word, the Bible. What a precious treasure You have given us. Thank You that all Scripture is God breathed, so that we have Your very Word, the saving truths You have revealed. May we receive it with great joy, read it, and meditate upon it day and night. Within the written Word, may we come face to face with the living Word, even our Lord Jesus Christ in whose name we pray. Amen.

Hymn for the day:
Holy Bible, Book Divine

PRAYERS & REMINDERS

Question #2: *What rule has God given to direct us how we may glorify and enjoy Him?*

Answer: The Word of God which is contained in the Scriptures of the Old and New Testaments is the only rule to direct us how we may glorify and enjoy Him.

Scripture Reading: Psalm 119:9-16

Isn't it wonderful to know that God has given us a book which enables us to know Him? The Bible is God's autobiography. He is the author and He is the subject. The Bible teaches many things. It tells us of the creation of the universe and the origin of life. It tells us who we are and how we came to be. It reveals the story of evil and how we became sinners. It traces the history of the human race in broad strokes and focuses on the lives of individual people who lived on earth long ago. These things and many more are found in the Bible, but above all things, events and people, the Bible reveals God, the one true and living God, Father, Son, and Holy Spirit. Because the Bible alone reveals Him, it is also the only rule (guide) to direct us how we may glorify and enjoy Him.

People search for truth in many places, but there is one and only one source of pure and totally reliable truth, and that is God's revealed Word as recorded in and through the Bible. Yes, God reveals Himself in nature and through the processes of history, but the Bible alone, God's written revelation, interprets natural revelation in a way that is always consistent with His written revelation. When we attempt to turn this around, and interpret the Bible through the eyes of science or history, or any other form of natural revelation, we will inevitably misread that natural revelation. It goes without saying (or it should) that we must never, never use the opinions and presuppositions of unbelievers, no matter how impressive their credentials, to discredit God's revealed Word.

PRAYERS & REMINDERS
_____
_____
_____
_____
_____
_____
_____
_____
_____

Prayer: Thank You, Father, for giving to us a reliable and infallible book of truth by which we may understand all truth. Thank you for revealing Yourself, Your majesty, power, and wisdom through creation and providence. Thank you for the Holy Spirit, Who enables us to see and understand the marvelous truths of Your Holy Word. We pray in Jesus' name. Amen.

Hymn for the day:
Open My Eyes That I May See

> **Question #2: What rule has God given to direct us
> how we may glorify and enjoy Him?**

Answer: The Word of God which is contained in the Scriptures of the Old and
New Testaments is the only rule to direct us how we may glorify and
enjoy Him.

Scripture Reading: Psalm 119:33-40

A popular song a few years ago made the proud boast, *I did it my way*. The
Christian knows the important thing is to live life God's way. What we must never
forget is that God's way may be found only in God's book, the Bible.

The Bible is a most remarkable book! God used many different people to write
His book. These people lived in different times and civilizations. They wrote in
many different styles and found themselves in many different circumstances. They
all had one thing in common. They were channels through whom God, the Holy
Spirit, revealed the Living Word. Although written in the languages of long ago,
the Bible has been translated into many languages all over the world and has lost
nothing in the translation! The Bible you hold in your hand and read with your
eyes or hear with your ears is God's Holy Word. Let the scholars debate which
translation is the best one. (They will disagree.) Ask your pastor to recommend a
good translation and read it as God's Word, for this is what it is. As you read it,
the Holy Spirit will open your mind and heart and you will learn from this book
how you may glorify and enjoy God.

In the Bible, God speaks to us not only through precepts, commands and
promises, He also speaks to us through the stories of people and events. In the
Old Testament we read about the lives of real people: Adam and Eve, Noah and
his family, Abraham and Sarah, their son Isaac, and his son Jacob. We read of
Moses, David, and all the kings and prophets. In the New Testament, we read about
Jesus and His disciples, and all the people to whom Jesus ministered. We read the
exciting story of the early church and how the
gospel began to spread around the world. In the
book of Revelation we read of the ultimate triumph
of God and good, over Satan and evil and of the
coming new and perfected creation in which believers will live and forever serve our glorious King and
Savior.

Prayer: Great and Gracious God, thank You for
Your wonderful and perfect revelation, the Bible.
Thank you for all the truth revealed in Your Word.
Help us to receive it by faith and live by its glori-
ous light, through Jesus Christ our Lord. Amen.

Hymn for the day:
Break Thou the Bread of Life

PRAYERS & REMINDERS

Question #3: What do the Scriptures principally teach?

Answer: The Scriptures principally teach what man is to believe concerning God, and what duty God requires of man.

Scripture Reading: Psalm 119:41-48

The Bible is God's Word. That Word is all-sufficient for all believers. The third question of the Shorter Catechism focuses on the central truths of Scripture. The key word here is what do the Scriptures *principally* teach. The Bible is mainly concerned with two matters: doctrine and duty, faith and life. It touches on many other things. It supplies the foundation on which all truth rests, and serves as glasses through which we may understand the truth that comes to us through nature or other avenues. By God's grace, there is much truth available to our minds for our good. But it must be understood in light of God's special revelation, the Bible.

Before looking at those matters the Bible principally teaches, let us say that wherever the Bible speaks, it speaks truth. When it speaks in the area of human nature, history, or the physical sciences, it speaks truth and is the only infallible interpreter of all other truth in these areas. When human learning and the teaching of Scripture appears to be in conflict, there are only two possibilities. Either human learning is in error or we have misunderstood Scripture.

Understand this. Most people in the world, even in the so-called Christian West, do not believe the Bible is true and infallible. To them it's just another religious book. You must make a choice between their opinions and the unchanging truth of God's Word. Sometimes the wisdom of the world seems so logical and attractive. *There is a way that seems right to a man, but its end is the way of death.* God's Word is the way of life everlasting.

Prayer: O Father, help us to trust Your word. Feed our hungry minds and hearts on the bread of life. Grant that our lives may bear witness to our confidence in Your Word, by our obedience to your commands, and faith in Your promises. Guard us from the danger of placing the opinions of man above the great truths of Your Word. We pray this in Jesus' name for His sake. Amen.

Hymn for the day:
How Firm a Foundation

PRAYERS & REMINDERS
_____
_____
_____
_____
_____
_____
_____
_____
_____

January 7

Question #3: What do the Scriptures principally teach?

Answer: The Scriptures principally teach what man is to believe concerning God, and what duty God requires of man.

Scripture Reading: Psalm 119:49-56

Now what are the major concerns of Scripture? First of all, the Bible teaches truth about God. It tells us what we must believe about Him and about ourselves. All human efforts to discover who God is have failed to give a clear and saving knowledge of the great Creator-God. All human concepts fall short of the true God and dishonor Him. This is true of the most primitive ideas derived from nature and of the most sophisticated concepts drawn from philosophical reasoning. Only in the Bible do we meet the true and living eternal God. In its pages alone do we see His true character and glorious nature, His sovereignty, His holiness and His grace. Never could nature or the mind of man discover the wonder of His love and saving power. It is only in the Bible we learn that *God so loved the world, that He gave His only begotten Son, that whosoever believeth in Him should not perish, but have everlasting life.*

Only in the Bible can we find such lofty concepts of God as are revealed in Genesis 1 & 2, in Exodus 1-20, and in the Psalms, such as Psalm 8, 19, 103, 119, and 139. The book of Isaiah is filled with lofty and glorious visions of God and His holiness and power. The revelation our Lord Jesus gave us about the Father both in the Gospels and in the book of Revelation fill us with awe and wonder. What a great and gracious God meets us in the pages of His written Word. The Bible, God's holy Word, opens for us a window into the throne room of God. There we may by faith behold Him who is our true God and our loving Father in heaven.

Prayer: Holy Father, how grateful we are for Your precious book, the Bible. Thank You for the glory we see in Your Word. Thank You even more for the grace which we learn from Your Word and experience by faith. Once more we pray that our lives will be shaped and molded by Your Word and our hopes secured by Your promises. Accept our prayers we ask in Jesus' name, and for His sake, Amen.

Hymn for the day:
Lord, Speak to Me That I May Speak

PRAYERS & REMINDERS

Question #3: What do the Scriptures principally teach?

Answer: The Scriptures principally teach what man is to believe concerning God, and what duty God requires of man.

Scripture Reading: Psalm 119:57-64

The Bible also reveals that this God requires certain duties of us. It comes as a surprise to the modern Christian to discover that God requires anything! We have become so accustomed to a gospel that speaks only of what God gives us that we tend to forget He also requires from us loving obedience to His commands. *He has shown you, O man, what is good; and what does the Lord require of you but to do justly, to love mercy, and to walk humbly with your God?* This verse from Micah is a beautiful, simple summary of all the Scripture teaches about our duty to God. The Christian who wants to please and honor, to glorify and enjoy God forever, will carefully search the Scriptures of both Old and New Testaments to discover the duty we owe Him, In so doing we will come to know that we must love the Lord our God with all our heart, mind, and strength, and our neighbor as ourselves.

The Bible tells us that God is infinite and eternal. This means He has always been and that He is everywhere. We cannot possibly know everything about God. We only know what He Himself shows us, and that is enough for our salvation. He is unchangeable. We may always depend upon God. Since He is absolutely perfect in every way, He has never changed nor will He. Something perfect cannot change for the better. The God who created the world is the God who sent His Son to die for sinners. God is not only infinite, eternal, and unchangeable in His being, He is all these things in all His attributes. His wisdom, power, holiness, justice, goodness, and truth are all forever perfect and complete. He will always be these things and you may know Him, trust Him, and love Him in complete confidence.

PRAYERS & REMINDERS

Prayer: Father, thank You for showing us in Your Word the duties you require of us. Help us to believe and obey all Your commands and precepts, and to accept all Your promises. We believe Your Word is truth. Help us to lovingly obey You always, and to live by Your holy law. In Jesus' name we pray. Amen.

Hymn for the day:
Trust and Obey

Question #4: What is God?

Answer: God is a Spirit, infinite, eternal and unchangeable, in his being, wisdom, power, holiness, justice, goodness, and truth.

Scripture Reading: Isaiah 40:18-31

What a question! Who and what is God? Dr. J. B. Green says in his *Harmony of the Westminster Standards: As a definition of undefinable deity, the Shorter Catechism is unexcelled, unequaled by any word of man.* This is high praise, but well-deserved. This question was a major concern of those saintly scholars at Westminster who wrote the Confession and the Catechisms. It is said that after many long hours of study and discussion, a prayer was offered to God for help in answering this most difficult of all questions. The prayer began, *O God, Thou who art Spirit, infinite, eternal and unchangeable in Thy being, wisdom, power, holiness, justice, goodness, and truth.* God answered the prayer for help in the words of the prayer itself.

It was Jesus who said, *God is Spirit.* This simply means that God exists forever and always as Spirit. He does not have a body like man, yet He knows, sees, speaks and hears, and loves and rejoices. This invisible Spirit God has no body like man, but He has character and personality. The Bible tells us that He is infinite and eternal. That means He has always existed and that He is everywhere. We cannot possibly know everything about God. We only know what He Himself shows us and that is enough for our salvation. He tells us that He is unchangeable. We may always depend upon God. Since He is absolutely perfect in every way, He has never changed, nor will He. When something is perfect, it cannot change, and God is perfect and complete in Himself.

Prayer: O God, You who are infinite, eternal and unchangeable in Your being and all Your attributes, we praise You for showing us who You are. Help us to love, honor and obey You always. For Jesus' sake. Amen.

Hymn for the day:
Immortal, Invisible, God Only Wise

PRAYERS & REMINDERS

Question #4: What is God?

Answer: God is a Spirit, infinite, eternal and unchangeable, in his being, wisdom, power, holiness, justice, goodness, and truth.

Scripture Reading: Lamentations 3:21-33

The God who created the world is the God who sent His Son to die for sinners. He is the God of wisdom, love and power. He invites us to Himself and draws us into a saving relationship with Him by grace which is irresistible. God is not only infinite, eternal and unchangeable in His being, He is all these things in all of His attributes. His wisdom, His power, His holiness, His justice, His goodness and His truth are all forever perfect and complete. He will always be all these things, and you may know Him, trust Him, and love Him in complete confidence. He will never change.

As a little child, I had the idea that my parents would always be there for me, that they would always be strong and healthy and wise and provide all my needs. As I grew older, so did they, and eventually they became old and feeble and dependent on others. Then when they were very old and very feeble, God took them home, and their *youth was renewed as the eagle.* Our great heavenly Father, who is perfect in Himself and in all aspects of His character, always will be perfect, and through His Son Jesus Christ we may know Him and become His beloved children. He has promised never to leave us nor forsake us. In Psalm 27:10 we read, *When my father and my mother forsake me, then the Lord will take me up.* It is sad but true that sometimes fathers and mothers may and do forsake their children to seek their own selfish and sinful pleasures, but God, our heavenly Father will not forsake His children for whom His beloved Son Jesus died on Calvary's cross. Do not be afraid. God is faithful and He will always be there for you.

Prayer: Dear Father, what a merciful and faithful God You are. Help us to know that *the eternal God is our refuge and underneath are the everlasting arms.* May we ever trust and lean on those everlasting arms of grace and help. Teach us to also be faithful to You and to each other. In Jesus' name we pray. Amen

Hymn for the day:
God Will Take Care of You

PRAYERS & REMINDERS

_____
_____
_____
_____
_____
_____
_____
_____
_____

Question #5: Are there more Gods than one?

Answer: There is but one only, the living and true God.

Scripture Reading: Jeremiah 10

After asking the question, *What is God?,* next comes the question, *Is He alone or are there more Gods than one?* The simple affirmation is expected, but it is far more profound and far more important than it may appear at first glance. Although the ancient forms of polytheism may no longer be evident, at least as they once appeared, yet the basic sin is still very much with us and that in many forms.

The one living and true God is the God who meets us in the Bible. He is the God and Father of our Lord Jesus Christ. The Muslim claims to have the sole knowledge of God, whom he calls Allah. He claims this God may only be known through his prophet Mohammed. We must never fall into the trap of thinking this is the same God we worship, but by another name. Many modern cults claim that the God they teach is the God of the Bible, but then they add their own ideas and subtract from the teachings of the Bible. Again we must recognize that their god is not the God of the Bible, nor the God our Lord Jesus came to reveal. So when those nicely dressed young men who are missionaries for some well disguised cult come to your door, just remember they do not represent the one living and true God. Their god is not the God and Father of our Lord Jesus Christ.

This may sound very intolerant in this day of political correctness, but God is the one and only great *I Am* who reveals Himself to us. It is neither sensible nor safe to reject God's own revelation of Himself in favor of a man-made image.

Prayer: Thank You, Father, for being who You are. What a mighty and glorious God You are. We accept Your self-revelation and reject all attempts to make You less than what and Who You are. You are our Creator, Redeemer and Friend, through Jesus Christ our Lord. Amen.

Hymn for the day:
O Worship the King

PRAYERS & REMINDERS

Question #5: Are there more Gods than one?

Answer: There is but one only, the living and true God.

Scripture Reading: Isaiah 40:12-31

False gods are not limited to pagan superstitions nor cultic misrepresentations. They exist in our sophisticated culture, too. These are the gods of materialism and self-indulgence, the gods of sex and drugs. In the Western world, atheism in the form of secular humanism has almost become the official religion of many nations, including the United States, and once great Christian nations such as Holland, Scotland and Sweden. Furthermore, whatever claims first place in our lives becomes our god. Yet these things are not gods, but vain imaginations and delusions.

In the book of Isaiah we read the prophet's scathing ridicule of idolatry. *To whom will you liken Me, and make My equal, and compare Me that we should be alike?* He then goes on to describe the futility of praying to a god who is made by the mind and hands of man, a god that must be carried from place to place, and set in its place so that people may bow down before it and offer it worship and ask of it help. *Though one cries out to it, yet it cannot answer nor save him out of his trouble.* Anytime we attempt to bring God down to a comfortable and manageable Deity whom we may manipulate to our own purpose and comfort, we are as pitiful as the ancient who bowed before his idol of wood, stone or precious metal.

There is but one only, the living and true God who reveals Himself in His holy Word and requires of us that we love Him with all our heart, strength, and mind. He is worthy, and He alone, to receive the worship, praise, and adoration of our hearts and lives. Let us bow before Him now and offer Him our prayers and praises.

PRAYERS & REMINDERS

_____

_____

_____

_____

_____

_____

_____

_____

_____

Prayer: Mighty God, heavenly Father, You alone are the true and living God. We worship and adore You. Protect us from the idolatry of thinking You are less than who You are as revealed in Your holy Word. Help us to walk before You today in a manner worthy of Your great name.

Hymn for the day:
Mighty God, While Angels Bless Thee

Question #5: *Are there more Gods than one?*

Answer: There is but one only, the living and true God.

Scripture Reading: I Kings 18:20-39

A little child was once asked, "How many gods are there?
He replied, "There is only one God."
"How do you know this?" he was asked.
"Because there is only room for Him alone, because He fills the whole universe."

Good answer, wise child. There is a beautiful and powerful story in the Old Testament which speaks to this truth. It is the story of Elijah and the prophets of Baal. On the slopes of Mt. Carmel, the man of God challenged the four hundred false prophets to prove the existence and power of their god Baal, to whom the people of Israel had turned as their god in place of the one true God. He suggested a contest. Two altars would be erected, one for Baal, and one for Yahweh. Sacrifices were to be placed on these altars, but no fire would be lit. The God who answered with fire from heaven to burn up the sacrifices would be known as the true God. The people of Israel consented to the test, and wicked king Ahab could not avoid the challenge.

In spite of their most frantic efforts, the four hundred prophets of Baal could not call down fire to consume their offering, for their god was but a figment of their imagination, an idol of stone. After their failure, Elijah prayed to the one living and true God. He prayed God would demonstrate His power and glory in such a way that no one could doubt He and He alone was truly God.

God answered Elijah's prayer with fire from heaven which consumed the offering and the altar and burned away the idolatry in the hearts of His people. So as we faithfully serve this same true God and prove by our redeemed lives His power and glory, we join hands with Elijah in the work of God, and lead others to cry out, *"The LORD, He is God! The LORD, He is God!"*

Prayer: O God, may our lives bear such a pure and holy witness to You and Your mighty power that the fatal grip of idolatry may be broken in the lives of many. We do not ask this for our glory, but for Your glory alone, through our Lord and Savior Jesus Christ. Amen.

Hymn for the day:
I Sing the Almighty Power of God

PRAYERS & REMINDERS

Question #6: How many Persons are there in the Godhead?

Answer: There are three Persons in the Godhead: the Father, the Son, and the Holy Spirit; and these three are one God, the same in substance, equal in power and glory.

Scripture Reading: John 1:1-18

After affirming that there is only one true God, the Catechism asks the question, *In how many persons does this one God exist?* It then goes on to affirm that there are three persons in the Godhead, the Father, the Son and the Holy Spirit, and also affirms that though there are three persons, yet the three are one. Of course we cannot fully understand this truth, but since it is revealed in Scripture, we dare not reject it as many do. If we reject everything in Scripture we cannot understand, we have little left. We reject the accusation that Christians believe in three Gods, but we only affirm that which Scripture affirms, that the Father is God, The Son is God, and the Holy Spirit is God.

There is no truth concerning God that is not relevant and urgent in the life of the believer. Everything He chooses to tell us about Himself has direct bearing on who we are and what we must know and believe about Him. This is most certainly true of the doctrine of the Trinity. Let's try to see how this truth applies to our salvation and our experience as Christians.

We begin in eternity, before the world was created. In the covenant of redemption, God, the Father, elected to Himself a people chosen before the foundation of the earth to be His own. God, the Son, in perfect unity and harmony with the Father's will, covenanted to win their salvation by His incarnation and atonement. God, the Holy Spirit, covenanted to apply both the electing grace of the Father and the atoning grace of the Son to each one of the elect. Thus the three persons of the Godhead are directly and immediately involved in our salvation. We see this glorious reality in the High Priestly prayer of our Lord Jesus as recorded in John 17. Jesus spoke to the Father and mentioned in that prayer, ... *the men whom You have given Me out of the world. They were Yours, You gave them to Me, and they have kept your word.*

PRAYERS & REMINDERS

Prayer: Great God, Father, Son and Holy Spirit, we come before You once more in awe and wonder of who You are. Help us to give You praise constantly for our salvation, and for the blessed covenant You made within the counsels of the Trinity for our salvation. In Jesus' name, Amen.

Hymn for the day:
Come, Thou Almighty King

Question #6: How many Persons are there in the Godhead?

Answer: There are three Persons in the Godhead: the Father, the Son, and the Holy Spirit; and these three are one God, the same in substance, equal in power and glory.

Scripture Reading: Matthew 28

Prayer is one of the most precious of God's gifts to the elect. It is our link with heaven, our lifeline to God. In prayer we come before the Father and address Him. Jesus taught us about prayer when He said, *In this manner, therefore, pray: Our Father in heaven.* Furthermore, the Lord Jesus told us that we are to come before the Father in His (Jesus') name. It is only through our Lord Jesus Christ that we may come to the Father. The good news is that we may come to the Father and that His Son gives us free access into the Holy Presence.

The Spirit's role in prayer is equally important. Even though we do not know how to pray as we ought, the blessed Spirit makes intercession for us *with groanings which cannot be uttered.* The Spirit convicts of sin, and at the same time assures us and encourages us to confess our sins in prayer to the Father by the name and blood of His Son. The normal pattern of prayer, then, is to come to the Father, through the Son, by the Holy Spirit.

But since all three, Father, Son and Holy Spirit, are *the same in substance, equal in power and glory*, we may feel free to call upon God the Son, or God the Spirit at need, and be assured that we are accepted through the merit and intercession of Christ, and the indwelling and interceding Holy Spirit. When we pray to the Father, *Your will be done*, we bring honor and glory to Him and to the Son and Spirit. In so praying we also acknowledge that our whole purpose for living is to bring glory and praise to our great triune God, Father, Son and Holy Spirit.

Prayer: Father, we come to You in Jesus' name, led by the Holy Spirit to seek You. May our lives be a testimony to Your almighty grace. May all our relationships with each other be patterned after the blessed unity which exists within Your triune nature. We ask these things in the name of our Savior, Your Holy Son, Jesus. Amen.

Hymn for the day:
Praise God from Whom All Blessings Flow
(Doxology)

PRAYERS & REMINDERS

Question #6: How many persons are there in the Godhead?

Answer: There are three persons in the Godhead: the Father, the Son, and the Holy Spirit; and these three are one God, the same in substance, equal in power and glory.

Scripture Reading: Genesis 1

Christian family life reflects the pattern of the Trinity. In the creation of our first parents, Adam and Eve, the Bible tells us: *So God created man in His own image; in the image of God created He him; male and female created He them.* So ideally in Christian marriage there is intended to be oneness of heart and purpose, intimate love and abiding peace and harmony. Yet there is distinction and respect of persons, just as there are distinct persons within the Godhead. The Son is eternally begotten of the Father, and the Spirit proceeds from the Father and the Son. So in God's plan for Christian marriage the parents are to beget children with whom they share nature and a loving relationship.

Yes, the doctrine of the Trinity lies at the very heart of all Christian theology, and underlies all Christian experience. It is an essential doctrine, and it is also a very precious truth. Be warned, beloved: any person or any system which does not clearly and forthrightly proclaim the Biblical doctrine of the Trinity is to be rejected and avoided. Let God be God, and let Him tell us in His Word of His glorious triune nature. Study diligently this great doctrine and all the many Scriptures which support it, both from the Old Testament as well as the New Testament. You will be surprised as you study to discover how many veiled yet sure references there are in the Old Testament, which support the doctrine of the Trinity. At the same time it is more clearly revealed through the words, prayers, and actions of the Lord Jesus. The command to *baptize them in the name of the Father and of the Son and of the Holy Spirit* came from the risen Lord and lays the foundation for the expansion of the Church, and the full development of the great Trinitarian creeds of the early Church.

PRAYERS & REMINDERS

_____

_____

_____

_____

_____

_____

_____

_____

_____

Prayer: O Lord, our Lord, how excellent is Your name in all the earth. We marvel at the glorious saving truth of the Trinity which You have revealed to us. May we always honor You and glory in this precious truth. For the sake and glory of our Savior, God the Son, Amen.

Hymn for the day:
God Our Father, We Adore Thee

January 17

> ## Question #7: What are the decrees of God?

Answer: The decrees of God are His eternal purpose, according to the counsel of His will, by which, for His own glory, He has foreordained whatever comes to pass.

Scripture Reading: Psalm 33

The expression *the decrees of God* has a strange and even ominous sound for many people. This is unfortunate and need not be so. The problem is that we associate the word *decree* with human authority, and even human despotism. God's decrees are entirely different from that. To understand this truth which the Catechism presents, you must begin with the nature and character of God. In our earlier studies we discovered that God who is Spirit is absolutely perfect in His being and in all His glorious attributes. He is the God of wisdom, power, holiness, justice, goodness, and truth. Apart from this understanding of God, the idea of His decrees might be frightening indeed. However, because of God's character we may rejoice in the concept and praise Him with great joy for His decrees.

Our God has an eternal purpose. This purpose is rooted in His own nature. He has a plan for all His creation. Everything He does, all His great and gracious acts, flow from this purpose. His purpose is consistent with His character. In His wisdom He has decreed that we must act as responsible moral beings, accountable to Him for our behavior. However, the ultimate outcome does not rest upon man's free will and human decisions and choices. The plan of the ages was not the product of a committee! (Praise God!) The book of Job raises the question, *With whom did He (God) take counsel?* It also answers that question with a resounding, *No one!* For in God alone is all wisdom and knowledge, and no one can add to or take away from Him.

Prayer: Lord, You have been our dwelling place in all generations. Before the mountains were brought forth, or ever You had formed the earth and the world, even from everlasting to everlasting You are God. Thank You for your great plan and purpose for Your people, and that our confidence is in You alone. Through our Lord Jesus Christ we pray. Amen.

Hymn for the day:
O God, Our Help in Ages Past

PRAYERS & REMINDERS

Question #7: What are the decrees of God?

Answer: The decrees of God are His eternal purpose, according to the counsel of His will, by which, for His own glory, He has foreordained whatever comes to pass.

Scripture Reading: Psalm 104

What does it mean to say that God foreordained whatever comes to pass? Simply that God is in control. He rules and overrules in all things. There is not one atom in this entire universe out of His control. Not a sparrow falls to the ground without the Father. He has numbered the hairs of your head and the stars in the heavens. Why has God done this? Why has He foreordained all things which come to pass? His is the highest and purest motive of all. For His own glory He has decreed all things. Again let it be said that His purpose is rooted in His character. There can be no higher motive than complete perfection.

Just a few swift glances at Scripture will show that this is not a new doctrine. It is not something the Westminster Divines dreamed up. It is a Biblical doctrine. One might say it is the Biblical doctrine of God. It is taught from the first to the last. It meets us in the first two chapters of Genesis in the account of creation. Nothing could be more obvious than to say that creation was according to a plan. As the Biblical record tells the story of creation, it reveals an orderly and well-planned world. This truth is also written into the very fabric of creation itself. Because God foreordains whatever comes to pass, we may observe His handiwork and see both purpose and plan in all His creation. As the beautiful creation unfolded, God said of this mighty work of His own hand, *Behold it was very good*, to which we add our own amen.

Prayer: How thankful we are, our God, that You are in control of the world You created, and also of all Your creatures. We are so very thankful that You concern Your great self with all the works of Your powerful hand. We are even more thankful that we are important to You, and the objects of Your eternal plan, even our salvation, through Christ our Savior. Amen.

Hymn for the day:
How Great Thou Art

PRAYERS & REMINDERS

_____

_____

_____

_____

_____

_____

_____

_____

_____

Question #7: What are the decrees of God?

Answer: The decrees of God are His eternal purpose, according to the counsel of His will, by which, for His own glory, He has foreordained whatever comes to pass.

Scripture Reading: Ephesians. 1:1-14

In God's covenant with Adam, a high and holy purpose is revealed. This purpose was written into the soul of Adam and Eve. It was to be their guide and motive for living. It held the promise of grace and glory for the whole human race. Even in the fall, God's purpose was not frustrated but rather fulfilled. With our finite minds, we may never be able to understand this, but we may trust the infinite mind of God, who works all things according to the counsel of His own will, ruling and overruling in all things.

The same is true in the story of Noah. God's plan included both judgment and mercy: judgment on the unbelieving world, mercy upon the man who found favor with God and who lived the life of faith and obedience. There are many, many prophecies in the Old Testament about the coming Messiah. How was this possible? Only because it was a part of God's plan and purpose which He revealed to the prophets. The New Testament adds its testimony to this doctrine. The book of Ephesians is one great example. In chapter 1, Paul tells us that God's gracious decrees mean that we have every spiritual blessing in Christ. We are chosen in Him before the foundation of the world. This choice of love results in our adoption into His family. By this we have redemption and the forgiveness of our sins. By this we are assured that we are heirs of God and joint-heirs of Christ. Now does the expression *the decrees of God* sound ominous? Far from it. It is a blessed word, a sweet and lovely sound in the believer's ear and heart.

Prayer: You have chosen us, dear Lord, to be Your very own from before the foundation of the earth. You have predestined us in Christ for adoption as Your beloved children. How blest we are! How infinitely gracious and kind You are. For these and all Your mercies, we bless Your holy name. In the name of Jesus Christ we pray. Amen.

Hymn for the day:
My Hope Is in the Lord

PRAYERS & REMINDERS

Question #8: How does God execute His decrees?

Answer: God executes His decrees in the works of creation and providence.

Scripture Reading: Psalm 147

What good is a plan or even a purpose if you lack the ability to carry out or execute that plan? Our God has decreed whatever comes to pass, and He is actively at work to carry out His decrees. This is a very important truth to understand. There are those who think of God as some sort of impersonal force or first cause who is not directly involved in His creation. The Deists thought of God as simply winding up the universe and then letting it run under its own power.

This is not the God of the Bible. God executes His own decrees. It is true that He uses secondary causes and He uses people to carry out His purposes, but it is God who executes His decrees by whatever means.

Many years ago (how many I refuse to say on the grounds it might tend to date me) our football coach used to say something like this: "Boys, I have a good game plan, but it will only win the game for us if you execute the plays." That is something of what we mean when we say that God not only purposes and plans, but He is constantly at work to carry through and carry out His plan. Because He is infinite, eternal and unchangeable in His wisdom, will, and power, He is abundantly able to accomplish all His holy will. Thus all that exists was created from nothing by the word of His power, and by that same power He upholds and sustains His creation and His creatures, and this includes you and me. How comforting to know our great heavenly Father knows and loves each one of His children, and will bring us all to glory in His good time.

Prayer: How great and wonderful are Your works, O God. How infinite is Your wisdom and power. We kneel in awe before You and give to You the praise and worship of which You alone are worthy. We rest in Your goodness and mercy forever. Through our Lord Jesus Christ we pray. Amen.

PRAYERS & REMINDERS

_____

_____

_____

_____

_____

_____

_____

_____

_____

Hymn for the day:
God, All Nature Sings Thy Glory

Question #8: How does God execute His decrees?

Answer: God executes His decrees in the works of creation and providence.

Scripture Reading: Job 36

Several years ago, a couple visited my study to ask for help in saving their marriage, which was about to come to a tragic and needless end. After a few counseling sessions, it became clear that one of their major problems was simply a lack of any understanding of an organized pattern of living. They had no family schedule, no budget, no plans for the present or future. I worked with them for some time, developing some organization to their lives. In short, we worked out a "game plan" for their marriage. They both agreed this was needed. They both worked with me to develop a mutually agreeable plan, and verbally committed themselves to it. I felt good about the future for them. However, within a few weeks, they were back again with more of the same problems as well as some new ones. They had a good plan, but they were unable or unwilling to work out the plan.

What if God were unable or unwilling to execute His decrees? They would have no meaning at all for Him or for us. Fortunately, this is not the case. In fact, the Catechism is very specific in answering the question, *How does God execute His decrees?* He executes His decrees in the works of creation and providence. Later we shall see in more detail what these works are, and how they individually serve to execute His decrees. For now, let it be said that God is personally involved in His creation and especially in the lives of His precious elect. He is the fountainhead of life itself. His great work of creation was simply the beginning of the execution of His eternal purpose. God, the grand designer, became God, the great contractor, when He began to say: Let there be…, and it was so.

Prayer: Father, we thank You that You not only purpose and plan all things, but that You work all things by Your wisdom and power. There is no limit to Your power to accomplish all Your Holy will. May we live in that confidence and rejoice in Your unfailing promises. We ask this through Christ, our Lord and Savior. Amen.

Hymn for the day:
Holy God, We Praise Your Name

PRAYERS & REMINDERS

_____

_____

_____

_____

_____

_____

_____

_____

_____

_____

Question #8: How does God execute His decrees?

Answer: God executes His decrees in the works of creation and providence.

Scripture Reading: Psalm 139

Upon the completion of this work of creation, after creating man, male and female, in His own image, God immediately began to execute His decrees in the work of providence. This work involved and still involves His provision and care for all His creation, His ordaining and foreordaining all events and circumstances which affect our lives. In the Bible you seldom, if ever, find an expression like *the wind blew* or *it rained.* Rather you may read, *God sent a great wind* or *God caused it to rain.* Even when the Scriptures do not specifically say that such things were done by the hand of God, the implication is clearly there.

God is not remote, or even far away. He is ever near and ever at work executing His decrees. What a blessing and comfort to know that it is God who works all things together for good to those who love Him and are called according to His purpose. This includes you and your life as it unfolds. Of course there are hard times and many questions in our hearts as to why God allows certain things to happen which seem to make no sense to us, or even worse which seem contrary to our understanding of His will. In the extremes of life we may even echo the noble words of faith, spoken by Job in the extremity of his suffering, *Though He slay me, yet will I trust Him.* As believers in Jesus Christ, we know that even when death approaches us, and our earthly life comes to an end, we may add to those words of Job by saying, *For we know that if our earthly house, this tent, is destroyed, we have a building from God, a house not made with hands, eternal in the heavens.*

Prayer: O God, there are many times we do not understand Your will and Your ways, but may we never fail to trust You with all our hearts, even when we do not understand. Help us to know that the Lord is our helper, therefore we will not fear. In Jesus' name we pray. Amen.

Hymn for the day:
All That I Am I Owe to Thee

PRAYERS & REMINDERS

Question #9: What is the work of creation?

Answer: The work of creation is God's making all things from nothing, by the word of His power, in the space of six days, and all very good.

Scripture Reading: Psalm 148

The whole matter and question of creation has been a major issue for the entire twentieth century and even before. Naturalistic scientists have disputed the biblical account of creation for many years. This has been especially true since the work of Darwin and his disciples. The capitulation of the believing community to this philosophy of unbelief has been and continues to be one of the major tragedies and scandals of modern-day Christianity. This surrender and compromise has not only included liberalism within the church, but a large portion of the evangelical sector as well.

However, in these latter days, God has raised up a band of dedicated scientists who are also Bible-believing Christians. These scholars have taken up the task of presenting the case for scientific creationism. They have called into question the basic assumptions of naturalism, and have exposed the folly of theistic evolutionism. Yet their greatest contribution is not their ability to debate the issues scientifically, but rather to call believers back to the statements of Scripture as the foundation for all truth and the starting point for the exploration of the natural world.

Many Christians fail to see the importance of accepting this biblical account of creation. *What difference does it make?* This question is frequently heard, and the implied answer is: *None whatsoever!* But wait! Isn't there a deeper issue involved? Isn't the real issue the reliability of Scripture as God has given it? If the biblical account of creation is only to be accepted as a broad literary framework by which we affirm that in some manner and at some time, and in some way God was involved in the world coming into being, then may we not also use the same principles in considering the incarnation, the cross and the resurrection?

Prayer: O Lord, our Lord, how manifold are all Your works. In wisdom You have made them all. Give us faith to believe Your word is truth and that You made all things of nothing in the space of six days, and all very good. We pray in the name of the Living Word, Jesus Christ. Amen.

Hymn for the day:
Praise Ye, Praise Ye the Lord

PRAYERS & REMINDERS

Question #9: What is the work of creation?

Answer: The work of creation is God's making all things from nothing, by the word of His power, in the space of six days, and all very good.

Scripture Reading: Hebrews 11:1-17

When the Catechism and the Bible speak of creation, they use the term in a very unique sense. We talk about creating a work of art. In the strictest sense this is not a creation at all, but a forming into other shapes of existing materials. We may talk of an author creating a novel or a poem, but again, this is not really a creation, but a use of things which have existed previously to produce a work of literature. The Catechism teaches us that God made all things of nothing. In the book of Hebrews we read these words: *By faith we understand that the worlds were framed by the word of God, so that the things which are seen were not made of things which are visible.* This teaches us that when God created the world, He brought into being things which did not exist before. He did not take primeval ooze and shape it into the world that now is. The Bible is very explicit in telling us that the Lord God spoke the Word, and those things described came into being then and there. The Gospel of John reminds us that it was by the eternal Word that all things were made, and that without Him was not anything made that was made.

Does it require faith to believe these things? Of course it does. But it also requires faith to believe in the very existence of a Creator, and of a Redeemer. This does not imply a blind faith in the presence of overwhelming evidence to the contrary. Faith in God as Creator, and faith in the Genesis account of creation is supported by much evidence written into the creation by the Creator Himself. The idea that nothing made everything is the basic assumption of naturalistic scientism, and for this basic assumption there is no evidence whatsoever to support such a naïve philosophy.

PRAYERS & REMINDERS

_____

_____

_____

_____

_____

_____

_____

_____

_____

Prayer: We thank You and praise You, O Lord, that Your glory is displayed in Your vast Creation. Guard our minds and hearts that we may not be carried away by the vain philosophies of this world. We pray in the name of Him in whom are hidden all the treasures of wisdom and knowledge, our Lord Jesus. Amen.

Hymn for the day:
For the Beauty of the Earth

Question #9: What is the work of creation?

Answer: The work of creation is God's making all things from nothing, by the word of His power, in the space of six days, and all very good.

Scripture Reading: Exodus 20:1-11

A word needs to be said concerning the time required for creation. Both the Bible and the Catechism make it very plain that it all took place in the space of six days. Since the ascendancy of Darwinian evolutionism in the scientific world, the Church has been frantically explaining to itself and to one and all that the word *day* in Hebrew does not always require a twenty-four hour period of time. It is pointed out that the word *day* appears several times in Scripture referring to an era, or period of time. This is true. But where in Scripture does the word *day* appear used in the same explicit, detailed way as seen in Genesis 1? Where in all Scripture does the expression appear: *And there was evening and there was morning, one day,* meaning an era, or an indefinite period of time? While it is not impossible to think of the word *day* as referring to an indefinite period of time, it is certainly a strained interpretation in the context of Genesis 1. If God is God, why is it a problem to believe His own description of creation without apology? If God did not make *all things of nothing in the space of six days and all very good,* why did He so explicitly say that He did? These words are not just found in Genesis 1 and 2, but also in Exodus 20 and Deuteronomy 5. Christians are not required to re-evaluate their theology to accommodate a naturalistic philosophy of science. Indeed quite the opposite, we are forbidden to place the wisdom of fallen man above the revealed Word of God.

One final word concerning creation, *it was all very good.* Of course it was, for it was made by the God who is Himself good, and wise and holy. Of all God's works we may say, *And behold it was very good.*

Prayer: O Lord, may we hold Your revealed Word in awe and reverence. Help us to stand on the solid ground of Scripture and not on the sinking sand of unbelief. We pray this through Christ, the solid Rock of Ages. Amen.

Hymn for the day:
Let All Things Now Living

PRAYERS & REMINDERS

Question #10: How did God create man?

Answer: God created man male and female, after His own image, in knowledge, righteousness, and holiness, with dominion over the creatures.

Scripture Reading: Genesis 1:26-31

God created man! This may well be the most significant statement in the entire catechism. It is foundational for every other truth we know concerning mankind. It is absolutely essential to know this and to say this before we ever discuss the doctrines of grace. The Christian faith as a body of revealed truth rests upon this foundation: God created man. The creation of man took place on the sixth day of creation, thus signifying that everything else in the order of creation was in preparation for the grand finale when God created man.

This biblical truth places us in direct and irreconcilable conflict with the evolutionary myths concerning the beginning of the human race. There is simply no meeting ground for the one who believes that an all-wise, powerful and holy God created man for His own glory and according to His eternal plan, and those who believe that man is the product of evolutionary chance with no meaning or purpose to his existence. All attempts at reconciliation between these two opposing philosophies end up in unacceptable compromise for the believer.

If we were created in God's image and for His glory, then life has meaning and purpose. Created to serve and honor the Creator is the highest possible view of the worth of human life and its sublime uniqueness. Of course all creation was made for God's glory and His purpose. But there is a vast difference between purpose for inanimate and non-rational beings, and the purpose for those created in God's image with self-consciousness and *in knowledge, righteousness and holiness, having the law of God written in their hearts, and the power to fulfill it.*

PRAYERS & REMINDERS

_____

_____

_____

_____

_____

_____

_____

_____

_____

_____

Prayer: O Lord our God, You created us in Your own image, and have promised a restoration of that image through the redeeming work of Christ, our Lord and Savior. Help us to conduct ourselves as those who have been thus created, and will be thus restored. In Jesus' name. Amen.

Hymn for the day:
Joyful, Joyful We Adore Thee

Question #10: How did God create man?

Answer: God created man male and female, after His own image, in knowledge, righteousness, and holiness, with dominion over the creatures.

Scripture Reading: Genesis 2:7-25

The Catechism notes the Biblical emphasis that both male and female were created in God's image. There are two things which deserve special attention at this point. In light of the present situation in our confused and lost culture, we need to affirm both. First, there is a basic equality between the sexes. Both male and female were created in God's image. The idea that either man or woman is somehow qualitatively superior to the other is not biblical. The biblical teaching of spiritual leadership that God has given to the husband and father may be, and often is, distorted into a non-biblical male chauvinism thinly veiled as the "reformed view." On the other hand, a radical feminist position which denies the role of headship to the husband and father is off-base as well.

The second thing we must affirm is the distinction between the sexes. The Bible repeatedly makes the point that there is a distinction between the sexes, and that distinction is built into the nature of man, both male and female. A clear understanding and affirmation of this biblical truth would go a long way towards refuting some of the most serious errors gaining acceptance in our society today, such as homosexuality and radical feminism. We are not male or female by some blind chance, nor do we have the right to decide which we shall be, or to attempt to alter that identification by some bizarre effort through medical science without a moral base derived from God's Word. Jesus very emphatically affirmed both the distinction between the sexes and the biblical norm for marriage in these words from Mark 10:6-8, *But from the beginning of the creation, God made them male and female. For this reason a man shall leave his father and mother and be joined to his wife, and the two shall become one flesh.*

Prayer: Lord, we rejoice in Your creation of us, whether male or female. We also rejoice greatly that You have ordered and established marriage for the welfare and happiness of mankind. May we always honor You in our gender, and the faithful acceptance of Your wisdom in so making us in Your image. Through Jesus Christ our Lord. Amen.

Hymn for the day:
All Creatures of our God and King

PRAYERS & REMINDERS

Question #10: How did God create man?

Answer: God created man male and female, after His own image, in knowledge, righteousness, and holiness, with dominion over the creatures.

Scripture Reading: Psalm 8

There has always been some confusion in the minds of many concerning the image of God in man. Some people think that the image of God in man refers to his physical appearance. This is not at all what is intended by this statement. Nor does it mean that we have the spark of divinity within us as the old liberal position claimed. What it does mean is that there are some things in the nature of man similar to God's nature. Some of the same characteristics found in God are also found in man. Man has the ability to think, to speak, to love and have fellowship. He can (in his created state before the fall) discern good from evil. He can act according to a plan and a purpose. All these things are found to perfection in God's nature, but only to a degree in man. The eternal God created man with an immortal soul.

One of the aspects of God's image in man is that of dominion. Man was created with both the ability and the mandate to rule over creation as God's steward. This dominion was not absolute, nor was it autocratic in the usual sense. It was a sacred trust, an internship of training for a future charge of far greater proportions. As Christians we will one day be restored to that position of dominion. We are destined to be heirs of God and joint heirs with Christ. The saints will judge the world and reign with Christ throughout all eternity.

Even now we have a responsibility under the Creator to be good stewards of His creation. We are to use those things God has provided for our being and well being, but we are always to remember whose we are, and whom we serve. We brought nothing into this world, and it is certain we can take nothing out. We are God's tenants, working the ground for His glory and our good, using the creation for its God-intended purpose with gratitude and careful responsibility.

Prayer: Help us, Lord, to remember that this is Your world by right of sovereign creation. Thank You for surrounding us with such plenty and such opportunity. By Your grace may we be good stewards of all You place in our care, through Christ our Lord. Amen.

Hymn for the day:
This is My Father's World

PRAYERS & REMINDERS

Question #11: What are God's works of providence?

Answer: God's works of providence are His most holy, wise, and powerful preserving and governing all His creatures, and all their actions.

Scripture Reading: Psalm 145

Next to the doctrines of predestination and election, this doctrine is the most difficult of all for the natural mind to understand or accept. Next to the doctrines of election and predestination, it is the most precious of all Biblical truths. The Shorter Catechism's answer to this question is a brief, but brilliant, summary of an entire chapter in the Confession of Faith, and two lengthy questions and answers from the Larger Catechism. This may give you some idea of the importance of this great truth in the minds of those who wrote the Confession and Catechisms.

The first thing to catch our attention is the emphasis on the character of God, before the work of providence is detailed. The words *holy, wise* and *powerful,* refer not just to the action of God in providence, but more importantly, to the character of the great God who preserves and governs all His creatures and all their actions. In many ways, these are the most important words in the answer. Before trying to deal with the staggering reality of God's omnipotence as seen in providence, we must remember that He is indeed holy, wise and powerful. This means that we may trust Him, even though we may not understand the "what and why" in the working out of His providence, especially in our own lives. As believers, it is important to develop an attitude of trust so that when evil times come, we may fall back on His truth, and trust Him as our holy, wise, powerful, and loving Father. Such living faith protects us from giving in to depression or despair when bad things happen to us or to those we love. Such faith also brings honor and glory to our God.

Prayer: Dear Father, How merciful and kind You are. We bless Your holy name for your providence and care for us and those we love. Thank You that we may trust You even when the way is dark before us and the trials of life threaten to overwhelm us. For Your name's sake, keep us from giving in and giving up in such times. We ask this in the name and for the sake of our Savior. Amen.

Hymn for the day:
Savior, Like a Shepherd Lead Us

PRAYERS & REMINDERS

Question #11: What are God's works of providence?

Answer: God's works of providence are His most holy, wise, and powerful preserving and governing all His creatures, and all their actions.

Scripture Reading: Exodus 3

A brief summary of this doctrine is in order. The Bible teaches us that God is sovereign in all things. We believe that our lives and the entire creation depend upon God for both origin and continuation. If it were not for the power of God, the universe would no doubt fly apart (literally) and we would no longer continue our own personal existence. All that is, is sustained by the power of God. His providence alone holds creation together, and sustains or preserves life. In this overall picture, He also governs all His creatures and all their actions. Both the Old and the New Testaments teach this explicitly and show this truth in action. Today we will look at the Old Testament.

The great example in the Old Testament is the account of the exodus from Egypt. In every step of this inspired narrative, we see this doctrine working itself out in real-life situations. It begins with the preparation and call of Moses, and continues through the actual exodus from Egypt and far beyond. Not only do we see God's providence at work preserving and governing all His creatures and all their actions, but we also see how His providence works. It includes events, circumstances, decisions, actions, and consequences. Special attention should be given to the fact that this includes obedience and disobedience, kindness and cruelty, the understandable and the inexplicable. At the same time, it should be carefully noted that the actors in this great drama are real people who are called on to make moral choices, and to act responsibly and responsively. Yet the one great truth that stands out above all others is that God is in control, not only of the final outcome, but of all the details. Pharaoh believed that he was in control and that he had no reason to acknowledge the God of the Hebrews, or to obey His commands. He paid dearly for his folly, as all do who defy the living God.

Prayer: Great and Sovereign God, we acknowledge Your mighty power and Your righteous decrees. May we willingly and lovingly accept Your Lordship over our lives, for Jesus' sake. Amen.

Hymn for the day:
Guide Me, O Thou Great Jehovah

PRAYERS & REMINDERS
_____
_____
_____
_____
_____
_____
_____
_____
_____

Question #11: What are God's works of providence?

Answer: God's works of providence are His most holy, wise, and powerful preserving and governing all His creatures, and all their actions.

Scripture Reading: Colossians 1:1-18

Yesterday we saw how the Old Testament teaches us explicitly that God is sovereign in all things and shows us this truth in action by delivering Israel from bondage in Egypt. No earthly power could have accomplished such a mighty miracle. Today we will look at the New Testament.

In the New Testament, the story of God's providence centers on the Lord Jesus Christ. We see this in two ways. First He acts out this truth in His ministry. He provides food for the multitudes, and healing for the leper. He calms the fierce storm and walks on the sea. He is not present when *the one whom He loves is ill*, but later calls him forth from the tomb. In all this and in many other parts of the story, we see Him in the role of the One by whom all things were made and continue to exist. We hear him as He expects and accepts the Father's providence to meet His needs. Satan tempted Him to doubt this providential care when he taunted Jesus in the wilderness temptation. *If You are the Son of God, command these stones to become bread.* The temptation was to take His life in His own hands, and misuse His power to that end. When Satan tempted Him to cast Himself from the highest pinnacle of the temple and then depend on the Father sending angels to bear Him up, this was a temptation to presume on God's providential care. Don't we also face the same kinds of temptation? We may not see immediate answers to prayer and so assume we must "take charge" of our own lives, rather than trusting in God's provision and living by His Word. Or we may easily presume on God's goodness and care and take daring chances even with our own lives, rather than living by faith in His clearly revealed will in Scripture. Believing in God's holy, wise and powerful preserving and governing of all His creatures and all their actions requires faith, obedience and submission, and supplies the strength we need for each day.

Prayer: O Gracious Father, You are great and You are good. Enable us by the indwelling Holy Spirit to understand and obey Your Word in our daily lives. We trust in Your kind providence even when we do not understand Your ways in our lives. Help us to ever trust You more. In Jesus' name and for His sake. Amen.

Hymn for the day:
Day by Day and with Each Passing Moment

PRAYERS & REMINDERS

Question #12: What special act of providence did God exercise toward man, in the estate in which he was created?

Answer: When God created man, He entered into a covenant of life with him, on condition of perfect obedience; forbidding him to eat of the Tree of Knowledge of Good and Evil, on the pain of death.

Scripture Reading: Romans 5:12-21

The human race was created for the glory of God. It was also created for joy and perfect fellowship with the Creator. Adam and Eve were not only creatures, along with the other forms of life which God had created; they were also children, in the image of the Father. They were His family. They were created in a state of innocence, nor were they guilty of any wrongdoing. Furthermore they were created with the ability to choose, which meant they could continue to perfectly obey the Father, and remain in a perpetual state of innocence with the implication of even greater things. They could also choose not to obey Him. When God required perfect obedience, He was not requiring the impossible. When man chose evil and disobedience, he was not choosing the inevitable. How all of this fits in with the doctrine of sovereignty is not explained in Scripture, nor should we attempt to explain the inexplicable. It is sufficient to note that Scripture affirms both the moral responsibility of man and the sovereignty of God. It is our duty therefore to also affirm both even though we may not fully understand.

The larger Catechism sheds a great deal of light upon this matter. In beautiful detail it describes the created estate of mankind, and the favorable surroundings which were a part of the covenant God made with Adam and Eve. It speaks of paradise, liberty, dominion, marriage, and communion with God. This reaffirms the contention that it was really possible for our first parents to keep the covenant of works.

PRAYERS & REMINDERS

_____

_____

_____

_____

_____

_____

_____

_____

_____

Prayer: Great and gracious God, our heavenly Father, we who were created in Your image have sinned and gone astray. We have lost the paradise You created for us. We accept with gratitude Your gracious salvation through Jesus Christ our Savior. Amen.

Hymn for the day:
How Great Our God's Majestic Name.

Question #12: *What special act of providence did God exercise toward man, in the estate wherein he was created?*

Answer: When God created man, He entered into a covenant of life with him, on condition of perfect obedience; forbidding him to eat of the Tree of Knowledge of Good and Evil, on the pain of death.

Scripture Reading: John 14:15-24

Obedience is never a matter of theory, but of practice. What could be more reasonable than for God to give to man a test of his obedience? The test was simple. Having surrounded Adam and Eve with all they needed, and far more, God required that they should not eat of the fruit of the tree of knowledge of good and evil. We are not to think of this as some sort of "magic tree," but rather as a simple test of obedience. This is where the knowledge of good and evil comes in. Obedience would bring good. There is every reason to believe that if they passed this test, they would have been confirmed in their state of innocence forever. Disobedience would bring evil; in this case evil so great as to surpass the imagination of man. This evil would mean the loss of paradise and liberty, dominion, and communion. It would mean the corruption of marriage, and the end of that perfect fellowship with the Father which had been enjoyed from the moment of their creation. Oh, how much there was to gain; how much there was to lose.

The same principles apply even in our fallen estate. Obedience to God's revealed will offers blessings. At the same time disobedience deprives us of so much that is good and especially of close fellowship with Him. Illustrations of these principles are seen throughout the entire Bible in the lives of God's people. It is very clear that we cannot earn our salvation by obedience, for we are saved by grace alone. But we may forfeit so much of the joy and peace of our salvation when we ignore God's Word, and live in disobedience at any given point. In the words of a very familiar hymn: *O what peace we often forfeit. O what needless pain we bear.*

Prayer: Father, we confess that so often we allow the things of this world, desires of the flesh, and the desires of the eyes and pride in possessions to lead us astray from Your will. Forgive us and help us to love You more than all these things, and to faithfully obey You in all things. We ask this for Jesus' sake. Amen.

Hymn for the day:
Trust and Obey

PRAYERS & REMINDERS

Question #12: What special act of providence did God exercise toward man, in the estate wherein he was created?

Answer: When God created man, He entered into a covenant of life with him, upon condition of perfect obedience; forbidding him to eat of the Tree of knowledge of Good and Evil, upon the pain of death.

Scripture Reading: Romans 8:28-39

Yesterday we looked at the test of obedience God gave man. It was simple. Adam and Eve had all they needed. God simply required that they should not eat of the fruit of the tree of knowledge of good and evil. Failure of the test would mean the loss of paradise and liberty, dominion and communion. It would mean the corruption of marriage, and the end of that perfect fellowship with the Father which they had enjoyed from the moment of their creation. Oh, how much there was to gain; how much there was to lose.

To a degree the same is still true. What blessing is ours if we trust and obey. What misery is ours if we fail in faith and obedience. Death was the final consequence of disobedience, and it still is. We may rightly mourn the loss of innocence which befell our first parents by their sin. We may try to understand what a world we would have if they had only obeyed. It is far more profitable, however, to be amazed by the grace of our God, who in love predestined all His sons and daughters to be redeemed from the curse of the fall, and, in spite of their and Adam's sin, to some day be restored to the image and estate from which our first parents fell. All the precious elect will be restored and redeemed through the Lord Jesus Christ, and His great work of grace. Even now God is at work through the grace of sanctification, preparing us for the final and full restoration of His image. As we grow in grace and knowledge of our Savior, we begin to show more of that image from which we fell. Rest assured, the final work of restoration will be glorious.

PRAYERS & REMINDERS

_____

_____

_____

_____

_____

_____

_____

_____

_____

Prayer: Gracious God, how grateful we are to know that Your mighty work of redemption will one day be fully accomplished in us. Help us each day to live in that hope, and to give evidence in how we live that Your work of changing us has already begun. Help us to live for the honor and glory of Your Holy Name, through Jesus Christ our Lord. Amen.

Hymn for the day:
Living for Jesus.

> ### Question #13: Did our first parents continue in the estate in which they were created?

Answer: Our first parents, being left to the freedom of their own will, fell from the estate in which they were created, by sinning against God.

Scripture Reading: Genesis 3:1-24

These words introduce us to a dark subject. This is the first tragedy in the tragic history of man. This is how Dr. J. B. Green began his comments on this question in his book, *A Harmony of the Westminster Standards.* He might well have added that this tragedy was the fountainhead of all subsequent tragedies, for truly it is so.

One of the basic flaws in modern anthropology and sociology is the failure to accept this fundamental truth about ourselves, that we are a fallen race. Any realistic study of human nature must face the truth that we are flawed. The evolutionist sees this as evidence that man is evolving into a more perfect species, and one day will be free of all defect. Grace and redemption have no place in this erroneous philosophy.

The Catechism is faithful to Scripture. It recognizes the truth of man's created estate. He was created sinless and righteous, in God's own image. He had a free moral will. He was not made to be either a puppet or a dumb beast, bound by created instincts to obey certain impulses. Nor was he created as a computer, to be programmed to automatically respond to certain commands. Commands were given in the covenant of works, but choices had to be made. Within the limits of our fallen nature the same thing is true in the new covenant. Salvation is by sovereign grace, but Jesus commanded, *Repent and believe, for the kingdom of heaven is at hand."* He also said, *If any man will come after Me, let him take up his cross daily and follow Me.* Both these commands imply that choices have to be made. Before this day is over you will be faced with a choice at some point to obey or to disobey the Lord. That choice will involve consequences too.

Prayer: Father, we all have many choices to make this day. Help us to choose Your revealed will in all we do. Forgive us when we fail to honor You with heartfelt obedience in all our choices. We ask this for Jesus' sake. Amen.

Hymn for the day:
I Have Decided to Follow Jesus.

PRAYERS & REMINDERS

Question #13: Did our first parents continue in the estate in which they were created?

Answer: Our first parents, being left to the freedom of their own will, fell from the estate in which they were created, by sinning against God.

Scripture Reading: Romans 7

Neither Scripture nor the catechism explains why God created man this way. Both affirm that He did so. We may venture some tentative thoughts on why God made us as He did. If He created us for joy and fellowship with Himself, there must be a willing, knowledgeable response to the Creator on the part of man. Love and fellowship are only possible where choice is involved. If you married your spouse because you had no choice, would true love and heart-to-heart fellowship be possible? In some Old Testament examples, it does appear that, by the grace of God, mutual love and choice followed rather than preceded marriage. But if you marry her (or him) because you mutually choose each other from all other people on earth, then the ground is laid for true love and lasting fellowship. There must be mutual choice at some point if there is to be mutual love. This is the most logical explanation why God gave man a free will, and a necessary choice.

The Catechism uses the expression, *being left to the freedom of their own will.* This does not imply desertion on God's part. It teaches there was no coercion. Obedience must be a choice. Even in our fallen nature this is still true to a degree. In the state of grace it is even more true. We are made alive in Christ. Our bodies are temples of the Holy Spirit. True, we still have our fallen natures in this life, but we also have new natures which enable us to make moral choices—not as totally free moral agents, but as redeemed and responsible children of the Father.

PRAYERS & REMINDERS

_____
_____
_____
_____
_____
_____
_____
_____
_____

Prayer: Thank You, dear Lord, for creating us in Your image with the ability to know, love and obey You. Forgive us for choosing our own ways and ignoring Your holy will. By Your mighty grace, give us the desire and will to obey You and honor You always. In Jesus' name we pray. Amen.

Hymn for the day:
O For a Closer Walk with God.

February 6

> **Question #13: Did our first parents continue in the estate in which they were created?**

Answer: Our first parents, being left to the freedom of their own will, fell from the estate in which they were created, by sinning against God.

Scripture Reading: Romans 6:15-23

By sinning against God, Adam and Eve lost Eden and far more. The fall includes the loss of innocence, corruption of the will, loss of freedom, and above all (and most tragic of all) loss of fellowship with God. The consequences of this fall are too catastrophic to even imagine. Death and hell are involved. Pain, disease, violence, crime, cruelty, and oppression are also part of that bitter fruit. Moreover, when our first parents fell, the rest of creation shared their awful fate. A curse fell on God's good earth that will not be lifted until the world is renewed by the finished work of Christ at His glorious return.

One final thought is in order. There is a very real sense in which each and every sin has this same effect. Someone has called sin "cosmic treason," and so it is. Never forget that your sin and my sin are just as odious in God's sight as the first sin. Flee from temptation. Pray with great seriousness of purpose, *Lead us not into temptation, but deliver us from evil.* Prayer to this end must be accompanied by practice. I mean this quite literally. It is important to establish habits of obedient response to God's commands. I often hear people say something like this: *Obedience to God means nothing if I don't feel deeply about what I am doing.* Obedience must be practiced whether we feel like it or not. I don't think Moses felt like going back to Egypt and confronting Pharaoh, but he was commanded by God to do just that. He refused at first, and only with the greatest reluctance did he finally obey, not because he felt like obeying, but because he knew he must obey the word of the Lord God. Make it your determined purpose today to obey the will of God as revealed in His Word.

Prayer: Great Father, how merciful and kind you are. You could have left us in our sin and misery. You could have kept the gates to Paradise closed forever, but You did not. We know our sins are inexcusable, and deserve death. Thank You that our Lord Jesus took that death upon Himself, that we might be forgiven. We pray in His Name. Amen

Hymn for the day:
Take My Life and Let It Be

PRAYERS & REMINDERS

Question #14: What is sin?

Answer: Sin is any want of conformity to, or transgression of, the law of God.

Scripture Reading: Psalm 51

The Westminster Shorter Catechism is one of the truly great theological documents ever written. Though short and concise, it is thorough, clear and always right to the point. It is remarkable that such a brief document could contain the wealth of material, the depth of insight, and the breadth of Biblical truth which the Catechism contains. This question and answer are perhaps the best illustration of this. Here we have a statement concerning the nature of sin upon which we may expand, but it is very doubtful if any other statement could properly replace it.

Ordinarily we tend to begin any discussion of sin at the point of lawbreaking, rather than failure. If we include the aspect of omission, it is usually as an afterthought. The Catechism begins with the treatment of sin where the Bible itself begins. Sin is basically failure. In fact the word *sin* has its roots in a word that means failure. It is taken from the ancient art of archery. It means shooting towards a mark and missing, or falling short. The Apostle Paul said, *For all have sinned, and come short of the glory of God (Romans* 3:23). While it is true that Adam disobeyed God, still the beginning point was failure to believe His Word. Satan in his crafty evil way, did not begin by telling Eve that God's Word was wrong. He simply asked, *Did God really say that?* He implied first that maybe Eve just had not really understood God. Once this doubt was planted in her mind, the next step was easy and even inevitable. Satan told her that God was wrong! Instead of relying on God's Word which she had heard, she fell back on her feelings to justify disobedience. You may be sure Satan will attempt to use these same tactics on you before this day is over. When Jesus was tempted by Satan He relied on the Word of God for His defense. So must we.

PRAYERS & REMINDERS

_____

_____

_____

_____

_____

_____

_____

_____

_____

Prayer: O Lord, truly we have sinned and broken Your Holy Law. We have failed to be what You have called us to Be. We have failed to do what You have commanded to do. Help us to see sin for what it is, rebellion against You. Forgive and cleanse us through Jesus our Lord. Amen

Hymn for the day:
God Be Merciful to Me.

Question #14: What is sin?

Answer: Sin is any want of conformity to, or transgression of, the law of God.

Scripture Reading: I John 1:5-2:2

Sin is more than just failure to act or to do. It is even more a failure to be what God wants us to be. It is failure to be as those created in His image. It is failure to be the persons we should be, those who have been redeemed. This works itself out into many forms of passive disobedience, which, I am convinced, are more hateful to God than active transgressions. For instance, we do not trust as we should, which leads to the transgression of worry. Because we fail to love the Lord our God with all our hearts, souls, and minds, we break His laws, and offend His grace. Because we fail to love our neighbors as ourselves, we steal, and bear false witness, and covet.

So sin begins with failure to be what God calls us to be, which leads to failure to do what He commands us to do. Far too often we shrug off our failures with, "No one is perfect," as if this makes it acceptable. Of course no one is perfect, and that is serious indeed. Our Lord summed up His treatment of the law when He said, *Be ye therefore perfect, even as your Father which is in heaven is perfect* (Matt. 5:48). That's really the whole point. Anything less makes us sinners in His sight. This calls for repentance on a daily basis. We cannot make up for our sins by trying to "be good", but we can and must confess our sins, and turn from them, trusting God's grace to forgive and cleanse us from all unrighteousness.

Prayer: Father, help us to walk in the light of Your Holy Word that we may see how far we fall short of Your glory. Keep us from ever saying or thinking that we have no sin. Enable us to confess our sins, knowing You are faithful and just to forgive our sins, and to cleanse us from all unrighteousness through Jesus Christ our Savior and Lord. Amen.

Hymn for the day:
No Not Despairingly, Come I to Thee

PRAYERS & REMINDERS

Question #14: What is sin?

Answer: Sin is any want of conformity to, or transgression of, the law of God.

Scripture Reading: Hosea 11.

We cannot ignore the second part of this definition of sin and still do justice to the Biblical teaching of it. The Catechism refers to transgression of the law. Another Biblical word is trespass, and these two words mean basically the same thing. Transgression implies willful disobedience, the intentional breaking of God's law. The Old Testament points out that even sins of ignorance, or unintentional breaking of God's law, are serious. How much more when we deliberately defy Him and offend Him! The sin of Peter, who was suddenly overtaken by unexpected weakness and temptation as he warmed himself at the fire of the enemy, was a serious offense, for which he had to repent and seek forgiveness. But how infinitely more hideous was the sin of Judas, who planned and plotted to betray the Lord.

Finally let me suggest that there is another aspect to sin that is not really brought out in this definition but which needs our attention. As believers, we know that God has become our loving Father through the grace of our Lord Jesus Christ. It is well to remember that when we break our Father's commands, we also break His heart. This alone should drive us to our knees, and even more to our Savior. As dear and loving children it should also break our hearts, and motivate us toward a more earnest endeavor to be and to do what God commands. Our sincere desire and determination must be that we will turn away from those things which offend our God and break our fellowship with Him.

Prayer: O Father, how foolish and sinful we are. You have shown us in Your Holy Word the good and right way to live. You have given us precepts and promises, and every good reason to trust and obey You. Yet we allow the whim of the moment and the call of the world to turn us aside. Please forgive and restore us. We pray this in Jesus' name and for His sake. Amen.

Hymn for the day:
Rock of Ages, Cleft for Me

PRAYERS & REMINDERS

Question #15: What was the sin by which our first parents fell from the estate in which they were created?

Answer: The sin by which our first parents fell from the estate in which they were created was their eating of the forbidden fruit.

Scripture Reading: I John 2:12-17

Sin is never in the abstract. It is more than a theological topic for discussion or debate. Sin is a reality in the story of the human race. It is the common denominator of all people, *for all have sinned and fall short of the glory of God.* (Romans 3:23). The origin of sin is never really discussed philosophically in the Bible, but the story is told in simple, straightforward narrative. The narratives relating to the early days of human life on earth are not in the form of parables. They are not prehistory; they are history, and tell what actually happened. The Catechism recognizes this important feature of Genesis by simply declaring what the Bible tells us, namely, that the first sin of our first parents was eating the forbidden fruit.

Why was this sinful, and what was the nature of that sin? Adam and Eve were created in God's image with freedom to obey God and to enjoy His immediate and blessed fellowship. In their created state, they were also free to disobey Him and go their own way. It was necessary, therefore, for their obedience to be tested at some definite, concrete point of behavior. God had surrounded them with goodness and plenty. They were given all they needed, and all that was best for them, in the beautiful garden of Eden. However, in the midst of the garden God had placed a special tree. It was called the tree of knowledge of good and evil. Whether there was some special physical property involved in the fruit of the tree, we are not told, but that is relatively unimportant. What was, and is important was the test of obedience. God did not tell them why He had given them this test. He did warn them of the severe consequences of disobedience, saying, *In the day that thou eatest thereof thou shalt surely die* (Gen. 2:17b).

Prayer: O God, so often with eyes wide open we walk the pathway of disobedience. We have no excuse, for You have shown us what is good, and what You require of us. Help us to *do justly, love mercy and walk humbly with our God.* In Jesus' name. Amen.

Hymn for the day:
May the Mind of Christ My Savior

PRAYERS & REMINDERS

> **Question #15: What was the sin by which our first parents fell from the estate in which they were created?**

Answer: The sin by which our first parents fell from the estate in which they were created was their eating of the forbidden fruit.

Scripture Reading: Psalm 95

The first test involved our first parents faced was a test of faith. Adam and Eve were required to believe God's Word for no other reason than that it was His revealed will. When they later questioned in their own minds, by the prompting of Satan, the reasonableness of God's command, they were but one step away from falling into ruin and death. We, too, are all faced with this same basic requirement — to believe and obey God's Word, just because it is His Word. He may give to us special reasons for believing and obeying, but sooner or later we are required to believe Him simply because He is God.

Humanly speaking, the cross by which we are saved makes no sense. It is not according to human wisdom, and is regarded as foolishness by the wisdom of man. But it is God's way and God's power for salvation, and we must believe it as such or be lost. Another aspect of the test for our first parents was love for God and respect for His authority over their lives. Disobedience to His commands always involves a lack of both love and respect, and is therefore always a personal affront to God. Of all our sins we must say as David said, *Against Thee, Thee only, have I sinned, and done this evil in Thy sight* (Ps. 51:4a).

Further, in yielding to Satan's persuasion, Adam and Eve chose their own will instead of God's will. Self-indulgence and self-gratification became a basic drive in fallen human nature. Any time we choose our own desires over God's revealed will, we are demonstrating this same basic failure, and flirting with death and alienation from God. We hear this warning in God's Word to which we do well to take heed: *Turn, turn away from your evil ways for why should you die?* Ezekiel 33:11.

PRAYERS & REMINDERS

_____
_____
_____
_____
_____
_____
_____
_____
_____

Prayer: O Lord, we acknowledge that all we like sheep have gone astray, we have turned, every one, to our own way. Thank You, Lord Jesus, You were willing for all our iniquity to be laid upon You, and that by Your blood, we are cleansed from all sin. Amen.

Hymn for the day:
Nothing but the Blood of Jesus

February 12

> ## Question #15: What was the sin by which our first parents fell from the estate in which they were created?

Answer: The sin by which our first parents fell from the estate in which they were created was their eating of the forbidden fruit.

Scripture Reading: Psalm 1

The final step Adam and Eve took in response to Satan's tempting was outright disobedience. The act was contemplated, the pros and cons debated, the consequences dismissed as improbable or of little importance, and then the fruit was eaten. God's goodness was discounted. His Word was ignored, and even His purpose and intent for His children were questioned in this first sin.

Who can read this story with dry eyes? Who can read this story and not be convicted of his own waywardness and folly? *If You, Lord, should mark iniquities, O Lord, who could stand?* (Ps. 130:3) We trace the same threads of this sad story in our own lives. We consider the law of God and then begin to wonder and debate within ourselves. Maybe the times have changed. Maybe grace has canceled the demands for righteousness. Perhaps we do not fully understand why our actions are really so wrong. Other people may tell us that we need not feel guilty, for right and wrong is really a matter of opinion. After all, they say, the Bible must not be taken literally. So we listen, so we consider, so we debate, and so we fall. The first sin of our first parents may seem trivial in the minds of modern man. But though fallen human reason may discount sin, it is never trivial in the eyes of God, and there is nothing trivial about it in human experience. We read in Romans 6:23, *the wages of sin is death.* Thank God we also read in this same verse, *but the gift of God is eternal life in Christ Jesus our Lord.* When it come to a choice, the real question is, what will it be for you, the wages of sin, or the gift of God?

Prayer: Great God and gracious Father, we come to You with a sense of our own sin heavy on our hearts. Never let us take the sin in our lives lightly or think it is of no consequence. Guard our minds from even debating Your commands, but enable us to lovingly submit, and gratefully receive Your forgiveness and grace through our Lord and Savior, Jesus Christ. Amen.

Hymn for the day:
And Can It Be?

PRAYERS & REMINDERS

Question #16: Did all mankind fall in Adam's first transgression?

Answer: The covenant being made with Adam, not only for himself, but for his descendants, all mankind, descending from him by ordinary generation, sinned in him, and fell with him, in his first transgression.

Scripture Reading: Acts 17:16-24

Fallout! This is one of the most dreaded words in the English language, especially when used in the context of nuclear warfare. During the so-called cold war, one of the most intense debates going on in the scientific community was concerning the extent of the potential damage of fallout from atomic bombs. While there were wide differences of opinion on the subject, all agreed that fallout would have worldwide consequences, with the potential destruction of all life as we know it. Some leading Christian thinkers suggest that this is the means God may use to fulfill end-times prophecies about the fiery judgment which is destined to destroy this present world.

The Catechism tells us of a more deadly form of fallout; the consequences of the sin of our first parents in the Garden of Eden. Since Adam acted not only as a responsible moral agent, but also as the representative for all future generations, his sin and fall affected the whole human race. The Catechism explains that the covenant made with Adam was both for himself and for his posterity. In the language of Reformed theology, He was the Federal Head of the human race. So it was not just Adam and Eve who were tempted and fell, but the whole human race of whom they were representatives. Of course this is not accepted either by the secular humanists or liberal theologians. They reject this out of hand as being silly and superstitious. This rejection of God's Word in no way changes the reality of the consequences of Adam's fall. In fact, it bears witness to the truth that fallen man shares in Adam's fall and the consequences of it.

PRAYERS & REMINDERS

_____
_____
_____
_____
_____
_____
_____
_____
_____

Prayer: O Holy Father, we are a fallen and sinful people. As we read of the great tragedy of Adam's fall into sin, and all he lost because of that fall, we see ourselves in him. We follow him both in sin and in guilt. Help us to remember that even in that awful moment, You provided covering for his nakedness, and a promise of redemption through Christ, who alone is our Savior. Amen.

Hymn for the day:
I Lay My Sin on Jesus, the Spotless Lamb of God

Question #16: Did all mankind fall in Adam's first transgression?

Answer: The covenant being made with Adam, not only for himself, but for his descendants, all mankind, descending from him by ordinary generation, sinned in him, and fell with him, in his first transgression.

Scripture Reading: Psalm 32

We must assume that the effects of Adam's fall affected his entire being, body and soul. There is every reason to believe that the body God created for Adam was a model of perfection, free from sickness, weakness, and capable of everlasting life. If so, then it follows that sin brought about dramatic changes with long-lasting effects genetically, as well as spiritually. In fact, there must have been devastating genetic changes which were passed on to future generations in the form of sickness, imperfections of body and mind, and the inevitability of aging and death.

In addition, there were even more deadly spiritual consequences. Mankind became a race of sinners under judgment of the holy God. Fellowship with God was broken so totally that never again could human beings come before this holy God by their own efforts. Lost, too, was their innocence. We often use the term "innocence" in referring to people. We speak of innocent bystanders, or innocent children. As a matter of Biblical truth, there are no innocents among the human race. We are all sinners by choice, but also by nature. Even our precious babies, though not guilty of sinful acts, inherit our sinful nature, which in turn expresses itself early in life in the form of actual sinful thoughts, words and deeds. This pattern of sin follows us and haunts us all the days of our lives. David the King warned of *the destruction that wasteth at noonday.* But in the noonday of his own life, he ignored his own words, and fell into destructive sins. Let us all be warned and follow David's good advice and not his example of sinful disobedience.

Prayer: Dear Father in heaven, we confess once more that we are sinners by nature and by choice. Save us from destructive patterns of sin in our lives, and forgive us for all our waywardness. We ask this in Jesus' name and for His sake. Amen.

Hymn for the day:
Yield Not to Temptation

PRAYERS & REMINDERS

Question #16: Did all mankind fall in Adam's first transgression?

Answer: The covenant being made with Adam, not only for himself, but for his descendants, all mankind, descending from him by ordinary generation, sinned in him, and fell with him, in his first transgression.

Scripture Reading: John 1:10-18

Several years ago, a young lady, who had just become a mother for the first time, angrily upbraided me for teaching that children are born with sinful nature. *You can't tell me that my baby is a sinner,* she shouted at me. Actually I wasn't saying her baby had committed sin, but simply that all people are born with a fallen nature. Even that failed to register ... for a while. Less than a year later, I was visiting in that home at what turned out to be a most inopportune time. The young mother was dressed to attend a church meeting, but had made the mistake of trying to feed the baby after getting herself all dressed up for church. I was never sure just where she had intended the pabulum to go, but it didn't get there. Instead it was all over the nice clothes, the hairdo, the kitchen table, as well as the cat and the dog. The baby was screaming, the mom was crying, and the preacher was wisely backing out the door, refraining from any discussion of *original sin.* As I remember, she threatened me with worse than death if I so much as mentioned the subject. While the incident was not without humor, the reality of sin and its hellish consequences are truths sad beyond a flood of tears.

One faint ray of hope appears in this Catechism answer. All of Adam's descendants, by *ordinary generation sinned in him and fell with him.* But remember there was a descendant of Adam who came by extraordinary generation, being conceived by the Holy Spirit, and born of the virgin Mary. He and He alone escaped the taint of original sin, and offers to us the way of escape. Of this and of Him the Catechism will have more to say.

PRAYERS & REMINDERS

_____

_____

_____

_____

_____

_____

_____

_____

_____

Prayer: Father, how very grateful we are that the "Seed of the Woman" was not born of ordinary generation, but being conceived by the Holy Spirit, He was born of the Virgin Mary, and without sin. Thank You that the Sinless One was willing to be the perfect sacrifice for our sins, that we might be saved. We pray in His name alone. Amen.

Hymn for the day:
Hark the Herald Angels Sing

Question #17: Into what estate did the Fall bring mankind?

Answer: The Fall brought mankind into an estate of sin and misery.

Scripture Reading: Genesis 6:1-12

When Adam and Eve disobeyed God and sinned, they fell. It was a dreadful fall. They fell from holiness and happiness into sin and misery. This is one of the most fundamental truths in the Bible. It is also taught in the history of the human race, and in the daily newspaper.

It seems impossible, but there are still people who believe that mankind is getting better and better, and will one day solve all the problems besetting us. Nothing could be further from the truth. The evidence to the contrary is overwhelming.

The Catechism tells us what the Bible teaches from cover to cover. The human race is a fallen race. In Jeremiah 17:9 we read: *The heart is deceitful above all things and desperately wicked, who can know it?* When the Catechism uses the word *estate*, it refers to our condition. Man was once the prince of creation, but by sin he became the pauper, utterly destitute the before holy God. He was once the hero of the story, but became the villain, and the victim as well. The effects of our sinful condition are seen everywhere. We read of terrorism, drug-related crime, sex scandals, corruption in high places, and disgraceful conduct on the part of well-known religious leaders. All this testifies to the sinful condition of the human race. But let us be careful about pointing the finger outward and at other people. This dreadful truth applies to all of us, *for all have sinned.* The Psalmist cried out, *There is none righteous, no not one.* We are included in this indictment, and we must all appear before the judgment seat of Christ.

Prayer: O great and gracious God, our Father in heaven, how we mourn the fallen estate of the human race. Truly You must be grieved to see how we have turned our backs on You, the great Creator. Thank You for the promise that one day we, and the whole defiled Creation will be restored through the merit and power of our Lord Jesus. Amen.

Hymn for the day:
Lo, He Comes with Clouds Descending

PRAYERS & REMINDERS

Question #17: Into what estate did the Fall bring mankind?

Answer: The Fall brought mankind into an estate of sin and misery.

Scripture Reading: Psalm 39

We need not look far away to see proof of the dreadful reality that the human race is fallen. We need look no further than our own hearts. When we would do good, evil quickly manifests itself. *The good I will to do, I do not do; but the evil I will not to do, that I practice.* Paul wrote of this in Romans 7:19, but we face it constantly in our own experience. It is not just that we commit sinful deeds, or even that we think sinful thoughts. We are sinful! That is our condition, that is the estate into which the fall brought us.

Scripture says, *all have sinned, and come short of the glory of God.* But sin brings with it misery. They are never separated. To be sinful is to be miserable. Look at Psalm 51. This was written after Nathan the prophet came before King David and denounced his sinful behavior with Bathsheba, and the murder of her husband Uriah. David thought his affair with Bathsheba would bring him pleasure, even joy. Yes, there are pleasures in sin for a season, but there is never joy, and the pleasures are fleeting at best. David's doleful lament is the inner experience of everyone who ignores God's law. *Against thee, thee only have I sinned, and done this evil in thy sight.* What David would learn through bitter experience was that he had also sinned against Bathsheba and her slain husband, dead by David's orders. Moreover he had sinned against his own family and the nation over which he ruled by God's grace. Sin has its consequences in all our relationships and within our own hearts and minds. Only the mighty, saving grace of God overcomes these dreadful consequences.

Prayer: Holy God, we are overwhelmed with Your holiness and our own sinfulness. All our efforts to be good fall short. All our determination to refrain from sin is swept away by our own desires and selfishness. Forgive us and cleanse us from all unrighteousness, through our Lord Jesus. Amen.

Hymn for the day:
God Be Merciful to Me

PRAYERS & REMINDERS

Question #17: Into what estate did the Fall bring mankind?

Answer: The Fall brought mankind into an estate of sin and misery.

Scripture Reading: Ezekiel 33:1-11

In Psalm 51:12 we hear David plead with God, *Restore unto me the joy of Thy salvation.* He knew what we all discover eventually. Fellowship with God is the source of joy, not sinful indulgence. The misery of our condition is clearly seen all around in the form of broken homes, abused and neglected children, forsaken elderly, incurable diseases, endless strife even in churches, and much, much more with which we are sadly familiar.

The greatest misery of sin is seen in none of this, however. The real misery, the source of all misery, is loss of fellowship with God. We were created by and for Him. Our purpose in life is to glorify and enjoy God, and anything less brings misery. I can still remember the misery in my childish heart when disobedience would break my parents' hearts, and mine as well. I can remember childhood spats with pals, and the misery of those broken relationships. I can remember feeling sad when my little children misbehaved, and our fellowship was broken. They no doubt can remember when their father was cross and unreasonable. All of these memories help me understand that the estate of misery into which mankind fell has far-reaching and long-lasting consequences that are experienced by all people everywhere.

May I also be so bold as to suggest that our Father in heaven is also grieved by our misery? This is the foundation of our hope. Soon we shall consider that part of the Catechism which tells us of God's answer to our sin and misery. For now it is enough to know He has the answer, and you, by His grace, may know that glorious answer.

Prayer: Father, forgive us when we grieve You and quench the Spirit. We long for a closer walk with You, and yet we stray away from You so quickly. Help us to know the joy of that close fellowship, and turn from the sins which separate us from You. Hear us and restore us, we ask in Jesus' name. Amen.

Hymn for the day:
I Am Thine, O Lord

PRAYERS & REMINDERS

> **Question #18: What is the sinfulness of that estate into which man fell?**

Answer: The sinfulness of that estate into which man fell consists of: the guilt of Adam's first sin, the lack of original righteousness, and the corruption of his whole nature, which is commonly called original sin, together with all actual transgressions that proceed from it.

Scripture Reading: Isaiah 53

We find the defendant guilty as charged. How many times has this verdict been heard in a court of law by a person charged with a serious crime? It must surely be a dreadful thing to hear. It is a dreadful thing to hear from the Judge of all the earth, and it is His declaration upon all people, *for all have sinned.* Guilt is a reality in every life.

Psychology may attempt to help people deal with guilt feelings. Often these are misguided efforts which never deal with guilt itself, only the feelings which guilt produces. Christianity deals with the real issue: We are all guilty sinners in God's sight.

The Catechism speaks of guilt as the inescapable consequence of sin. When we break a moral law, we become morally guilty. An act results in a condition, and repeated acts of sin harden us more and more in our guilty condition. Someone once said: *Sow a deed, and reap a habit. Sow a habit, and reap a character. Sow a character and reap a destiny.* Our condition is one of guilt before a holy God.

The story of amazing grace is that One who was never guilty of even the slightest sin or wrong doing, bore our sin and our guilt on the cross. When our Lord Jesus died on the cross He died as One condemned. For *He made Him who knew no sin to be sin for us that we might become the righteousness of God in Him.* Knowing how painful it is for us to deal with our own guilt, I believe one of the most painful things which our Lord suffered on the cross was the dreadful feeling of guilt which He bore for us.

Prayer: Thank You, Lord Jesus Christ, for bearing our sins, our sorrows and our guilt, and making them Your very own. Thank You that by Your sacrifice we are set free from our sin and guilt. Keep our hearts tender before You and our minds filled with the wonder of Your grace. Amen.

Hymn for the day:
Beneath the Cross of Jesus

PRAYERS & REMINDERS

Question #18: What is the sinfulness of that estate into which man fell?

Answer: The sinfulness of that estate into which man fell consists of: the guilt of Adam's first sin, the lack of original righteousness, and the corruption of his whole nature, which is commonly called original sin, together with all actual transgressions that proceed from it.

Scripture Reading: Psalm 130

Sin's consequences are not only guilt, but also a lack of positive righteousness. Because of sin, we are no longer righteous, nor are we free to be righteous. Once we sin, we can never again be innocent in our own strength, or by our own effort. God requires not only righteousness, but perfect righteousness for fellowship with Him. Adam and Eve lost their original righteousness, and we have never possessed it because we inherited a sinful nature. This does not mean that we can never be forgiven; it simply means we must be forgiven if we are to ever have a right relationship with God.

Forgiveness is what the gospel is all about. Daily forgiveness is an abiding necessity for believers in their walk with the Lord. In addressing Christians, 1 John 1:9 tells us: *If we confess our sins, He is faithful and just to forgive our sins, and to cleanse us from all unrighteousness.* Although believers aspire to true holiness and righteousness, we also recognize that we will never obtain this in our own strength, or in this life time. I have heard some believers say something like this: *I know I'm not perfect, but I have not committed any conscious sin for a long, long time.* But again from 1 John 1:8 we read: *If we say we have no sin we deceive ourselves, and the truth is not in us.* We have been redeemed, but we must still struggle with our old sin nature, which is filled with selfishness, pride and greed. Thank God that grace to cover all our sin is ours in Christ Jesus our Lord.

Prayer: Lord, You have told us to seek after holiness, without which we will never see You. But we can neither seek nor find this precious treasure unless You grant it by grace, and credit to us the righteousness of our Lord Jesus. Give us grace to eagerly pursue true righteousness day by day. In Jesus' name we pray. Amen.

Hymn for the day:
More Holiness Give Me

PRAYERS & REMINDERS
_____
_____
_____
_____
_____
_____
_____
_____
_____
_____

Question #18: What is the sinfulness of that estate into which man fell?

Answer: The sinfulness of that estate into which man fell consists of: the guilt of Adam's first sin, the lack of original righteousness, and the corruption of his whole nature, which is commonly called original sin, together with all actual transgressions that proceed from it.

Scripture Reading: I Timothy 6:6-19

Guilt and a lack of righteousness point us to a further result of Adam's fall — the corruption of our whole nature, or original sin. This means that our whole being is affected by sin. Our minds, our hearts, our wills, and even our physical bodies suffer because of sin. This does not mean that all people are totally and equally wicked in all they do, but it does mean that the poison of sin has permeated the entire being of all people. Thus we are disobedient, selfish, lustful, and controlled by our sinful nature. Even when we would do good, evil is present. When these natural inclinations are unchecked either by law or grace, they become more and more dominant, and we become more and more sinful. The Catechism does not overstate the case, if anything, it under states it.

As the words of the Catechism begin to sink in, and the Biblical truths taught by the Catechism become clearer, the amazing grace of our Lord becomes more and more precious. The greatest mystery of all time and eternity is why God loves sinners who are guilty of breaking His law, lacking in righteousness, and corrupt in their total beings. An equally unfathomable mystery is why He loves us so much that the Lord Jesus gave Himself for us. Mystery? Yes! But to that glorious mystery I cling, and by faith, trust in that saving grace. I Corinthians 1:30-31, tells the whole story. *But of Him, you are in Christ Jesus, Who became for us wisdom from God - and righteousness and sanctification and redemption- that as it is written, he who glories, let him glory in the LORD.*

PRAYERS & REMINDERS
_____
_____
_____
_____
_____
_____
_____
_____
_____

Prayer: "Forbid it Lord that I should boast, save in the death of Christ my Lord. All the vain things that charm me most, I sacrifice them to His Blood." This prayer we offer in Jesus' name and for His glory alone. Amen.

Hymn for the day:
When I Survey the Wondrous Cross

Question #19: What is the misery of that estate into which man fell?

Answer: All mankind, by their fall, lost communion with God, are under His wrath and curse, and so made liable to all miseries of this life, to death itself, and to the pains of hell forever.

Scripture Reading: Luke 16:10-31

Have you ever watched a cute young couple walk down the street hand in hand? Maybe they were very young, or even better, very old. In either case, wasn't your mind filled with thoughts of tenderness and admiration, and maybe even a little wistfulness? Well, here we see another sort of couple going hand in hand, and it is a terrible sight, filling us with dread and fear. Sin and misery always go together. They can never be separated. It may take a while for this to be seen and experienced, but there is no exception to this rule. It is a spiritual law that is totally inflexible. No matter what pleasures there may be in sin for a season, no matter how sweet the fruit may taste at the moment, the inevitable correlation is that sin always brings misery eventually. The full depth of that misery is pictured for us in the parable of the rich man and the beggar Lazarus.

The Catechism describes the nature and extent of that misery. Go back and read this answer again. Doesn't your own experience verify this, at least when it describes the miseries of sin in this life? Pray God the final misery will never be known in your experience. And it need not be. God has provided the answer to the misery of sin, and that is the joy of knowing Christ and being with Him forever in heaven. But even now, here on earth, we may know something of this joy and peace. As we remain in the Word, and in fellowship with each other, and as we bind ourselves together in the fellowship of God's Church, we begin to experience in part, what we shall know in fullness when we get to heaven. Even as sin always brings misery, so grace brings peace with God and peace within.

Prayer: Father, protect us from Satan's subtle lies that we will find happiness by disobeying You. Help us to understand that Your joy is far better than temporary pleasures the world, the flesh and the Devil offer us. In the name and strength of our Lord Jesus, we offer this prayer. Amen.

Hymn for the day:
Jesus Thou Joy of Loving Hearts

PRAYERS & REMINDERS

Question #19: What is the misery of that estate into which man fell?

Answer: All mankind, by their fall, lost communion with God, are under His wrath and curse, and so made liable to all miseries in this life, to death itself, and to the pains of hell forever.

Scripture Reading: Romans 6:15-23

The wages of sin is death ... These words from Romans are a verification of God's warning to Adam and Eve, *In the day that you sin, you will surely die.* The misery of sin begins with separation from God. Oh, how miserable we feel when there is separation from a loved one, especially if that estrangement has been caused by our sinfulness. But how much more miserable are we when there is separation from God. Sin does that. We know something of how Adam and Eve felt when they tried to hide from God. We sense our nakedness before the holiness of God. We realize the truth of His warning. We, like our first parents, fear to face God, and hide our faces in shame at our own weakness.

We may not always feel it at the moment. In fact, our own desires and emotions may blind us to this awful reality, and even lead us to believe that our sin is not really sin at all, or that it is somehow not quite so bad as others may think. We may even be deceived into thinking that in spite of our unconfessed sin we are still in close fellowship with God. We may even go on saying our prayers, reading our Bibles, and attending church. But, beloved, please hear and believe these words from the Shorter Catechism, believe me, and above all believe the Word of God. Sin brings loss of communion with God, and nothing is more miserable than that. This is why we must eagerly seek Him and confess our sins to Him quickly, that our sweet communion with Him may be restored and daily renewed. Even as God clothed sinful Adam and Eve with the skin of a slain animal, so He clothes us with the righteous robe of the slain Lamb of God, Jesus Christ, the Righteous.

Prayer: Father, we do not come before You to tell You how good we are, or to explain why we went astray. We come to confess our sins, seek Your grace and receive Your pardon through Christ, our Redeemer. Amen.

Hymn for the day:
Lead me to Calvary

PRAYERS & REMINDERS

Question #19: What is the misery of that estate into which man fell?

Answer: All mankind, by their fall, lost communion with God, are under His wrath and curse, and so made liable to all miseries of this life, to death itself, and to the pains of hell forever.

Scripture Reading: Psalm 42

There is more, much more, and it doesn't get better. Sin not only destroys our fellowship with the Lord, it brings upon us His wrath and curse. These are hard words, but is the Scripture any less hard? It is not until we deal with the full reality of sin that we may understand the fullness of grace. The Bible tells us, *God is angry with the wicked every day.* The wrath of God is a dreadful reality, even though many try to deny this Biblical truth.

Too often we hear some well-meaning, but ill-informed person say that the God of the Old Testament is a God of wrath, but the God of the New Testament is a God of love. There are no words in the New Testament which exceed some of the Psalms and other writings which describe the tender, Fatherly love of God. There are no words in the Old Testament which equal in terror the words of Jesus and the Apostles in describing the wrath of God. Do not be deceived, the God of the Bible is a Holy God. And because He is holy, He has terrible wrath against sin.

Therefore, we are made liable to all miseries in this life, and to death itself, and to the pains of hell forever. Dreadful words! Sobering words! True words! Correcting words! Yet blessed words, for they drive us away from confidence in our own goodness, and we flee into the gracious arms of God's forgiving grace through His Son, the Lord Jesus Christ. He has said, *Whosoever comes to Me, I will in no wise cast out.* If you are keeping God at arm's length because of shame over your sin, you are headed in the wrong direction. God invites you to draw close to Him in repentance and true faith that your sins are forgiven through our Lord Jesus.

Prayer: O Lord, there are times when we feel so deeply the pains of our sins, and many failures. Truly we may say, My tears have been my food day and night. All Your waves and billows have gone over me. Grant us true repentance that we may receive true forgiveness. We plead for this in Jesus' name. Amen.

Hymn for the day:
Out of My Bondage, Sorrow and Night

PRAYERS & REMINDERS

> ### Question #20: Did God leave all mankind to perish in the estate of sin and misery?

Answer: God, having out of His mere good pleasure, from all eternity, elected some to everlasting life, did enter into a covenant of grace, to deliver them out of the estate of sin and misery, and to bring them into an estate of salvation by a Redeemer.

Scripture Reading: Romans 8:28-39

The late Egbert Watson Smith, former secretary for foreign missions in the old Southern Presbyterian Church, wrote a book, *The Creed of the Presbyterians.* In this book he said that before God had ever found a place in this vast universe to hang this spinning globe called earth, He had already found a place in His great heart of love for the elect. This is the same truth taught in this question of the Catechism. In fact it is one of the great central themes of Scripture. It is the foundation of all our hopes, and the source of all joy. The theology of grace begins with the character of God, and as we learn in 1 John 4:8: *He who does not love, does not know God, for God is love.*

All God's purposes are consistent with His nature and flow from His nature. The motivation for God's gracious covenant is His mere good pleasure, and of course His sovereign grace. I think we tend to miss the meaning of the expression, *mere good pleasure.* To speak of God's mere good pleasure is to say that there was nothing in the fallen creature deserving of redemption. Nor is there anything a fallen person can do to merit God's good will. There are some, and even many theologians and commentators who insist that God's electing grace is based merely on His foreknowledge that some people will believe, and therefore He elects them to salvation. This makes man, not God the major player in the drama of salvation.

It is God's pleasure to show mercy and to express His love by sending His only begotten Son into the world to seek and save the lost.

Prayer: Father, we are in awe of Your grace towards us. You did not choose us because we were good and holy. You chose us because You are God and Your wisdom and ways are unsearchable. Humbly we acknowledge that in us dwells no good thing, but You are wholly righteous, and yet You have loved and saved us through Christ. We thank You for our Savior and our salvation. Amen.

Hymn for the day:
Amazing Grace

PRAYERS & REMINDERS

Question #20: Did God leave all mankind to perish in the estate of sin and misery?

Answer: God, having out of His mere good pleasure, from all eternity, elected some to everlasting life, did enter into a covenant of grace, to deliver them out of the estate of sin and misery, and to bring them into an estate of salvation by a Redeemer.

Scripture Reading: John 10:11-30

The reason for His grace lies within God Himself. It pleases Him to love us poor sinners. It is His goodness, and His goodness alone that moves Him to save lost sinners.

Another point the Catechism makes is that His grace is from everlasting to everlasting. From all eternity God has been the God of grace. He did not decide to have mercy on us after the fall. His electing grace is from all eternity. We are chosen in Christ from before the foundation of the world. There is mystery here we cannot understand, but in which we greatly rejoice.

It is well to pause for a moment and remember that God's electing grace comes to us through our Lord Jesus Christ. The name *Jesus* means *Jehovah's Salvation,* for that is who He is. There is a very real sense in which the covenant of grace is a covenant between God the Father and God the Son. Some theologians speak of this as the covenant of redemption, which is the foundation for the covenant of grace. Christ Himself speaks of this covenant in His great high priestly prayer, recorded in John 17, when He says to the Father: *Thine they were, and Thou gavest them to Me.* This indicates strongly that God's covenant of grace rests upon this eternal covenant of redemption. This gives to us added assurance that our salvation rests safely in God's hands, and not ours. In John 10: 29-30 we hear these words of Jesus: *My Father who has given them to Me is greater than all; and no one is able to snatch them out of My Father's hand. I and My Father are one.* Rejoice believer! There is no greater assurance than this.

Prayer: Thank You, Lord, for loving and saving us. Your power and grace have combined to do the impossible and for this we praise and will praise You for all eternity through Christ our Lord. Amen.

Hymn for the day:
How Firm A Foundation

PRAYERS & REMINDERS

_____
_____
_____
_____
_____
_____
_____
_____
_____
_____

> **Question #20: Did God leave all mankind to perish in the estate of sin and misery?**

Answer: God, having out of His mere good pleasure, from all eternity, elected some to everlasting life, did enter into a covenant of grace, to deliver them out of the estate of sin and misery, and to bring them into an estate of salvation by a Redeemer.

Scripture Reading: Romans 9: 1-24

Who are the objects of His gracious covenant? The elect. God's grace is sovereign. He will have mercy upon whom He will. In Romans 9:15 we read: *I will have mercy on whoever I will have mercy, and I will have compassion on whomever I will have compassion.*

Do not be foolishly tempted to lay the charge of injustice or unfairness to God. He is infinite in His wisdom as well as His goodness. Everything He does, every word He speaks, every thought in His mind is right and righteous and perfect. God alone knows why He chooses some to everlasting life. God alone is capable of understanding why. Don't be troubled by the foolish objections to election, or even the sincere misunderstanding of it. Rejoice in your own experience.

Does not the true believer understand that salvation is a gift? Do we not testify that our seeking the Lord was a response to prior seeking on His part? Do we not affirm, *we love Him because He first loved us*? The glorious end or purpose of the covenant of grace is described in these words: *to deliver them out of the estate of sin and misery, and to bring them into an estate of salvation.* The darkness and despair of our sin and misery is more than matched by the glory of our deliverance. The ultimate end of this covenant is that the elect are predestined to be conformed to the image of Christ, that *He might be the firstborn among many brethren.* Salvation from the curse and misery of sin will be complete when sin, misery, and death will have been forever banished from the new creation, and the covenant has been fulfilled.

PRAYERS & REMINDERS

Prayer: O Lord, our Lord, how grateful we are that our final destiny is to be conformed to the image of Christ. How thankful we are that You are working all things together for that glorious good. Hasten the day, we pray, when the gracious covenant has been fulfilled. We ask this for Jesus' sake. Amen.

Hymn for the day:
We Come, O Christ, to Thee

Question #21: Who is the Redeemer of God's elect?

Answer: The only Redeemer of God's elect is the Lord Jesus Christ, who, being the eternal Son of God, became man, and so was, and continues to be, God and man, in two distinct natures, and one Person forever.

Scripture Reading: Matthew 1:18-23

This is truly one of the most amazing statements in the Catechism. Amazing because of what it teaches about Christ, and amazing because of how much it teaches about Christ in a few well-chosen words. In the previous question we learned the good news that God did not leave all mankind to perish in sin and misery, but through a Redeemer, He purposed to save His elect. In this question the identity of the Redeemer is revealed. He is the Lord Jesus Christ, both God and man in two natures and one Person forever.

This great truth that meets our eyes is found in God's Word only. This is a major point of truth and should not be passed over lightly, especially in our day of easygoing toleration of almost any idea that poses in the dress of Christianity or any other religion. There is one Name and one Name only that deserves the title of Redeemer, for He alone can save us and bring us to God. That Name is Jesus, or more properly, the Lord Jesus Christ. It is always well to use that full expression when referring to our Lord, for it includes all that He is: God, Man, and Savior. When Joseph was told by the Angel that Mary was with child by the Holy Spirit, he was also told to *call His name Jesus, because it is He who will save His people from their sins.* In the original language the pronoun He is used in the emphatic, and exclusive sense of the word. The modern world of the "politically correct" despise the claims of Christ that He is the Way, the Truth and the Life, and that no one comes to the Father but by Him. However, this truth must never be denied nor compromised in any way.

Prayer: Great and gracious God, our Father in heaven, we come to You through our Lord Jesus, for He is the only way we may come. Help us to love and honor Him who first loved us, and brought us Your glorious salvation. In His name alone we pray. Amen.

Hymn for the day:
Jesus, What a Friend for Sinners

PRAYERS & REMINDERS

February 29

> *Hymn for the day: Hark the Herald Angels Sing*

PRAYERS & REMINDERS

_____

_____

_____

_____

_____

_____

_____

_____

_____

Question #21: Who is the Redeemer of God's elect?

Answer: The only Redeemer of God's elect is the Lord Jesus Christ, who, being the eternal Son of God, became man, and so was, and continues to be, God and man, in two distinct natures, and one Person forever.

Scripture Reading: Philippians 2:5-11

Our understanding of who Jesus Christ is must begin with His deity. He is God the Son, the second person of the Trinity. The first chapter of John's Gospel is the clearest statement of Christ's deity in all Scripture. He was one with the Father from all eternity. He joined with the Father and the Spirit in the creation of the world. Later He said of Himself, *I and the Father are one.* It was for this claim the leaders brought Him to trial and condemned Him to death. The heart and soul of Christianity lies at this point. Jesus is God. He is God the Son from all eternity. Before Abraham was, He is.

God the Son became man through the incarnation. How He became man is the subject of the next question, but for now we simply affirm with the Catechism, that He became man. Here is the great mystery of our faith. The Creator entered into creation. He in whose image man was created became man Himself. It was not that He appeared on earth as if He were a man, He actually became man. He was fully human in every way.

In doing this He did not cease to be God, not for one moment. The two natures were joined together in one person. This makes Him completely unique. Like others before Him, He was a prophet. Like others before Him, He was a great teacher of truth. Like others before Him, He was a great leader. But like none before or after Him, He and He alone was both God and man in two natures, yet one person forever. This is the heart and soul of Biblical Christianity, and our only hope of salvation.

Prayer: O Lord, You are our God and our salvation. The beauty of Your nature shines brightly through Your Son, our Savior. The mystery of Your glorious triune nature fills our hearts and minds with gratitude and praise through Christ our Lord. Amen.

Hymn for the day:
Fairest Lord Jesus

PRAYERS & REMINDERS

_____
_____
_____
_____
_____
_____
_____
_____
_____
_____

Question #21: Who is the Redeemer of God's elect?

Answer: The only Redeemer of God's elect is the Lord Jesus Christ, who, being the eternal Son of God, became man, and so was, and continues to be, God and man, in two distinct natures, and one Person forever.

Scripture Reading: Hebrews 4:6-16

This union of the human and divine has been the subject of theological inquiry and debate ever since the days of the Apostles. It is beyond human comprehension, but not beyond faith, for this is clearly taught in God's Word. While He was on earth, the Lord Jesus proved Himself fully human over and over again. He also proved Himself God at every turn. He was conceived in the womb of His mother, Mary, but His conception was by the Holy Spirit. He was born as all babies are born, but He was born of the Virgin Mary. He was hungry and thirsty, tired and troubled at time, but always relied on His Father in heaven to supply every need. He wept by the tomb of His dear friend Lazarus as anyone might do. But then He called dead Lazarus from the tomb as none save God could do. He was moved with compassion at the plight of the hopeless leper as anyone might be. But then He cleansed the leper as none save God could do. In God's appointed time and manner, He suffered death, as we all must do. But when He died on the cross, He endured the wrath and judgment of God in our place and for our salvation.

There is one final word which must be said. He is still both God and man, in two distinct natures, yet one person. Right now the Lord Jesus Christ is in heaven at the Father's right hand in the flesh of the resurrection body. He is God the Son as He has always been, but He is also the Son of Man as He became in the incarnation. Because He is still human, He knows our feelings. He is our merciful and faithful High Priest, who was tempted in all points as we are tempted (yet without sin). When we get to heaven and see Him, we will see the same Lord Jesus Christ the disciples saw on the first Easter morning and the sight will be glorious and blessed.

Prayer: O Lamb of God, who takes away the sin of the world, forgive us. O Son of God, who saves sinners, save us. O Savior of all, whom the Father has given You, take us at last to heaven to be with You forever. Amen.

Hymn for the day:
Does Jesus Care?

PRAYERS & REMINDERS

> **Question #22:** *How did Christ, being the son of God, become man?*

Answer: Christ, the Son of God, became man, by taking to Himself a true body and a reasonable soul, being conceived by the power of the Holy Spirit, in the womb of the Virgin Mary, and born of her, yet without sin.

Scripture Reading: Galatians 3:26 - 4:7

The Lord Jesus Christ was and is and ever will be God the Son, the second person of the Trinity. The Gospel of John begins by affirming this. *In the beginning was the Word, and the Word was with God, and the Word was God, And the Word became flesh and dwelt among us.* The Catechism's concern at this point is to answer the question: How did this happen? The answer lies very close to the heart of the gospel message.

First, the Catechism affirms that God the Son became a human being, a man. This is the incarnation. His body was a true human body in every sense of the word. Though He was sinless, yet His body reflected the fallen state of man, in that it was subject to weakness and pain, and even death. He did not therefore inherit in His incarnation the body of Adam before the fall, but of Adam after the fall. This was in order that He might become bone of our bone and flesh of our flesh. He hungered and thirsted even as we do. His was a true human body.

His assumption of human nature was complete, for His soul was a rational (reasonable) soul. He had the capacity to think, to reason, to remember the past, anticipate the future, and even to dread suffering. He had family and friends, joys and sorrows. He was tempted in every possible way a human being may be tempted, in body and soul. That was a great comfort to me as a teenager; it is even more a great comfort to me in these later years of my life. Yes, our Lord became a true man in the incarnation. The great Creator of all that is, became also a creature.

Prayer: Dear Lord Jesus Christ, what glory You left behind when You came into this sin cursed world. What wonder is ours when we read that You were tempted and tried in all points as we are. What gratitude fills our minds when we also read, yet without sin. Thank You for the perfect righteousness You have imputed to us who are so unworthy. Amen.

Hymn for the day:
Hark, the Herald Angels Sing

PRAYERS & REMINDERS

Question #22: How did Christ, being the Son of God, become man?

Answer: Christ, the Son of God, became man, by taking to Himself a true body and a reasonable soul, being conceived by the power of the Holy Spirit, in the womb of the Virgin Mary, and born of her, yet without sin.

Scripture Reading: Luke 2:25-38

Jesus was a very special man. He had no earthly father. His mother was a virgin at the time of His conception. Biological nonsense? Not at all; at least not for the creationist, and should not be even for one who calls himself a theistic evolutionist. The conception of Christ was an act of creation. The same Spirit who moved upon the face of the waters in the primeval creation, moved upon the body of the virgin Mary with the same creative power, and she conceived the earthly body of our Lord.

It has always amazed me that the same person who believes in the beginning God created a single-cell form of life that later evolved into a man, will not believe that the same God could energize a single cell in the body of Mary to cause conception. Of course we who are Biblical creationists have no problem with the miraculous conception at all, and this is a position I heartily recommend to one and all.

The Catechism says so much in so few words. It affirms that Christ was and is the Son of God. It tells us He became fully man both in body and soul. The expression, *true body and rational soul* simply means He became a man in every sense of the word save one, He was always without sin. As the book of Hebrews puts it: *He was in all points tempted as we are, yet without sin.* All of these Biblical truths are important and are well stated in this brief answer of our Shorter Catechism.

PRAYERS & REMINDERS

_____
_____
_____
_____
_____
_____
_____
_____
_____

Prayer: O God, we read in awesome wonder that You gave up Your precious Son for a season that we might have eternal life through Him. Thank you that the same power which caused the Virgin to conceive has also regenerated us who were dead in our trespasses and sins. We praise You for and through Christ our Lord. Amen.

Hymn for the day:
What Child Is This?

> **Question #22: How did Christ, being the Son of God, become man?**

Answer: Christ, the Son of God, became man, by taking to Himself a true body and a reasonable soul, being conceived by the power of the Holy Spirit, in the womb of the Virgin Mary, and born of her, yet without sin.

Scripture Reading: Luke 1:26-38

Let me tell you something. The Biblical truth of the virgin birth is a very important doctrine. It is very popular in some circles to deny and deride this great truth. It is popular in some other circles to affirm it, while saying it is not important to believe in the virgin birth so long as one believes in the deity of Christ. The Bible describes the manner of the Savior's birth in some detail. This alone tells us that God thinks it is important, therefore so should we. It is a gloriously simple and beautiful truth. We receive it with wonder and joy.

Sometimes an objection is raised as to the importance of the Virgin Birth on the grounds it is never mentioned or discussed in any of the Epistles. How many times does God need to tell us a truth before it becomes important to us? Certainly the detailed accounts given of Christ's birth in both Matthew and Luke indicate the importance of this revealed truth. Although the same detail is not given in John's Gospel, there certainly seems to be at least an allusion to the virgin birth in John 1:10-14. If this Gospel was the last one written as many scholars believe, the report of the manner of Christ's birth would already be established by the other Gospels which were written earlier.

So the above arguments against the Virgin Birth, and the importance of it, simply do not ring true. I have yet to hear or read the words of any Bible scholar who believes in the inspiration and inerrancy of Scripture and who argues against this doctrine, or who denies its central importance in the message of salvation. So far as I am able to conclude, those who have problems with the Virgin Birth, also have problems with the whole idea of the incarnation of our Lord Jesus Christ, not to mention the inspiration of Scripture.

Prayer: Lord, You have revealed the marvelous mystery of the Virgin Birth. We accept your Word with gratitude and praise for our Savior. Amen.

Hymn for the day:
Lo, How a Rose E'er Blooming

PRAYERS & REMINDERS

> **Question #22: How did Christ, being the Son of God, become man?**

Answer: Christ, the Son of God, became man, by taking to Himself a true body and a reasonable soul, being conceived by the power of the Holy Spirit, in the womb of the Virgin Mary, and born of her, yet without sin.

Scripture Reading: Luke 4:1-13

Yes, Jesus Christ, God the Son, became a man by means of the Spirit's power in the body of the virgin Mary. He became a true man in every way. But He was not a sinful man. He was a tempted man, but not a fallen man. He was without sin. That is so important for our salvation. When He offered Himself to God on our behalf, He was as a lamb without spot and without blemish. Born sinless, sinless He remained all His life. From His throne, He looks upon us poor sinners with compassionate grace, and will perfect that which He has begun in our hearts.

Some would argue that since He was God the Son, and since He was and is perfect in every way, He could not really be tempted to do evil. They miss the point that He was also truly man, and therefore He could be and was sorely tempted. At this point it is the better part of wisdom to discard human speculation and simply take the Scripture as it is presented. He was tempted by the Devil at the very beginning of His earthly ministry. This is reported in all three of the synoptic Gospels, Matthew, Mark and Luke. There is not the least indication in any of these three accounts that His temptation was just a charade or that it was a mere illustration that we too must face temptation. There is also every indication as reported in these same synoptic Gospels that He was sorely tempted in the Garden of Gethsemane to avoid the cross. His earnest prayers would indicate that this was a severe temptation indeed. Then of course we have the affirmation in the book of Hebrews in the following places. In Hebrews 3: 18 we read: *For that He Himself has suffered, being tempted, He is able to aid those who are tempted.* In Hebrews 4:15, we also read: *.but was in all points tempted as we are, yet without sin.*

PRAYERS & REMINDERS

Prayer: Thank You, dear Savior, for Your courage and strength to resist temptation and thus overcoming Satan's wiles for Yourself, and for all Your spiritual seed. Grant to us also courage and strength to resist him too. Amen.

Hymn for the day:
Tell Me the Story of Jesus

March 7

Question #23: What offices does Christ execute as our Redeemer?

Answer: Christ, as our Redeemer, executes the offices of a prophet, of a priest, and of a king, both in His estate of humiliation and exaltation.

Scripture Reading: I Peter 1:13-21

I will sing of my Redeemer and His wondrous love to me ... So goes the song known and loved by many who delight in Christ as their precious Redeemer. Here in the Catechism we learn that Christ is our Redeemer, and how He accomplished His role as such. The office is really one, but the functions are three. Before exploring the meaning of the three offices, let us first consider the word, *Redeemer.*

In the Bible we find the word used in several places, with various shades of meaning, all of which help us to understand Christ's work as our Redeemer. In the book of Exodus, God is Israel's Redeemer. This redemption takes place as a result of the Lord God coming to Egypt, and with a mighty hand defeating the gods of Egypt, and their puppet king, Pharaoh. This is redemption by conquest. Our Lord Jesus Christ entered this world in which His elect are held prisoner by sin, death, and Satan. He waged war upon our fierce foes. In the famous battles of Gethsemane, Calvary, and the empty tomb, He tore down the strongholds of Satan, defeated sin and death, and set the captives free.

In other places in Scripture, redemption is the result of a price paid. The slave is bought for a certain price, and becomes the possession of the buyer, or else is set free, or restored to a former position. We see this in the case of Hosea buying back his erring wife, Gomer, and restoring her to himself and to her home. We see this truth even more clearly in the words of I Peter cited above.

Prayer: Father in Heaven, we praise Your Holy Name. For You have redeemed us not with corruptible things such as silver and gold, but with the precious blood of Your Son, our Lord, in whose name we pray. Amen.

Hymn for the day:
When I Survey the Wondrous Cross

PRAYERS & REMINDERS

Question #23: What offices does Christ execute as our Redeemer?

Answer: Christ, as our Redeemer, executes the offices of a prophet, of a priest, and of a king, both in His estate of humiliation and exaltation.

Scripture Reading: Hebrews 9:11-28

In Isaiah, we hear God saying that He has redeemed His chosen ones by paying the ransom price. In the New Testament, both Paul and Peter make reference to Christ redeeming His people, by paying the price for their release. Paul reminds us: *for you are bought with a price.* Peter tells us*: we have been redeemed, not with corruptible things like silver or gold, but with the precious blood of Christ.* The purchase price for our salvation includes the whole story of the incarnation, and all the suffering and humiliation our Lord endured for us, beginning with the manger bed in Bethlehem, and including His life, His death, His resurrection, and His ascension.

Another concept of redemption is seen when the priest offers up a sacrifice to cover the sin and cleanse the guilt of God's people. This also includes the idea of substitution. God claimed for Himself all the firstborn of Israel, but provided that an offering of substitution was to be made instead of the firstborn. We even see this much earlier than the giving of the law, when God provided a substitute for Isaac on Mount Moriah.

Tracing this theme of redemption through the book of Leviticus we see how God provided His people with various sorts of sacrifices to cover every aspect and incident of sin. The book of Hebrews makes it abundantly clear that in the offering up of Himself, our Lord Jesus replaced all the ancient offering, and His once and for all sacrifice is a total and complete satisfaction for all our sins.

Prayer: Father, Your word tell us that without the shedding of blood there is no remission of sin. Thank You for the shed blood of our dear Redeemer, the Lord Jesus Christ. In His name. Amen.

PRAYERS & REMINDERS

Hymn for the day:
I Lay My Sins on Jesus

Question #23: What offices does Christ execute as our Redeemer?

Answer: Christ, as our Redeemer, executes the offices of a prophet, of a priest, and of a king, both in His estate of humiliation and exaltation.

Scripture Reading: Genesis 22

The doctrine of the substitutionary atonement lies at the very heart of New Testament theology as well as the Old Testament. Christ is the Lamb of God slain from before the foundation of the world to take the place of guilty sinners before a righteous and holy God. He is the lamb God promised through Abraham, who said to Isaac, *My son, God will provide himself a lamb for a burnt offering* (Gen. 22:8b).

Therefore, in every sense of the word, Christ is our Redeemer. He is our King who conquers sin and death. He is our Moses, our Prophet who proclaims the Word of God, and also demonstrates the mighty acts of God which mean salvation for the elect. He also reveals the law of the Kingdom, saying, *this is my commandment, that ye love one another* (John 15:12a). He is our great High Priest, who has made the once and for all perfect sacrifice for our sins, and who appears in the very presence of God, making intercession for us. He Himself is that sacrifice, the pure and spotless Lamb of God who takes away the sins of the world.

These offices He performs as our Redeemer, thus accomplishing our salvation, and preparing us for heaven. As we read and meditate on these words from our beloved Catechism, and even more from the supporting Scriptures it cites, we are overwhelmed with these truths concerning our blessed Redeemer. The refrain of that beloved hymn, *Man of Sorrows* comes to mind, *Hallelujah, What a Savior*!

Prayer: How perfect is Your plan of salvation, O God. How perfect is the Lamb of God without spot or blemish. How wondrous is Your amazing love and sovereign mercy. We believe, we repent, we accept Your only begotten Son as our Redeemer. Amen.

Hymn for the day:
What Wondrous Love Is This?

PRAYERS & REMINDERS

Question #24: How does Christ execute the office of a prophet?

Answer: Christ executes the office of a prophet in revealing to us, by His Word
and Spirit, the will of God for our salvation.

Scripture Reading: Malachi 3:1-7

When we think of a prophet, a mental picture forms in our minds. We probably think of long robes and beards, of fiery words and fierce looks, of thundering
messages and impending doom. We may think of Elijah, and his contest with the
prophets of Baal on the slopes of Carmel. We may think of bold Nathan, and his
fearless words to king David. Perhaps we may imagine Jeremiah, undaunted by
the wrath of kings and nobles, but weeping over the fallen city of Jerusalem. For
some, the picture of Isaiah comes into focus as he met with God in the temple
vision, marking his call to the office of prophet. Somehow we find it difficult to
fit the Lord Jesus into this picture.

Whatever mental picture we may have of a prophet, the Biblical picture of
a prophet (far more accurate than our mental images) fits the Lord Jesus well,
and the Catechism helps us to see why this is true. In fact, in His ministry, the
Lord embodies all the best in all the prophets of God. Isaiah saw the Lord in a
vision. The Lord Jesus has seen the Father face to face and has dwelt with Him
from all eternity. Brave Jeremiah faced the opposition of the king. Bravest of
the brave, our Lord Jesus Christ confessed His own deity to the High Priest,
knowing this confession would result in His own death. Elijah, who denounced
sin in high places, knew himself to be a sinner. The Lord Jesus preached boldly
against sin, and was Himself sinless. So the comparison and the contrast
between the Lord and the lesser prophets might be made in every case. All the
other Prophets were limited in what they revealed, but our Lord Jesus revealed
the Father perfectly and fully.

PRAYERS & REMINDERS

_____

_____

_____

_____

_____

_____

_____

_____

_____

Prayer: O God, Father, Son and Holy Spirit, how
perfect and complete is Your self revelation, the
Holy Bible. Lord Jesus, You are the great Prophet
of our God. Thank You above all for showing us
the Father in Yourself. Amen.

Hymn for the day:
Join All the Glorious Names

> ### Question #24: How does Christ execute the office of a prophet?

Answer: Christ executes the office of a prophet in revealing to us, by His Word and Spirit, the will of God for our salvation.

Scripture Reading: John 3:1-21

Just how does the Lord Jesus fulfill the role of prophet? In several ways. First, unlike a priest or king, the prophet of old was not anointed by any man to that holy office. The prophet was called by God alone and established as such in the eyes of the people by signs and wonders which accompanied the message from God. These attesting miracles bore witness that the man and the message were from God. So we see Moses bearing God's Word both to the unbelieving Israelites and stubborn, pagan Pharaoh. God granted him great signs to demonstrate to both parties that his message was from the Lord. To the Israelites who believed, they became testimonials to life, and to Pharaoh, who rejected the message, they were symbols of death.

When Jesus began His public ministry, He was anointed to the office of Priest by another Priest, John the Baptist, who inherited the office from his father, Zacharias. But His anointing as a Prophet came directly from God, when the Father said, *This is my beloved Son, in whom I am well pleased.* From that point on Jesus began to declare the will of God for our salvation, His preaching being accompanied by signs and wonders. Another aspect of the office of prophet, as seen in the Old Testament, was the endowing of the prophet with the Spirit of God, so that his words had authority and power. When the Holy Spirit came upon Jesus, and He went forth proclaiming the kingdom, the hallmark of His preaching was authority and power. *The people marveled, saying, 'Never has any man spoken as He speaks,' for He spoke as one having authority and not as the scribes.*

Prayer: Lord, help us always to accept Your authority over our lives. Your mighty miracles reassure us that You were not only a man sent from God, but that You are also God in human flesh, who came to save us poor sinners. Thank You, Lord Jesus. Amen.

Hymn for the day:
My Dear Redeemer and My Lord

PRAYERS & REMINDERS

Question #24: How does Christ execute the office of a prophet?

Answer: Christ executes the office of a prophet, in revealing to us, by His Word and Spirit, the will of God for our salvation.

Scripture Reading: Hebrews 2:1-9

During His earthly ministry, our Lord was God's prophet, declaring His Word and will. But the Catechism speaks in the present tense. He is still fulfilling that office as He speaks to His people by His Word and Spirit. As faithful pastors proclaim the Word under the power of the Spirit, Christ Himself is declaring the will of God for our salvation to His Church. Even when the Bible is read by the hearth or bedside, Christ is fulfilling His office as Prophet. The Bible speaks of Christ, but it also speaks for Christ, for He is the living Word, to which the written Word bears witness.

One final word is in order. The people of old were accountable for their response to the prophet's message. The issue was often life or death. So today, and far more, are we accountable for our response to the real and true prophet, the Lord Jesus Christ. The book of Hebrews tells us that *God spoke through His chosen Prophets at different times, and in various ways. But now in these latter days, He has spoken to us by His Son, whom He has appointed heir of all things, through Whom also He created the worlds.* Later, in chapter 2 of Hebrews we go on to read: *Therefore, we must give more earnest heed to the things we have heard lest we drift away.* It is truly a glorious thing to have available to us the full Word of God. It is also an awesome responsibility, for which we must give account. The more we see and understand God's precious Word, the more we are responsible to obey it and live by faith in all His promises and precepts.

Prayer: Father, may we show our gratitude for Your Holy Word, by living holy lives. We cannot do this in our own strength. Even at our best we fall so far short of that obedience You desire and command of us. Renew our minds, and fill our hearts with holy desires for Your glory. In the name of Christ we pray. Amen.

Hymn for the day:
O Word of God Incarnate

PRAYERS & REMINDERS

_____
_____
_____
_____
_____
_____
_____
_____
_____

Question #25: How does Christ execute the office of a priest?

Answer: Christ executes the office of a priest, in his once offering up of Himself a sacrifice to satisfy divine justice, and reconcile us to God, and in making continual intercession for us.

Scripture Reading: Hebrews 10:1-10

It is one thing to come before God with an offering or sacrifice. It is quite another to come before God as the sacrifice. As our great High Priest, the Lord Jesus Christ has done both for us. He is the once and for all perfect and complete sacrifice whose blood atones for sin and makes us fit for the presence of God, now and in heaven.

In the Old Testament, the office of priest was ordained by God, and regulated by His commands. God appointed Aaron, Moses' brother, as the first High Priest for Israel. His descendants were to maintain the office of priest in perpetuity, until Christ came and fulfilled the office. God intended Israel to be a worshiping people, and required that their worship be acceptable in His sight. The responsibility of the priest was to carefully follow God's directions for worship, and to lead the people of God in that worship.

The first step in acceptable worship involved the recognition of two things: God's holiness and man's sin. Those two things are still required of those who would worship the Father. He is holy, and we are sinful. Something must be done about these two realities before we may worship God in spirit and in truth. God' answer for Israel was an answer of pure grace. Sacrifices were made to atone for sin, and to bring the worshipers into God's presence. Atonement for sin required death, *for the soul that sins shall surely die.* But God in His grace accepted animal sacrifices as a substitute for the life of the sinner. Of course, the blood and life of dumb beasts could not remove sin, but God removed sin by His grace, and required the priests to offer the sacrifices in recognition both of His holiness and His grace.

Prayer: Help us, dear Lord, to worship you in Spirit and in truth. Help us always to remember that You alone can make us worthy to worship You. May we always and only worship You according to Your Word. In Jesus' name we pray. Amen.

Hymn for the day:
Holy, Holy, Holy

PRAYERS & REMINDERS

Question #25: How does Christ execute the office of a priest?

Answer: Christ executes the office of a priest in his once offering up of Himself a sacrifice to satisfy divine justice, and reconcile us to God, and in making continual intercession for us.

Scripture Reading: Hebrews 13:7-21

All Old Testament worship began with these rites of sacrifice, so the believers could know God and at the same time know themselves to be sinners in need of grace from the great God who had called them to Himself. This constant reminder of sin and grace gave both joy and solemnity to worship. The ceremonies of atonement and cleansing pointed to the realities of grace behind the symbols. Each act of the priest was to teach specific truth about God, His holiness, and His grace. I encourage you to read again and with great care the passages from Exodus and Leviticus which describe the priestly office and its primary function of offering acceptable sacrifices to God.

Jesus is our great high priest. He offered not symbolic substitutes for sinners but the true and perfect sacrifice, Himself in our place. He was the Lamb of God who takes away the sin of the world. He was sinless, perfect in His being and in His life of obedience. Thus when He went to the cross and offered Himself up to the Father, it was the one and only, once-and-for-all perfect sacrifice. His blood was the blood of the everlasting covenant that makes atonement for all the elect, and fits us to live with Him forever. No lesser sacrifice would be acceptable to God who is perfect in His holiness, and whose holy nature must be propitiated by the perfect sacrifice. I fear greatly that much of the modern church has lost that sense of God's holiness in favor of misguided ideas of His love. God's love, like His holiness is perfect, and is much purer and powerful than our fallen minds may ever imagine.

PRAYERS & REMINDERS

_____

_____

_____

_____

_____

_____

_____

_____

_____

Prayer: Great God of grace, help us to understand that You are truly holy and at the same time truly gracious. May we never presume on Your kindness by forgetting You holiness. Help us to remember that our Savior said, *Therefore you shall be perfect even as your Father in heaven is perfect.* Thank You that Jesus Christ is our perfection in Your sight. Amen.

Hymn for the day:
My Hope Is Built On Nothing Less

Question #25: How does Christ execute the office of a priest?

Answer: Christ executes the office of a priest in his once offering up of Himself a sacrifice to satisfy divine justice, and reconcile us to God, and in making continual intercession for us.

Scripture Reading: Hebrews 9:11-15

The priest had another function. His was the ministry of continual intercession. He prayed for God's people, seeking blessing and forgiveness. Here again we see the Lord Jesus fulfilling that function as our intercessor. We are told that He ever lives to make intercession for us. He became one of us. He knows and understands our nature and our needs. His ministry of intercession assures the blessing of God in our lives. His ministry of intercession also assures us that our own prayers are heard and answered as we come to the Father.

When He had made the perfect sacrifice for us, He opened heaven, and tore apart the veil of the temple. Therefore we may come boldly to the throne of grace, *dressed in his righteousness alone, faultless to stand before the throne.* With the rending of the magnificent and heavy veil of the temple, the Holiest of Holies within the temple became visible to the eyes of the worshipers for the first time. The greater truth was that by His perfect sacrifice for our sins, the way into God's immediate and holy presence was made possible for believers in Christ for all time. Never again would an offering in the temple of the old covenant have any efficacy. Never again would the blood of lambs, bulls and goats avail for the cleansing of sin. Those who insist that the Jewish temple should be rebuilt and someday will be rebuilt are trampling under foot the blood of God's dear Son, and counting it as insufficient for the cleansing of all sin. That is a sin of which no believer should ever be guilty.

Prayer: O Father, help us to see that the way into Your immediate presence is now opened for us through the atoning work of our Lord Jesus Christ on the cross. May we ever and often walk that blessed pathway that we might find grace to help in all times of need. This we ask for Jesus' sake. Amen.

Hymn for the day:
Alas! And Did My Savior Bleed?

PRAYERS & REMINDERS

_____

_____

_____

_____

_____

_____

_____

_____

_____

> ## Question #26: How does Christ execute the office of a king?

Answer: Christ executes the office of a king in subduing us to Himself, in ruling and defending us, and in restraining and conquering all His and our enemies.

Scripture Reading: Revelation 11:15-19

The late Dr. J. B. Green, in his *Harmony of the Westminster Standards,* said: *Christ as prophet meets the problem of man's ignorance, supplying him with knowledge. As priest, He meets the problem of man's guilt, supplying him with righteousness. As king, He meets the problem of man's weakness and dependence, supplying him with power and protection.* We come now in our study to the last of these, as we think of Christ executing the office of king.

Christ is King! Make no mistake about it. When questioned by Pilate about the charges against Him, that He made Himself out to be a king, Jesus affirmed two things about His kingship. First, He said of the charge, *To this end* [being a king] *I was born.* Secondly, He said of His kingship, *My kingdom is not of this world.* By both statements He was affirming in unequivocal language that He was indeed a king.

He was also affirming that the origin and nature of His kingdom were and are heavenly. This does not mean that His kingdom has nothing to do with this world. Indeed it does! When we see the glorious visions in the Book of Revelation, we see Christ enthroned, ruling over the new creation encompassing both heaven and earth. But even now His kingship is being exercised on earth among His people, and the Catechism does a beautiful job telling us how He carries out this office now and in the future. Thanks to His office as our King, Christ is even now thwarting the evil designs of Satan against you. Even now He is subduing your stubborn will to Himself. In the ages to come, when Satan has been cast into the lake of fire, the victory will be complete, and Christ shall reign forever and ever.

PRAYERS & REMINDERS

_____

_____

_____

_____

_____

_____

_____

_____

_____

Prayer: O Lord, may Your kingdom come, Your will be done in our lives. Defeat all our enemies within and without. Protect us from all the wiles of the evil one, and rule over us forever and ever. Amen.

Hymn for the day:
Come Christians, Join to Sing

Question #26: How does Christ execute the office of a king?

Answer: Christ executes the office of a king in subduing us to Himself, in ruling and defending us, and in restraining and conquering all His and our enemies.

Scripture Reading: Galatians 2:17-21

We use the word *sovereign* often, and often carelessly. It is a word that speaks of kingship. As our king, Christ has subdued our rebellious hearts by sovereign grace. I love the hymn which says, *I sought the Lord, and afterward I knew, He moved my soul to seek Him, seeking me. It was not I that found, O Savior true; no, I was found of Thee.* Truly this is the story of all who have sought the Savior king. He has found us. He has broken our stubborn wills with love. We are His people who have been subdued by a king whose crown was one of thorns, whose hands were nail-pierced. In subduing us to Himself, our king terrified us with the law, which brought conviction of sin and fear of judgment to come. Then when He drew us to His blessed cross, He cast out our fear with love, *for perfect love casts out fear.*

Once our King has brought us into His kingdom, we are His to rule and to defend. By His Word and Spirit, He teaches us His will, instructs us in His commands, and orders our lives for His glory and our good. Our Savior is also our Lord. We cannot have Him as Savior only; He is our Lord as well. The Christian life may be thought of as the process of learning to live under the Lordship of Christ. His commands are not burdensome, they are freeing. As we learn to live by His holy law of love we find great freedom to serve Him and to find ultimate fulfillment. This is something the pleasures of the world offer, but cannot give. We waste so much energy and time trying to find the meaning to our lives in all the wrong places, when it can only be found in Christ, and our willing surrender to Him.

Prayer: Thank You, Lord Jesus Christ, that You are our King. You have set us free from the law of sin and death. You have delivered us from the bondage of this world. Help us to use our freedom to obey and glorify You. Amen.

Hymn for the day:
'Tis So Sweet to Trust in Jesus

PRAYERS & REMINDERS

Question #26: How does Christ execute the office of a king?

Answer: Christ executes the office of a king in subduing us to Himself, in ruling and defending us, and in restraining and conquering all His and our enemies.

Scripture Reading: Ephesians 6:10-20

Christ as our King offers to us the gift of protection. This was and is one of the most important functions of government whether in a Monarchy or even a Democracy. Our enemies are Christ's enemies. The world, the flesh, and the devil all war against the believer's soul. Christ is the Captain of our salvation. He defends us against this deadly trinity of foes. Sin, death, and hell are our enemies, but Christ has defeated these dread foes as well, and defends us from them. Oh, yes, there are still battles to be fought, and as His people, we are called upon to resist our enemies, but not in our own strength. As Martin Luther sang, *Did we in our own strength confide, our striving would be losing; were not the right man on our side, the man of God's own choosing. Dost ask who that may be? Christ Jesus it is He, Lord Sabaoth His name, from age to age the same, and He must win the battle ... His kingdom is forever.*

Rejoice, the Lord is King! He has won us, He rules and defends us, and has willed that we will reign with Him. This is a part of what it means to say that we are heirs of God and joint heirs with Christ. His victories will become our victories. The battles of this world which we must fight as loyal subjects of our King will at long last be put behind us and we will enjoy the spoils of victory. We will know freedom from the assaults of Satan and the bondage of sin. Even now in this world the way to victory is in and through Christ. Christ alone has lived the victorious life, for we are incapable of it. But by His grace we will be given strength to overcome, and the glory will belong to Him alone. Right now in the midst of your battles and often defeats, look up for the Lord is on the throne and you will one day reign with Him.

PRAYERS & REMINDERS
_____
_____
_____
_____
_____
_____
_____
_____
_____

Prayer: We do rejoice, Lord Jesus, that even now You are on the throne of heaven, and will one day reign over all creation. We look for that day, we long for that day. Even so, come quickly, Lord Jesus. Amen.

Hymn for the day:
Lead On, O King Eternal

Question #27: What was Christ's humiliation?

Answer: Christ's humiliation consisted in His being born, and that in a low condition, made under the law, undergoing the miseries of this life, the wrath of God, and the cursed death on the cross; in being buried, and continuing under the power of death for a time.

Scripture Reading: Philippians 2:5-11

The human mind is incapable of grasping the truths set forth in this question and answer of the Catechism. It is impossible for mortal mind to understand what it cost our Lord Jesus Christ to enter this sin-cursed world, and win our salvation. The word *humiliation* is a good beginning point in our effort to at least try to see something of this purchase price He paid for the beloved elect. The plan was from all eternity. The submission to the Father's will was a part of His nature from all eternity. The fulfillment of the will and plan involved great cost, great loss, and terrible suffering.

The Catechism properly begins with His birth, not His cross. When you consider the pre-incarnate state of our Lord, when you hear the Apostle John begin his Gospel with the words, *In the beginning was the Word, and the Word was with God, and the Word was God ... all things were made by him, and without him, was not anything made that was made ... ,* then you begin to see that the Creator, entering His creation, by the process of human birth is in itself the very essence of humiliation. The distinction between the Creator and the creature is far greater than the distinction between man, and the lowest form of life on earth. Suppose for a moment that a human being became a lowly worm in order to save all worms. The distance between a man and a worm, which is also a creature would be less than the distance between God and man. Maybe this gives you some idea of the humiliation of our Lord when He became a man. The lowly circumstances of His birth serve to emphasize the humiliation. No room in the inn, the manger stall, the adoration of the shepherds, the flight into Egypt, all underscore the point: His was a lowly birth.

Prayer: Almighty God, Creator of all things, You humbled yourself beyond all measure when You became bone of our bone and flesh of our flesh in the incarnation. We stand amazed, Indeed we fall at Your feet and worship You who are blessed forever. We praise You, O beautiful Savior. Amen.

Hymn for the day:
Infant Holy, Infant Lowly

PRAYERS & REMINDERS

> ### *Question #27: What was Christ's humiliation?*

Answer: Christ's humiliation consisted in His being born, and that in a low condition, made under the law, undergoing the miseries of this life, the wrath of God, and the cursed death of the cross; in being buried, and continuing under the power of death for a time.

Scripture Reading: Matthew 27:27-44

When God met Moses at the burning bush, He identified Himself as "I AM," the Savior of Israel, the God of the Covenant. Later, on Mt. Sinai, He revealed Himself as the lawgiver. When our Lord Jesus was on earth, He claimed this same exalted identity for Himself saying, *Before Abraham was, I AM.* Furthermore He claimed for Himself the role of lawgiver, saying, *A new commandment I give you ...* Yet He was made under the law. He submitted to the law He had given, and kept it perfectly in letter and spirit, in form and substance. He honored the law in His teaching, and His living.

When Jesus came into this world, He did not exempt Himself from any of the trials and sufferings of humanity. He was subjected to the miseries of this life, just as we are. He was hungry, tired, misunderstood, rejected, disappointed, hurt by the failure of friends. He cruelly suffered, He wept, He was tempted and tried in every way as we are. He shared our common lot. Few of us living in today's world suffer the degree of want and privation to which He was subjected, but it was the common lot of the poor, and He endured it willingly. What great love! When He came unto His own, His own would not receive Him. They rejected and despised Him, refused to hear the message of salvation, and denied that He had come from the Father. Then they demanded His death at the hands of the Roman authorities and mocked Him as He hung on the cross. The ultimate shame came as they had judged Him to be a common criminal worthy of the most painful and accursed death possible. All of this humiliation He endured for your salvation and mine.

PRAYERS & REMINDERS

_____
_____
_____
_____
_____
_____
_____
_____
_____
_____

Prayer: "Ah Holy Jesus, how hast thou offended?" We hear of Your Humiliation and see our proud hearts still rejecting the cross You told us we must bear. Forgive us change us. Let this mind be in us which was also in You, that we might honor and serve You who are worthy of all honor and service. Amen.

Hymn for the day:
O Sacred Head Now Wounded

Question #27: What was Christ's humiliation?

Answer: Christ's humiliation consisted in His being born, and that in a low condition, made under the law, undergoing the miseries of this life, the wrath of God, and the cursed death on the cross; in being buried, and continuing under the power of death for a time.

Scripture Reading: I Corinthians 5:12-21

The Catechism speaks of the wrath of God, and the cursed death of the cross. It is more proper to reverse this order and speak first of the cross, and then the wrath of God. When the Lord went to the cross, He was in fellowship with the Father, and prayed that He would forgive those who crucified Him. Later, when in the mystery of His suffering, His soul was made an offering for sin, the righteous wrath of God fell upon Him and the fellowship was broken, as was His heart, for He cried, *My God, my God, why hast thou forsaken me?* That wrath and separation were so bitter, so devastating that we whisper in awesome wonder and with tears, *He descended into hell.* Calvin and many other Reformers all agreed that the words, *He descended into hell,* describe what happened on the cross, when he endured the wrath of God. The humiliation had reached its lowest depths.

He was despised by man, publicly disgraced and shamed, tortured, killed, and forsaken by the Father. Afterwards they laid Him in a borrowed tomb, and there He remained under death's dark sway for three days. These things constitute our Lord's humiliation. B*ut He was wounded for our transgressions, He was bruised for our iniquities, and the chastisement of our peace was upon Him ... and with His stripes, we are healed.* The depths of His misery and His humiliation constitute the heights of our hopes, for by His humiliation, the door is opened for our glorification. *For He made Him who knew no sin to be sin for us, that we might become the righteousness of God in Him.*

Prayer: What Thou, my Lord, hast suffered, was all for sinners gain: Mine, mine was the transgression, but Thine the deadly pain ... O make me Thine forever; and should I fainting be, Lord, let me never, never outlive my love to Thee. Amen.

Hymn for the day:
Ah, Holy Jesus, How Hast Thou Offended?

PRAYERS & REMINDERS

Question #28: What is Christ's exaltation?

Answer: Christ's exaltation consists in His rising again from the dead on the third day, in ascending into heaven, in sitting at the right hand of God the Father, and in coming to judge the world at the last day.

Scripture Reading: Matthew 28

The exaltation of Christ is one of the major themes of Scripture, and is the joy of the believer. Just before He left His disciples to go to the cross, the Lord Jesus promised them that they would see Him again, and when they saw Him, they would have great joy that could never be taken away. Later when Jesus appeared to these same disciples just after the resurrection and showed them His hands and His side, they were glad and rejoiced greatly. True to His word, the Lord gave them a joy they never lost again. The resurrection and the victory it represented became the cornerstone of the triumphant joy which has been characteristic of Christians for almost two thousand years.

The resurrection of our Lord Jesus from the dead is the most important event in the history of the world. It was a true, bodily resurrection of One who was dead and had been buried. It was the first giant step in the exaltation of our Lord. We celebrate this great event, not just on Easter Sunday, but on every Lord's day. The first day of the week has become the day on which believers celebrate the victory of our Lord. This has become the Sabbath of the new creation. Though some may cling to the Sabbath of the old covenant, the vast majority of believers recognize that the principle of the Sabbath has been transferred from the last day of the week to the first day. Let us make very sure that we give all honor to our Lord on His day. The principle of the Sabbath is still in effect, and should be as carefully guarded, and as joyfully celebrated as it was under the old covenant. What better way is there to recognize and rejoice in the exaltation of our Lord Jesus?

PRAYERS & REMINDERS

_____
_____
_____
_____
_____
_____
_____
_____
_____

Prayer: Father in heaven, thank You that You brought again from the dead, our Lord Jesus, the great Shepherd of the sheep. Thank You for His glorious exaltation we see in the resurrection. Help us to honor and worship Him on His blessed day of days. In Jesus name, and for His sake we pray. Amen.

Hymn for the day:
O Day of Rest and Gladness

> ## Question #28: What is Christ's exaltation?

Answer: Christ's exaltation consists in His rising again from the dead on the third day, in ascending into heaven, in sitting at the right hand of God the Father, and in coming to judge the world at the last day.

Scripture Reading: Acts 1:1-11

The resurrection, however, was not an isolated event. It may only be understood as the first in a series of events that are inseparable, and which comprise the exaltation of our Lord. Forty days after His resurrection, the Lord Jesus ascended into heaven. The ascension is properly recognized in the Apostles' Creed as deserving a prominent place in basic Christian doctrine. It is a neglected fact and truth in most preaching. The neglect of the ascension is most likely due to the fact that it is seen as a continuation of the resurrection. While this is true, it also has its own significance. This is seen especially in the book of Hebrews, which never mentions the resurrection, but makes the ascension the main focal point of Christology. The ascension to the right hand of the Father meant vindication for Christ. *The head that once was crowned with thorns, is crowned with glory now. A royal diadem adorns the mighty victor's brow.*

Like the resurrection, the ascension was bodily. The glorified body of Christ, still recognizable and bearing still the marks of His suffering, was lifted up to heaven, where Christ began both His reign and His intercession. It was the vision of the ascended Christ at the right hand of the Father that gave to Stephen the courage to face death, and the grace to forgive those who murdered him. Undoubtedly the reality of Stephen's vision led to an even greater vision seen by Saul of Tarsus on his way to Damascus. The light which blinded Saul was brighter than the noonday sun, for it came from the source of all light, the triumphant Christ seated at the Father's right hand. He is still there, and from there He will come again to judge the living and the dead.

Prayer: O Savior, from Your high throne of glory, look down with pity upon us here below. We are Your people, and the sheep of Your pasture. We long for Your return in glory. Help us to be prepared to meet You when You come. Amen.

Hymn for the day:
The Head That Once Was Crowned with Thorns

PRAYERS & REMINDERS

Question #28: What is Christ's exaltation?

Answer: Christ's exaltation consists in His rising again from the dead on the third day, in ascending into heaven, in sitting at the right hand of God the Father, and in coming to judge the world at the last day.

Scripture Reading: Revelation 1:1-8

Dr. J. B. Green's *Harmony of the Westminster Standards* statement on the ascension is worth quoting. *While the Scripture and the Catechisms represent Christ as sitting, they do not represent Him as idle. Sitting is the symbol of rest, rest from work finished. But atonement accomplished, must be applied. Christ must reign, administering the affairs of His church and kingdom till the restitution of all things.*

The final stage in Christ's exaltation has not yet taken place, and will not until the end of the age. He will come again to judge the living and the dead, and until that day, His exaltation must wait its final glory. This is the blessed hope of believers, and the fear and dread of unbelief. Rightly so, for it is a fearful thing to fall into the hands of the living God. Our Lord Jesus will return in power and great glory, even as He affirmed to the High Priest when He was on trial before the Sanhedrin. To omit this truth is to ignore large portions of Scripture, both Old and New Testaments. Much of what our Lord taught during His final days on earth has to do with this great truth.

The humiliation of the Lord Jesus Christ is forever ended. His exaltation begun at the empty tomb has yet to see its final glory, a glory beyond all human mind or thought. But though delayed, the final and complete exaltation of our Lord and Savior will be accomplished. It is on God's calendar of events yet to take place, but sure to take place. How glorious will that day be when the Lord Jesus sits on the throne of His glory. We see a grand vision of this glory in the first chapter of Revelation. You may wish to read again that same passage cited above.

PRAYERS & REMINDERS

_____
_____
_____
_____
_____
_____
_____
_____
_____

Prayer: How glorious, O God, is the throne of Your beloved Son, the Lord Jesus Christ. How wonderful to know His exaltation will be completed in Your good time. May we be found faithful in serving Him now, Whom we will serve forever in heaven. Amen.

Hymn for the day:
All Hail the Power of Jesus' Name!

Question #29: How do we take part in the redemption purchased by Christ?

Answer: We take part in the redemption purchased by Christ by the effectual application of it to us by His Holy Spirit.

Scripture Reading: Titus 3:1-8

Presbyterians have always believed that Christ did not come to make the salvation of all peoples possible, but to make the salvation of God's elect certain. If salvation is merely possible for any or all, then it is equally possible than none will be saved. In short condemnation would be a possibility for all. We believe that Christ's saving work assures the salvation of all those for whom He died. How could we believe less, and still hold to the sovereignty of God?

However, this certainty is not based on confidence in human ability to appropriate the grace of God, but in the power of God the Holy Spirit to apply the finished work of Christ to the elect. Again, we should understand that the elect are saved not because they are elect in themselves, but because Christ Jesus won their salvation by His perfect obedience in life, His atoning death on the cross and His blessed resurrection from the dead. The saving work of Christ resulted in God pardoning our sins, and declaring us to be righteous in His sight, and imputing to us the righteousness of Christ. We call this justification, the subject of a later study. But salvation is always an experience of grace and of Christ in the heart and life of the believer. This is the work of the Holy Spirit. He applies to us the benefits of Christ's work. By His work we are made partakers of what Christ has accomplished. This in turn assures us that we are now the children of God, heirs of God and joint heirs with Christ. The work of salvation in behalf of sinners, and in sinners is a work of the triune God, Father Son, and Holy Spirit. Each One has His role in our salvation, and all three Persons cooperate in this.

Prayer: Great and gracious God, Father, Son, and Holy Spirit, we bow before You and wonder that You should love us so much, and with such wisdom, love and power so as to secure our salvation. As You, great God, continue to persevere within us, may we also persevere in seeking You with all our hearts. We ask this for Jesus' sake. Amen.

Hymn for the day:
Seal Us, O Holy Spirit

PRAYERS & REMINDERS

_____

_____

_____

_____

_____

_____

_____

_____

_____

Question #29: How do we take part in the redemption purchased by Christ?

Answer: We take part in the redemption purchased by Christ by the effectual application of it to us by His Holy Spirit.

Scripture Reading: John 14:15-23

This truth is taught in a beautiful and comforting way in John 14. Jesus told His disciples that He was going away, but that He would send another Comforter to them. The Comforter would be the Holy Spirit, sent both from the Father and the Son to abide with His people forever. A part of His ministry would be to take the things of Christ, and make them known to the disciples. This is not only a promise of illumination of the mind but the application of saving truth to the heart. When Jesus promised that the Spirit would abide with us forever, He implied that He would be continually applying the benefits of His (Christ's) saving work to us. This would also assure our union with Christ, for the Lord promised that by the Spirit, He, too, would come to His disciples and be with them and in them. In fact He went on to say that the Father would also come and abide with them. The Trinity is always present when one Member is present.

Certainly fellowship with God is a part of the application of the benefits of Christ's redemption. This alone wins for us access to God and fellowship with Him. To be partakers of the benefits of Christ's redemption is to be heirs of God and joint heirs with Christ. What glory! What joy! Have you ever considered what an honor it is to be sought by God? Have you ever thought how utterly amazing it is that the thrice holy God desires fellowship with us, and beyond fellowship, desires us to be a part of His family? We are a blest people. We have a great salvation, and an even greater God! Hallelujah.

PRAYERS & REMINDERS

_____

_____

_____

_____

_____

_____

_____

_____

_____

Prayer: Heavenly Father, we will never understand why You love us so much. We are grateful beyond any words of praise for Your amazing grace. Thank You for the finished work of Your Son, the Lord Jesus, on our behalf. Thank You for the ongoing work of the Holy Spirit in applying His redemption to us. Our souls sing out, how great Thou art. We praise You in Jesus name. Amen.

Hymn for the day:
O For A Thousand Tongues

Question #29: How do we take part in the redemption purchased by Christ?

Answer: We take part in the redemption purchased by Christ by the effectual application of it to us by His Holy Spirit.

Scripture Reading: Philippians 3:1-14

I love the word effectual. It speaks of assurance and a hope that will not fail. It means that in Christ we will persevere unto the end. It means that we will be more than conquerors through Him who loves us. It means that even now we are the children of God, and that one day we will be like Him (Christ) for we shall see Him as He is.

Since it is the Holy Spirit who is at work to effectually apply the benefits of Christ's redemption to us, we must take heed to neither quench nor grieve the Spirit, whereby we are sealed unto the day of our full redemption. Rather it is ours to seek the constant filling of the Holy Spirit, and to obey Him as He opens God's Holy Word to our minds and hearts.

We should never get the idea that we are wholly passive in this process. There are so many exhortations in Scripture which forbid such an attitude. When Jesus was on earth He constantly called for willing response to His promises and precepts. The most notable of these is found in Matthew 16:24: *If anyone desires to come after Me, let him deny himself and take up his cross and follow me.* This requires conscious effort, even to the extreme of dying to self and sin. The great Apostle Paul reminded us: *By grace you have been saved through faith, and that not of yourselves; it is the gift of God not of works lest anyone should boast.* This same Apostle, in another place fervently exhorted us: *Work out your own salvation with fear and trembling, for it is God who works in you to will and to do according to His good pleasure.* How carefully Scripture guides us in our understanding of God's ways and works.

Prayer: Father God, may we to whom the Spirit has applied the saving work of Christ, be diligent and faithful in obeying You and accepting our responsibility to know and do Your holy will. This we ask in Jesus' name. Amen.

Hymn for the day:
Take Thou Our Minds, Dear Lord

PRAYERS & REMINDERS

Question #30: How does the Spirit apply to us the redemption purchased by Christ?

Answer: The Spirit applies to us the redemption purchased by Christ by working faith in us, and thereby uniting us to Christ in our effectual calling.

Scripture Reading: Romans 8:12-27

There is logical progression in the Catechism which is evident at every point. The last question dealt with how we are made partakers of Christ's redemption, namely by the Holy Spirit. In this question and answer, we see how the Spirit makes us partakers of the redemption purchased by Christ.

The Holy Spirit regenerates our hearts and enables us to have faith in Christ. More properly stated, the Spirit works faith in us. This speaks of sovereignty in salvation. This is entirely consistent with the Calvinistic theology of the Catechism, which ascribes our salvation not to us for anything we are or do, but wholly to God. Another way of saying almost the same thing is found in Ephesians 2:8-9: *For by grace are ye saved through faith, and that not of yourselves, it is the gift of God, not of works, lest any man should boast.* Salvation is of the Lord. The Father elected us, the Son died for us, and the Spirit applies these things to us, so that we actually experience the grace of God.

It is important to know that faith does not cause regeneration. Faith is the result of regeneration. In Ephesians 2: 1, we are told plainly that we were dead in our trespasses and sins. This would make faith impossible unless and until God regenerates us and makes us alive so we can respond to the Gospel. Many believers think faith precedes regeneration, but from what we read in Ephesians, and in many other places this would be impossible. Jesus said in John 6:44: *No one can come to Me unless the Father who sent Me draws him.* Until this happens no one can exercise faith. All of this is to simply say, God is sovereign in salvation as he is in all things.

Prayer: Father in heaven, truly we were dead in our trespasses and sins until You made us alive in Christ. Now we who were not Your people have by Your grace become Your people. Help us to live in such a way that all will know whose children we are. We ask this for Jesus' sake. Amen.

Hymn for the day:
I Am Not Skilled to Understand

PRAYERS & REMINDERS

> ### Question #30: How does the Spirit apply to us the redemption purchased by Christ?

Answer: The Spirit applies to us the redemption purchased by Christ by working faith in us, and thereby uniting us to Christ in our effectual calling.

Scripture Reading: Colossians 1:1-14

We may not be consciously aware of the Holy Spirit's role in our salvation. The faith He works in our hearts comes by hearing the Word of God. This may come to us by merely reading the Bible, or remembering something we have read in the Bible. It may come to us by the direct testimony of a loving friend who shares Christ with us from the Word. It may come as a faithful minister preaches a powerful gospel sermon that stirs our hearts, even as hearts were stirred at Pentecost by Peter's great message. Many learn faith at their mothers' knee, or from a loving Sunday School teacher. The point is that we are apt to be more aware of the means the Spirit uses to work faith in us than we are of the Spirit Himself. We may even be tempted to feel that faith is something we generated in our own hearts. Often the Gospel preacher in his zeal will lay the burden of faith on the sinner who is dead in trespasses and sin. However, we need to always remember that faith is a gift of the Spirit – a gift to be received, and a gift to use, but a gift, nonetheless.

But in whatever form the outward call may come to us, it is the inner call and regenerating work of the Spirit to which the Catechism points us. Many, many people hear the outward call of the Gospel, and many respond only in an outward way. This again points to the sovereignty of God in our salvation. Effectual calling takes place only when those whom the Father has given to His Son from all eternity come alive by the work of the Holy Spirit and answer His call truly. One reason why some people hesitate to believe in the security of true believers is that they confuse the outward call with the effectual and saving call by which we are born again from above.

Prayer: Thank You, mighty God and gracious Father, for Your unspeakable gifts of Christ and saving faith. It was not in us to repent and believe until You worked Your mighty work of salvation within. Thank You that because of You we are secure in our salvation. We offer You our grateful praise in Jesus' name. Amen.

Hymn for the day:
Jesus Paid It All

PRAYERS & REMINDERS

> ### Question #30: How does the Spirit apply to us the redemption purchased by Christ?

Answer: The Spirit applies to us the redemption purchased by Christ by working faith in us, and thereby uniting us to Christ in our effectual calling.

Scripture Reading: Colossians 3:1-4

What is the result of this effectual calling? It works faith in us, and unites us to Christ! We often refer to Christ as the great Physician, and he truly is. But is not the Holy Spirit also the great Physician who applies the saving work of Christ to our sin-sick souls? What an amazing thing to consider. How rich is our salvation. United to Christ! This needs some amplification and explanation. We are united to Christ in His death on the cross. By this we have died to sin, and the benefits of His death become ours. We are united to Christ in His resurrection. This means our justification and the promise of our own resurrection in God's good time. This also means *Christ in you, the hope of glory.*

Furthermore, it means we are heirs of God and joint heirs with Christ. This union with Christ means that we are united to Him in His death. So we hear Paul saying in Galatians 2:20 *I have been crucified with Christ.* He was not speaking of an emotional inner experience by which he was determined that he would be crucified with Christ. He was speaking of a judicial act on God's part, whereby He placed on the Lord Jesus all our sin and all its guilt. So that when Christ died for our sins, the sentence pronounced against us (*The wages of sin is death*) was actually carried out on Christ to whom we are united. Thus by that blessed union, He literally and actually bore our sin and punishment on Himself and they have been punished fully.

This in turn means we will be united to Him in glory forever and ever. This is the work of the Holy Spirit in applying to us the benefits of Christ's saving work. Once more we see how the blessed Trinity, Father, Son and Holy Spirit, are fully and equally involved in our salvation.

Prayer: Blessed be the God and Father of our Lord Jesus Christ who has blest us with all spiritual blessings in Christ Jesus. Thank You, O God, for such a rich and full salvation which you have won for us through Your Son, and applied to us by Your Spirit We praise You through Christ, our Lord. Amen.

Hymn for the day:
Loved with Everlasting Love

PRAYERS & REMINDERS

Question #30: How does the Spirit apply to us the redemption purchased by Christ?

Answer: The Spirit applies to us the redemption purchased by Christ by working faith in us, and thereby uniting us to Christ in our effectual calling.

Scripture Reading: II Corinthians 5

There is another side to this we often overlook in our joy over the blessings of this union. I speak of the awesome responsibility, and high privileges inherent in this union. In speaking to His disciples, Christ said, *The works that I do, shall ye do also, and greater works than these, because I go to my Father.* By these words we understand that our union with Christ involves us in His work and mission. This, too, is a result of the Holy Spirit applying to us the redemption purchased by Christ. After His resurrection, the Lord Jesus gathered His disciples around Him, and said to them, *Receive ye the Holy Spirit. As the Father hath sent Me, so send I you.* Being united to Christ, by the work of the Holy Spirit, we are made partakers of his redemption, and at the same time we become ambassadors of God and agents of the Holy Spirit, as He applies the benefits of Christ's redemption to all the elect.

The Apostle Paul understood this when he wrote to the believers in Corinth these words: *God was in Christ reconciling the world unto Himself, not imputing their trespasses to them, and has committed to us the word of reconciliation. Now then we are ambassadors for Christ, as though God were pleading through us.* In the book of Revelation, 21:17 we read: *And the Spirit and the bride say "Come!"* The bride, of course, is the Church. So speaking for our glorious Head and in His name we extend the offer of the Gospel. This is a part of our responsibilities and privileges as those who have been united to Christ by the Holy Spirit, who applies to us the benefits of Christ's atonement

Prayer: Father, we are so grateful that we have been united to Christ by Your Holy Spirit. Thank You for the high honor of representing Him in this fallen world. May we be found faithful to our holy task of being His ambassadors. We ask this in His name, and for His sake. Amen.

Hymn for the day:
So Send I You

PRAYERS & REMINDERS

Question #31: What is effectual calling?

Answer: Effectual calling is the work of God's Spirit, by which, convincing us of our sin and misery, enlightening our minds in the knowledge of Christ, and renewing our wills, He persuades and enable us to embrace Jesus Christ, freely offered to us in the Gospel.

Scripture Reading: Ezekiel 36:22-38

Sometimes the term, effectual calling, is used to describe the sovereign grace of God which brings to us the free grace of salvation. By these words, *effectual calling*, all honor and glory are given to God, and we claim no merit of our own in our salvation. Many people hear the outward call to salvation, and many outwardly respond in one way or another. But only those who have been chosen in Christ, and regenerated by the work of God's Holy Spirit are capable of responding to the inward call of the Spirit by repentance and faith.

The expression, *effectual calling*, is warm and full, but it does not and cannot really tell the whole story. First of all, this is the work of the Holy Spirit, the One promised by Jesus in the upper room to be our Comforter. Because of His great love and wisdom, He will not allow us to be content with false peace, nor fleshly security. It is His will for us to know real peace and true comfort. So as He awakens our hearts in God's gracious work of regeneration, we who were once dead in our trespasses and sins are made alive again. As we awaken to new life we see ourselves for what we are, miserable lost sinners, without God and without hope, save in His sovereign mercy. The awakening is very painful at first. After all who really wants to face the truth that we are all lost and under the sentence of death? Who wants to hear that all our righteousness is but filthy rags in God's sight? Who wants to hear that all have sinned and fallen short of the glory of God? But these truths must be faced and dealt with for what they are if there is any hope for us. And of course there is hope, but not just hope, even more, assurance, solid and true.

PRAYERS & REMINDERS

_____

_____

_____

_____

_____

_____

_____

_____

_____

_____

Prayer: Gracious and great God, our Father in heaven, You have called us to Yourself, and enabled us to hear, believe, and respond to Your gracious call. Thank You for the Holy Spirit by Whom we are effectually called into Your kingdom by faith in Your beloved Son, the Lord Jesus Christ. Amen

Hymn for the day:
Blessed Assurance

Question #31: What is effectual calling?

Answer: Effectual calling is the work of God's Spirit, by which, convincing us of our sin and misery, enlightening our minds in the knowledge of Christ, and renewing our wills, He persuades and enable us to embrace Jesus Christ, freely offered to us in the Gospel.

Scripture Reading: Acts 2:22-39

The first work of the Holy Spirit in our effectual calling is to convince us of our sin and misery. This almost sounds like a contradiction in terms. The comforter makes us miserable? Indeed He does, for He is the true Comforter. He must first bring us to the point of knowing ourselves to be sinners in the sight of God, justly deserving His displeasure, and without hope save in His sovereign mercy.

The Holy Spirit is like the skilled surgeon, who must inflict great pain if he is to bring about true healing. The malignancy of sin is deep-seated and life-threatening. We must see ourselves as condemned sinners before a holy God. The utter misery of knowing we are lost and without hope is a painful but very necessary experience, if we are to ever know the true comfort of forgiveness. This is precisely what Jesus meant when He said, *Blessed are the poor in spirit, for theirs is the kingdom of heaven.* Again He said, *Blessed are they that mourn, for they will be comforted.*

What hope is there for healing if the attending physician does not properly diagnose the true condition of the patient? What physician worthy of the title would knowingly tell you, you had a chest cold, when he knew you had lung cancer? What preacher who claims to be a true minister of God's word would dare tell people they have no need of a Savior, or that God would never allow anyone to be lost? So effectual calling begins with the deep conviction of sin as the necessary starting point of hearing and believing the message of salvation by grace.

Prayer: Father, we have sinned against You in so many ways. We are sinful by nature and by choice. Yet it is because of Your loving purpose for us, You have awakened us to our need and our sin and have brought us to repentance. Ever more convict us when we stray from You. We ask this in Jesus' name, and for His sake. Amen.

Hymn for the day:
Just As I Am

PRAYERS & REMINDERS

Question #31: What is effectual calling?

Answer: Effectual calling is the work of God's Spirit, by which, convincing us of our sin and misery, enlightening our minds in the knowledge of Christ, and renewing our wills, He persuades and enable us to embrace Jesus Christ, freely offered to us in the Gospel.

Scripture Reading: John 6:35-51

Thankfully, the conviction of sin is not the whole story in effectual calling. If it were, we would spend eternity in utter misery. However, a glorious next word, *enlightening our minds in the knowledge of Christ*, lifts the heavy weight off our hearts. Sin drives us to despair, the Holy Spirit leads us to Christ. As one Scottish preacher once said, *I looked into my own heart and saw nothing but sin and misery, darkness and despair. Then I looked to Christ and saw light and hope. It is good that we met.*

When the Spirit enlightens our minds in the knowledge of Christ, He convinces us that Christ is the Son of God and Savior of sinners. He enables us to understand that the Son of Man came to seek and save that which was lost. He points us to the Word of God, in which we read, *All that the Father giveth Me will come to Me, and him that cometh to Me, I will in no wise cast out.* Do you believe in the Lord Jesus Christ as the Son of God, and Savior of sinners; and have you looked in faith to the Lord Jesus Christ for your salvation? If so it is only because the Holy Spirit has enlightened your mind in the knowledge of Christ. The precious truth that was hidden from your darkened mind is now brought to light, and you understand that Jesus Christ is all He claimed to be, and that He is your Lord and Savior because of who He is, and what He accomplished by His death on the cross, and His resurrection from the dead. This enlightenment changes your whole outlook on life. It breaks your pride, but it gives you a new reason to boast, for as the Apostle Paul wrote, *God forbid that I should boast save in the cross of Christ Jesus my Lord...*

Prayer: Dear Father, You have afflicted us with the conviction of sin, and troubled our hearts by the knowledge we are without God and without hope apart from Your grace. But now You have revealed Christ to us, and have shown us Your salvation in Christ our Lord. Thank you for giving Your Son to be our Savior. Amen.

Hymn for the day:
In The Cross Of Christ I Glory

PRAYERS & REMINDERS

April 4

Question #31: What is effectual calling?

Answer: Effectual calling is the work of God's Spirit, by which, convincing us of our sin and misery, enlightening our minds in the knowledge of Christ, and renewing our wills, He persuades and enable us to embrace Jesus Christ, freely offered to us in the Gospel.

Scripture Reading: Acts 13:42-52

Once the mind is enlightened, then the will is quickened. We who were dead in our trespasses and sins, are made alive in Christ, by the Holy Spirit's work of regeneration. The desire for salvation is a gift. The will to respond to the free offer of the Gospel comes from above. The old will with the powerful pull of the world, flesh, and devil is still there, but now a new will is given, and we are enabled to repent.

The work of effectual calling is never complete, until persuaded by the Word and inner work of the Holy Spirit, we embrace the Lord Jesus Christ, receiving and resting upon Him alone for salvation, as He is offered in the Gospel. Drawn by cords of love, persuaded that I am a sinner, and that Jesus died for me, I open my heart to Him who has loved me from all eternity, and by whose Holy Spirit I have been effectually called to Him. My will, once so resistant to God has been renewed, and my mind has been enlightened and thus I am persuaded that the Gospel is true, and that the requirements of God's holy law have been met in two ways. First the full penalty for my law breaking has been paid by the death of Jesus Christ on the cross. The death He endured was both physical and spiritual, as His soul was made an offering for sin. As the perfect Lamb of God without spot or blemish of any kind, He took away my sin completely and forever. Secondly, the requirements of active obedience to the holy law of God were all met by the life Jesus lived. He obeyed in thought, word, and deed the full requirements of the law. He loved the Lord His God with all His heart, mind and strength, and His neighbor as Himself. All this active obedience has been credited to my account, and the law has been fulfilled.

Prayer: O Lamb of God who takes away the sin of the world, we come to You in simple but sincere faith that our debt has been paid by Your perfect sacrifice. Help us to rest in this confidence, and trust You wholly for our salvation. In Your name we pray. Amen.

Hymn for the day:
My Faith Has Found a Resting Place

PRAYERS & REMINDERS

> ## Question #32: What benefits are there in this life for those who are effectually called?

Answer: Those who are effectually called partake in justification, adoption, sanctification, and the other benefits that, in this life, do either accompany or flow from them.

Scripture Reading: Romans 3:21-31

Years ago I read a story of a man who bought a ticket on a river boat going from Cincinnati, Ohio, to New Orleans, Louisiana. He had barely enough money for the ticket, and was worried about hunger on the long trip, since he could not afford to eat in the ornate dining room on board the ship. Taking his last few dollars, he bought a supply of crackers and cheese, enough, he hoped, to last the long trip. Being embarrassed by his own poverty, he avoided the other passengers as much as possible and during meals would slip away to his cabin and eat his meager fare. Toward the end of the voyage a fellow passenger who had noticed his absence during the meals asked him why he never came to the dinner. Much ashamed, he finally confessed that he could not afford the cost. Gently, his newfound friend asked him to take out his ticket and look on the reverse side. Upon doing so, he found to his chagrin these words: All meals included. He had made the trip, but had missed out on some of the benefits of his ticket.

Those who are effectually called are blessed with many benefits which accompany and flow from this grace. Is it any wonder that those who have been effectually called by our great God have blessings and benefits from His hand? God is both great and good. He is a kind and gracious Father who delights to give His children good things. These good things are far more than just food and drink and shelter and clothing, as important as these things are. The benefits the Catechism talks about have to do with the eternal and the enduring. These benefits far surpass any benefits the world has to offer.

PRAYERS & REMINDERS

_____
_____
_____
_____
_____
_____
_____
_____
_____

Prayer: How You have showered blessing upon blessing on us O God. You have saved us by Your mighty grace. You have adopted us into Your family, and You have filled us with all spiritual blessings through our Lord Jesus Christ. In His name, we thank You and praise Your holy name. Amen.

Hymn for the day:
Great Is Thy Faithfulness

Question #32: What benefits are there in this life for those who are effectually called?

Answer: Those who are effectually called partake in justification, adoption, sanctification, and the other benefits that, in this life, do either accompany or flow from them.

Scripture Reading: Psalm 24

These benefits are summed up in three of the richest and sweetest words in the Christian's vocabulary. They are not words of theological abstraction, but of Christian experience and spiritual reality—justification, adoption, and sanctification.

What do these words mean, and how may we understand the doctrines taught by these words? It is often a temptation in this theologically illiterate day to simply abandon time-honored words which have been used throughout the history of the Church. The idea is that since no one understands the words any more, we need to find new words to explain Biblical truths. The problem with this historically is that when we abandon Biblical words, we also abandon Biblical truths. This is how heresy creeps into the Church, and how cults begin.

It is also well to remember that these are not separate experiences or truths, rather these words describe the sum total of the one great reality of salvation by grace. They are facets on the diamond of the Father's gift of life to us in Christ Jesus. In later studies we will consider each one separately, and see how each of these great words contributes to our understanding of the Gospel and our salvation. For now, just rejoice that the salvation which our Savior has won for us is full, rich and free, and includes everything we need to have a right relationship with God and a sure and certain hope for all eternity. Make this day a day of praise and thanksgiving to our God who bestows upon us such wondrous love, and showers upon us such good gifts of His mercy, grace and Fatherly kindness.

Prayer: Father, eternity will not be long enough to sing Your praise for all You have done for us, Your children. Your mercy is from everlasting to everlasting upon those You have chosen, called, and saved. You hear us when we pray, and answer all our prayers according to Your will in Jesus' name. Amen.

Hymn for the day:
Love Divine All Loves Excelling

PRAYERS & REMINDERS

Question #33: What is justification?

Answer: Justification is an act of God's free grace, in which He pardons all our sins, and accepts us as righteous in His sight, only for the righteousness of Christ imputed to us, and received by faith alone.

Scripture Reading: Romans 5:1-11

Next to the doctrines which have to do with the persons and nature of the Godhead, the doctrine of justification is probably the most important doctrine of Scripture. It has always been at the heart of most controversies in the church since the days of the apostles. In fact many of the writings of Paul, especially the books of Romans and Galatians, center in this doctrine. The Biblical doctrine of justification by faith is closely associated with the doctrine of predestination, and logically flows out of it. Luther's emphasis on justification by faith alone and Calvin's teaching on predestination are simply two ways of looking at the same truth, namely that salvation is of the Lord.

When Luther rediscovered this great truth by his study of Scripture, the lid blew off the medieval Church! The prevailing view of justification in the church of that era was that man is justified either by good works, or by the good will of the institutional Church, or both. There were those faithful souls who had been preaching salvation by grace through faith, but their numbers were few, and their voices stilled by the sword and stake. Luther's heralding of this Biblical doctrine became an historic event, a turning point in the history of Christianity. In God's providence, he lived to preach and write about this doctrine, and the truth spread like wildfire throughout Europe. It is unfortunate but true that this precious doctrine is once more under attack, and even from within Reformed circles. So take great care with what you read and hear. Often there is a thin line between truth and error at this point. The doctrine of justification by grace alone, through faith alone may be abused, and often is, but to surrender this Biblical truth because some misuse it is a tragedy.

Prayer: Help us, gracious Father, to always remember we are justified by grace alone through faith alone. We marvel at Your forbearance and mercy. We accept with gratitude and joy the truth of our justification, and pray we may always honor You in our faith and in our lives. Through the Lord Jesus we bring our prayers and praises. Amen.

Hymn for the day:
Nothing But The Blood Of Jesus

PRAYERS & REMINDERS
_____
_____
_____
_____
_____
_____
_____
_____
_____
_____

Question #33: What is justification?

Answer: Justification is an act of God's free grace, in which He pardons all our sins, and accepts us as righteous in His sight, only for the righteousness of Christ imputed to us, and received by faith alone.

Scripture Reading: Romans 5:12-21

What is this powerful truth? Why is it so important? It is important because it deals with the most basic issue in life. How can sinful man be right with the holy God? How is it possible to have my sin forgiven, and my guilt removed? Of course, if one does not take the Biblical doctrine of sin seriously, these may not seem to be overly important questions. But deep within the soul of every person, there is a dread and fear caused by sin, and the certainty of impending judgment. There is also a longing for God, and for the restoration of lost fellowship with Him—perhaps even a dim, shadowy memory of Eden when man walked with God in perfect harmony with the Creator, and the creation.

Justification means being right with God. It has to do with the forgiveness of sins, a right status and relationship with the Lord. The Bible makes it very clear that this is always based on God's sovereign grace. We are justified because God is God, and because He is good. It is His good pleasure to treat the elect just as if they had never sinned. In justification, God declares the unjust to be just. He pronounces the guilty to be not guilty in His holy sight. Incredible? Yes, but true. When Luther read with understanding these words: *The just shall live by faith,* the whole meaning of the Gospel of Christ became clear. His soul was set free from the bondage imposed on it by the false doctrines of the medieval Church. The more he read and studied, especially the book of Romans, and the book of Galatians, the clearer it became in his mind that this was the doctrine of salvation taught from Genesis through Revelation. His preaching took on more power, and this grand truth worked miracles of revival and reformation throughout Europe, and eventually around the world. Once you grasp this same truth, the doors of heaven are opened wide to you.

Prayer: Father, You are great and You are good. We worship You and love You for Your grace and mercy to us. May we see another mighty moving of Your Holy Spirit as the truth of justification by faith is once more heard throughout the whole earth. We pray this in Jesus' name and for His sake. Amen

Hymn for the day:
Grace Greater Than Our Sin

PRAYERS & REMINDERS

Question #33: What is justification?

Answer: Justification is an act of God's free grace, in which He pardons all our sins, and accepts us as righteous in His sight, only for the righteousness of Christ imputed to us, and received by faith alone.

Scripture Reading: II Corinthians 5:12-21

How is it possible for a righteous God to deal with sinners as if they were His pure and righteous children? How can He love sinners, and forgive them, and still be the holy God? Does He simply ignore our sins? Of course not! He must be, and is, true to His own character.

Now we come to the heart of the Gospel. God sent His beloved Son into the world to live a life of obedience and sinless perfection. He fully pleased the Father in all things, keeping the law in letter and spirit. Then at the end of this perfect life, He who was without spot and blemish became our sin offering. He died on Calvary's cross as the Lamb of God who takes away the sin of the world.

Thus by His sinless life, He imputes to us the merits of His obedience, and by His death, His blood covers all our sins. We therefore are justified. God imputed to Christ all my sins, and He died for me. God imputes to me all Christ's righteousness, and I live because of Him and, by God's grace, for Him. In Ephesians 2:8-9 we read: *For by grace you have been saved through faith, and that not of yourselves; it is the gift of God, not of works, lest anyone should boast.* Then the next verse goes right on to read: *For we are His workmanship, created in Christ Jesus for good works, which God prepared beforehand that we should walk in them.* Grace not only precedes good works, but is the fountainhead from which they flow. By grace we are brought into union with Christ, and thus we begin to do His works, no matter how imperfectly. Our assured hope is that one day we will be fully conformed to the image of Christ.

PRAYERS & REMINDERS

_____

_____

_____

_____

_____

_____

_____

_____

_____

Prayer: Thank You Lord Jesus Christ, our Savior, for the perfect life of obedience You lived on earth, and for the atoning death You died that we might have true righteousness and be forgiven for all our sins You are our righteousness and our peace with God. Amen.

Hymn for the day:
Channels Only

Question #34: What is adoption?

Answer: Adoption is an act of God's free grace, by which we are received as sons of God, and have a right to all the privileges of that standing.

Scripture Reading: Galatians 3:26-4:7

Of all the human experiences in this world, the act of adoption may well come the nearest to illustrating the amazing love of God for sinners. This truth has received very little attention in theological studies, but it deserves much more. The Apostle Paul develops the concept of adoption more fully than the other writers of Scriptures, though he derives much of his theology of adoption from the Old Testament. He also obviously calls upon his knowledge of the practice of adoption as seen in the Roman culture of his day and time.

The Catechism speaks of the nature of adoption, and the rights of those adopted. First of all, notice that it is described as an act of God's free grace. In this it is similar to justification. Once God has adopted the elect, they are adopted once and for all. To be a child of God by grace today, is to be a child of grace forever. Notice that the word *free* is used to modify grace. This simply means that the initiative is always from God. The comparison between God's act of adoption and the human act of adoption is seen most clearly at this point.

It is also at this point some dissimilarities may be seen. I know of one situation in which parents decided to adopt a child from another culture and another nation. It was a long and complicated process, but at last they were able to bring the little girl to this country and into their home. However they also discovered that she had some very serious health issues which had not been disclosed. Upon this discovery, they returned the child to the adoption agency, and repudiated their claim on her. Fortunately for the little girl, another couple adopted her, accepted the physical imperfections, made her their daughter and loved her with a much more perfect love than the former couple who had rejected her. God knows all about our many imperfections, but loves us and has a plan to make us perfect in holiness.

Prayer: Our Father in heaven, You have made us to be Your children. You have adopted us into Your family. Your only begotten Son has made it possible for us to be adopted. Thank You that we know our Father in heaven will supply our every need, and will never leave, nor forsake us. In Christ's name we pray. Amen.

Hymn for the day:
The King Of Love My Shepherd Is

PRAYERS & REMINDERS

April 11

Question #34: What is adoption?

Answer: Adoption is an act of God's free grace, by which we are received as sons of God, and have a right to all the privileges of that standing.

Scripture Reading: Romans 8:12-17

When human parents decide to adopt a child, they do not begin their search for someone who will love them, but for one whom they may love. The child to be adopted is usually unknown to the prospective parents. They are not obligated to adopt a particular baby, or any baby at all. They are motivated by love (ideally). Once the adoption is made legal, the child who was not a member of the adopting family is now a member with all the rights and privileges that go with the act of adoption. The little child is given the family name by way of identification. Moreover, whatever rights by birth a child of that family enjoys, so the adopted child also enjoys. And what is true in the eyes of the law, is also true in the hearts of the parents. Recently, a man with whom I was acquainted asked me to pray for his son who was very ill. It was later in the conversation I discovered the little boy was his step-son whom he had adopted. It was obvious from the look in his eyes, and the tone of his voice that the man held his son in his heart with no distinction between him and his children by birth.

So it is with God. Our adoption into His family is based on His free grace and sovereign love. We are made to be children of the Most High by His decree of adoption. In John 16:27, Jesus said: *For the Father Himself loves you, because you have loved Me, and have believed that I came forth from God.* In Romans 8:15-16 we find these words: *For you did not receive the spirit of bondage again to fear, but you have received the Spirit of adoption, whereby we cry, Abba, Father. The Spirit Himself bears witness with our spirit that we are the children of God.*

PRAYERS & REMINDERS

_____
_____
_____
_____
_____
_____
_____
_____
_____

Prayer: Father, thank you that You have sent forth Your Holy Spirit into our hearts that we may know You and call upon You as our dear Father who loves us with an everlasting love and delights to give us the good things needed for our salvation and peace. In Jesus' name. Amen.

Hymn for the day:
A Child Of The King

Question #34: What is adoption?

Answer: Adoption is an act of God's free grace, by which we are received as sons of God, and have a right to all the privileges of that standing.

Scripture Reading: I John 3:1-3; 4:7-19

I love the way the Apostle John speaks to this great truth when he says: *"Beloved now are we the sons of God, and it doth not yet appear what we shall be: but we know that when He appears, we shall be like Him: for we shall see Him as He is.* This reveals something of the privileges of being the sons of God. The first privilege is, of course, that even now we are the sons (and daughters) of God. The language of adoption is not only the language of love, it is also legal language. By adoption, we become heirs of God, and joint heirs with Christ, the only-begotten Son. We are given the family name, and a new status as well as a new relationship with the Father. This means we have access into His presence, and the privilege of prayer, with the expectation of being heard and answered. One thing many people do not seem to understand is that prayer is a privilege reserved for the Father's children. O yes, anyone may pray the sinner's prayer, *God be merciful to me, a sinner*, but that is a prayer which will only be prayed, in sincerity, by those who have been regenerated by the Holy Spirit.

This brings me to another privilege of the sons of God, namely the indwelling Holy Spirit to be our Comforter and Helper. Finally, we have the assurance that even as earthly parents delight to give their children good things, and will not mock their needs, so much more will our heavenly Father give good things to His beloved adopted sons and daughters. And the last and best of these good things is a heavenly home. How glorious it is to be the adopted sons and daughters of God!

Prayer: Father, from Your gracious and bountiful hand, we are given so much. Nothing we need will be denied us. Far beyond what we deserve, You have poured blessing upon blessing. Help us to live today as grateful and loving children of our heavenly Father. We ask this for Your sake and in Jesus' name. Amen

Hymn for the day:
Children Of The Heavenly Father

PRAYERS & REMINDERS

Question #35: What is sanctification?

Answer: Sanctification is the work of God's free grace, by which we are renewed in the whole man after the image of God, and are enabled more and more to die to sin and live to righteousness.

Scripture Reading: Romans 6:1-14

Here is a doctrine which needs much more attention by Presbyterians and all believers, and one which has been sadly neglected. If only the truth taught in this short statement of the Catechism could be widely taught in our churches, there would be much less confusion about this important doctrine. What is sanctification, and why is it so important to have a clear understanding of it?

To answer these questions we need to notice three key words which appear in this answer. The first of these is the word *work*. Sanctification is not an act either of God or man. It is not instant, as some teach. You may not make some sort of spiritual decision which results in immediate sanctification. It is the work of God the Holy Spirit in the hearts and lives of all believers, and it is a life-long process. It grows out of, and naturally follows, justification, but must always be distinguished from it. Like justification, sanctification flows from God's *free grace*. Unlike justification it is a work of grace and not an act of grace. The last of these three key words is *renewed*. This is a dynamic and powerful word which expresses a spiritual reality. Someone has said that sanctification is the justification of our justification. Maybe a better way of saying this is: sanctification is the ongoing testimony to our justification. However you may want to express it, the truth is that sanctification is taking place in all believers. Some grow in grace more rapidly and noticeably then others, but this work of God will take place and is taking place right now in you. Although it is a work of God's free grace, it also requires diligence on the part of the believer in *making your calling and election sure.* (2 Peter, 1:10)

PRAYERS & REMINDERS

_____

_____

_____

_____

_____

_____

_____

_____

_____

Prayer: O God, help us to grow in grace every day. Help us never to be satisfied with ourselves, but always longing for a closer walk with You, and a clearer testimony before the world. We pray this for Jesus' sake. Amen.

Hymn for the day:
Draw Me Nearer

Question #35: What is sanctification?

Answer: Sanctification is the work of God's free grace, by which we are renewed in the whole man after the image of God, and are enabled more and more to die to sin and live to righteousness.

Scripture Reading: Psalm 19

This work of sanctification is twofold. It is a work that produces death. It is a work that leads to life. By God's work of sanctification we are enabled to die more and more unto sin. Death is the only remedy for sin. It is the just punishment for sin. All people are born sinners, and thus born under the sentence of death, for *the soul who sins, it shall die;* (Ezekiel 18:4). Furthermore, it is by the propitiating death of Christ that our sins are atoned for, and we are delivered from death. In sanctification, what has happened for sinners begins to happen in sinners—the slow but sure process of dying to the habits and practices of sin. This gradual process is seen in these words: *and are enabled more and more to die unto sin.*

There is also a work of living in sanctification, for we are enabled to live more and more unto righteousness. Both the dying and the living are taking place simultaneously. The righteousness of Christ *imputed* to us is at the heart of justification. In sanctification God is at work to *impart* to us Christ's righteousness by the indwelling Holy Spirit. As we more and more die to sin, we are more and more enabled to live unto righteousness. The sequence is also important to understand. The dying unto sin produces living unto righteousness. Unless we are daily dying to sin, we find it very difficult to live unto righteousness. God in His wisdom understands our sinful foolish hearts and so orders the dying and living to be always taking place in us, until death finally ends the constant struggle. It is required of us to carefully examine ourselves with the constant questions: *Am I dying to the sin I see in my heart? Am I living unto the righteousness God requires of me?*

Prayer: Help us dear Father to live for You and by Your abundant supply of grace. Separate us from our sin, and our love of the world. Help us to live in such a way that other people will know whose we are, children of the heavenly Father. In Jesus' name we ask this. Amen.

Hymn for the day:
Living For Jesus

PRAYERS & REMINDERS

Question #35: What is sanctification?

Answer: Sanctification is the work of God's free grace, by which we are renewed in the whole man after the image of God, and are enabled more and more to die to sin and live to righteousness.

Scripture Reading: Ephesians 4:17-32

Another key expression in understanding the Catechism's doctrine of sanctification is: *in the whole man.* Sanctification affects the whole man. In this it is similar to total depravity, as Dr. J. B. Green points out in his commentary on the Catechism. Both are total in extent, though not in degree. In sanctification our souls are drawn closer to Christ, our minds are renewed after His image, and even our bodies are touched in anticipation of the resurrection.

Finally, the expression, *the image of God,* shows us the true goal of sanctification. When God created man in His own image, it was never intended to be temporary. It is His purpose, from the very beginning, that the elect should be conformed to His image. Sanctification begins the process of renewal that will be complete in our glorification. The righteousness imputed to us, the righteousness being imparted to us, will finally issue in the completed work of God in our lives when we will be restored to His glorious image, and fully enter the inheritance of the sons of God.

Anything less than full and total sanctification would be unthinkable. To be restored to the image of God which was placed in mankind in creation is the hope and expectation of all believers. In the book of Romans this is described as being conformed to the image of Christ. It was through Him all things were created, including mankind in God's image, therefore our predestined future is to be conformed to Him through whom and for whom all things were created. Our minds are incapable to taking in such wonder and glory, but by faith we claim for ourselves what God has promised to us.

PRAYERS & REMINDERS

_____

_____

_____

_____

_____

_____

_____

_____

_____

Prayer: O God, there are times when we must say, *the good that I would, I do not, and the evil I would not, that I do.* Please forgive us. Please cleanse us. Please train us by Your holy word to live lives that are true, and deliver us from the evil one by the power of Your Son, in whose name we pray. Amen.

Hymn for the day:
O Master Let Me Walk With Thee

> **Question #36: What are the benefits which in this life accompany or flow from justification, adoption, and sanctification?**

Answer: The benefits that in this life do accompany or flow from justification, adoption, and sanctification are: assurance of God's love, peace of conscience, joy in the Holy Spirit, increase of grace, and perseverance to the end.

Scripture Reading: Ephesians 3:14-21

When I read the answer to this Catechism question, I feel like a little child sitting under a Christmas tree opening up present after present of the most wonderful gifts. Or better still, I have the same exuberant joy that must have filled the heart of the Apostle John when he declared: *Behold what manner of love the Father hath bestowed upon us that we should be called the children of God!* Surely the Father has many gifts of love and grace for His children.

One of the deepest needs we all have is security and assurance in our relationships with others. How lost we feel when those whom we love and whose love we need make us feel uncertain and insecure. God never does this to His children. He gives to us assurance of His great love in so many ways. Above all He has given His Son. He constantly forgives our sins, and draws us to Himself by His kindness and grace. His word is filled with tender assurances from cover to cover. We think of just a few words from Scripture which bring this blessed assurance. In the twenty third Psalm we read: *The Lord is my Shepherd, I shall not want.* In Psalm 27 we find these words: *The Lord is my light and my salvation; Whom shall I fear?* In Isaiah 43 we read, *When you pass through the waters I will be with you; and through the rivers, they shall not overflow you, When you walk through the fire, you shall not be burned...for I am the LORD your God.* From the Apostle's words in Romans 8:28-39 we receive the assurance that nothing shall be able to separate us from the love of God which is in Christ Jesus our Lord. All these above promises speak to the blessed benefit of assurance of God's love.

Prayer: Father, You have brought us assurance and great joy by loving us and giving to us exceeding great and precious promises. Give to us courage to claim all Your wonderful promises, and steadfastness to live by them. We ask this in Jesus' name. Amen.

Hymn for the day:
The Lord's My Shepherd

PRAYERS & REMINDERS

_____
_____
_____
_____
_____
_____
_____
_____
_____
_____

> **Question #36: What are the benefits which in this life accompany or flow from justification, adoption, and sanctification?**

Answer: The benefits that in this life do accompany or flow from justification, adoption, and sanctification are: assurance of God's love, peace of conscience, joy in the Holy Spirit, increase of grace, and perseverance to the end.

Scripture Reading: Colossians 1:9-23

As a natural consequence of this assurance we also have peace of conscience. What a blessing and what a gift! The poet said, *Conscience makes cowards of us all.* God's gift of peace gives us boldness to come into His presence. *Perfect love casts out fear. Therefore being justified by faith, we have peace with God through our Lord Jesus Christ.* Only those who have been oppressed by a guilty conscience can really appreciate this gift of peace. A friend of mine recently went through a long period of sickness and infection from an unknown source. Though his body was filled with antibiotics, still the infection persisted and even became life-threatening. Finally the doctors discovered a small piece of metal in his lungs, and removed it in a relatively simple procedure. Once it was gone, the infection quickly cleared up, and within a few days he was well again. When God removes the curse of sin, and sentence of death by justification, He also gives us peace of conscience, and we are made whole.

It is our responsibility and privilege to take God at His word, believe in His promises, and claim the gift of peace of conscience. We will never know this peace simply by trusting in ourselves, or trying to do better. Unfortunately many believers are unable or unwilling to accept this gift of peace. They are troubled and upset with the severe circumstances which may befall us all in this world. They are troubled by the memory of sin and the inner remnants of the old fallen nature which we inherited from Adam and Eve, and which we have nurtured and cultivate by our own sinful practices. But when you begin to realize that you are truly and fully justified, that you are being sanctified, and will be glorified in God's good time, fear is overcome by perfect love.

Prayer: Forgive us Father, for giving into our doubts and fears. Forgive us for not trusting in Your words of grace. You are the Judge of all the earth, and You have justified us through the life and death of our dear Savior, in whose name we pray. Amen.

Hymn for the day:
Like A River Glorious

PRAYERS & REMINDERS

Question #36: What are the benefits which in this life accompany or flow from justification, adoption, and sanctification?

Answer: The benefits that in this life do accompany or flow from justification, adoption, and sanctification are: assurance of God's love, peace of conscience, joy in the Holy Spirit, increase of grace, and perseverance to the end.

Scripture Reading: John 15:9-17

Peace gives birth to joy, and this too belongs to the children of the Father. The Holy Spirit is the agent of our joy, just as He is the agent of our peace. By His ministry we are enabled to enjoy God. Christ promised His disciples that they would have joy when they saw Him again, and that joy could never be taken away. As the Spirit makes Christ known to us, and as He reveals the things of Christ to us, we share in that promised joy. This joy is in anticipation of the heavenly joy which we shall experience with the Lord. But even now this gift is ours to claim and to experience. Does this mean we will always be happy and content? Obviously it does not. Joy is so much deeper and more lasting than happiness. Happiness usually depends on favorable circumstance, and our circumstances are not always favorable. But *joy in the Holy Ghost* is a gift which accompanies justification, adoption and sanctification. This gift is a sort of down payment on the full joy we will know in heaven.

Many years ago when our family income was very low compared to the need of clothing and feeding a growing family, I received a letter from my father-in-law. Enclosed in the letter was a check for an amount that equaled half a month's pay! I was overwhelmed with gratitude. The letter was very short, it only said, this is an earnest of your inheritance. That dear, kindly man, my father-in-law, just wanted us to know his intention was to include us in his will when the time came, but he also wanted to encourage us with his generous gift. God gives to His children the gift of *joy in the Holy Ghost* to assure us of greater joy to come, and to encourage us along the way in this life.

Prayer: Our Father who art in heaven, we bless and praise You for giving joy to Your children. We know that the cares of this world and the deceitfulness of riches clouds our minds and hearts with doubts and fears. But You, dear Lord, have removed our fear and given to us joy in its place. For this and all Your mercies, we thank You through Christ our Lord. Amen.

Hymn for the day:
Joyful, Joyful We Adore Thee

PRAYERS & REMINDERS

Question #36: *What are the benefits which in this life accompany or flow from justification, adoption, and sanctification?*

Answer: The benefits that in this life do accompany or flow from justification, adoption, and sanctification are: assurance of God's love, peace of conscience, joy in the Holy Spirit, increase of grace, and perseverance to the end.

Scripture Reading: I Peter 1:3-9

The Catechism tells us that one of the benefits which flows from justification, adoption, and sanctification is *the increase of grace.* This simply means that the blessings and gifts from the Father do not diminish, but rather grow and increase as we walk with the Lord, in the light of His Word. But how does this actually work out in our lives? We would become more Christ-like in our attitudes, and actions, as well as our relationships with each other. Our focus would be increasingly on the things of the Lord, and less on the things of the world. The grace which has saved us would become the guiding principle in our lives.

The final benefit which flows from our justification, adoption, and sanctification is perseverance to the end. We persevere not in our own strength, but because God perseveres for and in us. *He that hath begun a good work in you will perform it unto the day of Jesus Christ.* I love to sing the hymn, Majestic Sweetness Sits Enthroned Upon the Savior's brow. One of the verses sings this way: *Since from His bounty I receive such gifts of grace divine, Had I a thousand hearts to give, Lord, they should all be Thine.* Though perseverance is a benefit flowing from justification, adoption, and sanctification, this does not imply that we are to be totally passive in perseverance. We are admonished in Ephesians 6:18: *...Being watchful to this end with all perseverance and supplication.* This at least suggests that believers must persevere in prayer. And again in 2 Peter 1:6: *...Add to your faith...perseverance.* These words come to us not merely as advice, but as an Apostolic command. So we hold in balance the promise and command from God's word that believers do and must persevere.

Prayer: Lord, were it not for Your sustaining grace, we would crumble and fall under the pressures of this life. But You, Lord, have won the victory for us and in us. So help us to persevere even as You persevere in us. In Jesus' name. Amen.

Hymn for the day:
Majestic Sweetness Sits Enthroned

PRAYERS & REMINDERS

> ## Question #37: What benefits do believers receive from Christ at death?

Answer: The souls of believers are at their deaths made perfect in holiness, and do immediately pass into glory; and their bodies, being still united to Christ, do rest in their graves till the resurrection.

Scripture Reading: Luke 16:19-31

Several years ago, when I was a young pastor (make that a bunch of years ago), one of the duties which was the most difficult for me was the graveside service following a funeral. It was my custom to try to make the funeral service itself a service of worship, but the burial service always seemed anti-climactic at best. The worst part of it was the reading of the inevitable *dust to dust, ashes to ashes*. Then one day in preparation for a funeral service I remembered the words of this question from the Catechism. What a contrast! Here we have a truly Biblical statement worthy to be read at the burial of a believer. I will always cherish the look of comfort on the face of the widow when I quietly quoted these words from the Catechism. I have used this in every burial service since, and always to good effect.

By these words, the Catechism refutes at least two erroneous ideas. (1) There is no room in these words, or in Scripture for the dogma of purgatory. This medieval doctrine long held by church of Rome and other Catholic bodies, finds no support in Scripture. Even if there was some biblical basis for this belief (and there is none!) to use this mistaken idea as a source for raising money for the church is most reprehensible. (2) The other idea which is widely held in some Protestant circles is that of soul sleep. This unbiblical doctrine teaches that at death, there is no conscious awareness of either heaven or hell. But here in the Catechism we learn that at death, our souls are made perfect in glory and do immediately pass into glory. There is abundant Scripture to support this truth. The clearest one of all is found in the words of Paul from 2 Corinthians 5:8 . *To be absent from the body and to be present with the Lord.* Doesn't this sound more biblical and hopeful than, *dust to dust and ashes to ashes?*

Prayer: Thank You Father for the blessed hope of passing into Your immediate presence when we leave this world. You have told us in Your word that to be absent from the body is to be present with the Lord, May we so live in faith that our fear of death will be replaced with trust in Your promises. In Jesus' name. Amen.

Hymn for the day:
Face to Face With Christ My Savior

PRAYERS & REMINDERS

Question #37: What benefits do believers receive from Christ at death?

Answer: The souls of believers are at their deaths made perfect in holiness, and do immediately pass into glory; and their bodies, being still united to Christ, do rest in their graves till the resurrection.

Scripture Reading: Revelation 21:1-5; 22:1-5

The question of what awaits believers beyond this life should be of utmost interest to all Christians. Death is the common experience of all people. Unless the Christian faith can speak to this, and speak with great hope and assurance, whatever else it has to say would be of little consequence. Let us look more closely at these marvelous benefits which believers receive from Christ at death.

First, there is the completion within the spirit of that which began with regeneration. The souls of believers are at death made perfect in holiness. Sin will have been utterly defeated at that moment. It will no longer mar our character, nor hinder our closeness with the Lord. Because we will be made perfect in holiness, we will be in full and loving fellowship with our perfect and holy God, Father, Son, and Holy Spirit. Temptation will no longer dog our footsteps. The bitter pain of remorse will no longer disturb our hearts. This is the absolute necessity which must take place before we may enter our heavenly home. God will not permit sin to enter His new creation. In His infinite wisdom and sovereignty, He allowed the entrance of sin into Eden. The new Eden will experience no such invasion, for Satan will have been cast into the lake of fire. The thought that we will be made perfect in holiness, and pass into the presence of our Lord and God creates hope, joy, and tremendous thrill. It also becomes a strong motivation for godly living and careful preparation for our heavenly home. This world becomes a training camp for the glories of heaven. I think Scripture clearly teaches that how well we do in "Boot Camp" will influence our enjoyment of heaven and our heavenly rewards.

Prayer: Help us to live in Your presence, dear Lord, as those who know they must give an account one day. Help us to do justly, love mercy and walk humbly with our God. We ask this for Jesus' sake. Amen.

Hymn for the day:
Jerusalem The Golden

PRAYERS & REMINDERS

_____
_____
_____
_____
_____
_____
_____
_____
_____

> ## Question #37: What benefits do believers receive from Christ at death?

Answer: The souls of believers are at their deaths made perfect in holiness, and do immediately pass into glory; and their bodies, being still united to Christ, do rest in their graves till the resurrection.

Scripture Reading: I Corinthians 15:12-26

There is no soul sleep known in Scripture. There is no purgatory which awaits believers. Our souls, being purged from sin by the blood of Christ, will at death enter into glory. By this the Catechism is reflecting the theology of the Apostle Paul who said: *To be absent from the body is to be present with the Lord.* The entrance into glory is entrance into the presence of the Lord. ... *We shall see Him as He is.* Truly it will be a passage to glory to see the Savior face to face.

But wait! The Catechism does not stop there, nor should it. Consider these words: *Their bodies, still be united to Christ, do rest in the graves until the resurrection.* The doctrine of the resurrection of the body is a vital and necessary truth which sets Christianity a part from all other religions. The full redemption promised in the word is not complete until the resurrection at the last day. This is clearly seen in the great work of redemption completed by our Savior. The Gospel centers in this great truth. The Gospels present it, the Epistles explain its meaning and its central importance. In I Corinthians 15 we are given the most complete and satisfying explanation of the meaning of Christ's resurrection for our assurance and hope, Paul argues that Christ's resurrection is an established historical event, and that it also assures believers they too will rise from the dead. He declared that a part from this hope we are of all people the most miserable.

He went on to explain that if we deny the resurrection of the body, we are left with no hope and that Christianity is powerless to save. He also said that the analogies seen in nature affirm the certainty of our resurrection, and give some hint as to its nature. The final words are: *Thanks be to God who gives us the victory through our Lord Jesus Christ.*

Prayer: We are so grateful, Lord, for the assurance You give us in the word, that there will be a resurrection in Your good time. Thank You that even now we may look back upon that first Easter Sunday long ago when our Lord Jesus came forth from the tomb, bringing hope and assurance that we too will one day rise from the grave. Amen.

Hymn for the day:
Come We That Love The Lord

PRAYERS & REMINDERS

April 23

Question #37: What benefits do believers receive from Christ at death?

Answer: The souls of believers are at their deaths made perfect in holiness, and do immediately pass into glory; and their bodies, being still united to Christ, do rest in their graves till the resurrection.

Scripture Reading: Philippians 3:17-21

Finally a word is included concerning the body. Our salvation is for the whole person. God has not abandoned the body He created for man. Though it has been horribly affected by the fall, it remains a very essential part of our being. The most important words in this statement concerning the body are these: *being still united to Christ.* How wonderful to know that the bodies of our precious dead are still united to Christ. How wonderful to know that God has a future for these bodies. Though now they *do rest in their graves*, there is a resurrection coming, and our bodies will then know the same glory. Of course the change which will take place between these present bodies of sin and death will be profound and dramatic. *It is sown in corruption, it is raised in incorruption. It is sown in dishonor, it is raised in glory. It is sown in weakness, it is raised in power.*

Do these words answer all our questions concerning the resurrection of our redeemed bodies? No, but they do answer the important questions. Because we believe in the resurrection of the body, and because we do believe our bodies, though dead, are still united to Christ, the way in which we bury our beloved dead becomes more important than many seem to believe. Church historians tell us that one of the major factors in the rapid growth of Christianity in pagan Rome was the way believers in Christ cared for the bodies of their dead, and the reverence they displayed towards the body. There is no "Thus saith the Lord" concerning burial verses cremation, but the symbolism of burial seems much more in keeping with our doctrine of the resurrection, and especially these words from the Catechism,: ...*their bodies, still being united to Christ...*

PRAYERS & REMINDERS

_____
_____
_____
_____
_____
_____
_____
_____
_____

Prayer: O God our help in ages past, our hope for years to come; our shelter from the storm blast, and our eternal home, we praise You for the resurrection and for our heavenly home, through Christ our Lord and Savior. Amen.

Hymn for the day:
Low In The Grave He Lay

> **Question #38: What benefits do believers
> receive from Christ at the resurrection?**

Answer: At the resurrection, believers, being raised up in glory, shall be openly acknowledged and acquitted in the day of judgment, and made perfectly blessed in the full enjoying of God to all eternity.

Scripture Reading: I Thessalonians 4: 13-18

The resurrection of believers will be glorious beyond our fondest and wildest imagination. There will be such joy, such holy hilarity at that time, we shall be filled with praise and love for the Savior. There will be reunion with loved ones. Above all, there will be immediate and blessed communion with the Lord. I read a story long ago that helps to illustrate something of that joy. A man and his young son were sailing on one of the Great Lakes when their small craft was caught in a sudden and fierce storm. In spite of the best efforts of the father, who was an experienced sailor, the small craft was overwhelmed, and the two were left clinging to the wreckage in mountainous seas. Within minutes, they were both swept away. The father's last glimpse of his son was the young lad disappearing beneath the waves. He awakened in a bunk on a Coast Guard vessel, realizing he had been rescued. His momentary joy was destroyed by the memory of his young son being washed away. As he turned his face to the wall to weep, he saw his son sleeping peacefully in the next bunk. He too had been rescued by the same ship. What joy was his in that moment of reunion!

Yet it is but a pale shadow of our joy when we awaken on the resurrection morn. We catch a glimpse of that joy as we read and study the Gospels' accounts of Christ's resurrection. We read of the great joy of Mary and the other women when they realized Christ was risen. They came to His grave expecting to anoint a beloved but dead body. They fell at the feet of the risen Savior. When they ran to bring the disciples word, they were met initially with unbelief and even scorn. But when it finally dawned on these men who were so reluctant to believe that Jesus had indeed arisen, they too discovered the same glorious joy. *Then were the disciples glad when they saw the Lord.*

Prayer: We too will be glad when we see You Lord, face to face, on that resurrection morning. You have rescued us from hopeless despair by Your own resurrection, and Your promises that one day You will speak the word, and all who are in the grave will come forth. Amen.

Hymn for the day:
When All My Labors And Trials Are O'er

PRAYERS & REMINDERS

April 25

Question #38: What benefits do believers receive from Christ at the resurrection?

Answer: At the resurrection, believers, being raised up in glory, shall be openly acknowledged and acquitted in the day of judgment, and made perfectly blessed in the full enjoying of God to all eternity.

Scripture Reading: I Corinthians 15:35-49

The Catechism does not dwell on the emotions of the resurrection, but on the immediate benefits which believers receive from Christ. The answer given by the Shorter Catechism at this point is something of a summary of several questions and answers from the Larger Catechism (86-90). Look these up and carefully study them to get the full picture. For our purposes, we shall consider only what the Shorter Catechism has to say.

First of all, we will be raised up in glory. This teaches the fact and form of the resurrection. We will experience a bodily resurrection and it will be glorious. Paul teaches us in I Corinthians 15, which you read today, that the body will be raised incorruptible, powerful, and in glory. This will be a spiritual body, but a real body nonetheless. Having said these words, we still do not fully comprehend it all, nor do we need to. If we have trusted the Lord for our salvation, may we not also trust Him for the resurrection body?

When the clever Sadducees, who did not believe in the resurrection, or much of anything else, came to Jesus to mock His teaching on the resurrection of the body, they brought a concocted story which in their minds made the resurrection seem absurd. They told the story of the woman who had seven husbands, all of whom preceded her in death. Then they asked the question, *whose wife will she be in the resurrection?* Jesus showed them the folly of their question, and the emptiness of their non-faith. He told them that in the resurrection there is no marriage, nor need of it. Then He pointed to the Old Testament passage concerning the appearance of God to Moses at the burning bush when God said, *I am the God of Abraham, the God of Isaac, and the God of Jacob,* as proof of the resurrection saying: *He is not the God of the dead but of the living.*

PRAYERS & REMINDERS

_____

_____

_____

_____

_____

_____

_____

_____

_____

Prayer: *Thine is the glory, risen conquering Son; endless is the victory, Thou o'er death hast won.* You won that victory for us dear Lord, and now we belong to You for all eternity. Thank You, Lord. Amen.

Hymn for the day:
For All The Saints

Question #38: What benefits do believers receive from Christ at the resurrection?

Answer: At the resurrection, believers, being raised up in glory, shall be openly acknowledged and acquitted in the day of judgment, and made perfectly blessed in the full enjoying of God to all eternity.

Scripture Reading: Matthew 25:31-46

Another wonderful benefit we shall receive from our Lord at the resurrection is acquittal, or the final vindication. Our justification will be affirmed anew, and we shall be acknowledged as being the Lord's own people. This does not mean there will be no accounting. Surely the Scripture teaches that we must all give an account as stewards on the day of judgment. As the Apostle Paul said in 2 Corinthians 5:10, *For we must all appear before the judgment seat of Christ, that each one may receive the things done in the body, according to what he has done, whether good or bad.*

For believers it will be primarily a judgment of rewards, and vindication. The Catechism uses the expression, *openly acknowledged and acquitted.* On what basis will these blessings be ours? Certainly not on the basis of perfect and sinless lives, but rather on the basis of Christ's righteousness imputed to us by justification and imparted to us by sanctification. At the same time, no sacrifice for the Lord's sake, no act of kindness in His name will be overlooked or forgotten. Even a cup of cold water given in His name has its reward. Care of the helpless, the hungry, the poor and needy, the sick and the prisoner will be extolled and rewarded by Christ Himself who lived that same kind of life on earth.

Finally, there is joy. We shall be made fully blessed. This means our relationship with the Lord will be completed. There will no longer be sin to mar our lives, nor sin to confess and be forgiven. We will no longer walk by faith, but we shall see Him face to face, and our joy will be complete, and forever.

Prayer: O what joy will be ours when we hear You say to us: *Well done, good and faithful servant. Enter thou into the joy of thy Lord.* We will give to You all the praise and glory then, even as we do now. Amen.

Hymn for the day:
When The Roll Is Called Up Yonder

PRAYERS & REMINDERS

Question #39: What is the duty that God requires of man?

Answer: The duty that God requires of man is obedience to His revealed will.

Scripture Reading: Deuteronomy 29:14-29

Duty! What a noble word. What a motivating word. For people in this generation, what a strange word, what an unwelcome word. For the most part, people are much more interested in learning about the benefits and blessings God has for us, rather than the duty He requires of us. But the two go together, and believers do have a duty they owe to God. However, duty need not be a word to fear, nor even a burdensome word. Unfortunately that is the connotation we have placed on this noble word.

In the Scriptures, duty grows out of a covenantal relationship between God and His people. The covenant is always predicated on the graciousness of God, and His initiative in establishing a relationship with His people. For instance, when He gave the law to Moses on Mount Sinai, He first reminded Israel that He was the God who had delivered them from bondage in Egypt. The gracious God of their salvation then gave them His ten words of instruction on how redeemed people are to live. The Ten Commandments are instructions from a loving heavenly Father to his children. By giving the law, God revealed much of His own character, and also the character He desires to see in His beloved children.

But that same covenantal relationship also requires a response of faith and obedience. God did not give His law simply on tablets of stone. He gave His law as a way of life and required Israel to obey His word. He promised blessings on those who did obey, and warned of consequences on those who disobeyed. The same principle is still at work. Obedience brings its own blessings. But disobedience has consequences.

PRAYERS & REMINDERS

_____

_____

_____

_____

_____

_____

_____

_____

_____

_____

Prayer: Lord, You have commanded us to love You with all our heart, mind, and strength, and to keep Your Commandments. We confess that we have not loved You as we should. Help us to love You more, and serve You better. For Jesus' sake we pray. Amen.

Hymn for the day:
Trust And Obey

Question #39: What is the duty that God requires of man?

Answer: The duty that God requires of man is obedience to His revealed will.

Scripture Reading: I John 3:10-23

By giving us the Ten Commandments, God revealed much of His own character, and also the character He desires to see in His beloved children. To see the law in this way does not lessen the duty we have toward it; indeed, it strengthens that duty. Love is always a stronger motivating force in the performance of duty than fear or even obligation. It is the duty of the parent to care for, and to provide for the child, but the motivation is that of love, not mere obligation. Even though the young child may obey his parents primarily out of fear of punishment, later the main motivation will change to love, and a desire to please. So as we grow and mature in our relationship to the Lord, our obedience is an act of love, more than a fear of punishment.

Nevertheless, we do have a duty to our Father, and that duty is summarized in one word, obedience. Obedience, ideally, is like the love which motivates it, in that it is unconditional. We do not come before God and say, "We will obey your will if it suits us." Rather we come to Him, saying, "All that the Lord has spoken, we will obey." Our duty is nothing less than this, to obey the entire will of God which He reveals to us. God has destined us to be conformed to the image of His Son, who is the express image of the Father. Obedience is our willing assent, and our eager anticipation of that glorious destiny.

The Lord Jesus said to His disciples, *If you love Me, keep My commandments.* In these words we see again the motivation for doing our duty: Christ's love for us, and our love for Him. He spoke another word, which also motivates us towards obedience, when He said, *By this will all men know that you are My disciples, if ye have love one for another.* Our duty is a duty of love. Our fulfillment of that duty is our most effective witness.

Prayer: O Savior, You have told us that if we love one another as You loved us, then the world will know we are indeed Your disciples. By Your grace, we would learn to love each other as You have loved us. Help us to do this. Amen.

Hymn for the day:
Though I May Speak With Bravest Fire

PRAYERS & REMINDERS

April 29

> ## Question #40: What did God at first reveal to man for the rule of his obedience?

Answer: The rule that God at first revealed to man for his obedience was the moral law.

Scripture Reading: Romans 5:12-20

The moral law did not begin with the giving of the ten words on Mount Sinai. When God created man in His own image He wrote on his heart the moral law. This is a part of what is meant when we hear God saying, *Let us make man in our own image.* Later, when the ten words were given to Moses, we discover that God was not only revealing His will, He was revealing His own character. Therefore, when man was created in the image of God, he was created with the moral law written into his very being. He was, by his created nature, a law keeper. Although he was given the freedom of choice in obedience to the Word of God, he was not neutral toward it. He was created to obey God and live in close fellowship with Him. This is why his disobedience was such a tragedy. By rejecting the moral law, he was renouncing his own innate character, and his relationship with his God.

God's moral law has always been the foundation for just and good laws among men. Many of the ancient codes of law bear some resemblance to the Ten Commandments. This is a testimony to the universality of God's moral law, written into the nature of mankind. Of course that law had become warped and perverted by the fall and the resulting sinful nature of man. But there still remained and remains some acknowledgement of right and wrong even among the most sinful and corrupt societies of humanity. Those of us who have been redeemed by God's grace have the testimony of God's word and of a conscience renewed by the Holy Spirit. So our responsibility to obey God is increased greatly. How are we doing?

PRAYERS & REMINDERS

Prayer: O God, Your law is pure and perfect, but we are not. Help us to live by that straight line You have drawn for us. Forgive us for our disobedience. Truly we have been saved to serve You. Help us to serve with glad obedience to Your holy word. For Jesus' sake we pray. Amen.

Hymn for the day:
Spirit Of God Descend Upon My Heart

**Question #40: What did God at first reveal to man
for the rule of his obedience?**

Answer: The rule that God at first revealed to man for his obedience was the
moral law.

Scripture Reading: Romans 2:1-15

God's moral law was still the only acceptable standard of conduct for
mankind, and he was held accountable for it, even though his sinful nature
made perfect obedience to it impossible. You would understand that murder
was wrong from the beginning, not just from the time when the Ten
Commandments were delivered to Moses. This would also apply to all areas of
human conduct. We see this concept quite clearly in the account of the flood. In
the days and years before the flood, mankind had become hopelessly corrupt.
God looked upon the human race and said, *Every imagination of his heart is
only evil continually.* The moral law was the standard that had been violated,
and for which the judgment of God fell upon the earth.

This description of human depravity before the flood has been repeated down
through the long ages of the human race. We see examples of this in the depravity
of the cities of Sodom and Gomorrah as recorded in the book of Genesis. No
doubt there were many other sins among the inhabitants of these cities, but the
one prevailing and corrupting sin of the whole culture was that of homosexuality.
This same corrupting sin, though often excused and even glorified in our culture
is having the same terrible effects on our culture today, and the same heavy judgment from God hangs heavy over our nation . Perhaps God is calling you to
become like Abraham and to pray for our failing culture with the same fervency
in which that Godly man of old prayed for those doomed cities. Most certainly
God is calling all believers to "come out from among them and be holy."

Prayer: Holy Father, help us to hate sin and yet
love sinners. Help us to love them enough to constantly intercede for them, that You will spare them
until they come to repentance. At the same time,
guard our hearts and deliver us from evil. We ask
this in Jesus' name. Amen.

Hymn for the day:
Jesus Calls Us

PRAYERS & REMINDERS

_____

_____

_____

_____

_____

_____

_____

_____

_____

_____

> ### Question #40: What did God at first reveal to man for the rule of his obedience?

Answer: The rule that God at first revealed to man for his obedience was the moral law.

Scripture Reading: Genesis 6:1-12

When the Catechism speaks of the moral law which God revealed, it takes into account His revelation prior to the giving of the commandments as recorded in the book of Exodus. There was in the account of the worldwide flood, another way in which God revealed His moral law, which we may tend to miss when we read of this in Genesis. God revealed His moral law through His faithful servant Noah. It cannot be said that Noah perfectly obeyed and exemplified the moral law of God, but in contrast to the rest of humanity, the direction of his life was consciously guided by God's law. The Scriptures tell us that Noah was upright and blameless, and that he walked with God. All these expressions simply tell us that God found in Noah a man who lived his life honoring God's word. Furthermore, the New Testament refers to Noah as a preacher of righteousness. This means he both lived and taught the moral law. He obviously instructed his own family in God's law, for they were saved with him in the ark. After the flood, God's covenant with Noah revealed further details of the moral law, including the appropriate punishment for murder.

From Noah to Abraham, and down through the patriarchs to Moses, God was revealing His moral law, and requiring obedience to it; blessing those who obeyed, and cursing those who would not. When He gave the formal ten words to Moses as the moral instructions for His covenant people, He was summarizing what was already known and given to mankind from the day of creation onward.

Prayer: Heavenly Father, You are just and holy. You have revealed Your will through Your law. Help us to be like Your servant Noah of old, upright and blameless in our walk before the watching world. We thank You that we have found grace in Your holy sight, through our Lord Jesus Christ. Amen.

Hymn for the day:
Teach Me Thy Way, O Lord

PRAYERS & REMINDERS

Question #41: *Where is the moral law found to be summarized?*

Answer: The moral law is found summarized in the Ten Commandments.

Scripture Reading: Exodus 20:1-17

When God delivered the Ten Commandments to Moses, and through him these same laws to the nation of Israel, He was restating in summary all the guidelines for living He had revealed to mankind from the days of Adam and onward. What He required in the Ten Commandments, He had always required. What He forbade in the Ten Commandments, He had always forbidden. Let me remind you again of two basic truths which are essential to the understanding of this summary of the moral law. (1) The Ten Commandments reveal not only the will of God, but also His character. This implies that the Commandments are intended to be not only guidelines for our conduct but also the mould for the shaping of our characters as God's image-bearers. (2) These commandments are not just a set of regulations but are primarily instructions from a loving Father to His children. The more we understand this, the more eager we are to learn them and live by them.

Our motivation for obedience must go beyond either fear or duty. We obey God because we know He loves us, and teaches us to walk in the way which will bring blessing and joy into our lives. When we have at last been conformed to the image of Christ, we will be perfect law-keepers, rather than law-breakers. By our sinful natures now, and our sinful choices, we constantly break God's law, and must seek forgiveness. But when God has finished His work of sanctification in us, we will be law-keepers by nature and by choice. Even now, we who are believers in Jesus Christ love God's law and long for more faithfulness in keeping it wholly.

Prayer: How Perfect is Your Law, O Lord. You have said: *Blessed are the undefiled who walk in the way, who walk in the law of the Lord.* Help us this day to claim that blessing by walking in Your way and will as revealed in Your word. For Jesus' sake we pray. Amen.

Hymn for the day:
Fight the Good Fight with All Thy Might

PRAYERS & REMINDERS

Question #41: Where is the moral law found to be summarized?

Answer: The moral law is found summarized in the Ten Commandments.

Scripture Reading: Romans 7:7-12

God gave His perfect law to imperfect people. It was never given as a way of salvation, but it was given to show saved people how to live a life that pleases God. God did not give His Ten Commandments to the Egyptians, but to His covenant people, the Hebrews. They were given as a part of the national covenant with Israel. In a sense, they were not new because they are basic laws which have always been incumbent on all people. But now they became an official document upon which the nation of Israel would be built, and their special relationship with God codified.

There is a clause in our own Declaration of Independence which reads, *We hold these truths to be self-evident.* So in another sense, these commandments of God are self-evident, for they are written into the moral fabric of creation and civilization. In fact, it is not going too far to say that apart from these basic laws, civilization would be impossible, and the human race would sink into chaos. I think this becomes obvious as we see our own Western civilization turn its back more and more on God's moral law, and the resulting lawlessness and moral disintegration which threatens to destroy our way of life.

The essential teachings of the Ten Commandments are as valid today as when they were given. It is true that they no longer comprise a national covenant in the same sense they once did with Israel, but woe unto the nation or the culture that jettisons these commandments and expunges their universal truths from the law of the land, either by decree or custom. Christian, pray that there may be a return to these principles in our nation. But first they must be proclaimed and practiced by the Church if we are to become the moral compass of our nation, as once we were.

PRAYERS & REMINDERS

_____
_____
_____
_____
_____
_____
_____
_____
_____

Prayer: O Lord, You have commanded us to keep Your precepts diligently. Oh, that our ways were directed to keep Your statutes. Then we would honor and love You as we ought, and You would delight in our ways. May this come to pass in each one of us, through Christ our Lord. Amen.

Hymn for the day:
Let All Things Now Living

> **Question #41: Where is the moral law found to be summarized?**

Answer: The moral law is found summarized in the Ten Commandments.

Scripture Reading: Deuteronomy 28:1-14

Although the Ten Commandments are primarily intended for believers, they also form the foundation upon which civilization itself rests. No society of mankind can long endure without these basic principles of law and order. Even among people who have no knowledge of God and therefore no ability nor desire to love and honor Him, the commandments are still foundational to organized society. Certainly most of the civil law in the Western world rests upon this foundation. There was a time, not too long ago, when some Law Schools had courses on the Ten Commandments, showing students that the basic law code of this nation rested firmly on God's Ten Commandments. I doubt very much if this is still true. Surely by now the ACLU would have filed suit in Federal court to forbid such a thing!

Although the promise of God to bless Israel as a nation if they kept His commandments was a part of that special covenantal relationship between God and His chosen people, the principle of blessing flowing out of obedience is still valid. God still honors those who honor Him. Just by way of illustration, what society of people could long endure if there were no respect for human life, or property? There would be disintegration, and eventually chaos. Our own western culture is headed in that direction largely because these protections are being removed, either by tacit agreement, and in some cases by laws which protect those who violate the principles mentioned above. Make it a point this very day to submit to the laws of our land, at least in so far as they do not violate God's law. A nation of law keepers is much more honoring to God than a nation of law breakers.

Prayer: Lord, you have told us in your word that *Righteousness exalts a nation, but sin is a reproach to any people.* Help us to respect those in authority over us, and to rededicate ourselves to Your law and Your love. In Jesus' name we pray. Amen.

Hymn for the day:
God of Our Fathers, Whose Almighty Hand

PRAYERS & REMINDERS

Question #41: Where is the moral law found to be summarized?

Answer: The moral law is found summarized in the Ten Commandments.

Scripture Reading: Psalm 53

A common cry from humanists and even unthinking Christians is, *You cannot legislate morality.* Yet in every society there are laws against stealing and murder, with severe penalties for lawbreakers. This is clearly the legislation of morality. The ultimate reason why stealing, murder, and adultery, and all other such crimes are wrong is because they violate the basic law of God. There is simply no escaping the fact that the moral law is summarily comprehended in the Ten Commandments.

God, in His holy word, definitely legislates morality. He does this by revealing to us in some detail the nature of sin and why it displeases Him. He is the sovereign Lord of creation and as such He has established laws which simply cannot and must not be broken upon pain of severe penalties. It is interesting and very helpful to go back to the Pentateuch, and see how God develops and applies His ten commandments in such clear detail. Another thing which I find so fascinating is that in only ten commandments God gives the basic laws which contain the principles which govern all human behavior.

When a nation or a culture buys into the false premise that you cannot legislate morality, that nation or that culture is doomed for destruction, destruction which will come sooner than later. Isn't this where we are headed in this nation of ours unless there is a dramatic turn away from the warped thinking and uncontrolled behavior which defies and even flaunts the authority of the Creator over His creation? Make it your determination today that you will begin to meditate day and night on God's word, with full intention to understand, respect and obey it.

PRAYERS & REMINDERS

_____

_____

_____

_____

_____

_____

_____

_____

_____

Prayer: Teach me, O Lord, the way of Your statutes, and I shall keep it to the end. Give me understanding and I shall keep Your law. Indeed I shall observe it with my whole heart. May this be my prayer and my promise today, for Jesus' sake. Amen.

Hymn for the day:
How Shall the Young Direct their Way?

Question #41: Where is the moral law found to be summarized?

Answer: The moral law is found summarized in the Ten Commandments.

Scripture Reading: Romans 13:1-10

For Christians, the ultimate authority for understanding and applying the Ten Commandments is none other than our King and Lawgiver, the Lord Jesus Christ. His Sermon on the Mount is the infallible interpretation of the Ten Commandments. In His sermon, He shows us the intention behind each of these ten words and what God requires in the hearts of those who accept His law as their standard of conduct. He never at any point puts His teaching in opposition to the law of God. What He does is reject the traditional interpretation which had led Judaism so far astray from the original intention of the law. In a simple, direct, but profound way, He explains the original purpose and intent of the law. Therefore it is the privilege and duty of all believers to know and understand the Ten Commandments from the perspective of the Sermon on the Mount.

As we shall see a bit later in our study of the Catechism, the entire law of God is summed up in two great commandments: to love God with all of our hearts, and our neighbors as ourselves. In the final sense, the moral law is summarily comprehended in these two commandments, which are a summary of the ten. This by no means sets us free from obedience to each of God's laws, but rather we begin to see that by specific obedience to each of His commands, we are showing love both to God and to our neighbor. Two illustrations serve to demonstrate this. (1) When we obey the command, *You shall not take the name of the Lord Your God in vain,* this is a demonstration of our love for the Lord. (2) When we obey the command, *You shall not covet,* we are showing love for our neighbor. So love supports and fulfills the law, but never negates it.

Prayer: Dear Father, help us this very day to honor and love You with all our hearts. Help us to demonstrate this by loving our fellow believers, and by showing love to those in need of grace and help, thus proving we are indeed Christ's disciples. In Jesus' name. Amen.

Hymn for the day:
We Are God's People

PRAYERS & REMINDERS

Question #42: What is the sum of the Ten Commandments?

Answer: The sum of the Ten Commandments is: to love the Lord our God with all our heart, with all our soul, with all our strength, and with all our mind; and our neighbor as ourselves.

Scripture Reading: Luke 10:25-37

Even as the moral law is summed up in the Ten Commandments, so the Ten Commandments are summed up by the law of love. This law has two directions; one toward God, and the other toward man. The Lord Jesus was so emphatic about this that He declared: *On these two commandments, hang all the law and the prophets.* Since we have already seen that the law is a reflection of the character of God, it is clear that the basic element in God's character is love. This is why the Apostle John said: *God is love.* This does not negate the holiness or justice of God. In fact, these attributes are more clearly seen in light of His love. Because God is love, He judges and punishes the sin which threatens His children, and which destroys their relationship with Him. God emphatically underscores the relationship of holiness and love in the cross. There justice and mercy meet and kiss each other. The Father in love sent His beloved Son into the world to seek and save the lost. The faithful Son assumed the role of servant, took upon Himself the sin of the elect, and endured the righteous wrath of the Father, whose holiness demands the punishment of sin.

Thus did our Lord sum up the law of God not only by His words, but by His life and death. For in dying on the cross, He provided the only sacrifice acceptable to cover all our sins. The life of Jesus was also a testimony of His love for the Father and for His neighbor, for He perfectly obeyed the Father, and at the same time showed great love and compassion for people. His life of loving service affirmed His wise teaching. May our lives of obedience bear witness to the truth we profess.

PRAYERS & REMINDERS

_____

_____

_____

_____

_____

_____

_____

_____

_____

Prayer: Father, may our love for You be shown to all as we obey Your commands from the heart. May our surrendered lives express this beautiful summary of the law even as our Savior showed us in His life. We ask this for His sake and glory. Amen.

Hymn for the day:
So Let Our Lips and Lives Express

Question #42: What is the sum of the Ten Commandments?

Answer: The sum of the Ten Commandments is: to love the Lord our God with all our heart, with all our soul, with all our strength, and with all our mind; and our neighbor as ourselves.

Scripture Reading: Luke 15:1-32

When our Lord gave His summary of the law in Matthew 22, His words carried great weight, and rang with sincerity because He had lived out His teaching in His life. Even when we are at our very best, there remains much inconsistency between what we say and what we do. Jesus practiced what He preached to perfection. Who could deny that His life was a demonstration of faithful love for His Father? Who could fail to see that He truly loved His neighbor as Himself? By His parable of the good Samaritan, He taught that one's neighbor is the one in need. He refused to restrict His definition of neighbor to the narrow confines Judaism had placed on the word. Furthermore, in His ministry, He lived out the teaching of His parable by ministering to the leper, to the Samaritan woman, and to many others who were outcasts and rejects. For Jesus, they were His neighbors and He loved them with healing and saving power.

We certainly cannot love with that same power, but we can and must show that same sort of self-forgetting love which will touch hearts, and point people to the Savior. Far too often we only love those who love us, and only do good to those who have the will and the means of returning that love. This is a difficult mental attitude to overcome, because we all tend to be very selfish by nature. But as the love of Christ sinks into our heart and permeates our will, then His great love will manifest itself through us, and He will be glorified. What a noble resolve to challenge us today, that others might see the Lord Jesus living in us. If this happens, you may know you have not lived this day in vain.

Prayer: Lord, help me live from day to day in such a self-forgetful way, that even when I kneel to pray, my prayer may be for others. We ask this not for our glory but for His, who loved and saved us. Amen.

Hymn for the day:
Others

PRAYERS & REMINDERS

Question #42: What is the sum of the Ten Commandments?

Answer: The sum of the Ten Commandments is: to love the Lord our God with all our heart, with all our soul, with all our strength, and with all our mind; and our neighbor as ourselves.

Scripture Reading: Ezekiel 36:22-32

In the new covenant God has written His law upon our hearts. This means that love, as defined by the Lord Jesus, has become a part of our new nature. Believers are renewed image-bearers. We have a special duty and the high honor of reflecting the basic character of God. We are those who love the Lord our God with all our heart, mind, and strength. It is our greatest joy and chief end to glorify God. We demonstrate this by obedience. We remember that Jesus said: *If you love me, keep my commandments.* We also remember that He said: *A new commandment I give you, that you love one another, even as I have loved you.* The second table of the law shows us exactly how our love for our neighbor is to be expressed. These commandments show us that love and righteousness go hand in hand. In fact, righteousness in our dealings both with God and man, is the best way to demonstrate true love.

Of course this kind of eager, heart obedience is not something we just decide to do. In the passage from Ezekiel we discover how such obedience is possible. God promises us that He Himself will cleanse us, saying: *I will sprinkle clean water on you, and you will be clean.* This passage may be rightly used to defend our view that sprinkling is the most likely biblical form of baptism, but let us not miss the point. It is not the outward form of baptism by whatever method which cleanses us. It is the inner reality symbolized by baptism that makes us clean. We are sprinkled with the blood of Christ in the heavenly realm, and this makes us clean in God's sight. This is also the beginning of inward renewal in which God writes His law upon our hearts, and puts His Spirit within us to enable us to love both Him and our neighbor.

Prayer: O God, wash us and make us clean. Write Your holy law upon our hearts. Take away these hearts of stone and give us hearts of flesh, that we may respond to Your grace and Your Law. We ask this for Your glory and in Jesus' name. Amen.

Hymn for the day:
Holy, Holy, Holy

PRAYERS & REMINDERS
_____
_____
_____
_____
_____
_____
_____
_____
_____
_____

Question #43: What is the preface to the Ten Commandments?

Answer: The preface to the Ten Commandments is in these words: "I am the LORD your God, who brought you out of the land of Egypt, out of the house of slavery."

Scripture Reading: Isaiah 42:1-13

Before God gave His holy laws to Israel through Moses, He first reminded them who He was. The authority and validity of any law depends upon the law giver. The laws were not the laws of Moses or of any other man. Often you may read of some who maintains that the Ten Commandments are only a summary of laws which had been developed by various civilizations over a long period of time. However, we read in God's word that they were given directly from God to Moses. That there are similarities between the Ten Commandments and various law codes is to be expected. The human race was created in God's image and, as such, they had the laws of the Creator written into their created nature. At the fall, though the image of God in man was shattered, it was not totally erased. In Romans 1:19-22 we read: ... *What may be known of God is manifest in them, for God has shown it to them. For since the creation of the world His invisible attributes are clearly seen, being understood by the things that are made, even His eternal power and Godhead, so they are without excuse, because although they knew God, they did not glorify Him as God ... but became futile in their thoughts and their foolish hearts were darkened.*

So some true knowledge of God was retained, but perverted by sin. It was this remnant of truth which remained in man which gave him the limited ability to think God's thoughts after Him and to write into the basic law of any given civilization some similarities to God's revealed and inerrant word. For us, we need to remember where God's perfect law came from, and who gave it to us. The Ten Commandments came directly from God's mind and heart and are given to us by the Creator and King of the universe.

Prayer: O Lord, You alone are God and the true law giver. Help us to love and obey You because You are God, and not for fear of hell or hope of heaven. Please guard our hearts that we may love and obey all Your holy word. For Jesus' sake we pray, Amen.

Hymn for the day:
O For a Heart To Praise My God

PRAYERS & REMINDERS

Question #43: What is the preface to the Ten Commandments?

Answer: The preface to the Ten Commandments is in these words: "I am the LORD your God, who brought you out of the land of Egypt, out of the house of slavery."

Scripture Reading: Romans 12

Why should the preface receive special attention before we begin to study the commandments? The answer is simply this: our attention to these commandments, and the degree to which we take them seriously, is in direct proportion to our knowledge of and reverence for the One who gave the law. Before God said: *Thou shalt* or *Thou shalt not,* He first revealed Himself as the living and true God of the covenant, who has redeemed His people.

It is significant that this preface begins with the same words by which God answered Moses' question before the burning bush: *What is his name? What shall I say unto them? ... Thus shalt thou say unto the children of Israel, I AM hath sent me unto you* (Exodus 3:13b, 14b). So now when God's chosen people are about to receive the law of the covenant, He repeats the same words again. As Dr. Green observed in his *Commentary on the Westminster Standards, He calls Himself their God by a threefold right: by right of His nature; by right of His covenant relation to them, and by right of redemption.* This affords a very good outline for us to follow in our consideration of the preface. The great triune God requires and deserves obedience from His people. He is worthy of worship and He is worthy of our loving and glad surrender to His will as He reveals it to us. Whenever we are faced with the choice of obedience or disobedience to His revealed will, we must remember that He is the sovereign ruler of His whole creation. To obey His given law is to obey Him. To disobey His given law is to disobey Him. This means that obedience to God's law is a very personal thing. It is your expression of love and devotion to Him.

PRAYERS & REMINDERS

_____
_____
_____
_____
_____
_____
_____
_____
_____

Prayer: Father, we love Your laws because we love You who first loved us. Help us today to be loving, obedient children who honor our Father in heaven by faithful obedience to Your laws. In Jesus' name, Amen.

Hymn for the day:
Savior, Teach Me Day by Day

Question #44: What does the preface to the Ten Commandments teach us?

Answer: The preface to the Ten Commandments teaches us that because God is the Lord, and our God and Redeemer, therefore we are bound to keep all His commandments.

Scripture Reading: Galatians 4:1-7

God reveals His nature through His name, JEHOVAH or YAHWEH. This implies that He is eternal and self-existent. He is the fountainhead of all life and being. He is the Creator and Sovereign of the entire universe. By His word and will, all things exist. It is He who sits upon the circle of the earth, and before whom all nations are as a drop in the bucket, or a speck of dust on the scales. By reason of His might, majesty, and power, His word is to be obeyed, His commands accepted as the law of life. This great and awesome God is the God of the covenant. He is Abraham's God, Isaac's God, and Jacob's God. Now to Israel, the covenant seed of the ancient patriarchs, He comes, saying, *I am the LORD thy God* ... There is an indication of the incarnation in these words. He is a personal God, who desires a personal relationship with those to whom He reveals Himself and with those whom He redeems. Such a relationship is only possible in the final sense because of the incarnation in which God becomes man in the person of our Lord Jesus Christ. One of the most amazing things about the incarnation is that the Law Giver subjects Himself to His own laws. He was born under the law as the above Scripture tells us. When Christ began His public ministry and called the first disciples to follow Him, He explained in great detail what obedience to God's law really requires, in His Sermon on the Mount. What could be more fitting than for the Law Giver to explain by life and word the meaning of God's law. Make it your purpose today to obediently follow Him.

Prayer: Father, help us to understand that obeying Your law must first come from within our hearts as a desire to honor and please You in all we do. You do not need our praise, worship and obedience, but You desire this of us, and we would offer You our grateful obedience. In Jesus' name, Amen.

Hymn for the day:
Before Jehovah's Awful Throne

PRAYERS & REMINDERS

_____

_____

_____

_____

_____

_____

_____

_____

_____

Question #44: What does the preface to the Ten Commandments teach us?

Answer: The preface to the Ten Commandments teaches us that because God is the Lord, and our God and Redeemer, therefore we are bound to keep all His commandments.

Scripture Reading: Matthew 5:21-29

The sovereign Lord, the covenant-keeping God, is the Redeemer of His elect. *I am the Lord your God, which has brought you out of the land of Egypt, out of the house of bondage.* This mighty act of redemption was accomplished by means of the plagues culminating in the Passover. In this act of redemption Israel escaped the angel of death and the cruel bondage of Pharaoh. God also saved Israel from the more deadly bondage of idolatry. In His loving election, and out of His eternal love, He saved Israel and brought them into the land of promise. Gratitude becomes the motivation for obedience to all His commands.

We who are of the new covenant recognize His rights of Lordship, too, and for the same reasons. We hear the voice of our Savior God saying, *If you love me, keep my commandments.* In the giving of the law, God first gives the reason above all other reasons why His covenant people should obey Him, namely that He is our Lord and our Redeemer. Gratitude combined with a sense of duty becomes a powerful motivation for believers under the new covenant. When we consider the price our Savior paid to set us free from bondage and eternal ruin, then we must place no limits on our response to His commands. Unfortunately, all too often we spend more time explaining why we did not or will not obey Him, than in actually obeying. Thank the Lord for His amazing patience with us, and His even more amazing promise that one day we will be conformed to the image of Christ, our Redeemer. Then our obedience and our love will both be perfected in glory, and His law will be our greatest joy and delight.

PRAYERS & REMINDERS

_____

_____

_____

_____

_____

_____

_____

_____

_____

Prayer: Great and gracious God, our Lord and our Redeemer, in love You have predestined us to adoption as sons and daughters. Help us to always serve and honor You and Your holy law. Thank You for the gracious covenant whereby we are redeemed and destined for glory through Christ our Lord. Amen.

Hymn for the day:
Jesus Calls Us

Question #45: Which is the First Commandment?

Answer: The First Commandment is, "You shall have no other gods before me."

Scripture Reading: Isaiah 44:1-8

The first commandment is the first in every sense of the word. It is first in order, first in importance, and the foundation upon which all other commandments rest. If this law is ignored, then it is impossible to give more than mere lip service to any other one. If, on the other hand, we take this law seriously, and sincerely try to obey it, then all others will fall in place, and we will delight in the law of our God. Think how much depends upon this commandment. Here is the foundation and fountainhead for godly living, for worship, for evangelism, and for all Christian virtues.

This word deals with the most basic and fundamental need of humanity ... to know God. Secular psychology tells us that man's most basic needs are physical. This commandment teaches us the exact opposite; namely that the more basic need is spiritual. Our Lord Jesus reinforced this truth, when He refused Satan's temptation to turn the stones into bread, saying, *Man shall not live by bread alone, but by every word that proceedeth out of the mouth of God* (Matt. 4:4b). To know God and His will for your life is the deepest need you will ever experience, and offers the greatest reward and satisfaction. All God's commandments speak to the needs of the human heart, and all speak to fulfillment of those needs which may only be found in our relationship to God. The first commandment tells us that God must come first in our lives, and that we dare not have other gods in our lives. This is not only a caution against false gods, but also against false mental images of the true God as we shall later see in our consideration of the second commandment.

Prayer: O God, You alone are God and we acknowledge and adore You as our God. Deliver us from all false gods, especially those of our own making. Help us to obey this commandment from our hearts, today and always. In Jesus' name we pray. Amen.

Hymn for the day:
Praise the Lord, Ye Heavens Adore Him

PRAYERS & REMINDERS

Question #46: What is required in the First Commandment?

Answer: The First Commandment requires us to know and acknowledge God to be the only true God, and our God; and to worship and glorify Him accordingly.

Scripture Reading: Matthew 19:16-22

In this commandment, God requires that He be given first place in your life. He requires you to know Him as He reveals Himself in His word and worship Him alone as the one true and living God. This means much more than just formal acts of public worship, though this is most certainly required. God's prophets of old said that His people worshiped Him with their lips but their hearts were far from Him. Such careless worship insults God. It does not honor Him nor does it meet the requirements of this command. It is relatively easy to give mental assent to this law, and to obey it superficially, but sincere heart obedience to it requires your whole mind, heart and strength.

The story of the rich young ruler who came to Jesus asking the question *Good Teacher, What good thing shall I do that I may have eternal life?,* helps us to understand this first commandment. Jesus told him to keep the commandments. When he asked Jesus which ones, the Lord responded with the second table of the law which speaks of our duty to our fellow man. To which the young man replied, *All these things I have kept from my youth. What do I still lack?* At this point the Lord turns his attention to the first table of the law, our duty to God. He did it in the most skillful way, by calling on the young man to sell all he had and give to the poor. This was Jesus' way of showing him his riches had become his god. Sadly, the young man turned away. I think he was sad because he knew Jesus was right, and he also knew he would not obey Him. Is there anything in your life that is more important to you than God? Are you prepared to confess this and repent?

PRAYERS & REMINDERS

_____
_____
_____
_____
_____
_____
_____
_____
_____

Prayer: Dear God, You have told us we shall have no other God before You. Yet we allow so many things to come into our lives which dominate our time, our income, and our lives. Please forgive us and teach us to love and serve you above all else. In Jesus' name we pray. Amen.

Hymn for the day:
Come, All Christians, Be Committed

May 16

Question #46: What is required in the First Commandment?

Answer: The First Commandment requires us to know and acknowledge God to be the only true God, and our God; and to worship and glorify Him accordingly.

Scripture Reading: Psalm 95

When we build our lives around this commandment, as God requires of us, the priorities we establish reflect this. Sadly, our practice seldom lives up to our profession. We teach our children more by our actions and visible priorities, than we ever do by our words of instruction, as important as these words may be. Oftentimes, a father may complain bitterly over Sunday dinner, when the worship service lasts past noon, but thinks nothing of spending hours watching professional sports being acted out on the television screen. And have you ever heard a complaint when the ball game goes into overtime? If we tell our children that God must come first in our lives, but then spend so much of our income on material possessions that we have little, if any, left for the truly important things such as missionary work, will they believe that God is really first?

Obedience to the first commandment means that God is at the center of my solar system; all revolves around Him. It is this commandment which is really the foundation for the grand statement at the very beginning of our catechism: *Man's chief end is to glorify God and to enjoy Him forever.* We will never know the joy of the Lord by seeking joy only in earthly things. We will most certainly never glorify God by putting the things of His kingdom at the very last of our priorities. When we obey this commandment, we will be diligent to attend to all our duties in the home and at work, but we will do all this for His glory and honor. The key to obeying this commandment is to remember it expresses the will of our Father who loves us, and it also reveals where our heart is. If we profess to love Him, as we do, we will express our love by careful attention and obedience to His laws, beginning with this first commandment.

Prayer: Father, our desire today is to bring You honor, praise and glory in all we do. Help us to search our heart before You to make sure we have not placed ourselves or our desires above Your revealed will. Glorify Yourself in and through us. We ask this for Jesus' sake. Amen.

Hymn for the day:
I Sing The Almighty Power of God

PRAYERS & REMINDERS

Question #47: What is forbidden in the First Commandment?

Answer: The First Commandment forbids the denying, or not worshiping and glorifying, the true God as God, and our God; and the giving to any other of that worship and glory due to Him alone.

Scripture Reading: Psalm 73

Atheism is a dreadful sin. It is a very common sin, and it is forbidden by the first commandment. Some might protest, saying, *You cannot command faith.* That misses the point. The acknowledgment of God is more than a matter of faith. It is a fundamental truth, essential to the very essence of human nature.

We are beginning to see the impossibility of any human system built on atheism. The communist world has crumbled all around us. This collapse is basically moral and spiritual. The economic failure is merely a symptom. However, any political or economic system which is built on philosophical or even practical atheism is doomed to failure. It is increasingly and distressingly clear that our own nation, and indeed the entire Western world, is rapidly embracing atheism. Unless this is reversed quickly and thoroughly, Western civilization and all its systems and institutions will collapse, too. God will not be mocked!

When we approve of what God forbids and hates, we show contempt for God and His word, and invite His wrath upon us. Even in the institutional church we see more and more disdain for God's word, and the lessening of its influence on the doctrines and practices of the church. To make matters even worse we are being told that God really approves of things the Bible says He forbids. We are horrified by this defection, but we must take great care that we are not guilty in other ways of ignoring God's word in how we actually live. We may find ourselves in danger of seeing the speck in our brother's eye, while ignoring the log in our own eye. May God help us love what He loves and hate what He hates.

PRAYERS & REMINDERS

_____

_____

_____

_____

_____

_____

_____

_____

_____

Prayer: Lord God, great Sovereign over all, we live in a time and culture when You holy laws are ignored and despised. We tremble and fear for this dear land we love. Turn us again, O God, and cause Your face to shine upon us. Bring revival to all our churches. Let it begin in me. In Jesus' name. Amen.

Hymn for the day:
God Of Our Fathers

Question #47: What is forbidden in the First Commandment?

Answer: The First Commandment forbids the denying, or not worshiping and glorifying, the true God as God, and our God; and the giving to any other of that worship and glory due to Him alone.

Scripture Reading: Isaiah 46

It is a fearful thing to realize that our nation, by its laws and courts, is more and more declaring itself to be one nation *out from under* God. Yet who can deny it? Christian citizens who have historically supported the public institutions of this country find themselves faced with more and more painful dilemmas. In fact, continued support of these institutions may force one into a position of denying God.

Philosophical atheism is a terrible sin, but there is another form of atheism which is also condemned and forbidden by the first commandment. I speak of subtle forms of atheism, such as confessing God outwardly, but then living as if God did not exist, or as if His existence were of little consequence. God Himself condemned this when He said of Israel, *These people honor me with their lips, but their hearts are far from me.* Insincere worship, though performed flawlessly in outward form, and though conforming to Scripture in a technical sense, is another form of atheism, as shocking as this may sound.

I would encourage you to read carefully Question and Answer 105 in the Larger Catechism which mentions the many offenses which this commandment forbids. It is a very humbling and convicting exercise, but a very profitable one. Among the other sins which are pointed out are such things as ignorance of God's word, the neglect of any duty required therein, hardness of heart, pride, presumption, lukewarmness, and deadness in the things of God, and delving into the occult. These are but a few of the sins mentioned in the Larger catechism which this commandment forbids. We would do well to make a thorough study of this section of the Larger Catechism, with the view of sincere repentance.

Prayer: Father, we are overwhelmed with the evil we see in our own hearts and practices. How easily we accept in ourselves and others what You forbid by this commandment. Teach us to avoid and hate all those sins which separate us from You. For Jesus' sake we pray. Amen.

Hymn for the day:
God Be Merciful To Me

PRAYERS & REMINDERS

Question #47: What is forbidden in the First Commandment?

Answer: The First Commandment forbids the denying, or not worshiping and glorifying, the true God as God, and our God; and the giving to any other of that worship and glory due to Him alone.

Scripture Reading: Psalm 77:1-15

The Larger Catechism catalogs a long and dismaying list of sins forbidden by this law, and believers would do well to study Question and Answer 105 in the Larger Catechism in great detail. Let me suggest a profitable way in which this might be done. First, go to your prayer closet alone. Get on your knees before God, and read Psalm 51 as your prayer of general confession. Then, with a broken and contrite heart, read the words of the Catechism, slowly, thoughtfully. As you do this, examine your heart before God, and ask Him to show you if you are guilty of any of these sins which break His holy law, the first commandment. You will, of course, discover that you are guilty of many, many of these sins. Confess them – each one. Pray for grace to overcome them. Seek His forgiveness for breaking His law and His heart. You will discover that, in so doing, this commandment will become alive and powerful in your life, and you will be motivated not only to avoid the sins forbidden by it, but even more to fulfill by sincere and diligent effort the requirements and the joys this law affords.

It is never enough to simply refrain from evil. We must replace sinful thoughts and deeds with that which pleases God. Jesus talked about this in His short parable found in Luke 11:24-26. He told of a man who had cleaned up his life, but had not replaced the evil with good. Being empty, his life was open to even more and worse evil than before. So in regard to this commandment, it is not enough to simply not violate the commandment, but seek to positively obey it from your heart.

Prayer: Great Father, we look into Your word and see all your righteous commandments. We look into our hearts and examine our lives and see all the many ways we have disobeyed and offended You. For Your great mercy's sake, forgive us and teach us to amend our sinful ways. For Jesus' sake we ask this. Amen.

Hymn for the day:
Wonderful Grace of Jesus

PRAYERS & REMINDERS

Question #48: What are we especially taught by the words, "before me," in the First Commandment?

Answer: These words, "before me," in the First Commandment, teach us that God, who sees all things, takes notice of, and is much displeased with, the sin of having any other god.

Scripture Reading: Psalm 139

In the child's catechism, there is a question which asks, *Does God know all things?* The answer is, *Yes, nothing can be hidden from God.* Our God sees and knows all things. Nothing is hidden from Him. We are all as open books before God. Therefore, everything we do, say, or even think, is *before Him.* Even the secrets of our own minds and hearts, which we ourselves do not fully understand, are known to Him. He is the God *with whom we have to do.*

The person who truly knows the Lord, is the person who understands this, and believes it. The person who fails to understand this may well be guilty of idolatry. Let me explain. If in all we do and are, we are conscious of the true and living God, our utmost devotion will be His. If we do not keep Him in our conscious awareness at all times, we will likely put other things in the throne room of our lives, and thus become idolaters. These idols may have many forms and many names, but unless God Himself comes first, another has taken His place of chief affection in our hearts. This is the very essence of idolatry.

The book of First John closes with this admonition, *Little children, keep yourselves from idols.* Though the immediate setting makes this plea seem out of context, the Apostle has been warning his readers over and over about false teaching. Anytime there is false teaching about God, there is the danger of idolatry. If we believe wrong things about God, we will replace the true God of the Bible with a false god of our own depraved thinking. This is why it so very important to know Scripture thoroughly. This is the only way to guard ourselves from false notions about God. The first commandment forbids this.

Prayer: Dear God, protect our hearts and minds from false ideas about You, lest we attempt to create a false God. Help us to avoid taking Your name in vain by ascribing to You characteristics which are untrue. May we seriously obey Your word which says, *Little children, keep yourselves from idols.* In Jesus' name we ask this. Amen.

Hymn for the day:
God Moves In A Mysterious Way

PRAYERS & REMINDERS
_____
_____
_____
_____
_____
_____
_____
_____
_____
_____

> **Question #48: What are we especially taught by the words, "before me," in the First Commandment?**

Answer: These words, "before me," in the First Commandment, teach us that God, who sees all things, takes notice of, and is much displeased with, the sin of having any other god.

Scripture Reading: Psalm 17

It is so very important to understand that God not only sees all things, but takes notice of them, too. He takes special notice of our obedience or disobedience to this first commandment. He is much pleased when His children attend to all its duties. He is much displeased and grieved when we are guilty of the sins it forbids. We live our lives in His sight. In Psalm 139 we are reminded of this truth. *O Lord, You have searched me and known me. You know my sitting down and my rising up. You understand my thought afar off.* The Psalmist was very much aware of the phrase from the commandment, *before Me.* What a difference it makes when we are aware that *The darkness and the light are both alike to You.*

The emphasis in this commandment is not only that God sees and knows all things, but that he is much displeased with the sin of having any other God. The people of Israel in the time of Ezekiel obviously thought if they hid their idolatries in the inner recesses of the temple, and in the dark places, they could hide their iniquity from the Lord. But God took Ezekiel into those hidden recesses and showed him all the abominations which were being practiced, even in His holy temple.

The application for us is to remember that nothing is hidden from God, even those things we may hide from our fellow man, and even those things by which we deceive ourselves. Resolve today that you will recall these words from Psalm 139, and live accordingly.

PRAYERS & REMINDERS

_____

_____

_____

_____

_____

_____

_____

_____

_____

Prayer: Lord, help us to walk in the light of Your word, and to live transparently before each other. Shine Your holy light into the hidden recesses of our hearts that we may know, acknowledge, and confess our sins. We ask this in Jesus' name, for His sake. Amen.

Hymn for the day:
Spirit Of The Living God

Question #48: *What are we especially taught by the words, "before me," in the First Commandment?*

Answer: These words, "before me," in the First Commandment, teach us that God, who sees all things, takes notice of, and is much displeased with, the sin of having any other god.

Scripture Reading: Ezekiel 8

We see something of this in the book of Ezekiel. In the eighth chapter we read of a vision which God gave Ezekiel – a vision in which he was taken in the spirit to the temple of the Lord in Jerusalem. There Ezekiel saw Israel committing detestable idolatry. In hidden places, even the spiritual leaders were engaged in secret idolatry. But God saw, and God knew, and God was grieved and insulted by what He saw. He said to Ezekiel, *I will deal with them in anger; I will not look on them with pity or spare them. Although they shout in my ears, I will not hear them.* God is no less displeased by our idols of materialism, wealth, and luxury. Even though we may make lip profession of true worship, and even attend with regularity the house of God, there may well be hidden rooms, where our affection, love, and desires are given over to our private idols. Please know that God sees this. Please understand He is insulted and grieved by it.

Even as I write these things, my heart is convicted. I trust your heart will be touched as you read and ponder. Join with me in the sincere prayer of the Psalmist of old, who cried out to God: *Search me, O God, and know my heart; try me and know my thoughts; and see if there be any wicked way in me, and lead me in the way everlasting.* Yes, *God knoweth the secrets of the heart.* If we are near the heart of God, we will be aware of our sin; and being aware of it, we will repent and have no other gods before Him. Of course we are not speaking of the kinds of idols which were secretly worshiped in ancient Israel. But the secret idols of our hearts are nonetheless idols which we may cherish, even above our outward profession of faith. Only you and God know what these idols are. Since God does know, isn't it wise to acknowledge and repent of these idols of pleasure, ambition, and pride?

Prayer: O God, once more we pray, *Search me, O God, and know my heart; try me and know my thoughts; and see if there be any wicked way in me, and lead me in the way everlasting,* for Jesus' sake. Amen.

Hymn for the day:
Jesus Calls Us O'er The Tumult

PRAYERS & REMINDERS

Question #49: *Which is the Second Commandment?*

Answer: The Second Commandment is, "You shall not make for yourselves a carved image, or any likeness of anything that is in heaven above, or that is in the earth beneath, or that is in the water under the earth. You shall not bow down to them or serve them, for I the LORD your God am a jealous God, visiting the iniquity of the fathers on the children to the third and the fourth generation of those that hate me, but showing steadfast love to thousands of those who love me and keep my commandments."

Scripture Reading: I Kings 18:20-40

Idolatry, in one form or another, has been the bane of humanity from the dawn of history, and is still with us even to this day. The genesis of idolatry is in the mind of man, fallen man. God created man in His own image, and after the fall, man set out to attempt to create God in his image. This is idolatry. Men of old sought out skilled craftsmen who fashioned idols from precious metal to give a visual representation to their mental and emotional images of what they wanted their god to be. Then they fell down and worshiped this god of their imagination. Though it was nothing more than cunningly designed metal, yet men ascribed to the idol great powers. They prayed to it as though its ears could actually hear. They sought guidance from it as though it had eyes that could see. They sought compassion from the cold statue with no heart. Poor men, who could not afford the golden gods, simply carved images from stumps, and worshiped with equal fervency, and equal futility. The story of the contest between Elijah and the four hundred prophets of Baal illustrates this powerfully. When Baal's prophets were challenged to call down fire from heaven by the name of Baal, nothing happened. Their efforts lasted the better part of a day and became more and more fervent and frantic. Towards the end they were leaping upon the altar, and cutting themselves with knives to get Baal's attention, to no avail. But when Elijah quietly and fervently called upon the name of the Lord, the fire came down, the sacrifice and the altar were consumed. God was victorious over the futile idol and its adherents. He always is.

Prayer: Thank You, Lord God, that Yours is the kingdom, the power and the glory forever. Help us to cast down every idol we have enthroned in our lives and worship You alone, for Jesus' sake. Amen.

Hymn for the day:
Faith Is The Victory

PRAYERS & REMINDERS

Question #49: Which is the Second Commandment?

Answer: The Second Commandment is, "You shall not make for yourselves a carved image, or any likeness of anything that is in heaven above, or that is in the earth beneath, or that is in the water under the earth. You shall not bow down to them or serve them, for I the LORD your God am a jealous God, visiting the iniquity of the fathers on the children to the third and the fourth generation of those that hate me, but showing steadfast love to thousands of those who love me and keep my commandments."

Scripture Reading: Psalm 115

Modern man, though more sophisticated, is no less idolatrous. He still worships gods of silver and gold, or now maybe gods of electronics and microchips. The gods of wealth, power, affluence, and sensuality have captured the minds and hearts of people today as no stone or metal image could ever do in ancient days. What thinking person could fail to see the tremendous hold these modern gods have on people today? Many Christians ignore this prohibition and worship, or attempt to worship, God through images, statues, pictures, and man-made rituals and forms. They would claim that these things are merely aids to worship, but by so doing they refuse God's authority to command the method and nature of true worship. Reformed Christians have always refused to countenance such practices, and see them as violations of this command. But are images, pictures, and statues the only way the command might be broken? Would it be possible to break the second commandment even though we did not use pictures or images as "aids to worship"? The question is self answering. So long as we retain mental or emotional ideas about God that are contrary to His word, or concepts of Him not directly taught in His word, we are also guilty of breaking this commandment. So we must guard our hearts against such violations. The so called regulative principle of worship is a very important and sound principle to follow. If God's word forbids it, do not practice it, and unless God's word teaches it, do not practice it.

Prayer: Father, help us to know You truly and serve You sincerely, not trusting in our own ideas and thoughts, but learning to think Your thoughts after You. Correct through Your word any and all false and unworthy ideas we have of You, that we may honor You in all our thoughts and deeds. In Jesus' name we pray. Amen.

Hymn for the day:
How Precious is the Book Divine

PRAYERS & REMINDERS

Question #49: Which is the Second Commandment?

Answer: The Second Commandment is, "You shall not make for yourselves a carved image, or any likeness of anything that is in heaven above, or that is in the earth beneath, or that is in the water under the earth. You shall not bow down to them or serve them, for I the LORD your God am a jealous God, visiting the iniquity of the fathers on the children to the third and the fourth generation of those that hate me, but showing steadfast love to thousands of those who love me and keep my commandments."

Scripture Reading: Psalm 97

It is possible to elevate our own ideas of what we think God is like to the level of Biblical revelation, and even above it. I have been in Bible studies with people who insist that their ideas of what God is like are more important than the doctrine of God found in Scripture. Such presumption is most insulting to God, who has faithfully revealed Himself in His word. How often I have heard people reject the Biblical concepts of God's righteousness, His absolute sovereignty, or His terrible wrath against sin. When presented with these truths they will respond, "I could never believe in a God who would send people to hell;" or "I don't think God would predestine some people to be saved." To reject any of the attributes or actions of God in favor of a god acceptable to fallen human reason is a clear and dangerous violation of the second commandment.

The God who reveals Himself in Scripture is the one true God, and anything less or other is an idol, a graven image of a corrupt mind. To such images we must not fall down nor offer worship. How subtle is this temptation. While we would never even think of bowing before an actual idol, we may still be guilty of idolatry when we substitute God's word with human concepts. We want a god who is easy to get along with, and who is very tolerant of our wishes and wants, no matter how ungodly they may be. Sometimes we try to create such a god by twisting Scripture to our desires, or simply by ignoring the whole counsel of God as revealed in His word.

Prayer: Father, what marvelous truths You have revealed in Your holy word. There, and there alone do we find truth that saves and transforms. May we always look into Your word that we may find You there. In Jesus' name. Amen.

Hymn for the day:
Creator God, Creating Still

PRAYERS & REMINDERS

Question #50: What is required in the Second Commandment?

Answer: The Second Commandment requires the receiving, observing, and keeping pure and entire all such religious worship and ordinances as God has appointed in His Word.

Scripture Reading: Psalm 119: 41-56

Worship is exceedingly important to God. He seeks those who will worship Him in spirit and in truth. The primary occupation of heaven is worship. The glorious climax of all human history is the gathering of the redeemed before the throne of God and of the Lamb, to offer grateful and joyous praise and worship. Is it any wonder that God should direct us in how He desires to be worshiped?

These questions and answers from the Catechism offer very explicit directions on how to worship God correctly and how to avoid offending Him by our worship. In this careless age of *every man doing what is right in his own eyes,* we would do well to give serious attention to this matter. There is a feeling abroad that everyone should have the right to worship God as he or she sees fit. This may be a right conferred by the laws of men, but it is not a right given by the law of our God. He requires that we worship Him as He sees fit, and as He directs in His word. Worship that is not according to God's word is worship that violates the second commandment. How sad to think that even in our most sacred moments we may offend God, if we stray from His word. A good rule for worship which some have suggested is this: read the word, preach the word, sing the word and pray the word. If we follow this pattern in all our worship, both public and private, we may sure that God is pleased, and we are blest. The examples we find in Scripture of worship which pleases God confirm that the above rule of worship is one we may safely follow.

Prayer: O God, unite our hearts to fear Your name. Help us to worship according to Your word. Help us to live according to Your word, that in worship or work we may glorify You in all we do. In Jesus' name we ask this. Amen.

Hymn for the day:
We Rest On Thee, Our Shield And Our Defender

PRAYERS & REMINDERS

Question #50: What is required in the Second Commandment?

Answer: The Second Commandment requires the receiving, observing, and keeping pure and entire all such religious worship and ordinances as God has appointed in His Word.

Scripture Reading: Psalm 111

The Larger Catechism gives details not covered by the Shorter, and is an effective commentary on the Shorter Catechism. Under the heading of what is required, the Larger Catechism spells out such elements as prayer and thanksgiving in the name of Christ. This would include not only prayers, but also thanksgiving in song, by singing, as the Apostle Paul instructed, *psalms and hymns, and spiritual songs.*

This commandment also requires that the Word be read and expounded. I was recently in a worship service in which a beautiful passage from God's Word was read. However, the sermon which followed had little if anything to do with that passage or any other passage from the Bible. On the other hand, I have attended worship services (yes, even Presbyterian worship services) in which only one verse of Scripture was read in the entire service, and that was belabored beyond reason or interest. In both cases there was an absence of some very necessary elements of worship. There are times when it is much more beneficial to simply hear the word of God read than to launch out into a long and specious interpretation of it. What God has said is far more important than our understanding of what it means, though it is most certainly necessary to understand His word. However, since corporate worship is ordinarily limited to one day each week, except on special occasions, family worship and individual worship should be daily, and always include the reading and at least a brief explanation of God's word. Never allow the devotional thoughts of mere men (or women) to replace the reading of God's word.

PRAYERS & REMINDERS

_____

_____

_____

_____

_____

_____

_____

_____

_____

Prayer: Father, all Your commandments are just and true. You have shown us through Your Son, the living Word, Your nature and Your will. Guide us by Your holy law as we journey on our way to heaven. Help us to love Your commandments and keep them diligently. We pray in Jesus' name. Amen.

Hymn for the day:
Break Thou The Bread Of Life

Question #51: What is forbidden in the Second Commandment?

Answer: The Second Commandment forbids the worshiping of God by images, or any other way not appointed in His Word.

Scripture Reading: Acts 5:1-11

The Larger Catechism is also helpful in understanding those things forbidden by this commandment. Not only are we to avoid any forms of worship contrary to the Word, but also any images of God, either inwardly of the mind, or outwardly in any kind of image or likeness. We are also warned against accepting traditions of worship which do not come from the Word. This is a sword with two edges, for it not only speaks against liturgical practices of non-Reformed traditions, but many worship practices defended on the grounds of Reformed tradition as well, with no real Biblical case for that particular practice.

What it all comes down to is this: God desires and requires of us that we worship Him in spirit and in truth, and He reserves for Himself alone the right to define and describe that true worship. He has revealed these things in His word, and expects His children to take this revelation seriously, even as they take worship seriously.

Taking God's revelation seriously requires that we exclude from worship whatever is forbidden in His word. This would include not only the outward acts of worship, but also the inner motivation as well. The classic example of this would be the case of Ananias and Sapphira as told in Acts 5. Remember how they noted the praise given to Barnabas when that worthy man sold some property and donated the proceeds from that sale to the needy in the congregation? So they, too, sold land, kept back part of the price for themselves, but claimed they had given to the church all they received from the sale. Their hypocrisy was discovered and they both paid the ultimate penalty for their sin. So we see that the spirit and the act must go together when we offer worship to God.

Prayer: Father, You know that even in our most sacred moment, we are as prone to sin as the sparks to fly upwards from the fire. Protect our minds and hearts that the worship we offer you may be sincere, and honoring to You. In Jesus' name. Amen.

Hymn for the day:
My Jesus, I Love Thee

PRAYERS & REMINDERS

Question #52: What are the reasons attached to the Second Commandment?

Answer: The reasons attached to the Second Commandment are: God's sovereignty over us, His ownership in us, and the zeal He has for His own worship.

Scripture Reading: Isaiah 29:13-24

When God gives a commandment to His people, it is to be regarded with respect, reverence, and eager obedience. When He gives specific reasons for the commandment, as He does with the second commandment, we are expected to give special notice and attention.

In the Lord's prayer, there is one petition which deserves special notice because it is the only one which our Lord reinforces with specific promises and warnings. That petition is, *Forgive us our debts, as we forgive our debtors.* He then added these words, *for if ye forgive men their trespasses, your heavenly Father will also forgive you: but if ye forgive not men their trespasses, neither will your Father forgive your trespasses* (Matt. 6:12,14). These words place special emphasis on this petition of the Lord's prayer.

So in the second commandment, we have additional words of special emphasis which focus our attention on the importance of obedience. We really must take special notice when our Lord gives us special reasons for obeying Him. So in this second commandment we are told that God is very concerned that we offer Him worship which honors Him and respects His right to order proper and God pleasing worship. The worship we offer God reveals our attitude of reverence and respect we have for Him. Improper worship reveals a lack of respect and reverence for Him. Idolatry in any form is unacceptable because it dishonors Him and ignores His specific command. Let us never be guilty of placing our opinions over the revealed will of God in worship and life.

PRAYERS & REMINDERS

_____

_____

_____

_____

_____

_____

_____

_____

_____

Prayer: Almighty and eternal God, our heavenly Father, You have been so gracious to show us how to worship and honor You. May this be our determination to obey this commandment, and to delight in worshiping You according to Your word. We ask this for the sake and honor of our Savior Jesus Christ. Amen.

Hymn for the day:
Savior, Thy Dying Love

Question #52: What are the reasons attached to the Second Commandment?

Answer: The reasons attached to the Second Commandment are: God's sovereignty over us, His ownership in us, and the zeal He has for His own worship.

Scripture Reading: Genesis 4:1-15

God gives us three reasons why idolatry is so odious to Him, and why proper worship is so important: (1) His Lordship over our lives; (2) His image in us; and (3) His own zeal for true worship. Any one of these reasons is compelling, all three together are overwhelming.

God is our sovereign Lord. He alone deserves our worship and praise. He brooks no rivals. He has every right to require our worship and to instruct us in proper worship. Idolatry is a denial of this right. It is a rejection of His sovereignty. It is questioning His authority and even His integrity. Eve's first step in sin was not eating the forbidden fruit; it was listening when Satan questioned God's good purpose in the prohibition of that fruit. Cain's offering was rejected because his heart was not right with God, but there may be some indication that neither was his worship right with God. In the parable of the wedding feast, Jesus told of the man who refused the wedding garment, and was expelled from the feast, presumably because his refusal was a denial of the prerogative of the host to invite and clothe his guests as he saw fit. May we not draw some lesson from this concerning worship? How dare we insult the character of God by offering to Him worship which is displeasing to Him? The lessons of Cain and Abel, and their offerings to God must not be lost on us. Abel's offering was acceptable because his heart was right with God, and this was expressed in his offering. Cain's offering was rejected because Cain's heart was not right with God. God said to Cain: *If you do well, will you not be accepted? And if you do not do well, sin crouches at your door. And its desire is for you, but you should rule over it.* This is a needed and timely warning for all of us as we come to worship God.

Prayer: Father, You know our heart's desire is to honor and worship You. If we discover sin crouching at the door, help us by grace to rule over it and not allow it to rule over us. Deliver us from the curse of Cain into the blessing of Abel, through Christ our Lord. Amen.

Hymn for the day:
Burn In Me, Fire Of God

PRAYERS & REMINDERS

Question #52: What are the reasons attached to the Second Commandment?

Answer: The reasons attached to the Second Commandment are: God's sovereignty over us, His ownership in us, and the zeal He has for His own worship.

Scripture Reading: Hebrews 12:18-29

The second reason annexed to the second commandment is stated this way: *His propriety in us*. This really speaks of the image of God in us which makes worship and the manner of worship so very important. Because we are image-bearers of the sovereign God, only God-directed worship is appropriate. Idolatry is a denial that we are image-bearers of the one true God. It would be most fitting for the evolutionists to worship a god made in the image of a monkey, or any other beast, since they insist we all evolved from lower forms of life. There is a sense in which all idolaters are evolutionists, and vice versa, though would be vehemently denied in both cases.

Finally our obedience to this commandment is important for us, because it is important to God. Since He is zealous for true worship, then so must we be. The Father seeks true worshipers, who will worship Him in spirit and in truth. In true worship we seek to honor the one true and living God. This means that our worship of God must not only be faithful and true to His word, but also it must come from those who seek to be true in their lives and conduct. Our acceptance before God in worship depends upon the perfect righteousness of Christ, and His intercession in our behalf. At the same time, when we come before the Lord in worship it must be an expression not only of our trust in Christ's finished work, but with the longing that God will continue His work in us until we are completely sanctified and glorified and His work in us is therefore completed. Then in heaven all our worship will be perfected, and God will be glorified.

PRAYERS & REMINDERS

_____

_____

_____

_____

_____

_____

_____

_____

_____

Prayer: Lord, purify our worship that we may honor, glorify and please You. Help us to offer You only true and deeply felt worship, praise and adoration. We anticipate with great and eager joy the time when in Your heaven, we will perfectly worship You alone, Father, Son and Holy Spirit. Amen.

Hymn for the day:
How Lovely Is Thy Dwelling Place

June 1

Question #53: Which is the Third Commandment?

Answer: The Third Commandment is, "You shall not take the name of the LORD your God in vain; for the LORD will not hold him guiltless who takes his name in vain."

Scripture Reading: Psalm 8

High on the list of God's priorities is the sacredness of His name. One of the evidences of a society dominated by atheism is a disregard for this sanctity. Needless to say, we are living in just this kind of society. The name of God is held in ridicule rather than reverence. We are living in a society that is openly defying God, and almost daring Him to do something about it. The warning, *for the LORD will not hold him guiltless who takes His name in vain*, is ignored and mocked.

Just because we do not see God immediately pouring His righteous wrath on those who take His name in vain, don't think for a moment that this command or its warning has been negated. Just what is meant by *the name of God?* God's name describes His character and all His glorious attributes. God's name is all the truth He has revealed about Himself in His word. It is the power of that name which keeps us from falling, and calls us back when we wander and go astray. I don't mean this in any sort of magical way, that we have but to say God's name in reverence, and all our trials will end. But rather in the assurance and strength of God's perfect revelation of Himself, we find grace and help in times of need. *He watching over Israel neither slumbers nor sleeps. The Lord is your helper.*

Claim the promises of His Fatherly love and care for you. Hold fast to that glorious name, and all the truth it implies. He will sustain and keep you in His own dear and precious name. Praise God from whom all blessings flow.

Prayer: Great God, our heavenly Father, we love and honor Your great name. We would keep Your name always holy, and never take it in vain. Yet we know our own sinful hearts, and how quickly we go astray. Forgive us and keep us in Your name. For Jesus' sake we pray. Amen.

Hymn for the day:
God Will Take Care Of You

PRAYERS & REMINDERS

Question #53: Which is the Third Commandment?

Answer: The Third Commandment is, "You shall not take the name of the LORD your God in vain; for the LORD will not hold him guiltless who takes his name in vain."

Scripture Reading: Psalm 115

Have you ever considered why God's name is so important to Him, and to us? The reason is simple: it is far more than just a word; it represents and reveals who He is. Your name is important to you for the same reason. Each individual within a family bears the family name and must faithfully represent the integrity of that name. Far more important than any earthly name is the name of our Father in heaven. He holds it in high esteem and requires the same of us. Any irreverent or flippant use of His name is offensive to Him, and invites His displeasure and even His wrath. At the same time, the use of His name in a reverent and loving manner honors and pleases Him. The ancient Hebrews seldom spoke or even wrote the name by which God revealed Himself to Moses. This is one reason why we find the word LORD (note the capital letters) so often in Scripture rather than the name *Yahweh,* or *Jehovah.* They were fearful of using that holy name improperly, and so avoided its use in most cases. Some scholars tell us that only the High Priest spoke aloud this name of God, and that only on special occasions of great solemnity.

Jesus taught us to call God, Father. Although we find this word in a few places in the Old Testament, we can discover no warrant in the Old Testament for calling God our Father. It was the Lord Jesus, God's only begotten Son who gave to us the right and privilege of calling God, *Our Father.* This was His most often used title for God, and all through His ministry we hear Him calling on God as His Father, and teaching His disciples to do likewise.

Prayer: Father, thank You for being our Father, and allowing us to know You as our Father. Thank You for adopting us into Your family, and giving to us the high and holy privilege of calling on You in all times of need. Thank You for Your Son, the Lord Jesus. Amen.

Hymn for the day:
This Is My Father's World

PRAYERS & REMINDERS

Question #53: Which is the Third Commandment?

Answer: The Third Commandment is, "You shall not take the name of the LORD your God in vain; for the LORD will not hold him guiltless who takes his name in vain."

Scripture Reading: Revelation 15

In contrast to the extreme (if indeed it was an extreme) of the ancient Jews, of never writing or using the name, Jehovah, lest they break this command, modern believers seem so influenced by the profane culture in which we live, to the extent that we join the world in its sin of taking God's name in vain. It never ceases to distress me to hear Christians using God's name lightly, and even irreverently. It has become a common expression to say, "oh God" or "good God" as a term of shock, dismay, or surprise. It is hard to say which is more destructive of the minds of the young, to be constantly exposed to the profane use of God's name on radio and television, or for Christian parents to fail in their duty to teach the sacredness of God's name and to hold it in loving esteem. As bad as it is to hear unbelievers take God's name in vain, it is infinitely more regrettable to hear believers use such language.

One of the great responsibilities which rests upon all believers is to live in such a way that God's name will be respected and honored because of our conduct. It was once said of king David that the heathen blasphemed the name of God because of his conduct. May this never be said of us! Rather, may people who see, hear and know us, bless the name of our God and even more, call upon Him for salvation and life. Thus we honor Him and give heart obedience to this commandment. May none ever say of us, "if that is what it means to be a Christian, I want no part of it."

Prayer: Dear Father, help us to honor Your holy name in all our speech and conduct. May our greatest joy be found in knowing You as our Father in heaven, and making You known both by word and deed to the people around us. In Jesus' name we pray. Amen.

Hymn for the day:
All Hail The Power Of Jesus' Name

PRAYERS & REMINDERS

June 4

> ### Question #54: What is required in the Third Commandment?

Answer: The Third Commandment requires the holy and reverent use of God's names, titles, attributes, ordinances, Word, and works.

> ### Question #55: What is forbidden in the Third Commandment?

Answer: The Third Commandment forbids all profaning or abusing of anything by which God makes Himself known.

Scripture Reading: Psalm 111

The third commandment which God has given to His people carries with it the responsibility of the right use of His name, and the avoiding of the wrong use. Both aspects of obedience are equally important; therefore, we will consider both questions from the Catechism together.

To understand the requirements for the proper use of God's name, we must deal with the words *holy* and *reverent*. We should take great delight and feel freedom in our use of God's name, so long as we keep in mind these two words. There is a hymn in which we sing, *How sweet the name of Jesus sounds In a believer's ear ... .* Truly the names by which our God has revealed Himself to us are sweet and glorious, and we love to repeat them over and over again. We do this in a spirit of reverent and holy joy, whether in the privacy of our own prayer closets, or in public assemblies of worship. The holy and reverent use of God's names and titles requires a knowledge and an understanding of who God is and what He has done in His works of creation, providence, and redemption. As we read His word and gain this understanding, we are awed by His holiness and majesty, as well as His grace and mercy. Therefore, when we speak or even think His name, we do so with reverence, and with love.

Prayer: O God, truly Your name is holy and reverend. Help us to hold it in the highest esteem and honor. All of Your glorious attributes inspire us to worship and praise. Your works of creation, providence and redemption are a reflection of Your Holy name and nature. Accept our praise and prayer, through Christ our Lord. Amen.

Hymn for the day:
The God Of Abraham Praise

PRAYERS & REMINDERS

> **Question #54: What is required in the Third Commandment?**

Answer: The Third Commandment requires the holy and reverent use of God's names, titles, attributes, ordinances, Word, and works.

> **Question #55: What is forbidden in the Third Commandment?**

Answer: The Third Commandment forbids all profaning or abusing of anything by which God makes Himself known.

Scripture Reading: John 17:6-19

To use His name properly, we must use it often in prayer and praise. We must speak it often in witness and testimony. How often and in what spirit we use the name of our God is a good indication of our relationship with Him. I think back years ago when my firstborn was on the mission field as a young single lady. She met a fellow missionary, who would one day be her husband. Her first reference to him in a letter was rather casual. Soon, however, his name was mentioned throughout every letter, and with growing and even glowing appreciation and affection. Her use of his name was a fair indication of the relationship which had blossomed into love. So the name of our Lord and our God becomes increasingly dear as we grow in our relationship with Him.

The little child learns to love God's name by hearing father and mother speaking often of Him in loving and glowing words of adoration, thanksgiving, and praise. When a person comes to a knowledge of salvation the name of the Savior becomes very dear, and that name is mentioned often and eagerly. When hard and trying times overtake us, we cry out to God, who is our refuge and our strength. When "sorrows like sea billows roll," our only refuge is the Lord, whose name keeps us from sinking under those waves. When age takes its toll, and the end of our earthly journey draws towards its end, our thoughts turn increasingly to our merciful and loving Father. Oh, yes! The name of God grows ever dearer to us and in that name we rest all our hopes in this world and the next.

Prayer: Lord, Your holy name is our strength and our delight. We call upon You day and night, for You are our hope, our only hope. We thank You for that dear name by which we may come into Your holy presence; and that name is Jesus. Amen.

Hymn for the day:
Blessed Be The Name

PRAYERS & REMINDERS

Question #54: What is required in the Third Commandment?

Answer: The Third Commandment requires the holy and reverent use of God's names, titles, attributes, ordinances, Word, and works.

Question #55: What is forbidden in the Third Commandment?

Answer: The Third Commandment forbids all profaning or abusing of anything by which God makes Himself known.

Scripture Reading: Ephesians 4:26-32

Needless to say, the improper or profane use of God's names or titles is forbidden by this holy law. In an age and society in which profanity and obscenity are commonplace, the believer is required to maintain a good testimony of pure, wholesome speech. Parents should not be overly surprised to hear profanity on the lips of their children if there is no parental supervision and even censorship of what their children watch on television or hear on the radio. It is almost impossible to watch a single program without hearing God's name taken in an irreverent manner. When this happens, either change the channel or turn it off, and tell your children why. Many children who attend public and private schools hear their teachers take God's name in vain constantly. They should be protected from this form of child abuse, even if it means changing schools or home schooling. Don't underestimate the devastating effect constant exposure to profanity will have on your children. It is unfortunate but true that many children and young people in our sports crazy culture first hear the name of God when it is taken in vain by their coaches. I have witnessed this over and over even at children's sporting events, such as baseball, soccer, track, basketball and football. Sometimes this profanity is heard more from the parents and grandparents who come to watch their children play. God have mercy on us.

PRAYERS & REMINDERS

Prayer: O God, surely You are deeply grieved when You hear even little children taking You name in vain. Please forgive and correct us, that Your name may be glorified in all we do. In Jesus' name, Amen.

Hymn for the day:
O, Could I Speak The Matchless Worth

> ## Question #54: What is required in the Third Commandment?

Answer: The Third Commandment requires the holy and reverent use of God's names, titles, attributes, ordinances, Word, and works.

> ## Question #55: What is forbidden in the Third Commandment?

Answer: The Third Commandment forbids all profaning or abusing of anything by which God makes Himself known.

Scripture Reading: Matthew 23:1-30

There is another more subtle sin which is seldom mentioned in connection with this commandment, yet lies at the very heart of its meaning. This is the sin of insincerity. When we use God's name in worship that does not come from the heart, we take His name in vain. When our basic profession of faith is insincere, we take His name in vain. When we offer prayers unworthy of our Savior's name, we take His name in vain.

Eternal vigilance is the price of freedom, and this same kind of commitment is required of those who would obey this law of God. How easily we slip into this sin of shallow insincerity. How ruinous of true faith it is. To bear the name Christian requires a conscious awareness of the honor of that title. Sometimes, the family name may be harmed by the conduct of members of that family. I'm sure you've heard it said of someone, "Oh, he's the black sheep of our family. We don't like to admit he's even a part of the family." How much more disgraceful it is for one who bears the name of God's family to behave in such a way that the name of our Savior, and His cause on earth is despised. When Jesus was on earth, the only people He called hypocrites were those very religious people who dishonored God by their contradictory behavior. He exposed the insincerity of their profession of faith by revealing how far from God's heart and will they were. This is always a tragedy when religious people who make great outward show of their faith, live before the world in a way which contradicts their profession.

Prayer: Father, save us from an insincere use of Your holy name. Help us to live up to what we profess, that Your name may be honored, and others may come to know You. In Jesus' name. Amen.

Hymn for the day:
Ask Ye What Great Thing I Know

PRAYERS & REMINDERS

June 8

Question #56: What is the reason attached to the Third Commandment?

Answer: The reason attached to the Third Commandment is that, however those who break this commandment may escape punishment from men, yet the Lord our God will not allow them to escape His righteous judgment.

Scripture Reading: Psalm 34

The seriousness of this commandment is underscored by the warning attached to it. It is the only commandment with such a warning. God takes the sacredness of His name very seriously indeed. The day has long ceased when there were laws against public profanity, though such laws were once on the books of almost every state and municipality in the United States. If such laws did not exist it was because they were not needed, since there was a public consensus that profanity was improper. God's laws are still "on the books" and in the Book.

Does this mean that the breaking of this commandment is the unforgivable sin? No, there is nothing in Scripture to suggest this. However, it is most certainly a heinous sin in God's sight and hearing. It is interesting to note that Jesus warned that blasphemy against the Holy Spirit would not be forgiven. Although theologians and other Biblical scholars disagree as to the exact nature of the *sin against the Holy Spirit*, certainly the sin of taking God's name in vain is closely akin to blasphemy. The point is that God gives a special warning against this sin, and this warning should be taken seriously. Any time God issues a special warning against any particular sin, we would do well to take this warning very seriously. Another example of this is when Jesus was teaching us to pray. He stopped when He came to the petition, *Forgive us our debts, as we forgive our debtors,* and warned us, saying, *For if you forgive men their trespasses, your heavenly Father will forgive you. But if you do not forgive men their trespasses, neither will your Father forgive you.* God's warnings are to be taken seriously, and this especially applies to the third commandment.

Prayer: Father, Your sacred name is holy, and we would not take it in vain. You have taught us to hold Your great name in reverence, and warned us against taking it in vain in any form. Forgive us when we do, and cleanse us from this sin for Jesus' sake. Amen.

Hymn for the day:
Take The Name Of Jesus With You

PRAYERS & REMINDERS

June 9

> ## Question #56: What is the reason attached to the Third Commandment?

Answer: The reason attached to the Third Commandment is that, however those who break this commandment may escape punishment from men, yet the Lord our God will not allow them to escape His righteous judgment.

Scripture Reading: Psalm 2

There are other consequences resulting from disobedience to this commandment. The loss of fellowship with the Lord is one of the more serious. When we carelessly or deliberately abuse the name of some earthly friend and fail to show respect and regard for their good name, our relationship is diminished and even seriously threatened. How much more will our disrespectful use of God's name hinder our fellowship with Him?

The fear of the Lord is the beginning of wisdom. Lack of reverence for Him and His holy name is the foundation of all folly. If we do not hold His name in reverence, if we do not honor and respect Him, are we likely to honor and respect those made in His image? Have you ever noticed how those who never seem to have anything but contempt for their fellow man frequently take God's name in vain? Profanity is the native tongue of the lawless and criminal elements. When all reverence and respect for God fall victim to profanity, disobedience to His other commandments is the next logical step, and almost always follows in due time. To dishonor God's name is to dishonor Him, and makes us guilty of holding God in contempt. The name of God represents all He is in His essential nature and all His attributes. So the sin of profanity and the careless use of God's name signifies that we have neither respect for God, nor fear of Him. Certainly the fear of the Lord is the beginning of wisdom, but fools make a mock of sin. God will not hold him guiltless who takes His name in vain.

Prayer: O great and holy God, help us always to hold Your name in great reverence. Deliver us from the great sin of our age, profanity. May our lips and hearts be clean and may we hold Your name as holy and very precious. In Jesus' name. Amen.

Hymn for the day:
O, For A Thousand Tongues To Sing

PRAYERS & REMINDERS

Question #56: What is the reason attached to the Third Commandment?

Answer: The reason attached to the Third Commandment is that, however those who break this commandment may escape punishment from men, yet the Lord our God will not allow them to escape His righteous judgment.

Scripture Reading: Proverbs 1:20-33

I think it is no accident or coincidence that those who are in the strident forefront of the so-called pro-choice crowd are often known by their loud and angry profanity. The unborn are just as truly image-bearers of God as are their parents, yet when the Lord of life is held in open contempt, so is life itself. In his film, *Whatever Happened to the Human Race?*, Dr. Francis Schaeffer pointed out the correlation between loss of reverence for God, and loss of respect for human beings as image-bearers. He also warned that the natural development from abortion is infanticide, finally followed by the so-called "good death" of euthanasia. Back in the 1970s when Schaeffer made these statements, many Christians thought he was an alarmist. No longer, for we see the development of these very abominable practices, their frequency is increasing at an alarming rate, and there is wide spread acceptance of these dreadful sins. Of course these horrors follow along right after the loss of respect for God and His holy name.

Is it not time to hear again the somber warning for the man *who takes His name in vain?* Parents, be very careful to teach your children the dangers of breaking this commandment. They are subjected to so many influences which might tend to deaden their consciences in this regard. In their schools, their community activities, on the television and internet, and in society as a whole, they hear God's name taken in vain constantly. Teach them diligently the importance of keeping this commandment, and the reason why. This is so important for their spiritual health and well-being.

PRAYERS & REMINDERS

_____
_____
_____
_____
_____
_____
_____
_____
_____

Prayer: O God, help us always to remember that it is only the fool who says in his heart "There is no God." Help us to understand it is only the spiritually blind who say, "The Lord does not see, nor does God understand." May we recognize and honor You in all our speech and ways. In Jesus' name. Amen.

Hymn for the day:
Gracious Spirit, Dwell With Me

Question #57: Which is the Fourth Commandment?

Answer: The Fourth Commandment is, "Remember the Sabbath day, to keep it holy. Six days you shall labor, and do all your work, but the seventh day is a Sabbath to the LORD your God. On it you shall not do any work, you, nor your son, or your daughter, your male servant, or your female servant, or your livestock, or your sojourner who is within your gates. For in six days the LORD made heaven and earth, the sea, and all that is in them, and rested the seventh day. Therefore the LORD blessed the Sabbath day and made it holy."

Scripture Reading: Mark 2:23 - 3:6

The Lord Jesus said, *The Sabbath was made for man, and not man for the Sabbath ... it is lawful to do good on the Sabbath.* The fourth commandment teaches us that God has set aside a special day in our lives for Him. This day is made for our good and blessing, and it is to be kept wholly and holy for Him. Jesus' words, His perfect example and interpretation of this commandment provide the key to our understanding of it, and obedience to it.

To get some idea of the importance of this commandment, and of this day in the sight of God, please remember that there are only ten commandments. God could have given us ten thousand laws, but He gave us ten. These ten words are very basic and fundamental. They provide the foundation for all law and for the conduct of God's people. For Christians, our holy Sabbath is now on the first day of the week. This is the day Christ rose from the dead, having completed His work of redemption. This is the beginning of the new creation. In the early days of the church, Christians continued to worship in the temple and to observe the Jewish Sabbath. However, even while the Apostles were still alive, a transition had taken place. As the Gospel spread throughout the Roman Empire, the majority of converts were Gentiles who for the most part were unfamiliar with the law of Moses. Furthermore, Christians were being severely persecuted by both the Romans and the Jews and forbidden access to the temple. By the time 2 Corinthians had been written, it is obvious that the practice of worship on Sunday, or the Lord's Day, was common practice among Christians.

Prayer: Father, thank You for giving to us the Sabbath principle in Your law. Help us to delight in it and observe it faithfully, that You may be honored by our obedience to Your Sabbath law. In Jesus' name, Amen.

Hymn for the day:
O Day of Rest and Gladness

PRAYERS & REMINDERS

Question #57: Which is the Fourth Commandment?

Answer: The Fourth Commandment is, "Remember the Sabbath day, to keep it holy. Six days you shall labor, and do all your work, but the seventh day is a Sabbath to the LORD your God. On it you shall not do any work, you, nor your son, or your daughter, your male servant, or your female servant, or your livestock, or your sojourner who is within your gates. For in six days the LORD made heaven and earth, the sea, and all that is in them, and rested the seventh day. Therefore the LORD blessed the Sabbath day and made it holy."

Scripture Reading: Amos 8:1-12

A strange thing has happened among God's people. It has happened before, and always to the detriment of His people, and the diminishing of their influence and testimony. Many in this generation of the church have decided that there are only nine commandments, and this is the one which has been voted out. There have been many attempts lately to prove that God no longer requires obedience to this law. If the same sort of hermeneutical gymnastics were applied to the rest of the commandments, we would be relieved of any responsibility of obedience. Though this may be the least regarded of all the commandments, it is still the fourth on the list of God's basic laws. In fact, the Sabbath law is older than Sinai. It is as old as creation itself. God not only established the Sabbath as a part of the creation, but observed it Himself by resting on the seventh day. It should come as no surprise, then, to find this law given on the Holy Mount as a part of the basic code of conduct for God's people. The fourth commandment serves to validate the Sabbath law given in Genesis 2:1-3. John Calvin's comment on this law is worth consideration. He said that God commanded us to rest on this day, that He might work in us. I often hear people claiming they have adopted the "continental view" of the Sabbath. By this they seem to mean: "anything goes" on the Lord's day. I wonder if these same people have ever taken time to see what has happened to the Church in Europe? Godly and respectful observation of God's holy day is essential to the health of His church. Are we really a healthy church?

Prayer: O God, help us to observe Your holy day as You have commanded us. May our careful observance of Your day be a testimony to the world around us. We mourn the loss of respect for You and Your gracious law even among Your people. Forgive us for Jesus' sake. Amen.

Hymn for the day:
Safely Through Another Week

PRAYERS & REMINDERS

Question #57: Which is the Fourth Commandment?

Answer: The Fourth Commandment is, "Remember the Sabbath day, to keep it holy. Six days you shall labor, and do all your work, but the seventh day is a Sabbath to the LORD your God. On it you shall not do any work, you, nor your son, or your daughter, your male servant, or your female servant, or your livestock, or your sojourner who is within your gates. For in six days the LORD made heaven and earth, the sea, and all that is in them, and rested the seventh day. Therefore the LORD blessed the Sabbath day and made it holy."

Scripture Reading: Isaiah 58:13-14

While it is true that in certain eras of history, there has been an overly legalistic view of the Sabbath, the opposite extreme is even more dangerous and harmful to our relationship to the Lord. In the Old Testament, the Sabbath was to be regarded with delight and joy, but it was to be regarded and taken seriously. God promised His people that if they would honor Him on His day, He would bless them and, conversely, He warned of sure punishment if they failed to so honor Him.

When the Lord Jesus came to earth, He taught by example and precept that it was right to do good on the Sabbath. It was right for Him to heal the sick and care for the needy. He allowed His disciples to pluck and eat the grains of wheat in the fields as they went along. So the principle of allowing and even encouraging deeds of mercy and necessity has set the standard for Sabbath observance even to this day. If only believers would follow His teachings, there would be little room for controversy, and less time for the sinful, selfish, pursuits of the world on God's holy day. We slip so easily into the patterns of this world. Convenience rules the day. I believe if only all professing Christians would follow the guidance of God's word, the blessings of the Sabbath would be extended to our whole culture. What places of commerce, or services, or sports could possibly stay open on the Lord's day if all believers would faithfully obey this law?

Prayer: Lord, since You rested on the Sabbath day after the work of creation, may we, too, rest on Your holy day that You might work in us. Teach us to call the Sabbath a delight, the holy day of the Lord honorable, that You may be glorified. We ask this in Jesus' name. Amen.

Hymn for the day:
This Is The Day The Lord Hath Made

PRAYERS & REMINDERS

Question #58: What is required in the Fourth Commandment?

Answer: The Fourth Commandment requires the keeping holy to God such set times as He has appointed in His Word; expressly one whole day in seven, to be a holy Sabbath to Himself.

Scripture Reading: Isaiah 56:1-8

The fourth commandment is far older than the ten commandments as given on Mount Sinai. As noted in our last study, God instituted the Sabbath at the dawn of creation. After finishing the magnificent work of creation, God rested on the seventh day, and set it aside as a day of rest and as a reminder that this world is a part of the Creator's handiwork, and that man is made in His image.

There is another part of this commandment which we overlook to our detriment, and the detriment of others. God required of His people that they not force or even allow others to work for them. *You, or your son, or your daughter, or your male servant, or your female servant, or your livestock, or the sojourner who is within your gates.* That is about as comprehensive as you can get, and about as clear, too, that God is not pleased when we require others to work for us on His special day. Of course we learn from Jesus that works of necessity and mercy are encouraged, but how does "running over to the mall," or the grocery store, or the restaurant, fit into necessity and mercy? Or have we just closed our minds to these things? All of these conveniences cause someone to work. If God is concerned even for the strangers and the cattle, is He not also concerned for the servers and servants? Think about it, Christians. How is our testimony seen before the world? Is this all just a matter of interpretation, or is it a matter of disobedience? I am not suggesting a long list of man made regulations imposed on you, but a commitment to the principles of God's holy day seen clearly in Scripture.

PRAYERS & REMINDERS

_____
_____
_____
_____
_____
_____
_____
_____
_____

Prayer: Father, make us willing to seek Your will in all that we do. We ask that we may be set free from the pressures our own culture brings to bear on us to ignore and disdain Your special day. In Jesus' name. Amen.

Hymn for the day:
Yield Not To Temptation

Question #59: Which day of the seven has God appointed to be the weekly Sabbath?

Answer: From the beginning of the world to the resurrection of Christ, God appointed the seventh day of the week to be the weekly Sabbath; and the first day of the week ever since, to continue to the end of the world, which is the Christian Sabbath.

Scripture Reading: Jeremiah 17:19-27

A question that inevitably comes up is: Why do Christians worship on the first day instead of the seventh? I assume that most if not all who read this will have already had that question answered, but in brief summary, let's state again why this is done. In the very earliest days of the church, believers gathered on the first day of the week for fellowship and worship. The resurrection was the beginning of the new creation, and the gathering for worship was an expression of their joy and faith in the triumph of Christ. Paul's letters to the churches make it clear that this was universal practice in the churches. Not only does Paul speak of believers worshiping on the first day, but John also records in the book of Revelation, *I was in the Spirit on the Lord's day*. This may be seen as an indication that this was the Christian's day of worship. The unbroken history of the church from its first days down to the present bears witness to the acceptance of the transfer of the Sabbath from the seventh to the first day.

Of course Christians may and should worship God every day of the week. But the formal gathering of the whole body for worship one special day of each week is in keeping with God's intention and ordering of one day in seven to be set aside for Him. Our observance of the Lord's day is a testimony before the world. It is day of joy and gladness, but it is also a day of reverence and reflection. It may also be well to consider that God did not just say, "Remember the Sabbath hour to keep it holy," but the Sabbath day!

Prayer: Dear Lord, may we never think of Your special day as a burden or an inconvenience, but as an honor and a great joy. Help us to remember that our Lord Jesus rose from the dead on the first day of the week. Help us to worship in grateful joy that He has conquered death for us. Amen.

Hymn for the day:
Christ The Lord Is Risen Today

PRAYERS & REMINDERS

Question #60: How is the Sabbath to be sanctified?

Answer: The Sabbath is to be sanctified by a holy resting all that day, even from such worldly employments and recreations as are lawful on other days; and spending the whole time in the public and private exercises of God's worship, except so much as is to be taken up in the works of necessity and mercy.

Scripture Reading: Colossians 3:1-11

Though there may be some minor disagreement on the specific day, there should be none on the principle that God requires one day for Himself to be set aside from the toil and pleasures of this world. What are some of the requirements for keeping the Sabbath? We must be careful not to fall into the error of the Pharisees and try to invent an artificial and extra-biblical list of do's and don'ts. However, guidelines are in order. God requires worship from His people. This is clearly taught in His Word. Public and corporate worship are essential for the proper keeping of the Sabbath. Service in the name and for the cause of Christ is another positive and proper use of our time on the Lord's day. The example and teaching of Christ on this subject are all we need for motivation and warrant. We may do such deeds as necessity may require and charity demand. Of course, rest is another requirement the commandment specifies. People are not machines, they are image bearers of God, created by His wisdom and power. Even before the fall of mankind into sin, God knew both the mind and body needed rest and refreshment from daily routine. How much more with the burdens imposed by the fall do we need this gracious provision for our good health and happiness. The frantic pace of life in this generation demands more than ever a day of rest and gladness. In Christian worship our minds and affections are raised from earth to heaven, and we are reminded that only the things of the Lord are eternal and of utmost importance. In light of this reality, is one day out of seven too much to offer the Lord in worship and obedience?

PRAYERS & REMINDERS

_____

_____

_____

_____

_____

_____

_____

_____

_____

Prayer: Father, may we understand that Your holy Sabbath day is a preparation for our eternal home where we will rest from our struggles against the world, the flesh, and the devil. Prepare us through earthly worship for the perfect worship of heaven. In Jesus' name. Amen.

Hymn for the day:
Joyful, Joyful, We Adore Thee

Question #61: What is forbidden in the Fourth Commandment?

Answer: The Fourth Commandment forbids the omission, or careless performance, of the duties required, and the profaning the day by idleness, or doing that which is in itself sinful, or by unnecessary thoughts, words, or works, about our worldly employments or recreations.

Scripture Reading: Psalm 112

There are some "don't" principles to be noted in our keeping of God's holy day. Again, this does not mean a detailed list, but biblical guidelines. First of all, we must avoid the wrong attitude of defiance and selfishness. Instead of defending everything we wish to do on the grounds of Christian liberty, we would do well to simply ask of all our activities, "Does this truly honor God on His day, and does it keep His Sabbath holy?" If we would honestly do this, most of our questions would be answered. One very important "don't" is this: Don't let popular opinion, even within the church, prevail over the clear teaching of God's Word. Commercialization of the Sabbath is a trap into which many believers have fallen. Clearly God is not pleased with this, any more than He is by the pursuit of selfish pleasures that leave no time to think on the Lord and His goodness. God has given us six days each week to accomplish our work and enjoy our pleasures. He has given us one day for special fellowship with Him, and for rest from our busy lives. He set the example by resting from His labors of creation. He also has given the command to honor Him and His day. How much more motivation do we need to keep the day holy?

Notice how Westminster divines loved and honored the Sabbath. More attention is given this commandment than any of the others. A total of six questions and answers are devoted to the fourth commandment. Isn't it time serious-minded believers of today reclaimed the Sabbath for God, and our rich heritage for ourselves and our children?

Prayer: Father, may our observation of Your holy day be much more than just a duty performed. May we with joy and thanksgiving and praise celebrate Your creation and even more the redemption You have given us through our Lord Jesus Christ. Amen.

Hymn for the day:
Let Us With A Gladsome Mind

PRAYERS & REMINDERS

Question #62: What are the reasons attached to the Fourth Commandment?

Answer: The reasons attached to the Fourth Commandment are: God's allowing us six days of the week for our own employments, His establishment of a special ownership in the seventh, His own example, and His blessing the Sabbath day.

Scripture Reading: Deuteronomy 11:18-32

Before moving on to the next commandment, it is time to stop and meditate on the reasons why keeping God's Sabbath are so important. The Catechism gives us four compelling reasons why this law must be obeyed. Notice that the command includes these words: *Six days you shall labor, and do all your work.* In a society that has grown more and more preoccupied with leisure and recreation, the whole idea of laboring six days is almost as foreign to the modern mind as observing the Sabbath one day. Our Reformed forebears taught that labor of any lawful kind is honorable and God honoring. But the work ethic that under girded western civilization has long since been lost. The point the Catechism is making is that we have ample time to pursue our vocations and avocations without intruding into the time God requires us to honor Him.

God, as Creator, Sustainer, and Redeemer is sovereign Ruler over His creation and His creatures. He has every right to claim "special propriety over the seventh day." God has created us in such a way that we must be constantly reminded of our dependence on Him for life and all its needs. What better way to be reminded of this than to honor His holy day? Many people are able to convince themselves and others that the Sabbath principle just doesn't make sense. Adam and Eve were able to convince themselves (with a little outside help) that the law forbidding them to eat of the forbidden fruit doesn't make sense either.

And what a price they paid! I think we are paying a much higher price than we realize when we abandon God's Sabbath law, and teach our children to do likewise.

PRAYERS & REMINDERS

_____

_____

_____

_____

_____

_____

_____

_____

Prayer: Holy Father, You have commanded us to keep all Your commandments, even those we do not understand nor like. Bring our rebel hearts in submission before You, and under Your gracious and just laws. For Jesus' sake we pray. Amen.

Hymn for the day:
Soldiers Of Christ, Arise

Question #63: Which is the Fifth Commandment?

Answer: The Fifth Commandment is, "Honor your father and your mother, that your days may be long in the land that the LORD your God is giving you."

Scripture Reading: Ephesians 6:1-9

The Word of God commands us, *Honor your father and your mother, and, Children, obey your parents in the Lord, for this is right.* It also says, *Fathers, do not provoke your children to wrath, but bring them up in the training and admonition of the Lord.* The fifth commandment is the hinge commandment. It stands between the two tables of the law and binds them together, forming a bridge between our duty to God and our duty to man. Obedience to this law will go a long way toward fulfilling the commandments to love God with all our hearts and our neighbors as ourselves. When parents fail to teach respect for authority to their children, they are doing their children greater harm than they seem to realize. We are living in a society which thinks discipline is child abuse, and the government is attempting to make discipline a crime. But next to abortion and infanticide, I believe the most harmful form of child abuse is the failure to discipline our children according to God's word. In the name of compassion, some parents will not discipline their children, and then wonder why their children create so many problems for themselves and others. Mankind is not smarter than God, and when we substitute our laws for God's laws we create chaos and bring destruction on ourselves and our descendents. Failure to keep this law is the surest proof of all. The sad thing is that many broken and miserable homes could be spared so much suffering and grief if only we would obey this family law. It is the only way a home can function successfully, and yet the fallen race of mankind has rejected it. Let us, who call ourselves Christians, obey this law gladly and consistently, and claim the blessing it promises.

Prayer: Father, You have taught us to love, honor and obey You. You have also taught us to obey our parents in the Lord. Help us to accept and respect all authority You place over us; in the home, state and church. For Jesus' sake. Amen.

Hymn for the day:
O Give Us Homes, Built Firm Upon The Savior

PRAYERS & REMINDERS

Question #63: Which is the Fifth Commandment?

Answer: The Fifth Commandment is, "Honor your father and your mother, that your days may be long in the land that the LORD your God is giving you."

Scripture Reading: Malachi 4

The purpose of this law is to lay a solid foundation for the family which is the most basic unit of society, and is the model and pattern after which all government is to be formed. This is true not only in the church, but in the civil state as well. The elders in the church are the spiritual fathers of the congregation. Therefore this commandment applies to them and to the congregation over which they rule. The elected officials in civil government ideally are as fathers to the citizens, and live under this law of God, too. Seldom is this ideal achieved; nevertheless, this is God's intention, and civil rulers are answerable to God, who alone gives them authority to rule. Our Lord Jesus Christ reminded godless Pontius Pilate of this reality when He said to him, *You could have no power at all against Me unless it had been given you from above.*

The survival of true government depends upon the survival of the family, and the survival of the family depends upon obedience to this law of God. The main reason why we are beginning to see the breakdown of law and order, and the increasing chaos of disorderly and rebellious conduct is the failure of the American family to function according to this law. The perfect law of God has been replaced by the very imperfect law of Dr. Spock and others like him, and we are paying a dreadful price. The youth rebellion which began in the sixties and the radical feminist movement since that time have both sprung from a rejection of this most fundamental law for an orderly and God-honoring society, and even more, rejection of the Law Giver, God.

PRAYERS & REMINDERS

_____
_____
_____
_____
_____
_____
_____
_____
_____

Prayer: Father in heaven, we look all around us and see a world in rebellion against Your laws and against all authority. We see children rebelling against their parents, and parents abdicating their responsibilities. Turn us again, O God, lest we fall under Your wrath. We ask in Jesus' name. Amen.

Hymn for the day:
Great King of Nations, Hear Our Prayer

Question #63: Which is the Fifth Commandment?

Answer: The Fifth Commandment is, "Honor your father and your mother, that your days may be long in the land that the LORD your God is giving you."

Scripture Reading: Mark 7:1-13

Someone with a gift for poetical expression once said, *My son, all you have on earth you owe to your parents. They have given you life, and thus have given you the privilege of seeing the majesty of the sun, the moon, the stars; the glorious beauty of the snow-capped hills, the blue ocean, and the endless beauty of the changing seasons.* God's Word says, *Honor your father and your mother.* It is precisely at this point the Ten Commandments have a unique feature which none of the ancient man-made codes have included. This is a requirement that mothers share equally in the honor and respect children owe their fathers. This reflects very important truths concerning mothers and women in general. First, women are image-bearers of God just as much as men, and secondly, mothers have an equally high place in God's plan for the family, though their roles differ from those of men. In one place where this law is repeated in the Old Testament, the order is reversed, and children are commanded to obey their mothers and their fathers.

This places upon the fathers the responsibility to set the example for their children by showing their wives honor and respect. Of course this also teaches that wives, too, must respect God's commands and teach their children by word and actions to honor and obey their fathers. In our next studies we will examine more closely what is required and what is forbidden in this commandment. For now it is enough to know that God requires respect for and obedience to our parents, and that He promises good upon the people who obey this command, and implies evil on those who ignore it or disobey it.

Prayer: Dear Father in heaven, You created man, male and female, in Your own image. You have commanded us to honor and obey both our fathers and our mothers. Help us to do this, that Your blessing might rest upon our nation, and that You will be honored in our obedience. For Jesus' sake we pray. Amen.

Hymn for the day:
Rise Up, O Men Of God

PRAYERS & REMINDERS

Question #64: What is required in the Fifth Commandment?

Answer: The Fifth Commandment requires the preserving of the honor, and performing the duties, belonging to everyone in their various situations and relationships, as superiors, inferiors, or equals.

Scripture Reading: I Peter 2:13-25

The Catechism makes it quite clear that this law of God not only includes the family unit, but also has much wider application to society as a whole. The Catechism is being faithful to Scripture in making this point. The first part of Ephesians 6 elaborates on this, and makes the application far beyond simply the family unit.

This law applies to the relationship between employer and employee, between the citizen and the state. By this law we are taught respect for all forms of authority which God may place over us. In I Peter, the Apostle points out that even though government may be unworthy, still it is God's agent of authority and must be obeyed. Of course, there are limits to this, and the attempt to discern those limitations has been a subject of debate and controversy down through history. For instance, both patriots and Tories quoted Scripture to justify their positions during the American Revolution. In more recent history, believers in Nazi Germany faced many hard choices in their resistance to tyranny. Many pastors, elders, and church members gave their lives protesting the inhuman and ungodly policies of that wicked regime. Others bowed to government pressure and found themselves participating by silent consent in the terrible atrocities associated with mass genocide. In our own country in more recent years, we saw many youths refusing to register for the draft on the grounds they might have to fight in wars they considered morally wrong. However, at the same time they eagerly accepted government handouts for their education and ignored the ironic contradiction they brought upon themselves.

PRAYERS & REMINDERS
_____
_____
_____
_____
_____
_____
_____
_____
_____

Prayer: O God, grant us wisdom, grant us courage for the facing of this hour, and the living of this day. Often we are confused and stumble along. Help us to understand Your word and cheerfully obey it for Jesus' sake. Amen.

Hymn for the day:
God Of Grace And God Of Glory

Question #64: What is required in the Fifth Commandment?

Answer: The Fifth Commandment requires the preserving of the honor, and performing the duties, belonging to everyone in their various situations and relationships, as superiors, inferiors, or equals.

Scripture Reading: I Samuel 3:11-14

Let us examine more closely the requirements of this law. First, it teaches the duty of parents to their children. The honor and obedience required of children toward their parents implies a prior duty of the parents to display the character and conduct worthy of that respect and obedience. God requires parents to be spiritual leaders and teachers of their children, both by example and by instruction. When we bring our children for covenant baptism, this responsibility is stressed in the vows we take. Among other things, we promise to set before them a godly example, and to instruct them in the Christian faith. When we do this, it is an expression of obedience to this commandment.

One of the often-overlooked and neglected duties of this law is that of godly discipline. Suffice it to say that we are reaping a terrible harvest from our failure at this point. I say again, that next to abortion and infanticide, both of which are practiced in our nation, the worst form of child abuse is failure to discipline our children according to God's word.

The other side of this commandment has to do with the duty which children owe their parents. What is this duty? Obedience is the first law of love toward parents and toward God. Jesus said, *If you love Me, keep My commandments.* The same thing is true in children's relationships to their parents. If you love your parents, obey them. This is the pathway to honor and respect, and to a right relationship with God. The Bible places disobedience to parents in the same category with murder, theft, witchcraft, and other heinous crimes.

Prayer: Father, thank You for Your godly discipline in our lives. Thank You that you love us enough to discipline and correct us when we go astray. May we never despise the discipline of our heavenly Father. In Jesus' name. Amen.

Hymn for the day:
All To Jesus I Surrender

PRAYERS & REMINDERS

Question #64: What is required in the Fifth Commandment?

Answer: The Fifth Commandment requires the preserving of the honor, and performing the duties, belonging to everyone in their various situations and relationships, as superiors, inferiors, or equals.

Scripture Reading: Deuteronomy 4:1-10

Not only does this law affect the family unit, but many other relations as well. However, a short review of some of the points concerning the family is in order. First, it is significant to note that this commandment includes both parents as objects of honor and obedience. This is unique among all the ancient law codes. In man-made codes, the father alone was accorded this place of honor, but in God's law, the mother shares equally. In fact, when the law is repeated elsewhere in the Old Testament, the order is reversed, and children are commanded to honor their mothers and their fathers. It is the duty of the Christian father to set an example for his children by honoring their mother. Unfortunately, this is not always done.

How does one show this honor to parents? When little ones first come into the world, they are totally dependent on parents for everything. This includes food, shelter, physical, emotional and spiritual care. As they begin to grow, they also begin to assert the desire and ability to move towards more independence and less dependence, and soon begin to express a will of their own. (Do they ever!) But this is natural and must be guided. The ultimate goal of believing parents will be to point their children toward more dependence on God and less on their parents. But all along the way they are to show honor, respect, and obedience to their parents under God, because He commands it, and because their testimony before the world requires it.

Prayer: Dear Father, give to us as parents the wisdom to guide our children closer to You. Give us wisdom as children to respect and obey our parents because You have told us this is right in Your sight. *Savior, like a Shepherd, lead us, much we need Thy tender care.* Amen.

Hymn for the day:
Savior, Like A Shepherd Lead Us

PRAYERS & REMINDERS
_____
_____
_____
_____
_____
_____
_____
_____
_____

Question #64: What is required in the Fifth Commandment?

Answer: The Fifth Commandment requires the preserving of the honor, and performing the duties, belonging to everyone in their various situations and relationships, as superiors, inferiors, or equals.

Scripture Reading: II Chronicles 36:11-21

Another word concerning discipline is necessary as we consider this commandment in the context of the family. Godly discipline is ordained by God, and is neglected only at terrible cost to the family and to society as a whole. The breakdown of law and order, loss of respect for authority, and moral chaos around us are largely due to the failure of parents to exercise discipline as God's Word requires. Children who are not properly disciplined by their parents will never learn self-discipline, and will become a menace to society. The book of Proverbs says, *He who spares the rod, hates his child.* How true this is. There are several tragic examples in Scripture.

Three generations of good men failed miserably in this. Eli, the priest, would not discipline his sons for their abuse of the priesthood, and so witnessed their deaths, and the end of his lineage. He failed to act, even though God, through young Samuel, specifically warned him of the coming tragedy. Samuel, sent by God to warn Eli of his failure and the terrible consequences to follow, failed to discipline his own sons, who in turn were rejected as leaders in Israel. Even David, whom Samuel anointed as King, followed in the tragic footsteps of Eli and Samuel. Of course, many modern day examples similar to these could be pointed out. But in spite of this more than abundant evidence of the terrible consequences which flow from failure to discipline, even many Christian families are obviously falling into the trap of secularism, with the resulting abandonment of godly discipline, and the inevitable chaos individually and for society as a whole.

Prayer: O Holy God, how far we have strayed away from Your laws and precepts. We have brought ruin on ourselves and our country by rebelling against Your word in so many ways. Forgive us and spare us, for Jesus' sake, Amen.

Hymn for the day:
My Soul, Be On Thy Guard

PRAYERS & REMINDERS

Question #64: What is required in the Fifth Commandment?

Answer: The Fifth Commandment requires the preserving of the honor, and performing the duties, belonging to everyone in their various situations and relationships, as superiors, inferiors, or equals.

Scripture Reading: James 1:22-27

Discipline means far more than punishment for wrongdoing. It involves instruction and encouragement in right doing. Martin Luther once said, *Keep both the rod and an apple handy in the training of children.* Failure to recognize and reward well-doing, is just as destructive as the failure to punish wrong behavior.

In our generation, honoring parents has taken on a whole new dimension. People are living much longer than in the past. The care of the elderly is not primarily the responsibility of the government, though many would like for it to be. The foremost responsibility falls upon the children. This may or may not mean that elderly parents live with their children until they die, but it does certainly mean that children must help provide for the care and well-being of the parents when they can no longer care for themselves. This may be costly and complicated, but it must be done. As a pastor, I often visit in nursing homes with elderly people who have not seen their children in years. I once visited a church member, living in a nursing home, whose pastor-son visited her once a year, yet he chided me for only going by once a month. Actually, between the other pastors on the staff, and the official church visitor, this dear lady had a visit almost every week but only yearly from her own son. As with all the commandments, the believer has the responsibility to understand and, more importantly, to obey all the requirements of the fifth commandment. The compassionate care of the elderly and infirm is most certainly one of many duties taught by this commandment.

PRAYERS & REMINDERS

_____

_____

_____

_____

_____

_____

_____

_____

_____

_____

Prayer: Compassionate Father, we hear the heart cry of the elderly, *Forsake me not when I am old and grey.* We know You hear their cry; help us to hear it, too, and to respond with loving kindness and care. In Jesus' name. Amen.

Hymn for the day:
O Gracious God, Forsake Me Not

Question #65: What is forbidden in the Fifth Commandment?

Answer: The Fifth Commandment forbids the neglecting of, or doing anything against, the honor and duty that belong to everyone in their various situations and relationships.

Scripture Reading: Colossians 3:18-25

The further development of the teaching of this commandment is brought out in this question and answer. The key words here are *neglecting*, and *doing anything against*. Just as the neglect of obedience to any law is breaking that law, so in this law particularly, neglect of the duty taught, is a serious violation of it. Let's begin by looking at this commandment from the perspective of parental duty. It requires parents to set a godly example before their children. This automatically forbids an unworthy example. In explaining the reasons for the wickedness of a king of Israel, the Scripture records, *For his mother was his counselor for evil.* What a terrible condemnation! In his case, this was a deliberate attempt by the king's mother to turn him away from the worship of the true God. However, it would be possible for well-meaning parents to become *counselors for evil* by default. Our children learn as much from what they see in us, as they do by what they hear from us.

Don't get the wrong idea. A good example, though very important, is not enough. The Bible commands us to teach our children by precept, too. Failure to teach our children the Word of God is a terrible violation of this commandment. Of course there are many other scriptures which also command us to teach them God's Word. We are to teach them of God's love, but we are to warn them that *the wages of sin is death.* We must make very sure we teach them the basic message of the Bible, and instruct them in its doctrines. If we neglect to do this, we are breaking this commandment. There is so much more which needs to be said of these things. The failure to love with a godly love that includes discipline is another serious breach of obedience to the fifth commandment.

Prayer: You have taught us Your truth, kind Father. Help us to pass that truth on from generation to generation. For Jesus' sake, Amen.

Hymn for the day:
Around The Throne Of God In Heaven

PRAYERS & REMINDERS

Question #65: What is forbidden in the Fifth Commandment?

Answer: The Fifth Commandment forbids the neglecting of, or doing anything against, the honor and duty that belong to everyone in their various situations and relationships.

Scripture Reading: Proverbs 3:1-12

Now let us look at the duty children owe their parents. In the previous study, we mentioned the sin of disobedience. We noted that the Bible places this sin in the context of the most serious sins we may ever commit. More needs to be said of this. Rebellion against parental authority is rebellion against God. Here again we may see how neglect of parental teaching and the failure to obey are just as serious as outright disobedience and rebellion.

Respect is a duty of this commandment, and the lack of respect for parents and other persons in positions of authority is forbidden by this commandment. Jesus Christ, to whom all authority has been given, placed Himself under the authority of His earthly parents. George Washington, who is one of the most respected figures in history, was a man who put great emphasis on respecting his parents' wishes. At one point, he gave up his intended career as a sailor out of respect for his mother's wishes. Needless to say, God greatly honored that respect. Unfortunately, respect for parents, and others in authority, has sadly diminished in these latter days. This is but a symptom of a growing lack of respect for God and His Word.

Finally, we should listen carefully to how this question is posed. What is forbidden in the fifth commandment? It is God who forbids neglect and doing things against the honor and duty owed to parents. *Forbidden* is a serious word which should be taken seriously by serious-minded believers. It is far more than mere suggestion, it is command from God.

Prayer: O God, forgive us when we act as if Your holy commandments were optional for us. Deliver us from the sins of presumption, and give us grace to obey You who loved us so much You gave Your Son to be our Savior. Amen.

Hymn for the day:
Children Of The Heavenly Father

PRAYERS & REMINDERS

_____

_____

_____

_____

_____

_____

_____

_____

_____

Question #66: What is the reason attached to the Fifth Commandment?

Answer: The reason attached to the Fifth Commandment is a promise of long life and prosperity (as far as it shall serve for God's glory, and their own good) to all who keep this commandment.

Scripture Reading: Jeremiah 35

The above mentioned passage from Jeremiah is an excellent commentary on this extraordinary promise which God makes to those who honor Him by honoring their parents. The faithful Rechabites were used of God to rebuke unfaithful Judah for breaking their covenant vows to God. The Rechabites were the descendants of a man who had vowed that neither he, nor any of his off-spring, would ever drink wine. Jeremiah brought them into the house of God and set wine before them, bidding them to drink. Even though Jeremiah was a prophet of God, they refused because of the vow of their father. Jeremiah cited their steadfastness to their father's vow as a rebuke to the men of Judah who had broken their fathers' vows and their own. He said, *They have obeyed their father's command, but I have spoken to you again, and again, and you have not listened to Me.* Then to the Rechabites God said, *Because you have obeyed the command of Jonadab your father, and kept all his commands, ... therefore thus says the Lord of Hosts, the God of Israel, Jonadab, son of Rechab, shall not lack a man to stand before Me forever.*

God honors those who honor His Word. The continuity of organized socie-ty in a large sense depends upon obedience to this law, with all its many impli-cations and applications. Remember the Catechism pointed out that this law applies to all in positions of authority and submission. The roots of the frag-mentation of our culture with all its many manifestations of lawlessness, lies in the breaking of this vital law which our God has given us. Disobedience to par-ents and to others in authority, especially those who conscientiously strive to be faithful, is disobe-dience to God. He is our Father in heaven, and the first duty this law requires is obedience to Him.

Prayer: Lord, help us to honor You by honoring all those who place in positions of authority over us, in the church and in the civil state. Above all, help us to carefully keep Your law and to do Your will. In Jesus' name. Amen.

Hymn for the day:
For The Beauty Of The Earth

PRAYERS & REMINDERS

> ## Question #66: What is the reason attached to the Fifth Commandment?

Answer: The reason attached to the Fifth Commandment is a promise of long life and prosperity (as far as it shall serve for God's glory, and their own good) to all who keep this commandment.

Scripture Reading: Psalm 90

Notice how the Catechism qualifies this promise. We need to hear this and understand it, and even go a bit beyond what the Catechism says. Although this is a law with general application to people, churches, generations, and nations, it is not an unqualified promise of long life on this earth in every individual case. There is indeed a principle here with broad application, but there are exceptions. So far as life on this earth is concerned, it is not always for the good of the believer, nor is it always for the glory of God, that all who obey this command, even within the limits of human possibility, live long lives. We must trust both the wisdom and the goodness of our dear Father in heaven to know and do what is best for His beloved ones. If He calls us home in the tender years of childhood or youth, or in the days of our strength in full manhood or womanhood, or if He allows us long and prosperous days on this earth, it is because in His great love and mercy He is doing for our good what is best.

However, like all the promises of God, this one is not limited to the short days of this life, nor even primarily concerned with them. This is a promise of eternity. Those who honor God the Father, by trusting in His Son, the Lord Jesus, and therefore seek to honor His precepts and claim His promises, will find that of all the good promises He has made, not one has ever, ever failed. God has established certain principles by which society is to function. One of the most important of these is recognition of authority, and respect for that authority. Without this, no family or nation can long endure. It begins in the home and family and extends to all relationships in the church and civil state.

PRAYERS & REMINDERS

Prayer: Father, our times are in Your hands. We would not have it otherwise. Teach us to number our days that we may apply our hearts unto wisdom. For Your glory we ask this, in Jesus' name. Amen.

Hymn for the day:
Faith Of Our Fathers

Question #67: Which is the Sixth Commandment?

Answer: The Sixth Commandment is, "You shall not murder."

Question #68: What is required in the Sixth Commandment?

Answer: The Sixth Commandment requires all lawful endeavors to preserve our own lives, and the lives of others.

Scripture Reading: Genesis 9:1-7

This commandment from God is very straightforward and direct. *Thou shalt not kill.* It teaches the sacredness of life and forbids the terrible sin of murder and all related sins. We live in a world and a time when this law is ignored to a shocking extent. In the eyes of many, human life is dreadfully cheap. For a handful of change, a street criminal kills his victim. Thousands die in drug-related crimes. Moreover, there is widespread indifference to such events. But God has never revoked His commandment.

One indication of turning away from this commandment of God is the reluctance on the part of our culture to hold people accountable for breaking this law. It is true that the law of God as given to us through Moses makes a difference between deliberate and accidental killing, and between premeditated murder and killing which might take place in an unguarded moment, but the distinctions which are now allowed by the laws of our land are totally without biblical sanction. For instance, often times the difference between a prison sentence and the death penalty (which is very rare indeed) is how much hideous torture the victim endured before he/she died. If it can be shown the victim died almost instantly, there seems to be great hesitancy to impose the death penalty. Another absurdity that exempts many from lawful punishment, is whether or not the murderer shows remorse. Another great failure in our culture is to allow parole and release even for criminals who have viciously murdered a victim. We pay the price for this foolishness when that released criminal almost invariably kills again. Criminal's rights seem more important than victim's rights in the convoluted thinking of our godless society.

Prayer: Father, You are the Lord and giver of life, and you have required that we hold life to be a sacred gift from You. You have forbidden murder, and required sure retribution upon those who break this law. Forgive us for any violation of this law, in thought, word or deed, for Jesus' sake. Amen.

Hymn for the day:
O Master, Let Me Walk With Thee

PRAYERS & REMINDERS

Question #67: Which is the Sixth Commandment?

Answer: The Sixth Commandment is, "You shall not murder."

Question #68: What is required in the Sixth Commandment?

Answer: The Sixth Commandment requires all lawful endeavors to preserve our own lives, and the lives of others.

Scripture Reading: Psalm 94:1-11

When this law was given, it was sorely needed. The tragedy of Cain and Abel had long been forgotten. God's commandment to Noah, *Whoso sheds man's blood, by man shall his blood be shed*, had been laid aside. As it is now, so it was then: Life was cheap. Moses, through whom this law was given, barely escaped with his life while still a helpless infant. Pharaoh had decreed that all male babies of the Hebrews were to be thrown into the Nile. Only the faith and courage of Moses' parents saved his life.

But is that shocking scene of infanticide any more terrible than the wholesale slaughter of the unborn in our own country? In the age of Moses, a master could kill his slave without accounting for the act. Fathers had life-and-death power over their children. Kings killed messengers who brought bad news. The ancient world desperately needed to hear God thunder from Mount Sinai, *Thou shalt not kill.* Is our modern world in any less need of this law? Recently, venerable Princeton University, once a strong fortress of biblical Christianity (but no more) employed a professor who openly advocates the murder of handicapped children by their parents. Moreover he is defended in his hideous philosophy by the university. Humanistic rationale will always find a way to justify even the most outrageous violations of God's law. Only people with a Reformed, biblical world and life philosophy can answer the godless thinking which all too often prevails in our culture. But we must be bold and courageous to speak out and stand up for God's truth.

Prayer: Dear Father, give to us courage and faith to stand by Your holy laws, and to stand up against those who would pass human laws which would negate Your laws. Give us courage to protect the helpless. In Christ's name we pray. Amen.

Hymn for the day:
Stand Up, Stand Up For Jesus

PRAYERS & REMINDERS

Question #67: Which is the Sixth Commandment?

Answer: The Sixth Commandment is, "You shall not murder."

Question #68: What is required in the Sixth Commandment?

Answer: The Sixth Commandment requires all lawful endeavors to preserve our own lives, and the lives of others.

Scripture Reading: Psalm 94:12-23

Who are we to cast stones at the mass killings and brutality of ages gone by? Our own indifference to human life is undeniable. We are so accustomed to violent death, we become immune to shock. Recently, a young man was killed while serving a prison sentence for a fairly minor offense. Public reaction was less than overwhelming. The only comment I heard was, "He got what he deserved. He shouldn't have been in prison in the first place."

Much of our concern in the Christian world for human life is limited by fads. Of course, we are all very upset about mass abortion. Yet in a recent survey at evangelical seminaries, many students admitted to drinking alcoholic beverages, despite the fact that over 10,000 teenagers are killed every year by drunken drivers. Many of the same students, however, are very vocal in their opposition to abortion. Some churches hold all-night vigils against capital punishment, but did you ever hear of a church holding a vigil for families of victims of murderers?

Truly we have been conformed to this world, rather than being transformed by the renewing of our minds. How quickly we see the sins of others while ignoring our own. We should be aware of all tendencies within ourselves and our culture which blind us to the far reaching implications of this law of God. God created man in His own image, and this alone makes life sacred and precious. This is why God forbids murder, and the failure to punish those who break this law in any way is a sin against Him.

Prayer: O Righteous Father, forgive us for taking this law so lightly. Forgive us for being so conformed to our lawless culture that we meekly accept our failure to honor Your holy Law. We ask this in Jesus' name. Amen.

Hymn for the day:
Blest Be The Tie That Binds

PRAYERS & REMINDERS

July 4

Scripture Reading: Psalm 27; Proverbs 14:34; Deuteronomy 6:10-15

Today is the anniversary date for the Declaration of Independence, which gave birth to the United States of America. I would suggest for your reading this day these words from our Confession of Faith, Chapter 23:4. "It is the people's duty to pray for those in authority, to honor them, to pay them taxes and whatever is owed them, to obey their lawful commands, and to be subject to them for conscience's sake." Unbelief or different religious views on the part of the civil authorities does not mean they are to be disobeyed by believers, including clergymen, in the pursuit of their duties.

These words written in the mid-sixteen hundreds by the Westminster Assembly are still as true and valid today as they were in those times. It is so easy to be supportive and to pray for those in authority when they agree with our point of view, or represent the political party of which we may be members. The Confession does not place such limits on our duty. Samuel prayed for Saul, and the other Prophets prayed for kings whom we consider unworthy of prayer. Several years ago, I was asked to go before the Senate of the United States, and offer a prayer for them as their day began. Here is the prayer I offered then, and I present it to you as a suggestion of how to pray for our Government today:

Almighty God, God of our fathers before us, by Your great and gracious hand we have been given this land of freedom and plenty. We humbly pray that we may prove ourselves to be a people who acknowledge You and Your goodness, and who are eager to do justly, love mercy and walk humbly with our God. Bless this dear land we love with honorable and upright leaders in government, industry, education and public life. Save us from all enemies and foes who would conquer and destroy. Save us from internal strife, discord and confusion, from pride and arrogance and from moral disintegration. Teach us to love and respect each other, who come from such diverse backgrounds, that we may truly be one nation under God. We especially pray for those to whom we have entrusted the authority and power of government. Grant them wisdom, courage and the humility to confess that all authority comes from above. May their deliberations and decisions be guided by Your almighty hand and tempered with charity towards one another. May they ever be mindful that "sin is a reproach to any people, but righteousness exalts a nation." In times of prosperity fill us with gratitude. In times of want and trouble, fill us with trust. When we must endure Your chastening hand because of waywardness, give to us a spirit of true repentance and humility. Grant us peace within and enable us to be peacemakers among the nations of this world. We ask these things in the name and by the authority of the Prince of Peace. Amen.

Hymn for the day:
My Country, Tis of Thee

Question #67: Which is the Sixth Commandment?

Answer: The Sixth Commandment is, "You shall not murder."

Question #68: What is required in the Sixth Commandment?

Answer: The Sixth Commandment requires all lawful endeavors to preserve our own lives, and the lives of others.

Scripture Reading: Romans 10:1-15

How may we as Christians obey this law? The answer must include obedience to the spirit of the law as well as the letter. Above all, the basic teaching of this commandment is summed up in these words, *I am my brother's keeper.* I am responsible for his life and well-being. Life is a sacred trust from God—both my own life and my neighbor's. Therefore, I must take all reasonable steps to preserve his life and mine. This commandment requires me to do all I can to express this responsibility to those around me. It also requires that I support laws designed to protect and defend life. Obedience to this law means I must support punishment of those who break it, and defend innocent victims.

There is, however, yet a higher duty in this commandment. According to the Bible, life in its fullest expression is a right relationship to God. We must never forget that all people apart from this saving relationship through Jesus Christ are under sentence of death. So, as a believer, I must do everything in my power to spread the good news of the Gospel to all men everywhere. We would all rise up and condemn a doctor who refused to treat a dying person. How much more reprehensible for Christians to ignore those who are spiritually dead and withhold the only cure for their condition? The God who said, *Thou shalt not kill,* commands us to preach the Gospel to all the world. We read these words from Romans 10:14-15 and realize that we do have a responsibility to tell the good news and to thus rescue the perishing. How are we doing?

Prayer: Father, You have given all to rescue us from sin, death, and the grave. Help us to be your servants and to tell a lost and dying world where it may find eternal life through Jesus Christ our Lord. Amen.

Hymn for the day:
Rescue the Perishing

PRAYERS & REMINDERS

_____
_____
_____
_____
_____
_____
_____
_____
_____
_____

Question #69: What is forbidden in the Sixth Commandment?

Answer: The Sixth Commandment forbids the taking away of our own lives or the lives of our neighbors unjustly, or whatever tends to do so.

Scripture Reading: Proverbs 3:21-35

The most obvious sin this commandment forbids is that of outright, premeditated murder. Long before this commandment was formally given, men knew that it was wrong and sinful to murder. Cain was the first murderer, and he was held accountable before God and man for his foul deed. Cain ignored God's warning and was overcome by the sin crouching at the door of his heart.

When God began again with Noah, and gave the fundamental laws which were to guide and govern the human race after the flood, a law concerning murder was one of the most prominent of these precepts. *Whosoever sheddeth man's blood, by man shall his blood be shed.* This law is an absolute necessity for the preservation of law and order, and the protection of human life. Unfortunately, we have decided we are smarter than God, and have all but eliminated this law. Even in states which still practice capital punishment, so many restrictions have been added as to make the law of little effect. And what a price we have paid, and will yet pay, for our disobedience. Murder, the sin expressly forbidden in this law, runs wild in our nation. Thousands fall victim to this crime every year, but our society seems more interested in protecting the rights of convicted murderers than in protecting the lives of their victims. When will we ever learn that God knows best? When we fail to follow the wisdom of His Word and the clear light of the Ten Commandments, we are inviting chaos and oppression. It is no longer safe to walk the streets of cities and towns after dark, or in some places even in daylight. When criminals are more protected than citizens, what else could we expect?

PRAYERS & REMINDERS

_____

_____

_____

_____

_____

_____

_____

_____

_____

Prayer: Once more, dear Father, we find ourselves living in a world such as Noah lived in long ago. Violence and oppression rule, and the weak and defenseless have no protection. Help us to rise up and reclaim our culture for Christ and Your holy law. In Jesus' name we pray. Amen.

Hymn for the day:
Rise Up, O Men of God

Question #69: What is forbidden in the Sixth Commandment?

Answer: The Sixth Commandment forbids the taking away of our own lives or the lives of our neighbors unjustly, or whatever tends to do so.

Scripture Reading: Matthew 5:21-26

This law also deals with sins which lead to murder. It is certainly possible to break this law by neglect and indifference. If I know that my neighbor is in great danger and do nothing about it, I have broken this law. If I were to see my neighbor's house afire and fail to warn him, or attempt rescue, would I not be guilty of breaking this commandment? There are so many other ways in which we may violate this law. The person who drives in a deliberately careless manner, ignoring the laws of safety and speed, or who drives while under the influence of drugs or alcohol may cause the death of another.

A young high school girl was the victim of careless gossip by some of her classmates. They told tales which implied that she was sexually promiscuous. Unfortunately, these lies were believed by many. She was so distraught that she finally took her own life, rather than face the taunts of her classmates. Although nothing was done to the gossipers, other than a severe lecture, surely in God's sight they had broken the sixth commandment.

Jesus taught us that there are sins which lead up to murder, and these sins also break this commandment. The Scripture listed above is a very clear and convicting exposition of this law. When we regard others as being beneath us and having no value in our sight, we are very close to breaking this commandment. When we allow anger and malice to control our attitudes and our tongues we come even closer to this dangerous precipice. The next step may well be a direct violation of the sixth commandment. So guard your heart carefully and do not allow Satan to lead you into this deadly trap.

Prayer: O Lord, You created man, male and female in Your own image, and therefore life is sacred. Help us to guard our hearts and our relationships with others lest we fall victim to the sin of Cain. For Jesus' sake. Amen.

Hymn for the day:
Gracious Spirit, Dwell With Me

PRAYERS & REMINDERS

Question #69: What is forbidden in the Sixth Commandment?

Answer: The Sixth Commandment forbids the taking away of our own lives or the lives of our neighbors unjustly, or whatever tends to do so.

Scripture Reading: Proverbs 14:1-12

Jesus used this law to show how one must obey not only the letter but the spirit of the law as well. According to Christ, anger, hatred, contempt may lead to murder and are a violation of this law. He sternly warned against these attitudes which break the spirit of God's law. Behind the angry hatred of another person lies the sin of an unforgiving heart. This blocks the work of the Spirit in your life, and leaves you open to the devil's deadly work. There are other slippery steps which may lead to murder. Envy, resentment, revenge, and retaliation are dangerous attitudes, and quickly dominate the thinking of one who surrenders to their influence. Indeed, most murders grow out of one of these four sins.

Surely we must recognize that we are a nation guilty of murder on a mass scale, when we think of the horror of mass abortion, the growing acceptance of infanticide and so-called euthanasia. As believers we must not only guard our own lives against any of the sins forbidden by the sixth commandment, but also join with others in resisting the rising tide of disobedience to this fundamental law God gave us to preserve and protect human life. Only a very few years ago, the idea that anyone in this nation would approve of mass abortions which number in the millions yearly would have been unthinkable. No one would have ever advocated the killing of babies with defects, or the so-called euthanasia of the sick and the elderly. Such ideas would have been considered depraved, and rejected out of hand. Moreover, any who thought this way would never have had a hearing before the public. How quickly we have sunk to a level of such depraved thinking! May God have mercy and may there be a thorough going rejection of these sins.

PRAYERS & REMINDERS

_____
_____
_____
_____
_____
_____
_____
_____
_____

Prayer: Help us, dear Lord, not to give in to the many pressures our culture brings to bear on us. Let us not give in to those who try to persuade us that wrong is right, and right is wrong. May we always defend the helpless. For Jesus' sake we pray. Amen.

Hymn for the day:
Soldiers of Christ Arise

Question #70: Which is the Seventh Commandment?

Answer: The Seventh Commandment is "You shall not commit adultery."

Scripture Reading: Matthew 5:27-32

There is a verse of poetry from somewhere which goes like this:

> "In vain we call old notions fudge
> and bend our conscience to our dealing;
> The ten commandments will not budge,
> and stealing will continue stealing."

And this of course applies not only to this one commandment.

In spite of all our frantic efforts to ignore or negate this commandment of God, it remains, unchanged and powerful. Let me remind you again of a principle of interpretation in understanding the commandments. The purpose of God's law is not to be understood as a code which prevents or forbids the fulfillment of our human nature. We are not even to think of them as a list of do's and don'ts. Rather they are God's guideposts pointing in the direction of true fulfillment, and ultimate joy. None of the commandments illustrate this principle more clearly than the seventh, *Thou shalt not commit adultery*. For all the sins forbidden by this commandment seem to offer happiness, freedom, contentment, and fulfillment. Deluded by these false hopes, modern man has abandoned this law, and embraced all forms of immorality as an acceptable way of life.

God loves His children too much to allow them to go unchecked along this way. What He wants for all His children is for them to know the meaning of love through the love of Christ for His Church, and to practice that principle of love in all our relationships. Of course we all fall far short of the ideal, but this law is given to bring us back when we stray, to lead us to repentance and to carefully guard our hearts and conduct.

Prayer: Dear and gracious Lord, there is nothing hidden from Your sight. You are a holy and wise God. You are also very compassionate and forgiving. Forgive our debts and lead us not into temptation. For Jesus' sake. Amen.

Hymn for the day:
Hiding in Thee

PRAYERS & REMINDERS

Question #70: Which is the Seventh Commandment?

Answer: The Seventh Commandment is, "You shall not commit adultery."

Scripture Reading: Luke 7:36-50

So what do we find? Rather than being able to fulfill all these apparent promises, this way of life leads to misery, bondage, and living death. Furthermore, it separates us from the true source and meaning of love, God.

If one of the primary purposes of the law is to convict of sin, this is one law which should bring us all to our knees, in sincere repentance, with a cry for mercy. Is there any one of God's laws more rejected and flaunted than this one? Is there any law more necessary for modern man to hear? Is there any law more universally broken than this law? If we consider the teachings of our Lord on this subject, we will all have to confess, *There is none righteous, no not one.* But because he will not hear it, and because he will ignore it, modern man is trapped in the chains of self-imposed bondage from which there is no escape except by the mercy and power of the Lord.

I think one of the greatest challenges facing the church in our day is how to deal with those whose lives have been devastated by this sin. On the one hand we must maintain a high standard, and on the other hand we must seek to reach out hands of healing, forgiveness and restoration to the fallen. Satan wins a great victory when this commandment is broken. He also wins a great victory when, unlike our Lord, we refuse to extend healing and forgiving love to those who have fallen, but seek help and cleansing. The only worthy example to follow in walking this narrow path is the example of Christ himself. He accepted the penitent prayers of those who had fallen, and called upon them to sin no more. Can we do less?

Prayer: Father, we have all sinned and broken Your commands at least in thought and mind. We grieve over our sins, we repent of them, and we ask for grace, and for strength to overcome and to honor You. In Jesus' name. Amen.

Hymn for the day:
Amazing Grace

PRAYERS & REMINDERS

_____

_____

_____

_____

_____

_____

_____

_____

_____

_____

July 11

> ## *Question #70: Which is the Seventh Commandment?*

Answer: The Seventh Commandment is, "You shall not commit adultery."

Scripture Reading: Romans 6:1-14

Any discussion of morality or marriage must begin with this commandment. Any study of human sexuality should begin at this point. All relationships between members of the opposite sex should be guided first of all by this commandment. There is a crying need for believers to become the light of the world and the salt of the earth at this point. Unfortunately, this is not always the case. The light of many believers no longer shines brightly with purity and steadfastness. We have been conformed to the world. Even if we have escaped the actual overt sins associated with this commandment, we have absorbed much of the lascivious lifestyle of the unregenerate. Yet believers committed to personal purity are the only ones who offer any hope of any light to guide people out of the darkness of immorality. If believers compromise the truth at this point, we serve only to increase the darkness and hopelessness of humanity.

As one begins to consider the terrifying statistics of broken homes, ruined marriages, blighted lives, confused and abused children, not to mention such horrors as venereal diseases, AIDS, teen pregnancies, rape, and other sexual crimes, it is truly appalling. What lies at the root of these problems? The rejection of God's law, which says, "Thou shalt not commit adultery." God refuses to accommodate His standards to the changing ideas and ideals of fallen man. It is past time for believers to join in this refusal and to rededicate ourselves to obedience in act and thought to this command.

Prayer: Father in Heaven, You made us in Your own image. You made us all, male and female, in the image of God. You have established boundaries between the sexes, but You have also ordained marriage, and protected that institution by Your holy Law. May we ever obey You in keeping this and all Your law. In Jesus' name. Amen.

Hymn for the day:
Be Thou My Vision

PRAYERS & REMINDERS

Question #71: What is required in the Seventh Commandment?

Answer: The Seventh Commandment requires the preservation of our own and our neighbor's chastity, in heart, speech, and behavior.

Scripture Reading: Genesis 2:15-25

When a commandment from our God begins with *Thou shalt not*, we may make the mistake of assuming there is only a negative emphasis in such a command. The Catechism rightly poses the question, *What is required?*, before it deals with *What is forbidden*? In dealing with the touchy and sensitive issues surrounding the seventh commandment, it is well to begin with the most positive of all exhortations we find in Scripture. *Husbands, love your wives as Christ loved the church ... wives be in subjection to your own husbands as unto the Lord.* What could be more positive than this? What better place to begin to explore the requirements of this command? Obedience to these words from Ephesians would go far in fulfilling the seventh commandment. If a man loves his wife in the way that Christ loved the church, and gave Himself up for it, there would be no room in his life for anyone else to share that kind of love. Even the temptations in this area to which all are subject, would lose much of their power.

As for the wife, especially one who is blessed by this kind of loving and self-sacrificing husband, her submission to her own husband, would eliminate the desire to be in submission to any other man. As she understood that submission to her husband was simply a part of her submission to the Lord, the yoke would be easy and the burden light. Unfortunately the influence of the world, in the form of the radical feminist movement, has caused many to despise and reject this biblical pattern of mutual love and respect. Both men and women have rejected God's pattern and law, and always to our hurt and the diminishing of true joy.

PRAYERS & REMINDERS

_____

_____

_____

_____

_____

_____

_____

_____

_____

Prayer: Father, because we have denied the authority of Your Word, and accepted the ungodly lifestyle of this world, the institution of marriage according to Your Word is in great danger. Please help us, who claim to be Your children, to obey this law from our hearts. We ask this for Jesus' sake. Amen.

Hymn for the day:
O Perfect Love

July 13

> ## Question #71: What is required in the Seventh Commandment?

Answer: The Seventh Commandment requires the preservation of our own and our neighbor's chastity, in heart, speech, and behavior.

Scripture Reading: I Corinthians 6

Philippians 4:8 speaks of the positive requirements of this law. *Finally, brethren, whatever things are true, whatever things are noble, whatever things are just, whatever things are pure, whatever things are lovely, whatever things are of good report, if there is any virtue, and if there is anything praiseworthy—meditate on these things.* This sort of Christ-controlled thinking will guard the mind against the impure thought, the temptations towards unchaste actions, and the overwhelming desires of our fallen nature. It is never enough to say no to these things. We must say yes to purity in thought, word, and deed.

The question before believers is simply this: who is our master, the Word or the world? We remember the challenge Elijah placed before the people of Israel as recorded in 1 Kings 18. He had proposed a contest between himself, as the representative of the one true God, and the four hundred and fifty prophets of Baal, the idol who was worshiped by many as the god of fertility. One of the chief features of Baal worship was the public flaunting of the seventh commandment. Without going into all the details of this contest, the words of Elijah as he made his challenge to the vacillating Israelites stir our hearts. He said, *How long will you falter between two opinions? If Jehovah is God, follow Him; But if Baal, follow him.* I think it is time for believers to face the same choice in the matters pertaining to this commandment. The worshipers of Baal, in all modern, yet ancient forms, are many. The followers of God are few. But be sure of this: God alone is Lord, and His Word must be obeyed.

Prayer: O Lord, the world beckons us to follow its way and to ignore Your commandment. Keep us true and pure as we struggle to obey You in this sensuous generation. Be our shield and defender for Jesus' sake. Amen.

Hymn for the day:
A Christian Home

PRAYERS & REMINDERS

Question #71: What is required in the Seventh Commandment?

Answer: The Seventh Commandment requires the preservation of our own and our neighbor's chastity, in heart, speech, and behavior.

Scripture Reading: Hosea 2:1-23

The words of Jesus also come to mind when He was asked, *what is the first and great commandment?* His answer, quoting from Deuteronomy, was: *You shall love the Lord your God with all your heart, with all your soul, and with all your strength.* Then he added, ... *you shall love your neighbor as yourself. Upon these two commandments hang all the law and the prophets.* In short, He was teaching us (among other things) that obedience to the seventh commandment, as well as all others, is summed up in loving God with all your heart, and your neighbor as yourself. This is truly what is required in the seventh commandment.

The world defines love as a very self-centered one dimensional sexual experience. God's Word places all human love in the context of the all-encompassing love of God, and love for God. When we accept the world's model of love we miss out on the full, and fulfilling experience of true love as ordained by God. What a perfect illustration this commandment is for the true understanding of God's purpose in all the ten commandments. The ten commandments are God's guideposts into true joy. They are warning signs along the highway of life to show us where the dangers lie, and how to avoid them. They restrain the baser instincts of our fallen nature so that we may experience the noble and the true. So even as obedience is an expression of our love for God, His giving us the commandments is His expression of love for us. Always remember this as you struggle in your efforts to keep God's holy law.

Prayer: Father, thank You for giving us Your law out of Your great heart of love. By these words You keep us from evil and in fellowship with You. You enable us to enjoy life to the fullest, and at the same time, You deliver us from the evil one. Thank You, in Jesus' name. Amen.

Hymn for the day:
Because I Knew Not When My Life Was Good

PRAYERS & REMINDERS

July 15

> **Question #72: What is forbidden in the Seventh Commandment?**

Answer: The Seventh Commandment forbids all unchaste thoughts, words, and actions.

Scripture Reading: Romans 1:18-32

The sins forbidden by this commandment are stated in some detail in the Larger Catechism. As you study that list you will discover a dismal catalog of the very actions and thoughts that are glorified in our corrupt contemporary culture. Beware, believers! All too many professing Christians are joining in the approval (and practice) of the many sins which fall under the condemnation of God's Word. Those who speak out against such terrible sins as adultery, fornication, rape, incest, homosexuality, and all contributing cases are now the villains of our society. Christians just don't seem to understand that when you engage in all the sinful pleasures and tendencies of our culture – reading and watching what the ungodly read and watch, dressing and talking as the ungodly dress and talk – that you will end up behaving as the ungodly behave. Hear these words and hear them well, *The wrath of God is revealed against all ungodliness.* So may our holy but humble wrath fall upon all the ungodliness of our lives. Let judgment begin in our own hearts and lives. Let us remove the log in our eye that we may see more clearly to help our brothers and sisters remove the speck we see in their eyes. This is not a call to hopeless despair, but to godly grieving that we may turn from our sins, and seek after holiness without which no one will see the Lord. What a tragedy this would be, to miss the greatest joy of all by substituting the empty pleasures of sin for a season.

Prayer: Jesus, Thou Joy of loving hearts, Thou fount of life, Thou light of men. From the best gifts that earth imparts, we turn unfilled to Thee again. Help us to drink so deeply of that blessed Fountain, we will never thirst after the waters of this world. For Jesus' sake. Amen.

Hymn for the day:
Take Time to Be Holy

PRAYERS & REMINDERS

Question #72: What is forbidden in the Seventh Commandment?

Answer: The Seventh Commandment forbids all unchaste thoughts, words, and actions.

Scripture Reading: Isaiah 1

The consequences of participating in the sins forbidden by this commandment are seen all around us. Vulgarity in speech has become commonplace. Crimes of sexual violence, especially against the weak and helpless, such as young children, have multiplied beyond our worst fears. The church's timidity in taking a strong Biblical stand on such issues as unlawful marriages, and unlawful divorces is undermining not only the church itself but the home as well. I have been appalled and amazed in recent years to realize how much more time I now spend in counseling Christians in troubled marriages, as compared with the time spent in this same ministry only a few years ago. The anger, resentment, confusion and hatred of children against their parents and step-parents are understandable, but alarming and devastating.

There is good reason why God forbids the many sins associated with the seventh commandment. These things dishonor God and corrupt human nature, and are destructive of Christian witness in a world of darkness and despair. *If the salt has lost its flavor, how shall it be seasoned? It is then good for nothing but to be cast out and trampled underfoot by men. You are the light of the world … let your light so shine before men that they may see your good works and glorify your Father in heaven.* These words of the Lord Jesus are a serious call to believers to live lives which point the way out of darkness and demonstrate that there is a way of life which leads to life and not death.

Prayer: Father of all mercies, God of all grace, forgive us, your erring children for the many ways we violate Your holy law every day. Thank You for the blood of Jesus that cleanses from all sin. Keep our hearts pure for His sake. Amen.

PRAYERS & REMINDERS

_____
_____
_____
_____
_____
_____
_____
_____
_____

Hymn for the day:
How Firm A Foundation

Question #73: Which is the Eighth Commandment?

Answer: The Eighth Commandment is "You shall not steal."

Scripture Reading: Ezekiel 34:1-10

The sin of stealing has become a national epidemic and a national disgrace. It is undermining our whole social and economic fabric; yet theft, along with all of its associated sins of dishonesty, has become so deeply ingrained into our way of life that many may be guilty of breaking this commandment without fully realizing they are doing so.

It would be possible simply to list many ways in which this commandment is broken and fill page after page. However, I will not do this lest I give you ideas you don't need. Though I do not have actual statistics, it is safe to say that stealing is the most commonly committed crime worldwide. It lies at the root of many other crimes, especially crimes of violence leading to injury and loss of life. Armed robbery has become so commonplace, it scarcely deserves an item in the newspaper. However, if you read any newspaper in any city in America on any day you will read at least one account of armed robbery and this account will probably include serious injury or death for the victims of the robbery. Theft by electronic manipulation, though not as violent as armed robbery, is nevertheless a crime so serious and so devastating it may well wreck the financial foundation of business, government and even charity. From time to time I am asked by an elderly person about certain charities which focus on fundraising by appealing to the elderly to make a donation to the supposed worthy cause. One such bogus organization suggested that God would go much lighter in His judgment if they would support this noble (?) work. *Thou shalt not steal*, especially in the name of Christ.

Prayer: Father, those of us who live in the lap of luxury are so prone to imagine that we deserve whatever we want at any expense to others. Help us to be content with our lot, grateful for it, and in every way to obey this law. For Jesus' sake. Amen.

Hymn for the day:
I'm Pressing on the Upward Way

PRAYERS & REMINDERS

July 18

Question #73: Which is the Eighth Commandment?

Answer: The Eighth Commandment is, "You shall not steal."

Scripture Reading: Matthew 5:38-48

There are many other forms of stealing which violate God's commandment. For example, a few years back there was a serious snowstorm in the Southeast. This storm left many thousands of travelers stranded on interstate highways. It was reported that in and around Atlanta the price of motel and hotel rooms doubled, tripled, and in some cases increased even more. Thousands of people paid unheard-of prices for refuge from the storm. Taking advantage of people in such situations is obviously stealing. In fact, the Larger Catechism mentions this as one form of violating the eighth commandment.

Do you realize that hundreds of small businesses are forced into bankruptcy because of stealing? Ordinarily, this is done by the employees of the company, or it may be simply in the form of shoplifting. Or it may take the form of customers refusing to pay their debts. I recently talked with a businessman who had been forced to close his business because the U.S. Government was so long in paying the bills he submitted for legitimate services rendered.

When churches and other organizations appeal for funds for some specific benevolent project, they must be very sure the money taken in is used for the purpose stated. Years ago, I was deeply involved in raising a considerable amount of money for a needed project within a certain organization. It was not until years later that I learned this money had been spent for an entirely different purpose within the same organization. I'm sure God overruled in all this for His own glory, but still the organization which did this was breaking the eighth commandment.

Prayer: Lord Jesus Christ, King and Head of Your Church, may we Your people always be faithful to care for those in need, the sick and elderly. May we care for them as good shepherds who must give account to the Good Shepherd. Amen.

Hymn for the day:
Living For Jesus

PRAYERS & REMINDERS

Question #73: Which is the Eighth Commandment?

Answer: The Eighth Commandment is, "You shall not steal."

Scripture Reading: Amos 5:1-15

There is another symptom of the national epidemic which deserves mention. Many criminals who are apprehended are never prosecuted. There is a system called plea bargaining by which some are allowed to plead guilty to a lesser crime to avoid being prosecuted for stealing. When there are riots in major cities, one of the first things to happen is people taking to the streets and breaking into shops and stores, stealing anything that may be carried away. They are seldom if ever prosecuted. In fact, such behavior is sometimes justified with the excuse that they are underprivileged and are expressing their frustrations. Because we reject any absolute standard of right or wrong, including the eighth commandment, we have developed an ethic which excuses criminal action on the basis of needs, real or imaginary. I fail to see how a stolen television set really meets a legitimate need.

In our culture persons who know a crime has been committed and fail to report it to the authorities are sometimes indicted for aiding and abetting the crime. Yet our whole culture is guilty of aiding and abetting crimes when the criminals are not properly punished for their crimes. The responsibility for enforcement of law and order rests upon the citizens who must require of their elected officials that law breakers be held accountable for stealing and all other civil wrongs. If we take this commandment lightly, we are not to wonder when our homes are ransacked, or our government agencies abuse their powers by unjust taxation and prolific waste of public funds.

Prayer: Father of all mercies, we ask You to deliver us from such bondage to possessions that we are tempted to ignore the eighth commandment. Save us from greed and discontent, and make us grateful for Your full provision of our every need. In Jesus' name. Amen.

Hymn for the day:
More About Jesus

PRAYERS & REMINDERS

Question #73: Which is the Eighth Commandment?

Answer: The Eighth Commandment is, "You shall not steal."

Scripture Reading: Proverbs 30:1-9

Now we are living in an era when technology has made it possible and relatively simple to commit major theft by electronic manipulation. This is usually referred to as white-collar crime, yet the criminal is just as guilty as the thug on the street who threatens his victim with gun or knife. Time would fail us to tell of the savings and loan disaster which threatened to wreck our whole economic structure. The evidence at this point suggests that over a trillion dollars was misappropriated through these now bankrupt institutions. The human mind is very ingenious when it comes to justifying taking from others to satisfy our desires. It should be noted that it is not usually the very poor who steal, but often the well-to-do, and even the very affluent. When our possessions possess us, we make ourselves slaves of a very cruel god who is never content or satisfied.

Another form of stealing is deliberately incurring debt when we know there is little likelihood we will ever be able to pay for what we charge. I know many lending agencies make it very easy to do this by almost forcing credit cards on a gullible public and making loans too easy to obtain. Yet in the long run, it is those who accept these offers who are ultimately accountable and responsible, and they are the ones who suffer the most for doing so. In Christian families parents and spouses must protect their children and each other from the abuse of credit, and the dishonest practices growing out of such abuse.

Next we will try to consider some ways in which we may be obedient to this law and thus fulfill the intention behind it.

Prayer: *O Lord, give me neither poverty nor riches. Feed me with the food allotted to me; lest I be full and deny You, and say 'who is the Lord'? Or lest I be poor and steal, and profane the name of my God. In Christ's name. Amen.*

Hymn for the day:
Trust and Obey

PRAYERS & REMINDERS

Question #74: What is required in the Eighth Commandment?

Answer: The Eighth Commandment requires that we utilize only lawful means in obtaining and furthering the wealth and outward estate of ourselves and others.

Scripture Reading: Psalm 24

The eighth commandment, which in the Hebrew literally says, *No stealing*, is rooted in the nature of man created in God's image. God is the ultimate owner of all things. The whole earth and all of its resources and all of its people belong to God. When God created man in His own image, He entrusted him with the stewardship of possessions. He conferred upon man the right and responsibility of possession. God built into the very fabric of creation the right to own, control, and use property and material wealth. Because of this, it is a sin against God for me to take what God entrusted to you.

Man in his relationship to God can never claim absolute ownership of anything. I have a farmer friend in South Carolina who is farming land which has been in his extended family for well over two hundred years. Yet this godly man testifies that he does not own the land, only God owns it and allows him to farm it. That is a philosophy of life we all need to adopt. Man in his relationship to man, however, has been given the right and responsibility of ownership. It therefore becomes our duty to possess, control, and use all our material wealth to the glory of God and for the benefit of ourselves and others. By implication, this commandment forbids that we should take from another any of his possessions unless our labor earns it or his love confers it. Once more it is well to point out that as a nation we have drifted far away from this principle, and by government control we often rob from the productive people in order to support those who refuse to work and take responsibility for their own well being. The whole philosophy behind the "entitlement" mentality goes against the Word of God.

Prayer: Father, thank You for Your bountiful provision for our every need. Help us to be good stewards of our land, homes, possessions and opportunities. May we teach each succeeding generation the value of work and the folly of claiming for ourselves the glory which You alone deserve. In Jesus' name. Amen.

Hymn for the day:
Take My Life, And Let It Be

PRAYERS & REMINDERS

Question #75: What is forbidden in the Eighth Commandment?

Answer: The Eighth Commandment forbids whatever does, or may, unjustly hinder our own, or our neighbor's, wealth or outward estate.

Scripture Reading: Acts 20:32-35

This commandment also forbids that I should even desire to take whatever belongs to other people. So there is a very close correlation between this commandment and the tenth which says, *Thou shalt not covet.* As a matter of fact, coveting usually leads to stealing in one form or another.

In the fourth chapter of Ephesians, the Apostle lays down a general pattern of honest living and then speaks quite specifically to the matter of stealing. He says, *Let him that stole steal no more: but rather let him labor, working with his hands the thing which is good, that he may have to give to him that needeth.* Of course, from this passage there are many other implications concerning our obedience to this commandment. According to Scripture, dishonest business actions are a form of stealing. In fact, it is surprising to discover how many of the writings of the Old Testament prophets deal with just weights and dishonest scales. The dishonest use of scales and balances is listed with such serious sins as murder and kidnapping and idolatry.

Another form of stealing is sloth, for the above word, *let him labor* is a command to be followed by all as health and opportunity present themselves. It is also interesting to see that the command to labor is not for the end that we might merely amass wealth, but that we might have the ability to share with those in need. What a difference between this godly impulse, and the demands made by the lazy that they be sustained by others who will work.

Prayer: Father, give to us generous hearts that we may be known as Your children who know it is more blessed to give than to receive. Keep us free from greed, that we may be free to hear the cry of the needy and to minister to them in Jesus' name. Amen.

Hymn for the day:
Oh, To Be Like Thee

PRAYERS & REMINDERS

July 23

> ## Question #75: What is forbidden in the Eighth Commandment?

Answer: The Eighth Commandment forbids whatever does, or may, unjustly hinder our own, or our neighbor's, wealth or outward estate.

Scripture Reading: Deuteronomy 24:10-15

The Bible also warns against defrauding the laborer of his wages. In Deuteronomy 24 we are told that if a poor man works for you, you must pay him that very day, lest he go hungry and have no place to sleep. The book of James warns that on the day of judgment the testimony of the laborer who has been denied his just wages will be held against the rich man. Those precepts still apply to us today. Consideration for the safety of those we employ must be a priority for Christians. I began my ministry experience in a section of the Cumberland mountains in east Tennessee where there are many small coal mines. They were kept small deliberately because if less than six men were employed in a mine, that mine was exempted from all the federal safety laws. Many died. They were denied protection on the basis of greed and indifference. May God keep us sensitive to the need for safety of all who work the hard jobs no one else will do.

The other side is that the worker may defraud the employer by failing to give an honest day's work for a day's wages. We cannot escape the fact that God is intensely concerned with simple, basic honesty. Our profession must mean more than just attending church or Bible studies or prayer meetings. These things are important, but they must lead us to practice godliness and honesty in the world in which we live. How often we compromise our testimony by failing to practice simple honesty in all our dealings, simple kindness in all our relationships, and proper humility for whatever successes God sees fit to grant us.

Prayer: O God, You show us how far we fall short of keeping either the spirit or the letter of Your holy law. Give us charity and honesty in all our dealings with our fellow man. Thank You that Your Son has paid the penalty for our breaking Your law and heart. In Jesus' name. Amen.

Hymn for the day:
I Need Thee Every Hour

PRAYERS & REMINDERS

Question #75: What is forbidden in the Eighth Commandment?

Answer: The Eighth Commandment forbids whatever does, or may, unjustly hinder our own, or our neighbor's, wealth or outward estate.

Scripture Reading: II Corinthians 9

One further comment on this commandment is in order. On a national level, we have pursued an economic policy that places intolerable burdens of debt upon succeeding generations. We are in effect requiring them to pay for our greed. Surely this is a form of stealing and is one reason why God's hand of judgment seems to be on our nation with all its economic problems. If we find ourselves guilty of breaking this commandment in any of the many forms suggested, our first step is repentance and our second step is obedience, including restitution where appropriate. And it is required of believers to take these steps if they are to walk in the way of the Lord. There is some indication that there is a growing realization among believers, at least, that economic (and spiritual) reality is beginning to seriously challenge our greed.

Where do we begin? We begin first of all with ourselves. The powerful tug of wanting to possess and to keep up with the world around us is difficult to resist. Bitter experience has taught many believers that God's Word must apply to our finances as well as to our hearts. We may not be able to mend the ills of our nation, but we can and should take whatever steps are needed to bring our personal finances under the authority of God's word. Our first priority is to make sure we are giving as the Lord prospers us. We are to strive to go beyond a sense of duty and learn to be cheerful givers, and eager to invest our money in the eternal kingdom which offers assured rewards for all eternity. Once this priority has been firmly established in our lives, then with diligence and honesty we can deal with all the other issues relating to finances, guided always by God's commandments.

PRAYERS & REMINDERS

Prayer: Father, You own the "cattle upon a thousand hills". The earth is Yours, and all its fullness. May we ever express obedience to Your command, "Thou shalt not steal" by confessing Your ownership of all we have, and honoring You in our financial affairs. In Jesus' name. Amen.

Hymn for the day:
He Is Able to Deliver Thee

Question #76: Which is the Ninth Commandment?

Answer: The Ninth Commandment is, "You shall not bear false witness against your neighbor."

Scripture Reading: Psalm 101

The ninth commandment forbids bearing false witness and it requires commitment to the truth. More than we like to admit, our attitude toward this commandment goes something like this: "If you lie to me, that is unforgivable. But if I lie to you, that is understandable. If I accuse you of lying, you ought to be ashamed, but if you accuse me of lying (even if I am guilty), it is a terrible offense."

It is said that the difference between an ordinary lie and a little white lie is whether I tell it or you tell it. But God sees all lying as just that, and He forbids it by this commandment. Actually, there are many, many places in the Bible which speak of God's dislike of lying. Some of these are as follows: *The Lord hates a lying tongue* (Proverbs 6:17); *He who tells lies shall not abide in my presence* (Psalms 101:7); *Put away lying and speak the truth* (Ephesians 4:25). Some of the most dreadful words of condemnation in the Bible are words which God speaks against false prophets who speak falsehoods in the name of God. Like all the other commandments, this one is more far reaching than appears on the surface. And like all the other commandments, the deeper we inquire into its meaning and application, the more we see our guilt and our sin of breaking this command.

This command was given to assure fair treatment in a court of law, but it goes far beyond that. However, even unbelievers recognize that justice depends upon truth in witnessing in courts. That is the reason witnesses are required to swear an oath that their witness is true. Even when we are not under an human oath, we are still required to tell the truth.

Prayer: Truthful Spirit, dwell with me, I myself would truthful be, and with wisdom kind and clear let my life in Thine appear; and with actions brotherly speak my Lord's sincerity. For Jesus' sake. Amen.

Hymn for the day:
O For A Heart To Praise My God

PRAYERS & REMINDERS

Question #76: Which is the Ninth Commandment?

Answer: The Ninth Commandment is, "You shall not bear false witness against your neighbor."

Scripture Reading: Psalm 101

Obedience to this commandment requires an enthusiastic love for the truth as well as hatred for falsehood. Christians all too often excuse themselves from obedience to this commandment and regard it as one of the lesser requirements for Godly living. Would you like to bring discord and strife and misunderstanding to break another person's career or reputation? All you have to do to accomplish these terrible things is to bear false witness, either by outright lies or implications and insinuations, or even simply by failing to tell the truth. Yes, you can accomplish all of this by disobedience to this commandment, but in doing so you will make it impossible to have a loving, trusting relationship with the Lord. This commandment is so basic to your own character that you really need to understand this law, repent of breaking it, and make a heartfelt commitment to keep it.

Like stealing, lying has become so deeply ingrained in our whole way of life that it is difficult to avoid this sin. In fact, it has become difficult for many people to know the difference between the truth and a lie. The father of our nation, George Washington, was quoted as saying, *I cannot tell a lie.* Some of his successors could not tell the truth. Some modern-day politicians seem to say, *I don't know the difference.* Most of us would agree that lying is sinful and dangerous to all concerned, but we tend to make personal exceptions. *I would never tell a lie except to protect myself or make a sale or keep from being fired or maybe to cover another lie.* Above all these exceptions we make, let us hear again, *Thou shall not bear false witness.*

Prayer: Father, forgive us, for we have all broken this commandment in so many ways and so many times. Help us who rely on Your revealed truth to be truthful people, as well as charitable in all our words and actions. In Jesus name, and for His sake. Amen.

Hymn for the day:
Breathe on Me, Breath of God

PRAYERS & REMINDERS

_____

_____

_____

_____

_____

_____

_____

_____

_____

Question #76: Which is the Ninth Commandment?

Answer: The Ninth Commandment is, "You shall not bear false witness against your neighbor."

Scripture Reading: I Samuel 21:1-10

There is another problem we face as we attempt to practice obedience to this law. We are living in a time in which most people reject the idea of absolute standards of right and wrong, of truth and falsehood. The humanist contends that what is true today may not be true tomorrow. He believes that what is true for him may not be true for you. This subjective approach to truth undermines the foundations of integrity and honesty. Moreover, people have discovered that if a lie is made to sound convincing and can be repeated often enough, it will be accepted as the truth by the vast majority of people. This was the ethic of both the Nazis and the Communists in their drive to dominate the world. They came dangerously near succeeding. Unfortunately it is rapidly becoming the ethic of our own country, which played such a major role in the defeat of these two false ideologies. Will we too fall because of the same sin?

Even Father Abraham placed himself in a position in which lying seemed to be the sensible way out of that difficult situation. The pagan king to whom he lied rebuked him for this sin. Later, he repeated the same lie, but never to his advantage. His son Isaac would follow in his father's footsteps with the same results. So even the best of God's saints must be on guard against this sin. The incident of David lying to the Priest as recorded in I Samuel 21 is very different in some ways to the cases referred to above. David was fleeing for his life from vengeful and angry King Saul. When he asked for help from Ahimelech the Priest, he deliberately deceived him into thinking he was on the king's business and so obtained his help. David's life was spared, but Saul ordered Ahimelech executed though he acted in innocent trust in David's word. *Thou shalt not bear false witness.*

Prayer: Father, keep us truthful even when dishonesty seems the only viable course of action. May our words be helping and healing and not destructive to others. In Jesus' name. Amen.

Hymn for the day:
Rise Up, O Men of God!

PRAYERS & REMINDERS

Question #77: What is required in the Ninth Commandment?

Answer: The Ninth Commandment requires the maintaining and promoting of truth between man and man, and of our own and our neighbor's good name, especially in testifying as witnesses.

Scripture Reading: Proverbs 14:20-35

What are the requirements for obedience to this commandment? What does God expect of His redeemed people?

If you really want to understand this commandment, you must approach it positively. It is above all else a commandment to speak the truth. Although there is a warning implied, still the main purpose of this commandment is to encourage us to speak truthfully. It is possible to break this law by guilty silence. If we keep quiet when God commands us to speak the truth, then we have broken the commandment. We must also be careful how we speak the truth. It is possible to take part of the truth and turn it into a lie, and this is often done. It is rightly said that a half-truth is the most dangerous form of a lie. We may also speak the truth for malicious purposes. A pastor whom I knew long ago was once rebuking a lady in his congregation for spreading unsubstantiated rumors about another member of the flock. Her response was: "I know these things are true, and I'm always bound to tell the truth. His response was simply: "Honesty is not the only virtue or even the highest virtue". It is obvious that this commandment forbids lying, but it does not command us always to tell all the truth we might know concerning a person or a situation. It is sad but true that often our desire to speak the truth or hear it is motivated by curiosity rather than benevolent love. We have all at one time or another listened to another person tell something hurtful to another, and repeat that information to others with a certain amount of glee. I truly believe this is breaking the spirit of this law.

One incident which comes to mind to show how true information may be falsely used was the criticism of the Pharisees against Jesus, intended to add to our Lord's suffering on the cross. *He saved others, but Himself he could not save.* Those were the most truthful words these evil men ever spoke, but the Pharisees only added to their own guilt by attempting to use that great truth to hurt and not help.

Prayer: God, help us to be both truthful and charitable in all we say. For Jesus' sake. Amen.

Hymn for the day:
A Charge to Keep I Have

PRAYERS & REMINDERS
_____
_____
_____
_____
_____
_____
_____
_____
_____

Question #77: What is required in the Ninth Commandment?

Answer: The Ninth Commandment requires the maintaining and promoting of truth between man and man, and of our own and our neighbor's good name, especially in testifying as witnesses.

Scripture Reading: James 3:1-12

This law teaches us that God has given us the priceless gift of speech. How we use this gift is very important. We must use it to promote the good of our neighbor by proper speaking of the truth and by refraining from false witnessing. We must protect our neighbor's good name and reputation. We must stand against error and resist evil speech and malicious tale-bearing. If we listen to idle and hurtful gossip in silence, we contribute to its spread and violate this commandment. Our use of the gift of speech should lead us to promote unity and understanding between people. Sadly, too often, the opposite is true. By words of doubt and suspicion we create a breach between friends, or rob those to whom honor is due.

In this passage from James we see something of the seriousness of an unchecked tongue. He told us that those who teach the Word will be held in more strict accountability for our use of the gift of speech. He went on to say that the human tongue could be compared to a bridle in a horse's mouth, or a rudder on a ship, in that these two small devices control larger bodies for good or ill. Then he uses the most startling of all comparisons for the harm and evil a loose tongue can bring. A small spark may set afire a great forest. We are all aware during times of drought how truly deadly a small spark can be. It may lead to hundreds of thousands of woodlands be burned. He said the tongue is a fire, a world of iniquity that can defile the whole body, set one's course of life on fire, and that is itself set on fire by hell. Strong words, but true words, and appropriate words of warning. Let us heed them well this very day.

Prayer: *Set a guard, O Lord, over my mouth; keep watch over the door of my lips.* This is our urgent prayer for this day and every day, that our Lord Jesus may be honored in all our conversations. In His name we pray. Amen.

Hymn for the day:
God of Grace and God of Glory

PRAYERS & REMINDERS

_____

_____

_____

_____

_____

_____

_____

_____

_____

_____

Question #77: What is required in the Ninth Commandment?

Answer: The Ninth Commandment requires the maintaining and promoting of truth between man and man, and of our own and our neighbor's good name, especially in testifying as witnesses.

Scripture Reading: Psalm 116

This law requires that we make promises and keep them. A good example of this would be the vows we take to God in the church when we become members. We all take the same basic vows, and we all tend to be quite selective in our obedience. It has been my experience over the years that the most often ignored vow we take is the last one, which reads: *Do you submit yourself to the government and discipline of the church and promise to strive for its purity and peace?* Modern day Christians seem to have a real problem with submission in any form or situation. Yet we have made the promise to be submissive. Another example would be a minister talking to a pulpit committee. It would be required of him to communicate honestly with the committee about his strengths as well as his weaknesses.

If we are to be faithful to this commandment, we are to speak the truth about Jesus Christ and His saving Gospel. This is the greatest truth we know and the best of all good news. If we fail to share that good news with others, we violate the ninth commandment. Of course, this places on us an additional responsibility of living out our profession so the words we speak ring true. A good question we might all ask at this point is: Are you able and willing to share the Gospel with others? I will say more of this in tomorrow's devotional, but there are other aspects of this command which deserve consideration. The Larger Catechism adds an interesting aspect of this law by saying that, among other things forbidden, are these: *Thinking or speaking too highly or meanly of ourselves, denying the gifts and graces of God and aggravating smaller faults.*
Ouch! That pinches pretty tight!

PRAYERS & REMINDERS

_____

_____

_____

_____

_____

_____

_____

_____

_____

Prayer: Keep us truthful in words, deeds and thoughts, dear Lord, that we may honor you, and keep this commandment sincerely for our own good, the good of our neighbors, and for the glory of Your precious name. Amen.

Hymn for the day:
Christ for the World! We Sing

July 31

Question #77: What is required in the Ninth Commandment?

Answer: The Ninth Commandment requires the maintaining and promoting of truth between man and man, and of our own and our neighbor's good name, especially in testifying as witnesses.

Scripture Reading: Ephesians 4:25-32

If you are seeking a perfect example of how to obey this law, look to the Lord Jesus Christ. His whole life was one of truthfulness and kindness. Think how He used the gift of speech. *Thy sins be forgiven thee ... rise up and walk ... Father, forgive them for they know not what they do.* Truly our Lord Jesus has the words of eternal life. By His words He gave help and hope. He caused light to shine in darkness and drove away falsehood. Even when it cost Him His life, He spoke the truth, saying, *I am the Christ.* The words which cost His life bring life to millions who believe His confession and accept Him as the Way, the Truth, and the Life.

Never think that you have exhausted the demands of this law, even if by God's intervening grace, you do not practice lying. Until you understand and practice sharing the truth about salvation with others around you, not only by word, but by deed as well, you have not fulfilled this law. Let me go one step further and say that even when you do meet this aspect of the law's demands, say to yourself, "I am but an unprofitable servant, for I have only done what my Lord commanded me." Beyond words of salvation, we are required to speak words of comfort, friendship, hope and help. Kindness, one aspect of the fruit of the Spirit, seems too lacking in the vocabulary and spirit of many believers when they confront each other. The attitude seems to be: "As long as I tell the truth, there is no need to be kindhearted about it." As my friend Steve Brown is wont to say, "That is a lie from the pit of hell, and it smells like smoke." We are commanded to be the salt of the earth, but not to be smoky!

Prayer: Lord, help us to always speak the truth in love and not allow any cruel or bitter words to proceed out of our mouth. For Jesus' sake. Amen.

Hymn for the day:
Christ Shall Have Dominion

PRAYERS & REMINDERS

Question #78: What is forbidden in the Ninth Commandment?

Answer: The Ninth Commandment forbids whatever is prejudicial to truth, or injurious to our own or our neighbor's good name.

Scripture Reading: Matthew 26:57-67

What does this law forbid? It forbids bearing false witness against our neighbor. The book of James has much to say about the wrong use of speech and the seriousness of sinning with our lips. James says that the tongue is tied to the heart and reveals the true condition of a person. He said the tongue is like the rudder of a ship guiding its course, or like a spark that sets off a great flame. Since we are children of God, who is Truth Himself, obedience to this law becomes a part of our basic testimony.

To misrepresent a situation for the purpose of personal gain is forbidden by this law. The political scene in this country reveals clearly that honesty in speech is sorely missing in our political system. I heard a man of honor address his fellow Senators recently and he was making a plea for integrity in their speaking and voting. He asserted that most of us see no further than the next election and say whatever it takes to retain our position and power. I was stunned at such honesty in his speech, and then sadly reflected that such honor and honesty is indeed rare among our elected officials. We flaunt this law at every turn. We wish to sell a product and feel we must exaggerate its value in our effort to sell. We claim great value for things which have little or none.

There is another aspect to this commandment to which the Catechism draws our attention. It says we are to avoid whatever might be injurious to our own or our neighbor's good name. When we pass on rumors about others, even if partially true, or true, knowing that what we say will be injurious to his or her good name, we have broken this commandment.

Prayer: "Truthful Spirit dwell with me, I myself would truthful be; and with wisdom kind and clear let Thy life in mine appear; and with actions brotherly speak my Lord's sincerity." For Jesus' sake. Amen.

Hymn for the day:
Join All the Glorious Names

PRAYERS & REMINDERS

Question #79: Which is the Tenth Commandment?

Answer: The Tenth Commandment is, "You shall not covet your neighbor's house; you shall not covet your neighbor's wife, or his male servant, or his female servant, or his ox, or his donkey, or anything that is your neighbor's."

Scripture Reading: Luke 12:13-21

The first commandment, *Thou shalt have no other gods before me,* and the last commandment, *Thou shalt not covet,* are very closely akin. They deal with the same basic aspect of human nature, though from differing perspectives. The Apostle Paul warns us, *Flee from covetousness which is idolatry.* So in effect the commandments end where they began. Have you ever tried to analyze the present world in which we live, to determine what lies behind the spirit of unrest which grips all humanity? Why is there an uneasy feeling of disquiet that infects the whole human race? Why is there a government-in-exile of terrorism throughout the whole earth which threatens international chaos? Why are we in the grips of a growing epidemic of violent crime which has become a personal threat to each one of us? Why is it that in almost every neighborhood it has become necessary to have some form of burglar insurance—perhaps an elaborate electronic device or at the very least a loud and obnoxious dog? Why is our national economy in shambles with deficits over $100s of billions a year and our budget completely out of control? Why does our national debt number in the trillions of dollars? Why have large corporations become so impersonal, treating their employees as if they were robots and casting aside those who have given years of faithful service as if they were no more than worn-out machines?

The answer to all of these questions lies in one word: covetousness—the all-pervasive sin of human nature. In 10,000 valleys, upon countless green hilltops, under many shady groves, and in the fathomless depths of every ocean lie the bodies of the best young men of almost every generation who have been killed in the mad struggle between warring nations. Behind all of these wars there is the passion to possess, the desire for more.

Prayer: O Father, "Cure Thy children's warring madness, bend our pride to Thy control; shame our wanton, selfish gladness, rich in things and poor in soul. Grant us wisdom, grant us courage, lest we miss Thy kingdom's goal, lest we miss Thy kingdom's goal." In Jesus' name. Amen.

Hymn for the day:
Dear Lord and Father of Mankind

PRAYERS & REMINDERS

Question #79: Which is the Tenth Commandment?

Answer: The Tenth Commandment is, "You shall not covet your neighbor's house; you shall not covet your neighbor's wife, or his male servant, or his female servant, or his ox, or his donkey, or anything that is your neighbor's."

Scripture Reading: Colossians 3:5-11

The sin of greed is so basic to human nature that no one is free from its demanding grasp. It is certainly the prevailing spirit of our present generation, perhaps more than any other. We are in bondage to covetousness. It is a self-imposed bondage, but one from which we are powerless to free ourselves.

Nevertheless, the commandment of God remains unchanged: *Thou shalt not covet.* It towers over the greed of humanity and the wreckage of human history. It condemns our madness to possess things and offers a more noble way of life.

The last of the Ten Commandments is unique, for it searches out the spirit of a man rather than his deeds. It does not say so much what you should or should not do as what you should or should not be. It deals with your heart more than any other commandment. This was the commandment which convicted Saul, who was to become Paul, of his sin and lost condition. He said in one place that he was unaware of sin and was not convicted of his sinfulness until he dealt with this commandment. It reached out and slew him and so brought him under bondage to the whole law, exposing his sinful nature and leaving him defenseless in the presence of our holy God.

This commandment, Thou shalt not covet, is used by the Holy Spirit even to this day to bring men and women to their knees in recognition and confession of sin. The greatest disgrace in the church of our generation is not so much the immorality of its people and pastors (as serious as this is). No, the great shame is the near-surrender to the sin of covetousness. May God through Christ set us free from this terrible bondage.

Prayer: Dear Lord, You gave Your all on Calvary's cross, that we might have the riches of Your grace. Forgive us for wanting what the world offers of its fleeting riches, more than we desire Your glory and heaven. We ask this in Jesus' name. Amen.

Hymn for the day:
I Am Resolved

PRAYERS & REMINDERS

_____

_____

_____

_____

_____

_____

_____

_____

_____

August 4

Question #80: What is required in the Tenth Commandment?

Answer: The Tenth Commandment requires full contentment with our own condition, with a right and charitable frame of spirit toward our neighbor and all that is his.

Scripture Reading: I Timothy 6:6-10

This commandment has rightly been labeled the catch-all commandment, for it catches us all and spares no one. It tells us we are sinful both by nature and by choice. Even if we could claim a surface obedience to all the other commandments, when we come to this one, we find ourselves unable to defend our innocence.

The sin of covetousness lies at the root of all disobedience. It was at the root of the fall of Adam and Eve in the garden. When Eve saw that the fruit of the tree in the midst of the garden was good for food, pleasant to the eye, and to be desired to make one wise, she ate of it and gave it to Adam, and he ate. Their covetousness led to their disobedience. Once again, the connection between the first and the last commandments becomes obvious, for we cannot love God with all our hearts and at the same time covet all else.

What does it mean to covet? In the neutral sense of the word, it simply means to strongly desire. But when that desire is misdirected or when it becomes our master, then it is sinful, and we are guilty of that sin.

This law not only forbids covetousness, but forbids the outward expression of it. Another expression of covetousness is the desire for something for nothing. We want reward without effort and this, too, is wrong. I think it is beyond argument to say that the sin behind gambling, the lottery, the sweepstakes, and all similar schemes is the sin of covetousness. Covetousness is a cruel master and brings ruin though promising plenty.

Prayer: "Search me, O God, and know my heart; try me and know my anxieties; and see if there is any wicked way in me, and lead me in the way everlasting." In Jesus' name and for His sake. Amen.

Hymn for the day:
All for Jesus

PRAYERS & REMINDERS

Question #81: What is forbidden in the Tenth Commandment?

Answer: The Tenth Commandment forbids all discontentment with our own estate, envying or grieving at the good of our neighbor, and all unreasonable motions and affections toward anything that is his.

Scripture Reading: Romans 7:7-12

There is a deeper meaning to this commandment. It forbids a worldly spirit that believes that life consists in the abundance of things one possesses. Jesus warned about this when He said, *Beware and take heed of covetousness for life does not consist of the abundance of things that one possesses.* He went on to tell the parable of the rich fool, in which He pointed out the danger of covetousness. Here we discover how covetousness erodes the character of a person, distorts his values, and in the end brings death and ruin.

Jesus also taught by His rebuke of Satan's temptation that man does not live by bread alone. He has a deeper and more urgent need: a right relationship with God. Do you know the one thing the covetous person wants? It is a four-letter word spelled m-o-r-e — more of anything and everything. That kind of covetousness makes contentment impossible. The constant desire to possess more and the lack of contentment add up to misery of the worst sort. The covetous person never knows peace within or with God.

The ultimate outcome of covetousness is seen in the life and death of Judas Iscariot. I'm sure Judas never intended to betray Christ when he first began to desire more worldly possessions. He did not set out to be remembered as the most infamous man in history. All he wanted was just a little more than what he had, but gradually that desire possessed him, until he betrayed Christ and killed himself.

Prayer: Lord, help us to see the power of covetousness in our own hearts and lives. Deliver us from bondage to things to the freedom of seeking first the kingdom of God, and Your righteousness, and trusting You for our daily bread. In Jesus' name. Amen.

Hymn for the day:
I Am Trusting Thee, Lord Jesus

PRAYERS & REMINDERS

_____

_____

_____

_____

_____

_____

_____

_____

_____

Question #81: What is forbidden in the Tenth Commandment?

Answer: The Tenth Commandment forbids all discontentment with our own estate, envying or grieving at the good of our neighbor, and all unreasonable motions and affections toward anything that is his.

Scripture Reading: Hebrews 13:1-17

In my own life I have found only one thing effective in overcoming the sin of greed, and that is the faithful practice of stewardship. The more I give, the less hold the things of the world have on me. When I forget and start holding on and trying for more, I find myself a willing captive of covetousness. Once you learn to put God first in a tangible way by tithing and giving offerings above the tithe, the stranglehold of covetousness is loosened and finally broken. The joy and fulfillment of giving replace the captivity of keeping. As you learn more of the grace of gratitude for that which God has placed in your care to be used for His glory, the things of the world have less hold on your heart. It boils down to a choice: either you will conquer the sin of covetousness or it will conquer you, an unthinkable thing for the child of the King.

Covetousness is also very deceptive. Often I have found myself focusing in on some item I think I just must have. Such desire can be all consuming. I remember back in the days of my folly and flirtation with boats, once I finally was able to get a boat in partnership with a friend. All seemed well, at first. However I began to notice that all my fishing friends had bigger, better, newer boats than I had. My prize possession, a 16 foot fishing boat, began to look small and very tawdry. I began to plot, plan, and come up with all sorts of noble sounding reasons why I needed to move up in the boating world. Necessity and the lack of time to fish finally motivated me to get rid of the boat. I was able to give it to one of my sons and let him deal with the problem of covetousness! (He handled it far better than me.) It was a very freeing thing to put covetous desire of a bigger, better, newer boat behind me, once for all. Looking back, I now realize that the object of my desire was nothing less than an idol!

Prayer: O God, in my heart cast down every idol throne. Reign supreme and reign alone. Forgive our wanton idolatry for Jesus' sake, we pray. Amen.

Hymn for the day:
Take My Life, and Let It Be

PRAYERS & REMINDERS

Question #82: Is any man able perfectly to keep the commandments of God?

Answer: No mere man, since the Fall, is able, in this life, to keep perfectly the commandments of God, but does break them daily, in thought, word, and deed.

Scripture Reading: Romans 3:9-20

One of the basic points of disagreement even among Christians is this question: Is anyone able to perfectly keep the commandments of God? In giving the negative answer to this, our Catechism takes seriously the Biblical teaching of the fall of man and the results of that fall in every area of his life.

There are many people who believe that mankind is basically good and that given the opportunity and the right environment, people will always do the right thing. On the other hand, there are those who believe that human nature is neutral, neither good nor bad, and that training and environment will determine whether the person is good or bad.

The biblical position is quite clear. When our first parents sinned, there was a fundamental change in human nature. Until that time, Adam and Eve loved God with all their hearts and were able to obey His Word and to live in perfect harmony with Him. In the garden before the fall, human nature was indeed good because our first parents were created in God's image. However, once sin entered into the world, that nature was changed and became totally affected by sin. We need look no further than the rest of today and we will discover that God's commandments lie shattered all around us. Remember these words from I John 1:8: *If we say that we have no sin, we deceive ourselves, and the truth is not in us.* Of course the greater truth beyond this stark sentence is the following verse from the same chapter in I John: *If we confess our sins, he is faithful and just to forgive us our sins, and to cleanse us from all unrighteousness.* Praise God!

PRAYERS & REMINDERS

_____

_____

_____

_____

_____

_____

_____

_____

_____

Prayer: Great and gracious God, our Father in heaven, You know us and our thoughts from afar. Nothing is hidden from Your sight. You know the hold the world has on our hearts. Help us to always remember that You have made us for Yourself, and our souls are restless until they rest in You. In Jesus' name. Amen.

Hymn for the day:
Praise the Savior, Ye Who Know Him

Question #82: Is any man able perfectly to keep the commandments of God?

Answer: No mere man, since the Fall, is able, in this life, to keep perfectly the commandments of God, but does break them daily, in thought, word, and deed.

Scripture Reading: Ecclesiastes 7:15-29

One of the five points of Calvinism is total depravity. Total depravity does not mean that everyone is equally and totally evil. It does mean that our whole nature is affected by sin and that no mere man is able to perfectly keep the commandments of God. The Apostle Paul talks about this in the book of Romans, showing how it is impossible for anyone to be righteous in God's sight through obedience to the law. Paul himself was a willing victim of this inability and spoke of his own frustration in trying to achieve righteousness through the law.

The Catechism tells us that we daily break the commandments of God in thought, word, and deed. This is most clearly taught in our Lord's exposition of the Ten Commandments contained in the Sermon on the Mount. His summary of the requirements of the law was this, *Be ye therefore perfect even as your Father in heaven is perfect.* However, before making that statement, He took several of the commandments and gave the traditional interpretation and then went on to show the full meaning of obedience to these commandments. In each of these He dealt with obedience from the heart and showed very clearly that no one is capable of obeying the law in thought, word, or deed.

If we fail to understand the importance of this truth, we are led into many areas of error. First of all, we could be tempted to think that we could earn our own salvation by obedience to God's law. It always surprises me how many people really believe this. Yet, to follow this pathway is to experience unending frustration and disappointment that will lead to despair and hopelessness.

Prayer: Dear Savior, You are our Priest who was tempted and tried in all points as we are, yet without sin. You know our frame. You remember that we are but dust. For Your mercy's sake, forgive us and cleanse us. Help us to love You and Your holy law. Amen.

Hymn for the day:
Take The Name of Jesus With You

PRAYERS & REMINDERS

August 9

> ## Question #82: Is any man able perfectly to keep the commandments of God?

Answer: No mere man, since the Fall, is able, in this life, to keep perfectly the commandments of God, but does break them daily, in thought, word, and deed.

Scripture Reading: Proverbs 20:1-9

Another danger is that we will simply fail to take sin seriously. If I believe that I am able to obey the law of God and yet see myself continually breaking it, I am tempted to rationalize my actions by believing that my failure is not serious or that what I am doing is not wrong at all. This is insulting to God, as it leads us to question His authority, wisdom, and holiness. If I take seriously what the Catechism teaches at this point, I will also take seriously the doctrine of grace; and if I take that seriously, then I understand my salvation is rooted in God's purpose and electing grace.

One final word is in order. Those who understand the inability of man to win his own salvation will inevitably strive to obey the law of God out of gratitude and so come nearer meeting its requirements. Grace is the foundation stone for obedience. Love for God is a more powerful force than any other human emotion. If one looks for the reason why the Lord Jesus was willing to endure the hell of the cross and at one point even complete separation from the Father, the only answer possible is His love for the Father, and His love for those whom the Father has given Him in the blessed covenant of redemption. As the powerful truth of this reality begins to penetrate deeply into our consciousness, then our love for our Savior increases greatly. Because we love Him we will strive to obey Him. When we fail miserably in our best efforts, we will be deeply grieved, and determined even more to honor and serve Him because He has loved us so. We love Him because He first loved us. We strive to obey Him because we love Him.

PRAYERS & REMINDERS

Prayer: Keep us close to Thyself, dear Savior. Help us to comprehend something of Your great love for the Father, that we may love Him more, even as You loved Him. May our loving gratitude for Your sacrifice manifest itself in renewed obedience every day. Amen.

Hymn for the day:
Jesus, I Am Resting, Resting

Question #83: Are all transgressions of the law equally wicked?

Answer: Some sins in themselves, and by reason of aggravating circumstances, are more wicked in the sight of God than others.

Scripture Reading: Matthew 23:1-15

First of all, let it be said that we reject the idea of the classification of sins as mortal and venial, because every sin is deadly. As someone has said, even the least sin is cosmic treason against the God of the universe. Every sin deserves the wrath and curse of God.

However, it is true that for several reasons some sins are more heinous in God's sight than others. What are these reasons? First, there is the matter of the person who is offending. It is one thing for a baby Christian to stumble and fall, but it is more serious when a mature Christian does the same thing. The reason for this is clear: the young Christian has not had the benefit of long years of bible study and prayer and the inner working of the Holy Spirit. On the other hand, the Christian who has had the benefit of all these things has greater responsibility to obey God in thought, word, and deed. Another consideration at this point is that a more mature Christian usually has a wider influence on other people. That is one reason why the Apostle Paul rebuked the Apostle Peter in the presence of the whole assembly. Peter's offense had a detrimental effect on the whole church because of his position of leadership. James warned us: *Let not many of you become teachers, knowing that we shall receive a stricter judgment.* Any pastor, teacher, choir member, leader in God's Church who does not tremble at that thought simply ignores this warning. If there is one truth which should cause all such people to fear and tremble, and walk humbly before God, it is this one.

Prayer: Savior, like a shepherd lead us, much we need Thy tender care. O Lord, help us to walk in paths of righteousness for Your name's sake. May You be glorified in our continual repentance and obedience. Amen.

Hymn for the day:
Savior, Like a Shepherd Lead Us

PRAYERS & REMINDERS

> ## Question #83: Are all transgressions of the law equally wicked?

Answer: Some sins in themselves, and by reason of aggravating circumstances, are more wicked in the sight of God than others.

Scripture Reading: 2 Samuel 22:26-37

This leads us to the second reason why some sins are more serious than others. We have to consider those who are injured by the sin. God is always offended by every sin, but sins that are directed toward Him are even more offensive. An example of this would be blasphemy. On the other hand, sins against weaker believers are also especially serious. When we cause weak Christians to fall by our conduct, then we have violated one of the commands of Scripture, namely, that we avoid offending weaker brothers in the faith. Even in the world, this sort of classification is recognized. Everyone abhors murder, but when the victim is a weak and defenseless person, it is regarded as being even more horrible. In fact, in the matter of capital punishment, this is often taken into consideration. In Leviticus 19, there are several verses which tell us that God is particularly concerned for the weak and afflicted, and has given definite laws to protect them. "You shall not curse the deaf, nor put a stumbling block before the blind, but shall fear your God; I am the Lord." This tells us that such sins are more grievous in God's sight because of the inability of the afflicted to help themselves. Another stark example of how some sins are more grievous than others because of the inability of the weak to defend themselves would be the murder of the unborn. They are the most helpless of all people, and must depend upon the justice of the righteous for their very survival.

Prayer: O God, You are the defender and provider of the weak and helpless. May we also be their defender. We ask this for Jesus' sake. Amen.

Hymn for the day:
Lord, Speak To Me

PRAYERS & REMINDERS

Question #83: Are all transgressions of the law equally wicked?

Answer: Some sins in themselves, and by reason of aggravating circumstances, are more wicked in the sight of God than others.

Scripture Reading: Genesis 4:1-12

The third reason why some sins are more heinous in the sight of God than others is the nature of the sin itself. It is a serious sin if in my heart I harbor hate against my brother, but if this hatred breaks out into violence, then the sin is complicated and becomes even more reprehensible. It is wrong for me to covet my neighbor's property, but if I steal that which I covet, I have complicated the offense. If I am overtaken by a sudden temptation this is serious enough, but if I do the same ill deed deliberately, willfully, and maliciously, then it is even worse.

The final "aggravation" that the Larger Catechism mentions is the circumstance of time and place. If the offense is on the Lord's Day, or during worship, that aggravates the sin. Another aspect of this would be whether the sin is public or private. Obviously, the consequences of public sin are much more widespread and, therefore, more disastrous. Ananias and his wife discovered that lying to God and his people is far more serious than other forms of dishonesty, though all dishonesty of words or actions is sinful and wrong. The Catechism does not teach situational ethics in any form, but it does recognize that the situation may indeed complicate the nature and effects of sin.

As we shall see in the next question of the Catechism, all sins make us liable to God's judgment, but in the Christian life, it is important to realize that there are complicated factors that make some sins more offensive than others. If this study does nothing else, it will remind us how dependent we are on the grace of God and how impossible it is to please Him in our own strength.

Prayer: O God, You are our refuge and strength, a very present help in trouble. We are deeply troubled by our sins of commission and omission. We plead only the blood and righteousness of our Savior, in whose Name we pray. Amen.

Hymn for the day:
Jesus, Thy Blood and Righteousness

PRAYERS & REMINDERS

Question #84: What does every sin deserve?

Answer: Every sin deserves God's wrath and curse, both in this life and that which is to come.

Scripture Reading: Psalm 51

This statement from the Catechism will probably sound extreme to many who hear and read it. However, a little serious consideration will help you to understand that there is nothing extreme or unbiblical at all about these words. In fact, the Larger Catechism inserts the expression: *even the least sin.*

Now, why is this true? First of all, we have to understand that all sin is sin against God. When David had committed the terrible sins of adultery and murder, his prayer was, *against Thee,Thee only have I sinned and done this evil in Thy sight.* Sin is always against God and His goodness and love. When we break His laws, we break His heart. This makes it a personal offense. It is only as we understand something of God's holiness and goodness that we can begin to comprehend the seriousness of sin.

God has given us a very clear pattern in His Word of acceptable conduct. We call this the Ten Commandments. It might well be said that much of what the Bible teaches is a commentary on these ten words. When we say that every sin deserves God's wrath and curse, we are recognizing something about the character of God that is often overlooked. God is the God of righteousness as well as the God of compassion. This statement from the Catechism emphasizes God's holiness and righteousness. Since we have every reason for obeying Him and none for disobeying Him, we therefore must reckon with His wrath when we sin against Him. The wrath of God does not mean that God gets mad at people. It does mean that God's wrath is constantly against sin and must be taken seriously. God certainly does!

Prayer: O Lord God, whenever we fail to take sin seriously, may the echo of Christ's lament on the cross, *My God, My God, why hast Thou forsaken Me*, shame us and break our hearts, too. In His name we pray. Amen.

Hymn for the day:
God Be Merciful To Me

PRAYERS & REMINDERS

Question #84: What does every sin deserve?

Answer: Every sin deserves God's wrath and curse, both in this life and that which is to come.

Scripture Reading: Mark 15:33-41

If there is one place in all the Bible that reveals the righteous wrath of God against all sin, it is in the accounts given of Christ's death on the cross. Here we see both the love and the wrath of God in proper balance. God's love sent His Son into the world to bear our sin. But when He, the sinless Son, took to Himself our sin, God's wrath was poured out on Him. The Apostle Paul said of Christ, *He was made sin for us.* This enables us to understand His heart cry from the cross, *My God, my God, why hast thou forsaken me*? There the unthinkable happened. The only begotten Son of God, the beloved Son in whom the Father was well pleased, was made our sin offering. He took all our guilt and all our sin upon Himself, and suffered the hell we so richly deserved by our sin and rebellion. Any time we are tempted to think lightly of our sin, we need to be reminded of that dreaded scene on Calvary's hill.

This of course means that only those whose sins are covered by the "blood of the everlasting covenant" are protected from the fierce wrath of God. The book of Revelation shows in graphic fashion the terrible wrath of God against unforgiven sin. The images of the seven seals, the seven trumpets, and the seven bowls of wrath all describe the terrible judgments of God against rebellious, sinful mankind. So the words of the Catechism are not at all an exaggeration, when they speak of the "wrath and curse of God against all sin in this life and the life to come". This great truth helps us to appreciate God's amazing grace, and at the same time serves as a deterrent against willful sinning.

Prayer: Holy Father, we know that all our sins deserve Your wrath and curse in this life and the life to come. Thank You that our Lord Jesus was willing to bear that awful load for us. Forgive us for His sake, and keep us from sin for Your glory and honor. We ask this in Jesus' name. Amen.

Hymn for the day:
Alas, And Did My Savior Bleed?

PRAYERS & REMINDERS

Question #84: What does every sin deserve?

Answer: Every sin deserves God's wrath and curse, both in this life and that which is to come.

Scripture Reading: 2 Corinthians 5:9-21

The Catechism adds the word curse to the concept of wrath. We need to understand the meaning of that word as it is used in Scripture. When our first parents sinned and fell in the garden, they came under the curse of death. In fact, this curse fell upon the whole of creation. Death became a principle, both for mankind and for all creation. When we think of the concept of the curse as a consequence of sin, we must go beyond just the temporal punishment that Adam and Eve suffered. The real curse associated with sin is everlasting separation form God. The Bible sometimes refers to this as death in the ultimate sense and sometimes as hell. Both words convey how dreadful sin is to God and for us.

This reality prepares us to understand the expression in the Apostles' creed, *He descended into hell.* When the Lord Jesus became our sin bearer on the cross, He placed Himself under the wrath and curse of God. He endured the punishment Adam and Eve had earned for themselves, for *the wages of sin is death.* Separation from God is by definition hell. So when we say in the Apostles' Creed, *He descended into hell,* we are confessing that in His death on the cross He endured the ultimate punishment for sin, complete and total separation from God, His beloved Father. When that dreadful penalty had been paid, and hell endured, our Savior could say, *It is finished. Father, into Thy hands I commit My Spirit.* In the words of that beloved hymn, *Alas, and did my Savior bleed,* we hear these words: *Was it for crimes which I have done, He groaned upon the tree? Amazing pity, grace unknown, and love beyond degree.*

Prayer: O Savior, help us to understand the depth of Your amazing love for us, as well as the depths of Your suffering, that we might praise You now and for all eternity. Amen.

Hymn for the day:
O Sacred Head, Now Wounded

PRAYERS & REMINDERS

_____

_____

_____

_____

_____

_____

_____

_____

_____

August 16

Question #84: What does every sin deserve?

Answer: Every sin deserves God's wrath and curse, both in this life and that which is to come.

Scripture Reading: Hebrews 9:23-28

The Larger Catechism has an interesting final word when it says, *and cannot be expiated except by the blood of Christ.* There are two important truths in that expression. First of all, God has provided a way for us to escape His wrath and curse which sin deserves. Secondly, it tells us there is only one way this may be done. The blood of Christ cleanses us from all sin and saves us from the dreadful wrath and curse which we have brought upon ourselves because of our disobedience. The good news of the Gospel must always be understood and claimed in light of this truth.

When we attempt to fully understand the importance of God's forgiving grace apart from His wrath and curse against sin, we make light of His mercy, and the debt of love we owe is not so great after all. A small sense of sin leads to little appreciation of Christ's atonement and our salvation. It may also lead us into the sins of presumption, and careless living. After all, if sin isn't really all that bad, why worry, or why repent? We need to pray every day that we will see sin as God sees it, and thus pray with greater fervency and urgency: *Forgive us our debts, as we forgive our debtors, and lead us not into temptation, but deliver us from evil.* In the foolishness of our depraved thinking, we seem to think that if we will "just be good", that will make up for the "bad" we have done. It is true that forgiven people want to show their gratitude for unmerited mercy, but that is quite a different thing than thinking our best efforts can make up for our sins. We come back to the words of the Larger Catechism which says of our sins: *And cannot be expiated except by the blood of Christ.* Thank God again this day for the precious, powerful, and atoning blood of Christ by which our sins are washed away, and we are saved from wrath.

Prayer: Holy Father, You have told us in Your Word that only the blood of Your Son, offered once for all, can take away our sin and guilt. How we thank You for this gift of love and cleansing You have given us through Your Son, our Lord. Amen.

Hymn for the day:
What Can Wash Away My Sin?

PRAYERS & REMINDERS

> **Question #85: What does God require of us, that we may escape His wrath and curse, due to us for sin?**

Answer: To escape the wrath and curse of God, due to us for sin, God requires of us faith in Jesus Christ, repentance unto life, with the diligent use of all the outward means by which Christ communicates to us the benefits of redemption.

Scripture Reading: Romans 5:1-11

The bad news is every sin deserves the wrath and curse of God. The good news is God provides a way of escape. The Catechism begins the study of salvation by asking, what is required to escape the wrath and curse due to sin? It is interesting that in a document in which the sovereignty of God and electing grace are the centerpieces of theology, a question like this could find a prominent place. For those who accuse Calvinists of ignoring or minimizing human responsibility, this question is a rebuke. The first requirement mentioned is faith in Christ. In a parallel passage in the Confession of Faith, the expression saving faith is justifying faith and justifying faith is faith in Jesus Christ.

The faith spoken of here is faith that believes in the truth of the Gospel and faith that receives the Gospel. It is more than mere assent to propositional truth, though of course that is necessary. This kind of faith receives and rests upon Christ alone for salvation. Receiving implies commitment and commitment speaks of relationship. So faith in Christ means we accept the truth God has revealed and we accept the Savior who meets us in the written Word. We cannot make up conditions upon which we will trust in the Lord for salvation. How many times have I heard words like this: *If only God will get me through this crisis, I will trust Him.* Or words like this: *If God will spare the life of my loved one, and make him(her) well again, I'll become a Christian.* God does not have to prove His sovereignty or His love by meeting any terms we may try to lay down. The words from Job come to mind: *Though He slay me, yet will I trust Him;* or, *Then Job's wife said to him, 'Do you still hold fast to your integrity? Curse God and die. But he said to her; Shall we indeed accept good from God, and shall we not accept adversity? In all this Job sinned not with his lips.*

Prayer: Heavenly Father, thank You for Your unconditional love. We have not earned this love in any way. We are undeserving of Your grace, but how we need it and how grateful we are for it. Through Christ our Savior we pray. Amen.

Hymn for the day:
Jesus, What a Friend for Sinners

PRAYERS & REMINDERS

_____
_____
_____
_____
_____
_____
_____
_____
_____

Question #85: What does God require of us, that we may escape His wrath and curse, due to us for sin?

Answer: To escape the wrath and curse of God, due to us for sin, God requires of us faith in Jesus Christ, repentance unto life, with the diligent use of all the outward means by which Christ communicates to us the benefits of redemption.

Scripture Reading: 2 Peter 3:1-9

The other requirement mentioned is repentance unto life. Repentance is called the missing doctrine in evangelical theology. However, it is only missing when evangelical theology is incomplete. It may be true many people minimize the need for repentance, but it is at the heart and soul of the Gospel we find in the Bible. The first public, recorded words of our Lord Jesus Christ are *repent and believe, for the kingdom of heaven is at hand.* The whole ministry of John the Baptist was built around this central theme of repentance. The preaching of repentance has played a prominent role in every major revival since Pentecost. In fact, preaching of repentance was also prominent in the few incidences of national revival we find in the Old Testament.

Repentance involves several ingredients. First of all there is an awareness of the holiness of God. That is the starting point for true repentance. It was Isaiah's vision of God and His holiness that led him to repentance. Repentance, however, not only looks upward to God but inward to our hearts. When Isaiah saw God, he immediately became aware of his own sinful condition and cried out for mercy and cleansing. From I John we read, *If we confess our sins, He is faithful and just to forgive our sins, and to cleanse us from all unrighteousness.* True repentance seeks both mercy and cleansing and we must never ask for one without the other, lest our repentance prove to be insincere.

Prayer: O God, Your holiness calls on us to repent of our sins. Your gracious love offers full pardon when we do. Help us to truly repent for all our sins, and eagerly pursue holiness of life. For Jesus' sake we pray. Amen.

Hymn for the day:
Jesus, Lover of My Soul

PRAYERS & REMINDERS

August 19

> ### Question #85: What does God require of us, that we may escape His wrath and curse, due to us for sin?

Answer: To escape the wrath and curse of God, due to us for sin, God requires of us faith in Jesus Christ, repentance unto life, with the diligent use of all the outward means by which Christ communicates to us the benefits of redemption.

Scripture Reading: Ezekiel 33:1-20

Repentance goes beyond awareness to confession. Confession is an open acknowledgment that we have sinned and fallen short of the glory of God. This, in turn, creates a spirit of sorrow, sorrow that we have offended God and that we failed to be all He has called us to be. This sorrow also includes recognition of what we have missed by our sinfulness.

But repentance is more than just a feeling or an attitude of regret and sorrow. Repentance is turning around from one direction and heading in another. A good example of this is the Apostle Paul. He started out for Damascus as Saul who hated Christ, but after meeting Him on the road, his life was turned around and he went to Damascus to proclaim Christ. Another example is found in the story Christ told of the prodigal son. For a part of his life, he went further and further away from his father. But when he came to himself, and realized how far he had fallen, he began to think about his father's kindness and goodness. Then he purposed in his heart he would return to his father. But none of these thoughts or feelings alone completed the act of repentance. It was not until he turned his steps back to his father, and actually came into his presence seeking pardon, that his repentance was complete. One final word, the Catechism says that we must make diligent use of all "outward means". That would imply the profitable use of every opportunity God affords for repentance and faith. The means of grace God has provided are the reading of and meditating on His Word; sincere prayer of confession and trust, regular worship in God's house with God's people, and the sacraments of Baptism and the Lord's Supper.

PRAYERS & REMINDERS

_____
_____
_____
_____
_____
_____
_____
_____
_____

Prayer: Father, we read in Your Word that you desire repentance from those who hear Your Word. We rejoice that You have said, *As I live, says the Lord God, I have no pleasure in the death of the wicked, but that the wicked should turn from His way and live.* By Your grace we turn to You for life, in Jesus name. Amen.

Hymn for the day:
No, Not Despairingly

Question #86: What is faith in Jesus Christ?

Answer: Faith in Jesus Christ is the saving grace, by which we receive and rest upon Him alone for salvation, as He is offered to us in the Gospel.

Scripture Reading: Ephesians 2:1-9

To understand the meaning of faith one must begin with another word, and that word is *grace.* The Catechism refers to it as saving grace. In the book of Ephesians we read, *For by grace are ye saved through faith; and that not of yourselves: it is the gift of God: Not of works, lest any man should boast.* Faith is a gift. It comes to us by the grace of God. We cannot of our own strength acquire faith. We cannot just decide; *I think I will have faith in God.* It is God who regenerates our hearts, and when He does, He also gives us the gift of faith, which we receive from Him, and for which we give Him praise and glory.

Grace implies a gift unearned and undeserved. The grace of God reaches out to lost sinners with the most precious gift of all, the gift of faith. However, faith is a gift that must be received and exercised. Once we become the objects of grace, we are regenerated by the power of the Holy Spirit. This gives to us the ability and the responsibility to exercise faith in Jesus Christ. Saving faith must have an object, and that object is Christ alone. Mere faith, apart from Christ, does not save us. Jesus Christ is our Savior and therefore faith must rest in Him. He is not only the author of our faith; He is the object of it as well. The Catechism is very careful to weave the word *faith* around the word *grace,* for the two may never be separated.

Prayer: Amazing grace, how sweet the sound that saved a wretch like me! For that grace and the gift of saving faith in Christ as Savior from sin, we thank You, O Lord, and praise Your holy name. Amen.

Hymn for the day:
Marvelous Grace of Our Loving Lord

PRAYERS & REMINDERS

Question #86: What is faith in Jesus Christ?

Answer: Faith in Jesus Christ is the saving grace, by which we receive and rest upon Him alone for salvation, as He is offered to us in the Gospel.

Scripture Reading: Philippians 3: 1-21

This gift of faith enables us, according to the Catechism, to do two things. First, we are enabled to receive Christ. In John 1:12, we read these words, *But as many as received Him, to them gave He power to become the sons of God, even to them that believe on his name.* Receiving means more than merely believing, though it includes this. It also means that we accept the Lord Jesus as our personal Savior. It means that we accept His gift from the cross. Receiving also implies a relationship. We receive friends into our lives and into our hearts. The husband and the wife receive each other into a relationship of intimacy. Parents receive children into their lives. So in the Catechism we are told that faith enables us to receive Christ and that receiving is very much like the above relationships.

The other word the Catechism uses is the word *rest.* Faith enables us to rest upon Christ alone for salvation. This resting is basically trusting. To say that there is only one way of salvation in no way diminishes that one great way. He is the only Savior, and He is the only One we will ever need. Resting upon Him only for salvation recognizes that great truth. When a believer rests upon Christ alone for salvation, there is a faint but sure parallel between our resting on Him, and His resting on the Father when He went into the garden of Gethsemane to surrender His will to the Father. His trust was sure, but He knew the dreadful price He would pay for our salvation. So He committed Himself into the Father's hands, trusting that His Father would raise Him from the dead. By faith we trust in Christ, knowing he will raise us from the dead.

PRAYERS & REMINDERS

_____
_____
_____
_____
_____
_____
_____
_____
_____

Prayer: We Rest on Thee, O Lord, our shield and our defender. "Our hope is in none other save in Thee. Our trust is built upon Thy promise free. O grant to us such stronger hope and sure that we can boldly conquer and endure." For Jesus' sake, Amen.

Hymn for the day:
My Faith Has Found a Resting Place

Question #86: What is faith in Jesus Christ?

Answer: Faith in Jesus Christ is the saving grace, by which we receive and rest upon Him alone for salvation, as He is offered to us in the Gospel.

Scripture Reading: I Corinthians 15:1-11

A final phrase in this statement, *as He is offered to us in the gospel*, is one that should be carefully considered and understood. Christ is offered to us in the gospel in a particular way. We are not free to pick and choose, nor to suggest to God another way or another gospel. In the gospel, He is presented to us as God the Son. One of the failures of many modern-day cults is the failure to recognize the full deity of Jesus Christ. Even though some very popular cults refer to him as the Son of God, they do not mean what the Bible means by that expression. Christ is God the Son and in His own words, *I and the Father are one.* At the same time we are told that He was and continues to be also man, truly man. Furthermore, His saving work is that of a substitute. Christ died for our sins according to the Scripture. He was raised again from the dead and ascended into heaven. He will also come again to judge the living and the dead. In Isaiah 33:22 we read these words, (*For the LORD is our Judge, The LORD is our Lawgiver, The LORD is our King; He will save us);....* This prophecy speaks of the Lord Jesus Christ and this is what the Catechism means when it says, *as He is offered to us in the gospel.* Believers are to make very, very sure of two things. One, that they have received the Lord Jesus Christ as He is offered in the gospel and two, we must be very sure that when we offer Him to other people, our offer is according to the Word of God.

Evangelism that honors God always presents Christ as *He is offered in the gospel.* Anything less or more than this does not honor our Lord, and will not be blessed by Him. There are no shortcuts into the kingdom of God, there is only one path and one door. God's Word alone is a lamp unto our feet and a light upon our path to heaven.

Prayer: Father, we come to You the only way we may come, through Him who is the way, the truth and the life. We can come in no other way, nor do we desire another way. For Your beloved Son's sake, receive us as Your very own children, adopted and born again from above through Christ. Amen.

Hymn for the day:
We Come, O Christ, to Thee

PRAYERS & REMINDERS

Question #87: What is repentance to life?

Answer: Repentance to life is a saving grace, by which a sinner, out of a true sense of his sin, and understanding of the mercy of God in Christ, does, with grief and hatred of his sin, turn from it to God, with full intention of, and endeavor after, new obedience.

Scripture Reading: Psalm 32

Faith and repentance are twin graces and they may be said to be born simultaneously. They may be separated in thought but not in experience; in logic but not in life. Faith of a kind precedes and produces repentance, and faith of another kind follows and is the effect of repentance. So writes Dr. J. B. Green in his *Harmony of the Westminster Standards.* The Catechism's answer to the question deals basically with the grounds and ingredients of repentance.

Let us first of all consider the grounds of repentance. The Shorter Catechism refers to repentance as saving grace. The Larger Catechism inserts these words, *wrought in the heart of a sinner by the Spirit and Word of God.* Right away we are given to understand that repentance is a product of regeneration. The unregenerate can never repent of sin in the true sense, nor can the regenerate ever live comfortably with it. Sovereign grace is the fountainhead of all the graces we experience. However, as the Catechism points out, the sinner is not passive in this process, far from it. Two overwhelming realities face the penitent sinner. The first one is found in these words; *Out of a true sense of his sin.* When this happens a person comes under conviction of sin, and sin appears in all its ugliness and evil, and the convicted sinner sees himself as vile, helpless, and deserving God's wrath and displeasure. At this point, the gospel becomes sweet music, and the realization of God's mercy is even greater, and so repentance comes rushing in, and the sinner turns to God in loving gratitude, and hatred for the sin once cherished. God welcomes us even as the father welcomed the prodigal son back home again.

PRAYERS & REMINDERS

_____
_____
_____
_____
_____
_____
_____
_____
_____

Prayer: We stand amazed in Your presence, O Holy God, that You should receive and welcome us who have broken Your law and heart. We love You who first loved us, and we rejoice with glad hearts and lightened minds in Jesus' name. Amen.

Hymn for the day:
Christ Receiveth Sinful Men

Question #87: What is repentance to life?

Answer: Repentance to life is a saving grace, by which a sinner, out of a true sense of his sin, and understanding of the mercy of God in Christ, does, with grief and hatred of his sin, turn from it to God, with full intention of, and endeavor after, new obedience.

Scripture Reading: Psalm 25

Humanly speaking, repentance springs out of two kinds of knowledge. First, there is the knowledge of the true sense of sin which is so basic to repentance. If we never see ourselves as sinners in the sight of God, we will never sense a need to repent. However, once we see ourselves through the eyes of God and see our sin as God sees it, then we are on the way to repentance. Jesus said, *Blessed are the poor in spirit: for theirs is the kingdom of heaven.* He also added, *Blessed are they that mourn: for they shall be comforted.* By these words our Lord described both the necessity and the essence of repentance. The one who is poor in spirit is the one who sees himself as a sinner in the sight of God. The one who mourns his condition will be comforted by the grace of forgiveness.

The other kind of knowledge involved in repentance is the knowledge of God's mercy in Christ. This comes about through understanding the gospel. Paul wrote these incredible words concerning Christ: *He became sin for us who knew no sin that we might be made the righteousness of God in Him.* When we understand the mercy of God, then our repentance moves us into a saving relationship with the Lord Jesus Christ. However, we must remember it is all a work of God's sovereign grace and not of our own works. Therefore, since our salvation is by the grace and power of God, we do not rest in our own ability or even our own repentance and faith, but in the God who gives to us these saving graces. This is a more sure foundation and a safer harbor than all the good intentions and good works of men.

Prayer: Truly, O Lord, Your mercies are great. *Remember, O LORD, Your tender mercies and Your loving kindnesses. According to Your mercy, remember me, for Your goodness' sake, O LORD,* for Jesus' sake. Amen.

Hymn for the day:
Rock of Ages

PRAYERS & REMINDERS

Question #87: What is repentance to life?

Answer: Repentance unto life is a saving grace by which a sinner, out of a true sense of his sin, and understanding of the mercy of God in Christ, does, with grief and hatred of his sin, turn from it to God, with full intention of, and endeavor after, new obedience.

Scripture Reading: Hosea 6:1-11

The ingredients of repentance are likewise twofold. The first one is a grief and hatred for sin. When we realize that our sin offends God and was the cause of the death of our Lord Jesus Christ, then we can truly grieve over our sin. Too often our grief is superficial because it is grief over the consequences we must suffer. That is remorse, but not repentance. Our real grief over sin is the grief that we have caused God.

The second ingredient of repentance is turning from it unto God. Repentance is reversing our direction in thought as well as deed. Like faith, our repentance may be imperfect, but it may also be sincere. Repentance is not just a once-and-for-all experience; it is a daily turning to God. Unless the turning from sin involves a turning to God, with the full purpose of new obedience, then it will spend itself in emotion alone. There is emotion involved, but the emotion must prompt us to action or our repentance will be short-lived. Genuine repentance involves the whole man—his mind, his heart, and his will.

One final reminder is in order at this point. God alone can produce this kind of repentance in our lives. Man-made repentance will not endure. As soon as the emotion of the moment is past, so is the false start towards repentance. Our sorrow for sin must go beyond regret that our sin has been found out, and reach the point at which our greater grief is that we have offended God, and broken His holy law.

PRAYERS & REMINDERS

_____

_____

_____

_____

_____

_____

_____

_____

_____

Prayer: O Lord, may we ever understand that sin creates a barrier between us and our Father in heaven. Only You can break that barrier down, and You did this at awful cost to Your Son, our Savior Jesus Christ. In His name we offer our thanksgiving. Amen.

Hymn for the day:
O For A Thousand Tongues

Question #88: What are the outward means by which Christ communicates to us the benefits of redemption?

Answer: The outward and ordinary means by which Christ communicates to us the benefits of redemption are his ordinances, especially the Word, sacraments, and prayer, all of which are made effectual to the elect for salvation.

Scripture Reading: I John 5:1-13

This section of the Catechism follows the treatment of repentance and faith. The Catechism raises the question: What does God require of us to escape His wrath and curse because of sin? The answer is faith in Jesus Christ and repentance unto life. The same section of the Catechism refers to a diligent use of all the outward means that Christ uses to communicate to us the benefits of His redemption.

Now the Catechism deals with the question: what are these outward means? When the Catechism uses the two words, *outward* and *ordinary,* it does not mean to say *insignificant* or *of little importance.* These words refer to the ways in which faith and repentance become living realities in the lives of believers.

Three of these outward means are mentioned—the Word, sacraments, and prayer—and all of these are used by Christ to communicate to us the benefits of His redemption. The Word, of course, refers to our use of the Word of God and what it does in the life of the believer. In order for the Word to be operative in our lives, it must be read, understood, and applied. Later the Catechism will emphasize the necessity of the Word being preached. Ordinarily, God calls the elect to Himself through the preaching of the Word. When the Word is read or heard in faith, there is a supernatural power at work in that process to draw us to God and to experience the actual working of His grace in our lives. It is therefore both dangerous and foolish for believers to neglect the Word. Reading the Word and seeking the Lord in prayer go hand in hand, and both are necessary for us to honor and obey God.

Prayer: Great and gracious God, we praise You for Your holy Word. By that word You have revealed yourself and brought us the knowledge of Christ and salvation. Help us to abide constantly in Your Word faithfully. In Jesus' name. Amen.

Hymn for the day:
Holy Bible, Book Divine

PRAYERS & REMINDERS

> ## Question #88: What are the outward means by which Christ communicates to us the benefits of redemption?

Answer: The outward and ordinary means by which Christ communicates to us the benefits of redemption are his ordinances, especially the Word, sacraments, and prayer, all of which are made effectual to the elect for salvation.

Scripture Reading: Ezekiel 36: 22-32

Another expression the Catechism uses is the sacraments. These are two: Baptism and the Lord's Supper. It is interesting to note that in the context of the times in which the Catechism was written, the Westminster Divines did not allow the Roman Catholic misuse of the sacraments to distort their own view. Although they rejected the superstition associated with the sacraments, they recognized their value as a means of grace.

Baptism, being a sign and seal of the covenant, was given by the Lord and therefore becomes a means by which the truth of the gospel becomes effective in our lives. The worth of this sacrament does not depend upon the one who administers it or even upon the one who receives it, but rather it derives its meaning from the God who gave it. It signifies cleansing from sin by the Holy Spirit applying the sacrifice of Christ to us. The Holy Spirit is poured out upon us, and with His coming we are sprinkled with clean water, we will be cleansed from all filthiness and idols.

The Lord's Supper, the other sacrament recognized by Presbyterians, is a means of grace calling us to remember the atoning work of Christ. It reminds us of our relationship to Him and communicates the reality of His presence with His people. While we reject the unbiblical teaching that the elements of the Lord's supper, bread and wine, are turned into the body and blood of Christ, we affirm that by faith Christ is present with His people at His supper, not in a physical manner, but in a spiritual way. Since God is a Spirit, then the spiritual presence of Christ is far more beneficial than any physical presence could ever be.

Prayer: Gracious Lord, You take the simple things of life, water, bread, and wine, and by these things you demonstrate the most profound and saving truths of our salvation. Thank you for stooping down to our weakness and giving us strength. In Jesus' name. Amen.

Hymn for the day:
Here, O My Lord, I See Thee

PRAYERS & REMINDERS
_____
_____
_____
_____
_____
_____
_____
_____
_____

August 28

Question #88: What are the outward means by which Christ communicates to us the benefits of redemption?

Answer: The outward and ordinary means by which Christ communicates to us the benefits of redemption are his ordinances, especially the Word, sacraments, and prayer, all of which are made effectual to the elect for salvation.

Scripture Reading: I Timothy 2:1-7

The final expression is prayer. Although these three—the Word, the sacraments, and prayer—are joined together, there is a special significance to the last of these. Prayer is a means of grace when the sinner prays for forgiveness and it is granted. Prayer continues to be a means of grace as the sinner confesses his sins and is assured that God is faithful and just to forgive us our sins and cleanse us from all unrighteousness. Prayer is a means of grace as the believer confesses his sins and is assured that God is faithful and just to forgive us our sin and cleanse us from all unrighteousness. Prayer is a means of grace when we seek the guidance of the Holy Spirit in understanding the Word. Prayer is a means of grace when we intercede for fellow believers and pray for the coming of Christ's Kingdom. All three—the Word, sacraments, and prayer—are important in the lives of believers and the neglect or misuse of them is a serious matter indeed. However, as we grow in the knowledge of the Word, our appreciation of the significance of the sacraments and our exercise of prayer, we experience the benefits of Christ's redemption.

It is so easy to write and talk about prayer, but real praying is exacting, demanding, and difficult in many ways. It requires a deliberate sacrifice of time. It is true that we are to "Pray without ceasing", but it is also true we need to set aside significant times to seek the Lord in prayer. If we study the prayer life of Jesus (a very neglected, but profitable study), we discover that he devoted long hours and even days to prayer. Dare we do less?

Prayer: Lord, we echo the request of the disciples of old, "Teach us to pray". Help us to understand what You have taught us in Your Word and apply this teaching diligently, and thus grow in our ability to pray and our love for praying. Amen.

Hymn for the day:
Prayer is the Soul's Sincere Desire

PRAYERS & REMINDERS

Question #89: How is the Word made effectual to salvation?

Answer: The Spirit of God makes the reading, but especially the preaching, of the Word an effectual means of convincing and converting sinners, and of building them up in holiness and comfort, through faith to salvation.

Scripture Reading: Isaiah 55

The Bible is not just another book; it is the Word of God. Holy men of old spoke and wrote as they were moved by the Holy Spirit. These writings are literally God-breathed. This is what we mean when we say that the Bible is inspired.

The Catechism asks: *How is the word made effectual to salvation?* The answer begins with the Holy Spirit. Even as the Spirit inspired the writing of the Word, so He must be active in the reading and hearing of the Word. His work is absolutely necessary to make the work of God effective in our lives. I have known many people who are well-read in the Bible and who have studied the Scriptures in depth and yet are not Christians. They can discuss and debate the finer points of the Scripture as if they were good theologians, but they have never been converted by those same Scriptures.

In theory, all Bible-believing pastors are committed to preaching the Word of God. However, when less than two minutes are given to the reading of God's Word, and much time is spent (wasted?) with opinions and observations about the world in general, and the state of religion in particular, we have to wonder about the degree of true commitment to Scripture. The words of Scripture are the only words God has promised to bless. So the challenge facing all of us who preach and teach the Word is to make sure that God's words fill our sermons and lessons. The great challenge facing those who hear the sermons and lessons is to make sure we listen with faith and full intention to obey.

PRAYERS & REMINDERS

Prayer: Father, thank You so much that You have promised to bless Your Word and make it accomplish the purpose for which You send it. May we always trust Your wisdom over our own, and learn to think Your thoughts after You. For Jesus' sake. Amen.

Hymn for the day:
Brethren, We Have Met For Worship

Question #89: How is the Word made effectual to salvation?

Answer: The Spirit of God makes the reading, but especially the preaching, of the Word an effectual means of convincing and converting sinners, and of building them up in holiness and comfort, through faith to salvation.

Scripture Reading: I Corinthians 2:1-16

One aspect of the work of the Holy Spirit is to so illumine and empower the Word as to regenerate the lost and edify the saints. The Catechism puts special emphasis on the preaching of the Word as a means of converting sinners and edifying believers. Preaching by definition is expounding the Word of God. Anything less than this is simply not preaching in the biblical sense. It may be informative and entertaining, but it is not preaching. In biblical preaching, the style may vary, the application may be made by way of illustration, but at the heart of true preaching is the proclamation of God's Word. At its best, preaching is a supernatural event in which the living God meets with and speaks His Word to His people. This is not the work of man; it is the work of the Holy Spirit. The preacher's role is simply to be a servant of the Word and the Holy Spirit.

According to the Catechism, the preaching of the Word has two major thrusts. One is the convincing and converting of sinners. All too often this is overlooked in Presbyterian circles. However, the Bible always emphasizes the reaching of the lost through the preaching of the Word. Presbyterian preaching, like all biblical preaching, must include an effort to convince and convert sinners. The other emphasis is on building up believers into holiness of life. Most preaching has this as its primary purpose and focus. The Catechism also mentions the word *comfort*. This too should be a major concern in all preaching, that God's people receive the comfort God offers in His Word. In any given congregation, there will be faithful souls who live in quiet grief constantly. Sometimes we overlook the need for comfort from the pulpit, but it should not be so.

Prayer: Gracious Father, we thank you for your Word of peace and comfort through the gospel of our Lord and Savior, Jesus Christ. We pray that your servants will always minister to those who are in sorrow and distress. In Jesus' name. Amen.

Hymn for the day:
Wonderful Words of Life

PRAYERS & REMINDERS

Question #89: How is the Word made effectual to salvation?

Answer: The Spirit of God makes the reading, but especially the preaching, of the Word an effectual means of convincing and converting sinners, and of building them up in holiness and comfort, through faith unto salvation.

Scripture Reading: II Timothy 4:1-8

The other major theme of preaching is building up believers in holiness and bringing them comfort. One of the reasons why God converts sinners is to change them into His own image that He might have fellowship with them through all eternity. This requires that we grow in holiness, for in this we grow in likeness to our Father in heaven. The Scripture tells us to be holy, for the One who called us is holy. Holiness may be understood to be simply a reflection of the character of God. As children of God, His character grows in us through the work of the Holy Spirit and this comes about primarily through the preaching of the Word. The Catechism also uses the word *comfort.* Comfort should be always in the mind of God's messengers when the Word is preached, for our God is a God of all comfort. In our own experiences we are surrounded constantly by pressure and sorrow and this is the common lot of all mankind. The preacher who does not understand this is not reflecting the heart of the God whom he represents. In conclusion, the Catechism uses two words, *faith* and *salvation.* The end and goal of all preaching is to produce faith that leads to salvation. When this is done, then the Spirit of God is making the Word of God effectual to salvation. Without the powerful work of the Holy Spirit, both in the one who proclaims the Word, and in the ones who hear the Word, all preaching is vain. God uses preaching to communicate His Word, but the preaching and the preacher are only the vessels through which His Word comes to us. So let all glory be His alone.

PRAYERS & REMINDERS

_____

_____

_____

_____

_____

_____

_____

_____

_____

_____

Prayer: How grateful we are, dear Father, that You have chosen to reveal Yourself through the written Word. What a joy to know that the Bible we hold in our hands is Your inerrant and inspired Word. In Jesus' name we pray. Amen.

Hymn for the day:
Jesus Loves Me

> ### Question #90: How is the Word to be read and heard, that it may become effectual to salvation?

Answer: That the Word may become effectual to salvation, we must attend to it with diligence, preparation, and prayer; receive it with faith and love, lay it up in our hearts, and practice it in our lives.

Scripture Reading: Psalm 119:1-16

A man once gave a friend a copy of the Bible. On the flyleaf he wrote four words which guided him in how to read it. These words were admit, commit, submit, and transmit. Whoever reads or hears the Bible with the view of doing these four things will find the reading and the hearing a blessed experience.

The way in which the Word is read or heard determines the value of that reading or hearing. The reader or hearer's attitude toward the Bible is of fundamental importance. The Larger Catechism is an excellent commentary on the Shorter at this point. It teaches us that the Bible is to be read and heard with a desire to know, believe, and obey the will of God revealed therein. If one reads and hears with such a motive, then one will truly read with attention and diligence, with prayer and meditation, and will discover the truth the Bible teaches; but it is not enough that the Word would be read by all, it must be preached as well.

The Catechism puts a high degree of importance on the preaching of the Word. The Larger Catechism develops this much more fully than the Shorter Catechism, and I encourage you to read and reflect on the Larger Catechism, questions 158 through 160. However, more can be said about the simple, straightforward statement which is found in the Shorter Catechism. We are told that there must be preparation and prayer in reading and hearing the Word. The kind of preparation that is necessary is that of prayer and a willing heart to understand and obey that Word.

Prayer: O Lord, help us to love Your Word and to meditate upon it day and night. We waste so much time reading the thoughts of sinful man. May we ever treasure Your Word above all else, for in it You reveal pure, unadulterated, and saving truth. In Jesus' name. Amen.

Hymn for the day:
Wonderful Words of Life

PRAYERS & REMINDERS

Question #90: How is the Word to be read and heard, that it may become effectual to salvation?

Answer: That the Word may become effectual to salvation, we must attend to it with diligence, preparation, and prayer; receive it with faith and love, lay it up in our hearts, and practice it in our lives.

Scripture Reading: Psalm 119:17-40

The Catechism teaches us that the Bible must be received with faith and love. Faith in the Word of God means believing that it is true and that it has authority in your life. Faith in the Word means that you trust the Bible in all that it says. This means believing that the Scriptures are God-breathed, and therefore are beyond error or doubt. It saddens me very much to hear Christians concede so very much to the non-theistic philosophy which has dominated western culture for at least the last two centuries. I even hear learned people saying we must re-evaluate how we interpret the Bible in light of "recent scientific findings" which make the traditional methods of reading and studying the Bible out-of-date. The Catechism insists that faith in the Bible as God's Word and, therefore, as truth, must guide us as we read and study it.

Furthermore, we are to receive the Word with love. This speaks of an attitude of gratitude. We love God because He first loves us. We love His Word because through it we discover a personal relationship with God Himself. As the psalmist says, *Oh, how I love Your law! It is my meditation all the day.* In the long run you will discover that love for God and for His Word is the only enduring motivation to read and hear it. Although duty may make us diligent for a short while, only love will persevere and give us an eagerness of spirit that will allow nothing to replace the reading of God's Word or give into unbelief in how we interpret it.

PRAYERS & REMINDERS

_____
_____
_____
_____
_____
_____
_____
_____
_____

Prayer: Father, You have spoken through Your revealed Word. Help us to come to Your holy Word with faith and love, with diligent preparation, and prayer, knowing that it is truth itself, and therefore to read it, study it, and by the Holy Spirit, apply it to our lives. In Jesus' name. Amen.

Hymn for the day:
How Precious Is the Book Divine

**Question #90: How is the Word to be read and heard,
that it may become effectual to salvation?**

Answer: That the Word may become effectual to salvation we must attend to it
with diligence, preparation, and prayer; receive it with faith and love,
lay it up in our hearts, and practice it in our lives.

Scripture Reading: Psalm 119:41-56

The Catechism teaches us that we are to lay up God's holy Word in our
hearts. Once more we quote the psalmist who said, *Thy Word have I hidden in
my heart that I might not sin against Thee.* When Jesus said, *lay up for yourselves treasures in heaven*, He undoubtedly intended the laying up of God's
Word in our hearts as a part of this investment. Laying up God's Word in our
hearts requires meditation and reflection. When I read or hear the Word of God,
I must ask myself, what is God saying to me and how does this affect my life?
What needs changing? Of what must I repent and seek forgiveness? What
promises may I appropriate and claim?

The final instruction in the Catechism is that we are to practice it in our
lives. Failure to do this will result in the loss of the knowledge that we might
otherwise gain in the reading and hearing of the Word. So the Catechism teaches us that those who read and hear the Word have a great responsibility and an
even greater privilege. When we understand that so much of the human race is
bound up by chains of ignorance of God's revealed Word, we may begin to see
how blest we are to have it so freely available. Just think! There are multiplied
billions of people in the world today who, if they only knew a fraction of what
we have before us in God's Word, would undoubtedly rejoice in the discovery
of such powerful, life-changing truth. It is a very sobering thing to remember
the words of Scripture, *To whom much is given, much will be required.*
Certainly this applies to a knowledge of God's Word above all else.

Prayer: Father, we read Your Word, and know it is
true. Yet we resist its teachings, ignore its precepts,
and forfeit its promises. Help us to eagerly seek
Your truth that we may store it up in our hearts,
and work it out in our lives. For Jesus' sake we
pray. Amen.

Hymn for the day:
Holy Bible, Book Divine

PRAYERS & REMINDERS

> **Question #91: How do the sacraments become effectual means of salvation?**

Answer: The sacraments become effectual means of salvation, not from any virtue in them, or in him who administers them; but only by the blessing of Christ, and the working of His Spirit in those who by faith receive them.

Scripture Reading: Matthew 3:13-17

The place and importance of the sacraments in the Christian life has long been a subject of debate and division within the Church. There are Christians who believe that the elements of the sacraments themselves are the means of grace, while other believers place little importance at all upon the sacraments. Presbyterians have always tried to maintain a biblical balance when it comes to the place and importance of the sacraments. We have already seen that the Bible as a means of grace must be heard in a certain way. The same thing is true of the sacraments. In order to receive the blessing of Christ through the sacraments, there must be a proper understanding of their meaning and importance. It is through the sacraments that God bestows benefits and blessings upon His Church and His people. The Catechism makes it very plain that the blessing does not come through the ceremony of the sacrament or even through the one who administers them.

When we read of how the sacraments, baptism and the Lord's Supper were given in such beautiful simplicity, we regret that we have often surrounded them with man-made ceremonies. I think of that heart-touching account in Matthews' Gospel of how the Lord instituted His supper at the last Passover celebration with His disciples. The power of that account lies, at least in part, in its utter simplicity. The several accounts in the book of Acts of baptism are equally unadorned with human ceremony. The baptism of Cornelius and his household is an example of this simplicity, as is Philip's baptizing the Ethiopian eunuch. I know both sacraments must be administered in a solemn and reverent manner, but let us take care not to surround them with too much human pomp and ceremony.

Prayer: Thank You, gracious Lord, for showing us such profound truth in such simple ways as we see in the drama of the sacraments. We rejoice that You have made Your deep truth so wonderfully simple for us to understand. In Jesus' name. Amen.

Hymn for the day:
Here, O My Lord, I See Thee Face to Face

PRAYERS & REMINDERS
_____
_____
_____
_____
_____
_____
_____
_____
_____

September 5

> ### Question #91: How do the sacraments become effectual means of salvation?

Answer: The sacraments become effectual means of salvation, not from any virtue in them or in him who administers them; but only by the blessing of Christ, and the working of His Spirit in those who by faith receive them.

Scripture Reading: Matthew 3:1-12

Sometimes Christians make the mistake of assuming that because the one who administers the sacrament is not a worthy servant of Christ, there is no virtue in the sacrament itself. I have talked to believers who wanted to be rebaptized because they believed the one who administered baptism to them was not a true minister of Christ. This is to totally misunderstand the meaning of the sacraments. It is Christ who blesses the sacraments, not man. Therefore, baptism is received in the name of the triune God. The same thing is true of the Lord's Supper. Its virtue depends solely upon Christ working through it to produce repentance and faith in men's lives.

The Catechism goes on to point out that the work of the Holy Spirit is essential for the sacraments to become effectual means of salvation. The role of the Spirit is to interpret the meaning of the sacraments to those receiving them. It is through the baptism that we have been cleansed from sin by the blood of the everlasting covenant. In the Lord's Supper, He shows us that we are united to Christ both in His death and resurrection and that we are sustained by His grace. But apart from the work of the Holy Spirit in and through the sacraments, they are but outward symbols of truths we do not understand. The next time you are in a worship service in which the sacrament of baptism is administered either to a believer or the covenant child of a believer, ask the Holy Spirit to work grace in the hearts of the recipients and all who are present. At the next communion service, seek His blessing upon your own heart and of all those present in the service.

Prayer: Father, we thank You for the visible signs of the covenant of grace. May the blessed Holy Spirit apply the benefits of these sacraments to the hearts of all believers who are present. For Jesus' sake. Amen.

Hymn for the day:
The Spirit Breathes Upon the Word

PRAYERS & REMINDERS

Question #91: How do the sacraments become effectual means of salvation?

Answer: The sacraments become effectual means of salvation, not from any virtue in them or in him who administers them; but only by the blessing of Christ, and the working of His Spirit in those who by faith receive them.

Scripture Reading: Hebrews 11:17-29

Finally, the Catechism points out the role of faith in the proper use of the sacraments. While it is true that the child of the covenant is incapable of exercising faith at the time of baptism, still the parents by faith look to the Lord Jesus for the salvation of their covenant child. Then as they are faithful in keeping their vows, the Holy Spirit works faith in the life of the covenant child in due time until that one comes to a saving faith in the Lord Jesus. Again, in the Lord's Supper we accept by faith the atonement that is demonstrated in the broken bread and the cup of the New Testament. We may go through the routine of the Lord's Supper a hundred times without the experience of even one blessing. When we come to the table in faith believing that Jesus died for us, then the sacrament becomes an effectual means of salvation in the life of the believer.

The Scripture tells us that without faith it is impossible to please God. It is also impossible to understand the work of grace illustrated by the sacraments unless they are received by faith. In these services, faith sees beyond the outward signs, and understands that the things which are seen are temporal, but the things which are not seen are eternal. Grace that saves and edifies is offered to us and symbolized by the elements of the sacraments. It is well to remember that these are symbols with rich and deep meaning, and as such they are to be received with gratitude and the understanding which is given in God's word. Here is the biblical order: the Word, the symbol, and faith.

PRAYERS & REMINDERS

Prayer: Father, please grant us the faith to see beyond the mere elements of the sacraments, and to comprehend the graces they represent. May the blessings You intend through these outward signs be ours, by faith. In Jesus' name. Amen.

Hymn for the day:
Faith of Our Fathers

Question #92: What is a sacrament?

Answer: A sacrament is a holy ordinance instituted by Christ, in which, by perceptible signs, Christ and the benefits of the new covenant are represented, sealed, and applied to believers.

Scripture Reading: Hebrews 9:11-15

When we were very young, we learned that a sacrament is an earthly sign with a heavenly meaning. That is fine so far as it goes, but it obviously does not go far enough. The Shorter Catechism gives a concise but far more complete definition, while the Larger Catechism and the Confession fill out the complete definition which we seek.

The first and most important thing which is taught in this statement from the Catechism is that a sacrament is instituted by Christ Himself. This is what gives the sacraments their meaning and validity. It is not the prerogative of the Church to institute sacraments, any more than it is her prerogative to claim her words are on par with Scripture, or that the deliverances of the Church are new revelation beyond Scripture. It belongs to the Church to proclaim the revelation already given, and to observe the sacraments already instituted. This means that we must be diligent to observe these sacraments and not neglect them. There are people who think that neither baptism nor the Lord's Supper are really important, and that the only thing important for the Church is the preaching of the Word. Yes, the preaching of the Word is important, and God's Word teaches us that both baptism and the Lord's Supper are important, too, and that they are to be observed until the Lord returns, because He has given them and commanded His Church to observe them. Preaching is the Word proclaimed. The sacraments are the Word dramatized.

Prayer: Dear Lord, help us to obey You in all You command. Grant to us an increasing appreciation of the sacraments You have ordained, that we may better understand what our Savior has done for us. In His name we pray. Amen.

Hymn for the day:
Shepherd of Souls, Refresh and Bless

PRAYERS & REMINDERS

Question #92: What is a sacrament?

Answer: A sacrament is a holy ordinance instituted by Christ, in which, by perceptible signs, Christ and the benefits of the new covenant are represented, sealed, and applied to believers.

Scripture Reading: Hebrews 9:16-22

The sacraments are called holy ordinances. This means they are actions and ceremonies which are God-ordained, and to be held in wonder and adoration because they depict the truths taught in God's Word. As Dr. J. B. Green wrote in his *Harmony of the Westminster Standards: The Word is the Gospel addressed to the ear, and the sacraments are the Gospel addressed to the eye.*

When the Catechism refers to the sacraments as sensible signs, it simply means they are signs or symbols which may be discerned at least in outward form by the physical senses. They may be seen, felt, and tasted. They would be meaningless without the Word, but as they are presented, in company with the Word, they accomplish God's purposes. Only in extraordinary cases are the sacraments to be observed apart from the preaching of the Word. When faith is replaced by superstition, the "sensible signs" make no sense. One may wonder why God gave us these "sensible signs" in addition to His written word. God created us in His image and this has so many implications. We are not one dimensional creatures. We have been created with imagination, the ability to see and relate what we see to spiritual realities. God created majesty and beauty and tells us in His Word that His power and glory may be seen in His creation. So when He would teach us the truth of such words as baptism, and the Lord's Supper, we can understand the meaning of these words more fully as we consider the "sensible signs" which He has chosen to be associated with the saving sacraments. In short, He has given us these signs to help us comprehend the message of the Gospel.

PRAYERS & REMINDERS

_____

_____

_____

_____

_____

_____

_____

_____

_____

Prayer: Dear Father in heaven, help us to appreciate and understand the truths You have revealed through the "sensible signs" of the sacraments Christ has given to His Church. In His name. Amen.

Hymn for the day:
According to Thy Gracious Word

Question #92: What is a sacrament?

Answer: A sacrament is a holy ordinance instituted by Christ, in which, by perceptible signs, Christ and the benefits of the new covenant are represented, sealed, and applied to believers.

Scripture Reading: Hebrews 9:23-28

What are those purposes of God that are accomplished through the sacraments? There are several mentioned here and more in the other documents of our standards. In these sensible signs, Christ and the benefits of the new covenant are made known to believers.

First, Christ and these benefits are represented. That is to say, when we see the water of baptism we are to understand that this represents cleansing. Water is the universal agent of washing or cleansing, and when the water of baptism is poured out upon believers and their infant seed, we are reminded of our need for cleansing, and God's grace in providing it. But there is far more than mere representation in this act. There is a sealing, a real act whereby the believer or the covenant child is sealed unto the day of redemption. Of course, this is not by the act alone, but rather by the grace of God working in and through the sign. Beyond sealing, there is also application of covenant blessings. When the act of baptism is accompanied by words of instruction and promise from the bible, and when these words are received by the faith of the believer for himself and/or for his covenant seed, then grace is truly given, and the sacrament of baptism becomes effective in believing hearts for the cleansing from sin. We would not make the mistake of thinking that the very act of baptism assures one of eternal life as some do, but neither would we minimize the effectiveness of the God-appointed means of grace. Thank God for your baptism and pray that what has been symbolized in this sacrament, may be a living reality in your life.

Prayer: Lord Jesus, You commanded Your disciples to baptize in Your name. May we always take seriously Your every command, and give due diligence to practice all You have commanded. Amen.

Hymn for the day:
See Israel's Gentle Shepherd Stand

PRAYERS & REMINDERS

Question #92: What is a sacrament?

Answer: A sacrament is a holy ordinance instituted by Christ, in which, by perceptible signs, Christ and the benefits of the new covenant are represented, sealed, and applied to believers.

Scripture Reading: I Corinthians 11:17-22

What we have said of baptism is also true of the Lord's Supper. This is again a covenant act. It is a believer's feast. Since we are admonished in Scripture that we must discern the Lord's body, we first instruct our covenant children and admit them to the table upon their own profession of faith and examination by the Session.

While it may be true that some harm has been done and some of the splendor tarnished by too frequent observation of the Lord's Supper, it is equally true that we are spiritually impoverished by failure to observe the sacred meal more frequently than most of us do. Pastors and Sessions would do well to study and pray fervently concerning this. Is our present practice of monthly observation of the Lord's Supper really sufficient to encourage the saints in their walk with the Lord? Or is it too frequent to the point we take it for granted? These are questions each congregation must decide for itself. The more important question, however, is with what seriousness of purpose we partake of this holy meal, and with what discernment we approach the table. It is not the frequency with which we observe the sacrament which makes it effective, but our response of faith and obedience to all it teaches us. One principle that must be followed is that the Word and the sacrament should not be separated, lest we fall into the trap of thinking the ceremony itself carries some special power, and forget that without the word, the sacrament easily becomes nothing more than a ceremony.

Prayer: Father, as we partake of the holy sacrament we long to experience the spiritual feast which only You can give us. Help us to receive the grace You give in gratitude and love. Through Christ alone we pray. Amen.

Hymn for the day:
Bread of the World in Mercy Broken

PRAYERS & REMINDERS

September 11

> **Question #93:** *Which are the sacraments of the New Testament?*

Answer: The sacraments of the New Testament are Baptism and the Lord's Supper.

Scripture Reading: I Corinthians 11:23-34

When the *Westminster Confession of Faith* and Catechisms were written, the Reformed churches were in deep conflict with the Roman Catholic Church over the question of the sacraments. The Roman position was that the church had the authority to establish sacraments. Furthermore, the Church of Rome decreed that there were seven sacraments — Baptism, the mass (the Lord's supper), marriage, confirmation, penance, orders, and extreme unction. The Reformers held that there were only two sacraments as opposed to the seven of Rome. They came to this conclusion on the basis of the necessary tests to establish the nature of a sacrament.

First of all, it is required that a sacrament be instituted by the direct authority of Christ. Although the Lord gave approval of such things as marriage, there is never any indication that it was to be a means of grace to communicate salvation. Thus it could not possibly meet the requirement of direct institution by the Lord. So far as the other sacraments of the Roman church go, there is little, if any, biblical ground for them, and certainly none suggesting that Christ directly instituted these things.

On the other hand, both Baptism and the Lord's supper came to us by direct commandment of the Lord to the disciples. In Matthew 28:19, we have one record of the command to baptize. This was part of the Great Commission and was to be administered in the name of the triune God. When Christ instituted the Lord's supper, He commanded us through His Apostle that this be observed until He comes again.

Prayer: Lord Jesus Christ, You are the Head and Savior of Your Church. Your law alone is our guide and rule. By Your command we baptize, and at Your word we gather around Your table. Amen.

Hymn for the day:
The Mighty God, The Lord

PRAYERS & REMINDERS

Question #93: Which are the sacraments of the New Testament?

Answer: The sacraments of the New Testament are Baptism and the Lord's Supper.

Scripture Reading: Colossians 2:1-10

The Lord's supper was instituted by Christ in the Upper Room shortly before His arrest, trial, and death. Later, the Apostle Paul gave instruction concerning the Lord's supper, saying, *I have received from the Lord that which I also delivered unto you.* So it is obvious that these two sacraments meet that test of direct institution by the Lord.

The second test was that in the sacrament there must be an outward visible sign. Again, the additional five sacraments of the church of Rome do not meet this test. It is obvious that the two sacraments accepted by the Reformers are built around the outward visible signs. In the case of baptism, the sign is water, and in the case of the Lord's supper, bread and wine.

The third test has to do with the inward grace signified. The sacraments teach us by sensible signs the meaning of the saving and keeping grace of God. When this test is applied to the extra-biblical sacraments instituted by the Church of Rome, again we find them failing to meet that biblical standard. In the case of Baptism and the Lord's supper, their whole meaning is derived from the grace signified. In Baptism, we signify the cleansing from sin. This cleansing is signified not only by the application of water as the universal agent of cleansing, but also as an illustration of the anointing of the Holy Spirit by which we are born again into the Kingdom of God.

Prayer: How kind and gracious You are, dear Savior, to show us such great truth through such simple signs. Truly You have stooped to our weakness and have given light to our dark minds. Illumine our minds to understand all You teach us. Amen.

PRAYERS & REMINDERS

_____

_____

_____

_____

_____

_____

_____

_____

_____

Hymn for the day:
O The Deep, Deep Love of Jesus!

Question #93: *Which are the sacraments of the New Testament?*

Answer: The sacraments of the New Testament are Baptism and the Lord's Supper.

Scripture Reading: Colossians 2:11-23

The Lord's supper signifies the death and resurrection of our Lord. The bread and cup signify the body broken and the blood shed, but since Jesus added the promise that He would eat this meal again in the Kingdom of God, we also understand it speaks of the resurrection. Further, it signifies our enduring communion with the Lord. Just as we receive the bread and the fruit of the vine physically, so we receive Christ spiritually by faith and are nurtured by His abiding presence. So the sacraments of the New Testament are two only — the Lord's supper and Baptism. These alone fulfill the requirements for a true sacrament. Though there are only two sacraments of the New Testament, yet in them we discover more truth and power than all the many sacrifices and ceremonies of the Old Testament. In fact, all the more elaborate ceremonies of the law are summed up so beautifully in these two simple sacraments of the New Testament.

Therefore it becomes the duty of the church to instruct its members in the full meaning of these gifts of grace, lest we somehow miss the powerful messages they contain. Every time we baptize a believer, or a child of the covenant, there should be adequate explanation of what we do, and why we do it, lest we fail to comprehend the importance of this act of faith. When we come to the Lord's table, once more the meaning of this act should be opened up to the hearts and minds of the people.

Prayer: "Open my eyes that I may see, glimpses of truth Thou hast for me. Place in my hand the wonderful key that shall unclasp and set me free." In Jesus' name. Amen.

Hymn for the day:
Searcher of Hearts, From Mine Erase

PRAYERS & REMINDERS

September 14

Question #94: What is Baptism?

Answer: Baptism is a sacrament, in which the washing with water, in the name of the Father, and of the Son, and of the Holy Spirit, does signify and seal our grafting into Christ, and receiving of the benefits of the Covenant of Grace, and our engagement to be the Lord's.

Scripture Reading: Romans 6:1-14

As we start to explore the meaning of the sacraments beginning with Baptism, we see how thoroughly consistent the Catechism is with the teaching of Scripture. Baptism is a sacrament which has been instituted by Christ not only as a sign but also as a seal of the benefits of the new covenant to believers.

The Catechism begins by describing Baptism in these words, *the washing with water in the name of the Father, the Son, and the Holy Ghost.* Although the mode of baptism is not dealt with in the Catechism, it is worth a moment of our time to consider this a bit further. In both sacraments of the New Testament there is representation of a reality that is greater than that which we see on the surface. Just as the blood of bulls and goats could not atone for sin, so the actual practice of Baptism cannot wash the soul and make it clean. Therefore, it is proper to symbolize this washing in a way that is appropriate for all believers and their children under any circumstance. Only sprinkling or pouring meet this criteria. In all the sacrifices and ceremonies of the Old Testament, the oil, the water and the blood were all sprinkled on the furnishings of the Tabernacle, and on the priests who served therein. In the prophecies of the Old Testament concerning the new covenant which would come, the same language of sprinkling and pouring was used. For example, in Ezekiel 36 as the inspired Prophet looked to the spiritual restoration of Israel, he quotes God, saying: *I will sprinkle you with clean water, and you will be clean; I will cleanse you from all your filthiness, and from your idols.*

PRAYERS & REMINDERS

_____
_____
_____
_____
_____
_____
_____
_____
_____

Prayer: Thank You, most gracious Lord, for the sprinkling with clean water we have received from Your hand. We are so grateful that the reality of true cleansing that is symbolized with water baptism is ours to claim. In Jesus' name. Amen.

Hymn for the day:
My Faith Looks Up to Thee

Question #94: What is Baptism?

Answer: Baptism is a sacrament, in which the washing with water, in the name of the Father, and of the Son, and of the Holy Spirit, does signify and seal our grafting into Christ, and receiving of the benefits of the Covenant of Grace, and our engagement to be the Lord's.

Scripture Reading: Acts 9:10-19

Baptism by sprinkling or pouring is the mode of baptism that fits best the biblical descriptions in both the Old and New Testaments. Two brief examples will serve to illustrate this. In the tabernacle, the altar and the various implements of worship were ceremonially cleansed by the sprinkling of blood and water. It is not to be imagined that such a ceremony actually cleansed either the altar or the other furnishings of the tabernacle. Rather, this was a symbolic representation that God had purified the tabernacle for His own use. In the New Testament, the baptism of the Apostle Paul is one of the most significant events recorded. The command to Paul was to arise and be baptized and his response was immediate. The Bible says he arose and was baptized. There is no indication he left the location to accompany Ananias to a pool or river. He simply arose and was baptized on the spot. It is an interesting fact that Ananias is only identified as a "certain believer". There is no indication that he was a significant leader in the church, or that he ever had any special recognition for baptizing the most significant convert of the first century. How unlike the twenty first century scene! Can't you imagine if this had happened in the present, Ananias would be praised, interviewed, photographed and have his own website, complete with pictures, and detailed description of how he had been chosen to baptize brother Paul, and maybe even an offer to travel far and wide so that the hand that baptized Paul, can baptize you, too. Seriously, we have to guard our hearts and seek only glory for God, and count our service to Christ as being a duty owed, and love returned.

Prayer: O God, You were pleased to give us the blessing of Baptism and the greater blessing of what it symbolizes. Make that inner cleansing also be an ongoing experience by Your grace and the sacrifice of our Lord Jesus Christ. Amen.

Hymn for the day:
My Hope is Built on Nothing Less

PRAYERS & REMINDERS

Question #94: What is Baptism?

Answer: Baptism is a sacrament, in which the washing with water in the name of the Father, and of the Son, and of the Holy Spirit, does signify and seal our grafting into Christ, and receiving of the benefits of the covenant of grace, and our engagement to be the Lord's.

Scripture Reading: Romans 6:1-11

However, the real significance of Baptism has little to do with the mode or method. It is obvious the mode was not the major preoccupation of the Westminster scholars, since the Shorter Catechism does not speak to this at all. Their intent was to explain what is symbolized by the act of Baptism.

Three things are signified by Baptism as explained in the Shorter Catechism. First of all, there is our ingrafting into Christ. This simply means that Baptism is to show that we have not only identified with Christ but have become part of His body on earth, the Church. The second thing signified by Baptism is that we are partaking the benefits of the covenant of grace. These benefits are several: justification, adoption, regeneration, sanctification, and finally, glorification. So Baptism anticipates things that will take place in the life of believers as well as the gracious acts of God on their behalf. Finally, the Catechism refers to our engagement to be the Lord's. That expression is meant to convey that Baptism is a public announcement of our relationship with Christ. In this ceremony, we publicly and willingly commit ourselves to Christ and to His Kingdom, and by this outward sign we bear testimony to the inward grace which has taken place in our lives.

The Catechism also refers to Baptism as more than just a sign; it is also a seal. This means that beyond the outward ceremony of Baptism, there is real grace imparted to and experienced by the believer. The "engagement to be the Lord's" will be consummated at the wedding feast of the Lamb.

PRAYERS & REMINDERS

_____

_____

_____

_____

_____

_____

_____

_____

_____

Prayer: Father, You have placed Your sign and seal on us in Baptism. By this we have made public our commitment to Christ and His kingdom. By this also You have identified us as being Yours. Thank you, Father, in Jesus' name. Amen.

Hymn for the day:
Loved with Everlasting Love

Question #95: To whom is Baptism to be administered?

Answer: Baptism is not to be administered to any who are out of the visible church, till they profess their faith in Christ and obedience to him; but the infants of those who are members of the visible Church are to be baptized.

Scripture Reading: Joel 2:28-29; Acts 2:38-39

It sounds like an innocent enough question, but the answers have been causes of fundamental division within the Christian church. Before the Reformation, infant baptism was seldom if ever questioned. It was historical fact from the days of the Apostles that believers and their infant seed were baptized into the church. However, in the development of the Reformation, there arose a sect known as the Anabaptists that maintained only believers were to be baptized and then (among many of them) only by immersion. This was an extreme reaction to the abuses of baptism that existed in the medieval church.

The Catechism in answering this question speaks to the issue of the objects of baptism and also the meaning of baptism. We believe it is also proper for the children of believing parents to be baptized. At God's command, Abraham received the sign of the old covenant, which was circumcision. God also commanded him to have his infant son circumcised to indicate that he was a child of the same covenant. Though the covenantal sign has been changed to baptism, the promise given to Abraham and his children is now offered to believers in Christ and their children. In the Presbyterian Church we do not baptize all children but only the children of Christian parents. A child is accepted for baptism even if only one parent is a professing Christian.

Probably every Presbyterian minister has been asked at one time or another, "Will you *christen* our baby next Sunday?" We do not christen children in the church, for that is a rite by which a name is given. We do not confer a name upon a child, but by the name given to the child by the parents we baptize the child into the name of Christ Jesus.

Prayer: O Lord, we are so glad You have included our children in the covenant of grace. Truly Your goodness and promises endure from one generation to another. May the gracious Lord who said, *Let the children come unto me and do not forbid them,* accept our children, too. In His name. Amen.

Hymn for the day:
Our Children, Lord, in Faith and Prayer

PRAYERS & REMINDERS

September 18

Question #95: To whom is Baptism to be administered?

Answer: Baptism is not to be administered to any who are out of the visible church, till they profess their faith in Christ and obedience to him; but the infants of those who are members of the visible Church are to be baptized.

Scripture Reading: Acts 16:25-34

What is the meaning of baptism, especially as it applies to the baptism of infants? First of all, we acknowledge that they are a part of the body of Christ on earth. We refer to our baptized children as noncommuning members. This means they are not entitled to all of the privileges of church membership, but they are acknowledged to be a part of the family. When they come of age they must make their own profession of faith and at that time will be received into the church as full members with all the privileges and rights of membership.

One illustration of this is seen when a child who is born of American parents in a foreign country comes under the protection of the United States government. Until the age of 18, that child is regarded as a citizen by birth, but if he wishes to retain that membership he must sign papers confirming his citizenship before he can vote, and he must also take a vow of allegiance to the United States. This is an excellent illustration of a child's membership in the body of Christ. That child is to be regarded as being a member under the protection and care of the church, but when he comes of age, he must make his own profession of faith and take his vows of membership. This is frequently called validating our baptism. The Jewish people followed this principle too. When their sons reached a certain age, they were fully instructed in the meaning of the covenant, and then had to declare themselves to be "Sons of the Law". This was practiced in the time of Jesus, and so He, too, went through this training and ceremony. So our baptized children must be instructed in the meaning of church membership and confess their own faith in the Lord Jesus before becoming communing members.

PRAYERS & REMINDERS

Prayer: Dear Lord, You have told us that our citizenship is in heaven. So we look for a city whose builder and maker is God. You have placed Your sign and seal on us. We belong to you, and for this we are so very thankful. In Jesus' name. Amen.

Hymn for the day:
Around the Throne of God in Heaven

Question #95: To whom is Baptism to be administered?

Answer: Baptism is not to be administered to any who are out of the visible church, till they profess their faith in Christ and obedience to him; but the infants of those who are members of the visible Church are to be baptized.

Scripture Reading: I Corinthians 7:10-16

The baptism of infants is a sign and seal of the covenant of grace. When we present our children for baptism we claim for them the benefits of the covenant and the blessings which God has promised to believers and their children. The most important of these is found in these words, *I will be a God unto you and unto your children after you throughout all generations.* How blest we are to be able to claim the promises of God for our children. How much we deprive them when we fail to do this. God places great importance on the ordinances which He has ordained for His church. It is not ours to use human "wisdom" to down-play in any way these "sensible signs" of the covenant. In fact, it would seem we are guilty of presumption and even disobedience when we fail to claim God's promises for them, and place on them the privileges and the responsibilities of the covenant.

Finally, we baptize our children as a sign of our own dedication to their upbringing in the Lord. The outward sign then is not only upon the child, but upon the parents who make promises to God on behalf of their children. In this ceremony the parents acknowledge that their child belongs to God and that it is their responsibility to teach their child the truths of the Christian faith. One of the most glorious privileges and solemn responsibilities Christian parents have is to claim the benefits of the covenant for their children as well as themselves. The simple vows taken by believing parents are rich in their meaning, and demanding in the responsibilities placed on the parents of covenant children.

Prayer: Father, we pray that we may honor the vows our parents made for us when we were still infants. We pray that we may also honor the vows we took in behalf of our infant children, and that they may come to faith in the Savior, and faithfully fulfill those vows which they have made. In Jesus' name. Amen.

Hymn for the day:
Baptized Into Your Name Most Holy

PRAYERS & REMINDERS

September 20

Question #96: What is the Lord's Supper?

Answer: The Lord's Supper is a sacrament, in which by giving and receiving bread and wine, according to Christ's direction, His death is shown forth; and the worthy receivers are, not after a corporal and carnal manner, but by faith, made partakers of His body and blood, with all His benefits, to their spiritual nourishment and growth in grace.

Scripture Reading: Matthew 26:26-30

When the Catechism explains the meaning of the Lord's Supper, it begins by mentioning the elements involved. According to the Catechism, bread and wine are given and received. There is an ongoing debate in Christian circles as to the exact nature of the substance of the cup. Nowhere in Scripture is this clearly stated. Ordinarily the expression the cup is all that is used. The only other words were the words of Jesus when He referred to the contents of the cup as "fruit of the vine."

Probably more has been made than is wise or necessary over this matter. However, a word of caution is in order for those who insist on the use of wine. People who have had a problem with alcoholism in the past have mentioned to me on several occasions that both the taste and the odor of the wine has been a real stumbling block for them in the observation of the Lord's Supper. This should cause us to be very careful lest in the observation of the Lord's Supper occasion be given for unnecessary temptation to be placed before a weaker brother. Certainly in situations in which it is known that alcoholics are present, it would seem best to avoid fermented wine. At the very least the alternative of non-alcoholic grape juice should be made available and made known by instruction from the host pastor. Having said all this, the proper observation of the Lord's Supper goes far beyond the question of juice verses real wine. There are also those who believe that only unleavened bread should be used in the Lord's Supper. Again, this is a detail which should be left up to conscience trained by the truth of God's Word, and need not be a matter of controversy.

Prayer: Father, help us to see beyond the outward symbols, and understand that which they represent. Help us to constantly feed upon Christ by faith and be strengthened to live for Your glory. For Jesus' sake. Amen.

Hymn for the day:
When I Survey the Wondrous Cross

Question #96: What is the Lord's Supper?

Answer: The Lord's Supper is a sacrament, in which by giving and receiving bread and wine, according to Christ's direction, His death is shown forth; and the worthy receivers are, not after a corporal and carnal manner, but by faith, made partakers of His body and blood, with all His benefits, to their spiritual nourishment and growth in grace.

Scripture Reading: Mark 14:12-26

The Catechism, in explaining the meaning of the elements, mentions two basic truths. First, that the giving of the bread and the wine are a showing forth of the death of Christ. Presbyterians have always rejected the doctrines of transubstantiation and consubstantiation as being unBiblical. While we believe that the elements themselves simply represent the body and blood of Christ, we believe that it is a true representation, and although Christ is not present in the physical sense, He is most surely present in a spiritual sense. Therefore, when we feed physically upon the elements, we are feeding spiritually upon the reality of Christ and His atonement. Furthermore the Catechism tells us that we are made partakers by faith of His body and blood and all His benefits. To partake of the body and blood of Christ is to have a part in His body the church and to be in the family of God. The Apostle Paul said in Romans 8:17 that we are heirs of God and joint heirs with Christ.

When we think of the benefits that Christ has given to His people, we think in terms of forgiveness and justification. In this way the Lord's Supper becomes a means of grace to communicate to us the blessings of salvation. Remember the Passover event in the book of Exodus? The slain lamb, whose blood protected the Israelites from the death angel, also provided the food which would strengthen them for the long journey towards the promised land. Every time Israel celebrated the Passover from then on, there was a reminder of the death of the lamb of God, whose shed blood had protected them from death, and whose body provided food and strength. By the elements of the Lord's Supper, we too are reminded of these same truths.

Prayer: Faithful Savior, as we partake of the holy supper You have given us, we would be reminded of Your sacrifice, and by faith we would partakers of Your flesh and blood with all the benefits of that spiritual feast. Amen.

Hymn for the day:
Beneath the Cross of Jesus

PRAYERS & REMINDERS

September 22

Question #96: What is the Lord's Supper?

Answer: The Lord's Supper is a sacrament in which, by giving and receiving bread and wine, according to Christ's direction, His death is shown forth; and the worthy receivers are, not after a corporal and carnal manner, but by faith, made partakers of His body and blood, with all His benefits, to their spiritual nourishment and growth in grace.

Scripture Reading: Luke 22:14-23

The expressions *spiritual nourishment* and *growth in grace* naturally go together. When the child is nourished physically, that child grows physically as well. When believers are spiritually nourished, they also grow in grace and in likeness to Christ. So the Lord's Supper then becomes one of the ways in which we grow as believers. It is sad but true that Protestants in general and Presbyterians in particular have tended to minimize the importance of the Lord's Supper and thus have denied themselves one form of spiritual nourishment and the growth that results from it.

When the elders in Geneva denied John Calvin's request to include the Lord's Supper in every worship service and limited its observation to four times a year, they set a pattern for Presbyterians that has been to our detriment. When we properly prepare ourselves and instruct our people in the true meaning of the Lord's supper, then a more frequent observation of this sacrament would seem to be in order. In many Reformed and Presbyterian churches the Lord's supper is celebrated on at least a monthly basis, and in some churches more often. But just an increase in frequency of celebration alone will not assure us of added blessing from this holy meal. Indeed it could even lessen our understanding and appreciation of it unless we are careful. We are spiritually nourished by this sacred meal only as we more fully understand what we are doing and why, when we come to the table. It is by understanding the Scriptures related to the Lord's supper, and acting upon this knowledge and the Biblical instructions that we are spiritually nourished and thus grow in grace.

PRAYERS & REMINDERS

Prayer: Help us O Lord to grow in grace and knowledge of You through Your Word, and Sacraments. Enable us to fully appropriate by faith all that You intend for us in these blessed sacraments. In the name of Jesus Christ our Lord. Amen.

Hymn for the day:
A Parting Hymn We Sing

Question #97: What is required to be worthy of receiving the Lord's Supper?

Answer: It is required of those who would receive the Lord's Supper worthily that they examine themselves, as to their knowledge to discern the Lord's body, as to their faith to feed on Him, and as to their repentance, love, and new obedience; lest, coming unworthily, they eat and drink judgment on themselves.

Scripture Reading: John 13:18-38

Who is worthy to come to the Lord's table? The answer is simple: No one is worthy. Who may come to the Lord's table in a worthy manner? All believers may partake in a worthy manner, but not all do so.

The question of worthiness to partake of the Lord's Supper has been a thorny issue and a matter of debate from the beginning of the Christian church. There have been (predictably) two extremes on the question and, like most extremes, both are wrong.

Some err on the side of having no restrictions placed on the Lord's table. In some churches there is never a word of warning, exhortation, or even explanation for those who come to the Lord's table. John Calvin insisted that all who came to the table must be endeavoring to lead holy lives, and he attempted to deny this supper to the city fathers of Geneva who seemed to have no knowledge of salvation, or any evidence of repentance. His insistence on proper preparation and forbidding the unrepentant from coming to the table resulted in Calvin's banishment from Geneva by the resentful city fathers. Three years later, when Calvin was restored as the spiritual leader of the church in Geneva, the Lord's supper was celebrated with much more understanding of the need for faith and repentance as requisites for partaking. It is hoped that we too would take this privilege and responsibility much more seriously than we do, and thus receive greater blessing. There may even be times when you feel led to discipline yourself by refraining from the Lord's table until you confess and repent of your sins.

Prayer: Lord, You have told us that if we would judge ourselves we would not be judged, but rather disciplined that we might not be condemned along with unbelievers. May we sincerely do so. In Jesus' name. Amen.

Hymn for the day:
Not Worthy, Lord, To Gather Up The Crumbs

PRAYERS & REMINDERS

Question #97: What is required to be worthy of receiving the Lord's Supper?

Answer: It is required of those who would receive the Lord's Supper worthily that they examine themselves, as to their knowledge to discern the Lord's body, as to their faith to feed on Him, and as to their repentance, love, and new obedience; lest coming unworthily, they eat and drink judgment on themselves.

Scripture Reading: I Corinthians 11:17-22

There are those who, in their zeal to "fence the table," make it all but impossible for any, save a select few believers, to partake of the Lord's Supper. In the early days of my own ministry, I served a congregation of people who had been taught that no one should come to the Lord's table unless they were totally free from sin. So on a given Communion Sabbath, out of a congregation of well over one hundred, no more than a half-dozen or so would ever partake of the Lord's Supper.

The Apostle Paul dealt with this whole question when he wrote to the church in Corinth. He warned against a frivolous observation of the Lord's Supper and instructed all those who would participate to examine themselves. You will note that Paul did not tell believers to examine each other, but rather to examine their own hearts. There has been a tendency in Presbyterian circles to reverse that priority. I am not saying it is improper for Sessions to exercise spiritual leadership or even discipline, but self-examination is the primary requisite in preparation for the Lord's Supper. The responsibility of the Pastor to; (1) instruct believers; (2) encourage the weak, and (3) warn the heedless is absolutely necessary at each communion service. We have to be careful to keep a balance between the three, but all are needed. The Lord's Supper emphasizes God's saving grace above all else, and motivates us to respond to grace with gratitude and obedience. Let's make sure we properly prepare ourselves to come to the Lord's table.

Prayer: Father, help us to examine ourselves in light of Your word. Search us and try us O Lord, and see if there is any wicked way in us, and lead us in the way everlasting. Through Jesus Christ our Lord. Amen.

Hymn for the day:
O Jesus, Thou Art Standing

PRAYERS & REMINDERS

_____

_____

_____

_____

_____

_____

_____

_____

_____

> **Question #97: What is required to be worthy of receiving the Lord's Supper?**

Answer: It is required of those who would receive the Lord's Supper worthily that they examine themselves, as to their knowledge to discern the Lord's body, as to their faith to feed on Him, and as to their repentance, love, and new obedience; lest coming unworthily, they eat and drink judgment on themselves.

Scripture Reading: I Corinthians 11:23-34

The Catechism emphasizes proper preparation for communion when we are exhorted to examine ourselves as to knowledge, faith, repentance, love, and obedience, before coming to the table of our Lord. The knowledge that we are instructed to have is the knowledge that enables us to understand what we do when we come to the table and what the elements signify. This is one reason why traditionally Presbyterians have required covenant children to be trained and examined by the session before they are admitted to the Lord's table. In some circles of Presbyterianism, this time-honored practice is being abandoned and even the smallest of children, who understand little if anything about the meaning of the Lord's Supper, are allowed to participate. This would seem to violate both our own standards, and the clear teaching of Scripture. This is just one example of how the thinking of the world creeps into the counsels of the church. In this present generation there is a tendency to put aside any thought that there are some things which are appropriate for children only as they mature and develop beyond early childhood. One extreme example of this is seen in the promotion of the most detailed sex education programs, even for kindergarten children. Believers know it is inappropriate for our children of any age to receive such instructions in the context of an amoral culture for which there are no restraints, and no absolutes of right and wrong. But this idea is especially reprehensible for very young children. For believing parents to insist on their very young children to be allowed to partake of the Lord's Supper before being examined by the Elders of the church as to their understanding, and ability to "discern the Lord's body" may be one example of how the thinking of the world intrudes into the church. May God protect us!

Prayer: Guard our minds dear Lord. Spare us from the foolish wisdom of this world, and teach us Your pure and true wisdom. How beautifully You have shown us our Savior in the blessed sacrament. Amen.

Hymn for the day:
Father, We Thank You for the Night

PRAYERS & REMINDERS

Question #97: What is required to be worthy of receiving the Lord's Supper?

Answer: It is required of those who would receive the Lord's Supper worthily that they examine themselves, as to their knowledge to discern the Lord's body, as to their faith to feed on Him, and as to their repentance, love, and new obedience; lest coming unworthily, they eat and drink judgment on themselves.

Scripture Reading: I Corinthians 11:27-34

Another requirement for worthy participation in the Lord's Supper is repentance. When we examine ourselves in light of God's Word, the most obvious thing we discover is that we are all sinful people and need forgiveness. Repentance means that we acknowledge this and seek God's pardoning grace and His power to overcome the sin in our lives.

We are also required to renew our love, faith, and obedience. None of us love the Lord as we should, nor is our faith as strong as it ought to be. However, the Lord's Supper affords a wonderful time to pledge again our love to Christ, to renew our faith, and to determine the practice of more faithful obedience. It is interesting to note the Larger Catechism encourages weak, doubting Christians to come to the Lord's table in order that their faith might be strengthened and their doubt resolved. If we did more to encourage this, we might find our people blessed and strengthened by participation in the Lord's Supper, rather than being discouraged by their insufficiencies. One of the lingering effects of perfectionism in its various forms is an unhealthy preoccupation with our own sinfulness rather then a full trusting in the merits of Christ, and the forgiveness He has won for us. The Devil loves to take advantage of our wounded conscience and afflicted the forgiven sinner with doubts and fears about his/her salvation. Of course the Holy Spirit convicts of sin, and we are commanded to examine ourselves that we might confess and repent. But the doubts we raise about ourselves in this process may, and often does, lead us to doubt the promises of our Lord. The Lord's Supper enables us to focus on Christ and His saving transforming power, rather than on our miserable selves.

Prayer: Gracious Lord Jesus, we look into our own hearts and often despair, for the good we would, we do not, and the evil we would not that we do. But we look to You and see our hope in Your shed blood. Amen.

Hymn for the day:
Jesus, Thy Blood and Righteousness

PRAYERS & REMINDERS

September 27

Question #98: What is prayer?

Answer: Prayer is an offering up of our desires to God, for things agreeable to His will, in the name of Christ, with confession of our sins, and thankful acknowledgment of His mercies.

Scripture Reading: Psalm 62

The three means of grace mentioned in the Catechism are the Word, the sacraments, and prayer. We come now to the last of these—prayer.

In the Shorter Catechism we have an answer to the question: What is prayer? This shows the Shorter Catechism at its finest. The answer to this ninety-eighth question ranks in quality with the magnificent first question and answer.

The practice of prayer requires an understanding of its essential nature and that's what makes this statement from the Catechism so important. Here we have precise instructions on the nature of prayer, the manner of prayer, and the content of prayer. The expression, *offering up* is the language of sacrifice borrowed from the Old Testament. The Patriarch Abraham was willing to offer up Isaac, his beloved son, in obedience to God's call. All through the Old Testament we hear over and over again about sacrifices being offered up to the Lord. Now when the Catechism uses the expression, *offering up* in relation to prayers, we see that prayer is a sacrifice in a very real sense of the word. Prayer is offered up before the righteous and Holy God who Himself has provided the once for all perfect sacrifice by the gift of His beloved Son to take away our sin and guilt. It is offered up in the same spirit of humility and of faith that because of Christ's sacrifice, our prayers are heard and answered according to the will of God. As you go to the Lord in prayer now, make your prayer a sacrifice, a holy offering to God of your life and will to Him and His kingdom. Then you may make known your petitions, your praise, and your grateful expectation that he will hear and answer.

Prayer: Holy Father, Your Son paid for our salvation by offering up His life for us poor sinners. We come now to offer up our prayers and praise to You, the God of our salvation. We humbly ask that You will accept our prayers and our prayers. In Jesus' name. Amen.

Hymn for the day:
From Every Stormy Wind That Blows

PRAYERS & REMINDERS

Question #98: What is prayer?

Answer: Prayer is an offering up of our desires to God for things agreeable to His will, in the name of Christ, with confession of our sins, and thankful acknowledgment of His mercies.

Scripture Reading: Philippians 4:4-9

First of all, the Catechism acknowledges the reality of our communication with God through prayer. Because prayer is an offering up of our desires unto God, this implies both an emotional and knowledgeable exercise. Prayer must never be offered to any save God alone. As Protestants and Presbyterians, we reject the concept of praying to the saints. However, upon closer examination, we will discover that many of our public prayers are precisely that. Far too often we are more aware of those with whom we pray than Him to whom we pray. While we should pray for the benefit of others who hear our prayers, we must never fall into the trap of praying to be heard and seen by them. The perfect model of public prayer is the high priestly prayer of our Lord. There in the presence of His disciples, the Lord Jesus lifted up His eyes and heart to heaven and prayed to the Father. Every word He spoke was addressed directly to the Father, and every word was a blessing and encouragement to His disciples. He obviously wanted them to hear His every word spoken to the Father. The Holy Spirit brought to John's mind every word the Lord had prayed on that night so long ago. Under the Spirit's guidance, John carefully wrote down all those blessed prayer words, so that we too, like those faithful men who were with Him in the garden, might also hear His prayer to the Father. How impoverished we would be without this most precious of all prayers. How impoverished our children are who do not hear their parents pray for them every day. I still remember more of my parent's prayers than any other thing they taught me through their teachings. Will our children remember us for the prayers they heard us pray?

PRAYERS & REMINDERS

_____

_____

_____

_____

_____

_____

_____

_____

_____

Prayer: Thank You gracious Lord that You heard the request from Your Disciples of old, *Lord, teach us to pray.* We thank You that when You answered that request, You also have taught us how to pray. You are the Door through which we enter into the Father's presence. Amen.

Hymn for the day:
Come, My Soul, Thy Suit Prepare

Question #98: What is prayer?

Answer: Prayer is an offering up of our desires to God for things agreeable to His will, in the name of Christ, with confession of our sins, and thankful acknowledgment of His mercies.

Scripture Reading: I John 5:14-17

When we bring our desires before the Lord, we are to do so openly and sincerely. At the same time, these desires must be tempered by two important considerations: the will of God and the name of Christ. These two considerations are closely entwined. To pray for things according to the will of God is to pray for those things for which Jesus taught us to pray. Why is it so important to pray in the name of Christ? The answer is twofold. Christ is the sinless and perfect and only mediator between God and man, while we are sinful and cannot enter the presence of the Holy God apart from Christ's righteousness and intercession. It is also important to pray in His name and seek from the Father only those things which will honor that name. Thoughtful consideration of all that our Lord taught us by His life and ministry will temper our prayers, and lead us closer to the ideal He taught us by word and deed. How could I possibly pray selfishly and heedlessly of others and close my prayer in Jesus' name? How could I fervently pray for Him to pardon and forgive me, if I refuse to forgive from my heart those who have offended me?

Knowing the will of God will only come from careful and continual study of His Word. Yet knowing that will is possible as we diligently study the Ten Commandments, the Sermon on the Mount, and the other discourses of Jesus, the Epistles of the New Testament, and the Prophets of the Old Testament. We may not find direct answers to each decision we face, and indeed we will not. But we are given guiding principles which enable us to make choices which will honor the Lord.

Prayer: Father, may we never sink so low that we will insist that our will be done, rather than Your will. We know that Your will is far better than our will. Help us to joyfully seek only Your will in our lives. For Jesus' sake. Amen.

Hymn for the day:
The Lord's Prayer

PRAYERS & REMINDERS

_____
_____
_____
_____
_____
_____
_____
_____
_____
_____

Question #98: What is prayer?

Answer: Prayer is an offering up of our desires to God for things agreeable to His will, in the name of Christ, with confession of our sins, and thankful acknowledgment of His mercies.

Scripture Reading: Psalm 92

The content of all our prayers may be summed up in three phrases: *Offering up of our desires; Confession of our sins*; and *Thankful acknowledgment of his mercies*. It is so very important that we not allow the confession of sin and the offering up of our desires to consume all of our time in prayer. Of course, these things are important, but not so important that we can afford to ignore the thankful acknowledgment of God's mercies. This means that much of our time in prayer should be spent in praise and adoration. We should thank God for His own character and faithfulness. We should thank Him for His mighty works of creation and redemption, and, as we seek His blessing, we should also thank Him without ceasing for the blessings already received. If we really understand and practice what the Catechism teaches about prayer, we will discover a greatly enriched prayer life and a closeness to the Lord which we have not known before.

If you feel inadequate to express your praise and adoration, then turn to the book of Psalms, for there you will discover in God's perfect word, the words you need to express the thoughts of your mind, and the joys of your heart. You don't need to stop with just the Psalms, as helpful as they are. You can go to the Prophets, such as Isaiah and Daniel, and all the others and find glowing phrases of praise you may adopt as your own. And if these are not enough, turn to the Epistles and read the ascriptions of praise you will find in each one of them. Finally, walk into the throne room of the book of Revelation, and you will see and hear soaring words of praise and adoration. Try it. You will like it!

PRAYERS & REMINDERS

_____
_____
_____
_____
_____
_____
_____
_____
_____
_____

Prayer: O Living Word of the Father, thank You for the wonderful passages from the written word which gives to us words to sing Your praise, and to offer our thanksgiving in Your holy name. Amen.

Hymn for the day:
Praise the Lord, Ye Heavens Adore Him

Question #99: What rule has God given for our direction in prayer?

Answer: The whole Word of God is of use to direct us in prayer; but the special rule of direction is the form of prayer that Christ taught His disciples, commonly called "the Lord's Prayer."

Scripture Reading: Luke 22:39-46

The Catechism mentions prayer as a means of grace. While it may not be technically correct to regard prayer as a means of grace, it is certainly a most essential part of worship. It is also undeniably an avenue of great blessing.

When the question is asked, what rule has God given us for our direction in prayer, it is interesting to note that the *Larger Catechism* refers to prayer as a duty while the *Shorter Catechism* does not use the word, though it supports the *Larger Catechism* in the concept that prayer is a duty as well as a privilege. As someone has said, a prayerless person is essentially a Godless person.

However, unless our prayers are guided by the Word of God and aided by the Spirit of God, they may go far astray from the will of God. There is a tendency in some evangelical circles to use prayer as a demand on God. It is not too rare to hear people say, *In the name of Jesus, I demand that this person be healed*, or a similar statement. Such prayer is not Biblical and insults God's sovereignty. No one has any claim on God except that which His sovereign grace confers. There are many examples in Scripture of urgent desperate prayers, but no examples of anyone demanding that God answer a request, however urgent that request may have been. When our Lord was praying in the Garden of Gethsemane His heart was broken, He was filled with anxiety and dread, yet still He prayed, *Not my will but Thine be done.* When He was hanging on the cross and His enemies mocked Him and demanded that if He was the Christ, He must come down from the cross, still He demanded nothing of the Father, but offered submission and accepted the just punishment which was due us for our sins.

Prayer: Lord Jesus, even as we pray, "Teach us to pray," we are reminded that You have already taught us this throughout Your Word and by Your example. Help us to lovingly come into Your presence often and eager to commune with You. Amen.

Hymn for the day:
The Lord's Prayer

PRAYERS & REMINDERS

Question #99: What rule has God given for our direction in prayer?

Answer: The whole Word of God is of use to direct us in prayer; but the special rule of direction is the form of prayer that Christ taught his disciples, commonly called "the Lord's Prayer."

Scripture Reading: Matthew 6:9-15

Our Catechism teaches us that the whole Word of God is to be used as a primer on prayer. To be able to pray according to Scripture requires us to know Scripture and especially those parts of Scripture that deal with prayer. We find the prayers of God's people recorded in the Word from the very beginning to the end. One of the more profitable ways to learn to pray is to study these prayers and to learn to pray as men of old. Daniel's prayers are outstanding examples of effective prayers of intercession and confession of sin. Many Psalms are prayers and it is appropriate to adopt the language and spirit found in the Psalms. Every possible form of prayer may be found in the Psalms. There are prayers of praise and adoration. There are prayers of deep contrition and sorrow for sin. There are prayers of fear and frustration, of depression and gloom. There are prayers of petition for help and blessing. There are even prayers for God to overcome and punish evildoers and enemies of His people.

The Catechism, however, points us in particular to the Lord's Prayer as our model. Again, the Larger Catechism addresses the question of how the Lord's Prayer is to be used. It points to the Lord's Prayer as a pattern, but also as a prayer that may be offered by believers. Our primary concern in the study of the Lord's Prayer will be to learn how it may be used as a pattern for all our praying. However, we will also attempt to understand the words themselves, since we pray this prayer so often. May it never become just a routine or ritual. May it always be a prayer from our minds and hearts, a prayer we truly pray and not just recite.

PRAYERS & REMINDERS

_____

_____

_____

_____

_____

_____

_____

_____

_____

Prayer: Gracious Lord Jesus Christ, You have taught us to pray this perfect prayer which You, Yourself gave to us long ago. Thank you for the words and the spirit You have set before us, that we may pray aright, and learn to pattern all our prayers after this one. Amen.

Hymn for the day:
Prayer is the Soul's Sincere Desire

Question #99: What rule has God given for our direction in prayer?

Answer: The whole Word of God is of use to direct us in prayer; but the special rule of direction is the form of prayer that Christ taught his disciples, commonly called "the Lord's Prayer."

Scripture Reading: Matthew 7:7-12

In the Lord's Prayer, we discover that prayer is to be addressed to God and to God as our Father. The Lord's Prayer is the prayer, therefore, of children. There is an exclusiveness about the Lord's Prayer because not everyone may properly address God as heavenly Father. This is a right reserved for believers in Jesus Christ and for them alone. So the beginning point of prayer is to make sure of the proper relationship with God that affords us a hearing. While it may be true that in the general sense God hears the prayers of all people, this is true only in a very general sense. Certainly God is aware of all prayers for He is all-knowing. But true communication and fellowship come only through our Lord Jesus Christ. Some people object to the use of the Lord's Prayer in corporate worship on the grounds that not everyone who attends church is necessarily a believer. It seems to me that this is unnecessarily judgmental. God knows those who are His and accepts their prayers as a Father hearing his children. The church is the body of Christ on earth; and, therefore, it is proper for the church to address the Father in the language which was taught us by our Lord Jesus Christ.

Little children learn to pray this prayer long before they understand the meaning of it, or even before they understand the meaning of salvation. Should we prohibit our children from saying this prayer before they come to the knowledge of Christ and salvation? Of course not. So let us not be too quick to criticize the public use of this prayer on the grounds someone might say these words who is not a believer. For Christians, it is not enough just to say the words of the Lord's Prayer, but to be taught the art of prayer by its form, its content, and its spirit. These things we will explore further in our study.

Prayer: Father, we are so thankful that You are more eager to answer our prayers than we are to pray. You delight to give good gifts to Your children, and we delight in Your gifts to us, especially the gift of the Holy Spirit, by whom we are born anew. In Jesus' name. Amen.

Hymn for the day:
What a Friend We Have in Jesus

PRAYERS & REMINDERS

Question #100: *What does the preface of the Lord's Prayer teach us?*

Answer: The preface of the Lord's Prayer, which is, "Our Father in heaven," teaches us to draw near to God with all holy reverence and confidence, as children to a father, able and ready to help us; and that we should pray with and for others.

Scripture Reading: Luke 11:1-13

The Lord's Prayer is an answer to prayer. It was given at the request of Jesus' disciples who said, *Lord, teach us to pray.* This is how Jesus taught His disciples and us to pray. If we follow His formula for prayer and understand its meaning, we will truly know how to pray. If we know how to pray, we will know God. He will bless us. All the infinite resources of heaven will be placed at our disposal. Our faith will increase and we will develop a warm and personal relationship with the living God.

The preface to the Lord's prayer teaches us that we may address God as our Father; however, this is not an open invitation to people apart from Christ. We must remember that Jesus taught His disciples to pray in this manner. He was the one who said, *No man comes to the Father but by Me.* The privilege of calling God our Father is a gift from Jesus Christ to those who love and trust Him as their Savior and Lord. We probably have no idea how wonderful it is to belong to God, and to be His own beloved children. We say *Our Father* so easily, without thinking the price our Lord Jesus paid to make this possible, and to reconcile us to God. In the very depths of His suffering, when His soul was made an offering for sin, Jesus cried out from the cross, *My God, My God, why hast Thou forsaken me?* Because He was willing to bear that dreadful curse for our sins, we may know with confidence that God will never forsake us. Not only so, but for now and forever we have been given the right to call God, *Our Father,* and to avail ourselves of His infinite resources of provision and help for every need. What a blessing! How sad that we use such a precious gift so seldom!

Prayer. O Father, to think that we who are so sinful and lacking any righteousness of our own are able to be Your beloved children. How wonderful that You have given us the right to pray, and the understanding of how to pray. We are so indebted to our Savior, and we pray in His name alone. Amen.

Hymn for the day:
How Sweet the Name of Jesus Sounds

PRAYERS & REMINDERS

_____

_____

_____

_____

_____

_____

_____

_____

_____

October 5

> **Question #100: What does the preface of the Lord's Prayer teach us?**

Answer: The preface of the Lord's Prayer, which is, "Our Father in heaven," teaches us to draw near to God with all holy reverence and confidence, as children to a father, able and ready to help us; and that we should pray with and for others.

Scripture Reading: John 14:1-18

Christ made it very clear in His teaching that not everyone can call God Father. He even said to those who opposed Him, *You are of your father, the devil.* He constantly reminded His disciples that there is coming a day of final separation, which will divide people for all time. Some will go to be with their Father in heaven and others will be expelled from His presence. So as soon as we begin to pray, *Our Father,* we are to pause and ask, *Is He my Father? Have I claimed His Son as my Savior so that I may call Him Father?*

Once this issue is settled and we know that we belong to Jesus Christ, then we may truly call God our Father and know that He loves and cares for us. We may be assured that He is more eager to bless us than we are to receive the blessing. We may know that our sins have been forgiven and that we have a Father and a home; our Father's house of many mansions.

In this world, our parents bear us, raise us, and pray for us, but sooner or later they pass on and we are left without their love and comfort. But our Father in heaven will always be our loving parent. He never changes. He does not grow old, nor does he grow weary of our constant need of Him and dependence upon Him. As earthly parents we try to train our children to be less and less dependent upon us as they mature and grow. But our Heavenly Father teaches us to be more and more dependent upon Him, and more submissive to His will. The mark of maturity as believers is that we become less and less dependent upon ourselves, and more dependent on God, our Father.

Prayer: O Lord our God, You have called us to Yourself. You have adopted us into Your family. You have caused us to be regenerated and born anew by Your mighty power. You are truly our Father because Your only begotten Son is our Savior. In His name we pray. Amen.

Hymn for the day:
Children of the Heavenly Father

PRAYERS & REMINDERS

Question #100: What does the preface of the Lord's Prayer teach us?

Answer: The preface of the Lord's Prayer, which is, "Our Father in heaven," teaches us to draw near to God with all holy reverence and confidence, as children to a father, able and ready to help us; and that we should pray with and for others.

Scripture Reading: Hebrews 12:3-11

When we pray, *Our Father,* we do not stop there but go on to say, *who art in heaven.* This adds a dimension to our prayer life that is sorely missing in many prayers. Yes, we may have an intimate, personal relationship with God and we may call Him our Father, but He is also the Almighty, the ever living God of eternity, sovereign in all His ways. He is the great and able God to whom we come when we pray, *Our Father who art in heaven.* He is able to do far more abundantly than we are able to ask or think. He has a perfect will and the power to perform it. He knows just what answer to your prayer is best for you and will accomplish His will in your life. When you pray, you pray to a holy, almighty and powerful God who in Jesus Christ has become your Father in heaven.

The words, *who art in heaven,* are especially important in a culture which has glorified the macho man image to the extent that the traditional role of fathers has been greatly damaged in the minds of many. How will a little boy who has seen his earthly father play the role of a selfish tyrant ever have a proper understanding of God as a Father without the words, *who art in heaven?* How will a little girl be able to understand the beauty and wonder of her heavenly Father, when her earthly father ignores her, or worse? We must never limit our understanding of God as our Father to the image we have of earthly fathers. Even the best of men and fathers fall far, far short of the ideal we find in God alone. Thank God for godly earthly fathers, but God, our Father in heaven, is the one perfect Father and the ideal role model for all who are called father on earth.

Prayer: Father, we are so very grateful that we have a Father in heaven who loves with a perfect love, and who cares and provides for us so abundantly. Help all who are earthly fathers to strive constantly to follow the example of our heavenly Father in loving care for their families. In Jesus' name. Amen.

Hymn for the day:
This Is My Father's World

PRAYERS & REMINDERS

_____

_____

_____

_____

_____

_____

_____

_____

_____

> ## Question #100: What does the preface of the Lord's Prayer teach us?

Answer: The preface of the Lord's Prayer, which is, "Our Father in heaven," teaches us to draw near to God with all holy reverence and confidence, as children to a father, able and ready to help us; and that we should pray with and for others.

Scripture Reading: I Corinthians 10:1-13

This Father loves you. He knows you, and both His knowledge and His love are perfect. Your every need is known before you request His help. Every tear that falls from your eye is felt by Him. He hears every weary sigh, every inward groan. He desires to heal you. He waits for you with eager arms of love and acceptance. He has given you His Son; will He not also freely give you all things? When you pray, be still and know that He is God. Before you confess a single sin, before you ask one blessing for yourself or another, call upon your Father in heaven. Be aware that you are in His presence, rejoice in Him, and be glad.

Know also that His gracious love may be expressed in His Fatherly discipline of His children. The father on earth who fails to discipline his children according to God's Word demonstrates a lack of love for them. Unfortunately we often react to God's fatherly discipline of us, just as little spoiled children react to parental discipline. We whine and complain that "life isn't fair", by which we really mean, "God isn't treating me fairly." I often hear people complain, "What have I done to deserve this?" when hurtful things happen in their lives. Of course none of these things make us happy, but when we realize God's purpose for us is always for the good end of making us like our Savior, we may endure these hurtful things in patience and hope. God will do everything necessary to prepare us for heaven, and he will bring us there in His good time.

When you pray, say, *Our Father, who art in heaven.*

Prayer: Father in heaven, we love You who first loved us. You delight to give us the good gifts. Help us to know that all Your gifts to us are good and for our good because our heavenly Father loves us. In Jesus' name. Amen.

Hymn for the day:
Day By Day, and With Each Passing Moment

PRAYERS & REMINDERS

Question #101: For what do we pray in the first petition?

Answer: In the first petition, which is, "Hallowed be your name," we pray that God would enable us, and others, to glorify Him in all the means by which he makes Himself known, and that he would arrange all things to His own glory.

Scripture Reading: John 12:27-36

One of the great lessons of the Lord's Prayer is to be found in its order. In this prayer, first things come first, and each part logically follows the other. There is the beauty of symmetry in this prayer, and the even greater beauty of truth.

The first petition focuses not upon the need of the one who prays, but on the God to whom we pray. This is always a must in true prayer. If our attention is not focused upon the Lord, our prayers are little more than wishes spoken aloud. But if we are aware of the great God before whom we come, then prayer is a reality of communication and relationship with the Most High. So when you pray, think first of God, your heavenly Father.

We began our devotional walk through the Shorter Catechism at the beginning of the year, with the first question and answer. *What is the chief end of man? Man's chief end is to glorify God and enjoy Him forever.* Now as we consider this first petition in the Lord's Prayer, we are brought back once more to the beginning. If our highest purpose in life is to glorify God and enjoy Him forever, then it follows that our first concern in prayer is to seek the honor and glory of our great Father in heaven. Thus we begin by praying *Hallowed be Thy name.* This is a request that God would be glorified and that His great name would be honored by our prayers and by our lives. This is a large prayer. By that I mean we do not just pray for God's name to be hallowed by us, but that he would be recognized and honored by all His creatures and creation throughout the whole world. The whole purpose of the life and ministry of the Lord Jesus was that His Father and ours would be honored and glorified. This is our prayer and purpose too.

Prayer: Great Father in heaven, our heart's desire and petition is that You would be honored, extolled, and glorified throughout the whole world, and by all Your creatures. But Lord let this begin with us who claim You as our beloved Father in heaven. We pray this in Jesus' name and for His sake. Amen.

Hymn for the day:
Immortal, Invisible

PRAYERS & REMINDERS

Question #101: For what do we pray in the first petition?

Answer: In the first petition, which is, "Hallowed be your name," we pray that God would enable us, and others, to glorify Him in all the means by which he makes Himself known, and he would arrange all things to His own glory.

Scripture Reading: Psalm 62

I think it would be clear to all the readers of this devotional guide that this prayer is truly for children only, and we are only children of the Father by faith in His Son, the Lord Jesus Christ. For children, the Father Himself is our first concern in prayer. Our desire is to know Him and to glorify Him. This petition expresses that desire. By these words we are asking that we, and, indeed all people, might truly know God through His own self-revelation, and that knowing Him, we might also honor and glorify Him.

In the Bible we meet the one true God who is Creator and Savior. He is sovereign, gracious, and holy. He is the one who said, *Let there be*, and the universe came into existence. Yet He is also the Good Shepherd who tenderly cares for His sheep and seeks out those who have gone astray to return them to the fold again. He is the God of the covenant who works all things together for good to those who love Him, to those who are called according to His purpose. So when we pray, *Hallowed be thy name*, we are asking that we may know Him as He thus reveals Himself. The psalmist sings, *O magnify the Lord with me, and let us exalt his name together.* We do not, and, indeed, cannot, add to the glory and greatness of His name, but we may, and must, ascribe to Him that greatness and glory. We are commanded to proclaim His name and wonders throughout the whole earth. Furthermore, we who are called by the name of His Son (Christians) pray that our lives may indeed honor that great name. This commitment to the honor and glory of our great God must lie at the very core of our being.

Prayer: Father, our desire is to magnify and glorify Your holy name. We know that we cannot add to Your glory, but by Your grace we may and must exalt Your name, and that is our heart-felt desire and prayer we offer in Jesus' name and for His sake. Amen.

Hymn for the day:
All That I Am, I Owe to Thee

PRAYERS & REMINDERS

Question #101: For what do we pray in the first petition?

Answer: In the first petition, which is, "Hallowed be your name," we pray that God would enable us, and others, to glorify Him in all the means by which he makes Himself known, and he would arrange all things to His own glory.

Scripture Reading: Revelation 4

Lack of reverence for God's name is one of the most terrible sins of this generation. Be warned! God will not hold him guiltless who takes His name in vain. Profanity and blasphemy are so common that some people never hear the name of our God save when it is taken in vain. What a tragedy! We pray that the name of God may be reverenced, for the name of God reveals the character of God.

All other petitions flow from this one. Whatever requests we may bring before the Lord must honor Him and His great name by which we make our requests known. We have no right to ask for anything that in anyway dishonors God and does not contribute to His glory and honor.

This is a petition of great hope and promise. For when we pray, *Hallowed be thy name*, we are reminded that the day will come when every knee shall bow and every tongue confess that Jesus Christ is Lord, to the glory of God the Father. When we read through the book of Revelation, we find that the conflict between good and evil, God and His enemies, will end in total victory and the exaltation of our great God will be the song of the redeemed. So we never pray this prayer with anything less then complete confidence that God's name will be hallowed in all the earth and creation. But here and now His blessed name is mocked and scorned. Our purpose must always be that God's name will be honored in and through us. So this becomes also a prayer of surrender and commitment on our part.

PRAYERS & REMINDERS

_____
_____
_____
_____
_____
_____
_____
_____
_____

Prayer: Great and gracious God, we fervently pray, *Hallowed be Thy name.* This is our heart's desire, that You, O God, be honored and praised throughout the whole creation. We also pray that we will contribute to that praise and worship that honors You. Through Christ we pray. Amen.

Hymn for the day:
Sing Praise to God Who Reigns Above

October 11

Question #102: For what do we pray in the second petition?

Answer: In the second petition, which is, "Your kingdom come," we pray that Satan's kingdom may be destroyed; and that the kingdom of grace may be advanced, ourselves and others brought into it, and kept in it, and that the kingdom of glory may be hastened.

Scripture Reading: Psalm 2

One of the universal dreams of all people everywhere has been the dream of a golden age. Some look back to the good old days of long ago—but they were never really that good. Others speak of a coming age of peace and perfection. All through the ages people have written about an ideal kingdom, a hidden Utopia.

There is a reality behind these dreams. It is the kingdom of God. This kingdom was foretold by the prophets and proclaimed by Christ and His Apostles. In its completed form, it is truly the fulfillment of this age-long dream. It will be a kingdom of righteousness, of peace, of fulfillment, and perfection. But notice how the Catechism addresses this petition, by first pointing out that for God's kingdom to come, Satan's kingdom must be overthrown. We tend to overlook this and even wonder if it is right to pray for the downfall of evil systems and rulers who defy God. The second Psalm is an excellent guide in praying against the conquests by Satan and His minions. There are many more of these imprecatory Psalms in which we are taught to pray against evil institutions and evil people. Of course we must take great care in what spirit we offer such prayers lest we become self righteous and think we have the right to pray against everyone who disagrees with us. One way to guard against this would be to ask God to overthrow whatever control Satan may have over our lives, and then be willing to surrender more fully to God's control. Such praying could result in major changes in the way we think, talk and live. Does that need to happen in your life?

Prayer: Father, deliver us from bondage to the kingdom of this world. Set us free to serve the King of kings. By Your grace and power overthrow the control of self and Satan in our hearts. In Jesus' name. Amen.

Hymn for the day:
The Son of God Goes Forth to War

PRAYERS & REMINDERS

Question #102: For what do we pray in the second petition?

Answer: In the second petition, which is, "Your kingdom come," we pray that Satan's kingdom may be destroyed, and that the kingdom of grace may be advanced, ourselves and others brought into it, and kept in it, and that the kingdom of glory may be hastened.

Scripture Reading: Revelation 19:6-16

In these words which Christ taught His disciples to pray, the hopes and dreams of mankind become the prayer of the believer: *Thy kingdom come.* Notice again the logical order of this prayer. We began by addressing the great God of heaven as our Father. We adore and worship Him and pray that His name might be honored. Immediately following this we pray, *Thy kingdom come.*

The theme of much of Christ's preaching and teaching was the Kingdom of God. His first public proclamation was, "Repent and believe, for the Kingdom of heaven is at hand." Most of His parables had to do with the Kingdom of God, sometimes referred to as the Kingdom of heaven. Almost His last conscious act on earth was to receive a dying thief into His Kingdom. The study of what is meant by the Kingdom of God is a fascinating one indeed. Many books have written on this subject, with many different opinions on just what is meant by this term. In the simplest language the Kingdom of God means the rule of God over the lives of His people. That definition has many aspects and it is beyond the purpose of this devotional to do a long dissertation on the meaning of this term. But if we are to pray, *Thy Kingdom come,* we need to have some idea of just what we are asking God to do. We are not only ask-ing for the overthrow of Satan's evil kingdom, but for the establishment of God's rule over all His creation and over all realms. In Revelation 11:15 we read the announcement of the seventh trumpet: *The kingdoms of this world have become the kingdoms of our Lord and of His Christ, and He shall reign forever and ever.* At this great news the saints in heaven rejoice and give God glory and praise.

Prayer: Father, we are so thankful You have an everlasting Kingdom, and that our Lord Jesus is proclaimed as King of Kings and Lord of Lords. We look forward to joy at the full revelation of that Kingdom when our King returns in power and glory. Amen.

Hymn for the day:
Jesus Shall Reign

PRAYERS & REMINDERS

Question #102: For what do we pray in the second petition?

Answer: In the second petition, which is, "Your kingdom come," we pray that Satan's kingdom may be destroyed, and that the kingdom of grace may be advanced, ourselves and others brought into it, and kept in it, and that the kingdom of glory may be hastened.

Scripture Reading: I Chronicles 29:10-20

There are two very important questions to be answered if we are to understand what it means to pray, *Thy Kingdom come.* What is the Kingdom of God? In what sense do we pray for its coming? The simplest answer is that the Kingdom of God is the rule of God in the lives of His people. This may be expanded to include factors such as extent, time and nature, but basically the kingdom of God is a relationship between God and man.

To pray, *Thy kingdom come*, is a prayer for things in the present tense. We pray for God to extend His Kingdom into the hearts and minds of people everywhere. Thus, this is a missionary prayer. It should ever be in the heart and on the lips of every believer. We cannot bring the Kingdom in ourselves, but we can pray that God will cause His Kingdom to come, and we may be used of Him to advance His Kingdom. The throne upon which our King now sits is not visible to the human eye, but according to Scripture, our Lord Jesus is even now sitting on the right hand of God the Father, Almighty. This means He is recognized in heaven as the One who is *worthy to receive power, and riches, and wisdom and strength and honor and glory and blessing.* Therefore it is proper for us to unite with the creatures in heaven and on earth saying: *Blessing and honor and glory and power be unto Him who sits on the throne and to the Lamb forever and ever.* As we understand the majesty and glory of our Savior, we may with renewed assurance and confidence pray, *Thy Kingdom come.* But we do well to look into our own hearts and ask: *Do I want the Lord to have His way with me, and does my life reflect the rule of God over me?*

Prayer: Lord, when we pray *Thy Kingdom come* may it be a prayer of hope and a prayer of surrender. Help us to be loyal servants of our King and faithful citizens of His Kingdom. For Jesus' sake we pray. Amen.

Hymn for the day:
Ye Servants of God, Your Master Proclaim

PRAYERS & REMINDERS

Question #102: For what do we pray in the second petition?

Answer: In the second petition, which is, "Your kingdom come," we pray that Satan's kingdom may be destroyed, and that the kingdom of grace may be advanced, ourselves and others brought into it, and kept in it, and that the kingdom of glory may be hastened.

Scripture Reading: Isaiah 37:1-20

John Calvin posed the question, *In what sense do we pray 'Thy Kingdom come'?* His answer reads, *That day by day the Lord may increase the number of faithful, that day by day He may increasingly bestow His graces upon them until He has fulfilled them completely.* By this prayer, we pray for the success of the gospel and the conversion of the lost. To make this prayer more meaningful for us, we could pray for certain missionaries and ministries by name. We could pray for our own congregation and for the proclamation of the Word from the pulpit, that God would attend it with converting power in the lives of all who hear. We could also pray for all those who teach in our Sunday School, as well as neighborhood Bible studies. There are so many opportunities to pray *Thy kingdom come.*

At the present time, the Kingdom of God is in conflict with the powers of darkness and sin. Satan and sin rule the heart of natural man. Paul referred to Satan as being *the god of this world*, so the Kingdom of God and the kingdom of Satan are at war when we pray, *Thy Kingdom come.* We are aware of this conflict and pray for the overthrow of evil. As Christians, we have an obligation to join sides in this war. Neutrality is impossible. And our prayers should extend far beyond our own little circle of concerns. Try praying for the overthrow of false religions and for the doors now closed to be opened to the Gospel. Pray for the overthrow of spiritual strongholds which are opposed to our Lord and His gracious Kingdom.

PRAYERS & REMINDERS

_____
_____
_____
_____
_____
_____
_____
_____
_____

Prayer: Father, protect us from all the forces of evil which seek to destroy and discredit us and wreck our witness. Open those doors which are closed to the Gospel. Root out, we pray, the false gods and idols from the minds and hearts of people. May You rule in our hearts, and may Your Kingdom come now and always. For Jesus' sake we pray. Amen.

Hymn for the day:
We Gather Together

Question #102: For what do we pray in the second petition?

Answer: In the second petition, which is, "Your kingdom come," we pray that Satan's kingdom may be destroyed, and that the kingdom of grace may be advanced, ourselves and others brought into it, and kept in it, and that the kingdom of glory may be hastened.

Scripture Reading: 2 Peter 3

This can be a dangerous prayer for you. Do you really want the overthrow of evil within your own heart? Do you really want to give up your pride and greed, your evil thoughts and hasty tongue? To pray, *Thy Kingdom come,* in a personal way may lead to change, upheaval and disruption in your life. You must be prepared to face the consequences of this prayer. It was right and proper for believers all over the world to pray for the downfall of the "Iron Curtain" in Eastern Europe and the "Evil Empire" of the Soviet Union. God heard that prayer and we saw His answer unfold before our very eyes. But with equal zeal we should pray against the evil forces in this nation which are assaulting the Judeo-Christian values and ideals upon which this nation is founded. And with even more zeal should we pray that God will guard our hearts against the influences brought to bear on us by our rapidly disintegrating culture in which we live day by day.

Finally, this prayer has a future dimension. In the Scripture we read today, Peter said we are *looking for and hastening the coming of the day of God.* So in this petition, we are praying for the return of Christ and the ushering in of the Kingdom in all of its glory and wonder. I mentioned above how believers prayed for the downfall of the Iron Curtain, and how God dramatically answered that prayer. We have already been assured that God will also answer our prayers for the return of our Lord and Savior and for all evil empires and influences to be forever destroyed. The promises of the Word concerning this should urge us on in confidence and certain hope every time we say: *Thy Kingdom come.*

Prayer: Lord, give us faith to believe that You will conquer all Your and our enemies. Help us to search our hearts and discover all the many ways the forces of evil threaten our walk with You and our testimony before the world. Then help us to pray for Your power to overcome all evil in our lives. For Jesus' sake. Amen.

Hymn for the day:
Make Me a Captive Lord (May be sung to the tune of Crown Him with Many Crowns.)

PRAYERS & REMINDERS

Question #103: For what do we pray in the third petition?

Answer: In the third petition, which is, "Your will be done, on earth as it is in heaven," we pray that God, by His grace, would make us able and willing to know, obey, and submit to His will in all things, as the angels do in heaven.

Scripture Reading: Ephesians 6:1-20

When one of the great Puritan ministers lay dying, his last words were, *Lord, what You will, where You will, and how You will.* In these words, he was expressing not only his faith but a summary of his entire life. He had lived to do the will of God and was happy to die in the will of God.

When we pray, *Thy will be done,* we are praying a prayer that will always be answered. God is sovereign; He rules and overrules in all things and in all places. In the drama of human history, He is the leading actor and all people no matter how great or small play a supporting role to Him.

There is, however, another sense in which this prayer is not being answered yet. There is so much in the world that opposes God and is contrary to His will. There is so much hatred, so many wars, so much violence, so much infidelity to truth, so much pollution of the mind, so much abuse of the weak and the helpless. No, we cannot say God's will is being done on earth as it is in heaven. Which one of us can honestly say that in all things, God's will is being done in my life. O Yes, I believe in God's sovereignty and in His providential ordering of all things to His own glory, but this does not relieve me from my duty to seek and do His will as He reveals it in His Word, and in the circumstances of life His providence ordains. So I am taught by the words of this prayer to seek and obey God's will. We should do this willingly and joyfully and in full submission, even when God's will may be costly for us, as it was for our Lord Jesus in the Garden of Gethsemane.

PRAYERS & REMINDERS

_____

_____

_____

_____

_____

_____

_____

_____

_____

Prayer: Lord Jesus, for the sake of us poor, lost sinners You prayed to the Father, *Not My will, but Thine be done.* In gratitude for Your great, saving sacrifice, may we pray to You, *not our will, but Thine be done.* We ask this for Your glory and honor. Amen.

Hymn for the day:
Searcher of Hearts, From Mine Erase

Question #103: For what do we pray in the third petition?

Answer: In the third petition, which is, "Your will be done, on earth as it is in heaven," we pray that God, by His grace, would make us able and willing to know, obey, and submit to His will in all things, as the angels do in heaven.

Scripture Reading: Matthew 26:36-45

In this petition, we find an affirmation of faith. This is our firm belief, our cherished conviction, our life experience with God. We believe in God's authority and power and deny that either chance or evil is in control. We believe the providence of God is actively at work. Though evil may seem to be in control, in the final sense we can never accept this illusion.

God is Lord. This is the only life-view that makes sense or can deliver us from despair. The Christian believes every joy or sorrow, every victory or defeat is part of the often mysterious but always-loving plan and purpose of God. This does not mean we surrender to apathy or evil, but rather that in the end God will triumph. We may not always be able to explain the events of the moment or how they fit into God's loving purpose, but we do believe that God is in control and ultimately His will will be done. What if it were otherwise? What hopelessness we would know and experience. When our Lord Jesus was praying in the Garden of Gethsemane, He was able and willing to pray to the Father, *Thy will be done*, because He had complete confidence that the Father was still in control of all events, even His arrest, trials, humiliation, suffering and death. He also knew that it was the Father's will to raise Him from the dead, and restore Him to His former position of power and glory. He knew it was the Father's will for His death to be the atoning sacrifice for the sins of all His beloved elect. He knew the cost, but still He prayed the prayer, *Thy will be done.* Our willingness to pray this same petition is based on our confidence that God's will is best for us, and that He has ordained that *all things work together for good to those who love the Lord, and the called according to His purpose.*

Prayer: Father, when we are faced with the really hard times, and difficult decisions which test our love for You, give us grace to pray as Jesus prayed, *Thy will be done.* In Jesus' name and for His sake. Amen.

Hymn for the day:
My Jesus, As Thou Will

PRAYERS & REMINDERS

Question #103: For what do we pray in the third petition?

Answer: In the third petition, which is, "Your will be done, in earth as it is in heaven," we pray that God, by His grace, would make us able and willing to know, obey, and submit to His will in all things as the angels do in heaven.

Scripture Reading: Acts 21:1-14

This prayer is more than just an affirmation of faith—it is an act of commitment. When we pray, *Thy will be done*, we are engaging in a personal act of dedication and commitment which has great significance in our own lives. We are saying in effect that we want to know God's will and pledge ourselves to do it. This will mean a surrender of self and a forsaking of sin. This will also mean a readjusting of priorities. When I pray, *Thy will be done*, I must mean "in me." The idea is to present our bodies as living sacrifices unto God, holy and acceptable, which is our reasonable service. Martin Luther once prayed, *Oh Father, do not let me fall so low as to insist that my will be done. Break my will, put obstacles in my way, that come what may, not my will, but Thine be done.*

It is easy to say these words. It is much more difficult to sincerely mean them. Our example is that of the Lord Jesus Christ in the Garden of Gethsemane when He gave His will over to the will of the Father. I think also of the example of Paul on his last journey to Jerusalem. He knew that bonds, prison, and probably death awaited him there. His friends begged him not to go. But somehow Paul knew it was God's will for him to make that fateful trip, So he resisted the pleas of his friends, and overcame his own anxieties and set out for Jerusalem. Even his friends finally accepted his decision. Though fearful of the consequences they too said of his decision, *The Lord's will be done.* May that ever be our prayer as well.

PRAYERS & REMINDERS

_____

_____

_____

_____

_____

_____

_____

_____

_____

Prayer: O God, we echo the prayers of Your servant Martin Luther of long ago. Please let us never fall so low that we will insist on our will being done. Rather may we always seek You will in all decisions, actions and plans, that the Lord Jesus might be honored in our lives. We ask this for His sake and glory. Amen.

Hymn for the day:
Living for Jesus, A life That Is True

Question #103: For what do we pray in the third petition?

Answer: In the third petition, which is, "Your will be done, in earth as it is in heaven," we pray that God, by His grace, would make us able and willing to know, obey, and submit to His will in all things as the angels do in heaven.

Scripture Reading: Hebrews 11:1-16

Finally, this prayer is an ideal for which we long. The petition is not complete until we add, *in earth as it is in heaven.* By these words, we look in faith for the sure and certain future. This petition contains an eternal dimension. Although it points to a future age, it has bearing on the present age in which we live. We pray for the perfections of heaven to be at work in our lives even now. God has promised a new heaven and a new earth wherein dwells righteousness. When we pray this prayer, we claim that promise and commit ourselves to that ideal.

I fear there are few Christians who really build their lives around the hope of heaven. We are so tied into this world. We delight in the things of the world and not in the Lord. We believe in heaven, but unlike the great people extolled in Hebrews 11, for whom heaven was their goal and hope, we think of it as a safety valve, just in case things don't go well for us on earth. Often times I will hear people say of an aged, dying saint who has been suffering terribly with some terminal illness like cancer, *Well he will be better off in heaven.* They make heaven sound as if it may just be a little bit better than suffering, pain and death here on earth. Actually, for a believer, no matter how healthy, wealthy, comfortable, and young that believer might be, if that one is taken suddenly in an accident or illness, she will be a thousand times better off in heaven than the very best the world has to offer. I remember years ago when an older minister was being examined before Presbytery, prior to his move to a new church, he was asked, *What do you believe about heaven.* In answer he stamped his foot hard on the floor and replied, *It's a lot more real then the floor I'm standing on.* I hope you know that too!

Prayer: Gracious God, our heavenly Father, rescue us from bondage to the lusts of this world. Help us to know that heaven is real and that it is our ultimate home. May we live in that blessed hope. In Jesus' name. Amen.

Hymn for the day:
O That Will Be Glory

PRAYERS & REMINDERS

_____

_____

_____

_____

_____

_____

_____

_____

_____

Question #104: For what do we pray in the fourth petition?

Answer: In the fourth petition, which is, "Give us this day our daily bread," we pray that, of God's free gift, we may receive a sufficient portion of the good things of this life, and enjoy His blessing with them.

Scripture Reading: Genesis 1:26-31

In the Lord's Prayer, there is an abrupt transition from the lofty things of God and His Kingdom down to the everyday needs of people. One might expect the Lord to deal first with needs of the spirit, with forgiveness and cleansing, but this is not the case.

The Lord was being perfectly logical and consistent. After all, the spirit resides within a human body. That body must be fed and its needs met. There could be no piety or dedication without the food which nourishes and sustains our bodies. There could be no act of worship, no self-denying piety, no winning souls for Christ unless the body is maintained. Never forget that the human body was created by a direct exercise of God's creative power. Greek philosophy taught that the body was evil and the soul was good. That is not the teaching of God's word. He created first the body of man, and then breathed into that body the breath of life.

There are other petitions immediately following this one which remind us, *man does not live by bread alone.* However, in this petition attention is turned toward the physical and material needs which God has promised to provide. This fourth petition is the practical consequence of the first three. Only one who calls upon God as his Father, seeks God's glory and kingdom, and prays for the will of God to be accomplished in his own life can pray with expectation, *give us this day our daily bread.* This petition recognizes the goodness of God. He is our Father who gives to His children good gifts, and provides every need of body, mind, and spirit.

PRAYERS & REMINDERS

_____
_____
_____
_____
_____
_____
_____
_____
_____

Prayer: Dear God, You are a good and loving Father. How we thank You for all the bountiful goodness You have poured out upon us, Your children. Thank You for our food, shelter, clothing, and so much more. We are so dependent on You, and You never fail us. We thank You in Jesus' name. Amen.

Hymn for the day:
We Plow the Fields and Scatter

Question #104: For what do we pray in the fourth petition?

Answer: In the fourth petition, which is, "Give us this day our daily bread," we pray that, of God's free gift, we may receive a sufficient portion of the good things of this life, and enjoy His blessing with them.

Scripture Reading. Luke 12:13-21

The eternal God, creator of the universe, knows and cares about your every need. The hairs of your head are numbered. The thoughts of your mind are known. Isaiah says all nations are but a drop in the bucket before God. But the same Bible tells us not even a sparrow falls to the ground without your heavenly Father. God provides and cares. Therefore, you may call upon Him for your own personal needs with the same confidence by which you pray, *Thy Kingdom come.*

There are other passages in the Bible which teach that it is proper for us to call on God for our physical needs. With the right attitude and purpose, we may pray for God to bless us materially if we are willing to accept the fact that He may choose not to do so. God knows our every need and in His wisdom and sovereignty He will supply whatever is best for us. We must also remember that the Bible constantly warns against allowing material things to be of utmost importance. The parable of the rich fool found in Luke's Gospel is a good example of such a warning. We get the idea that this man was at first content with his lot up to a point. But when his land produced a really plenteous crop, he began to consider how he might preserve his new found wealth, and prosper even more. Of course you remember that right in the middle of his contemplation on how he could best benefit from this bounty, he suddenly died. Jesus used this as a warning against covetousness, and reminded His hearers (and readers) that the meaning of life is not to be found in the abundance of things one possesses.

It is so easy to come under bondage to things. Jesus said, *Seek first the kingdom of God and His righteousness and all these things will be added unto you.*

Prayer: Dear Father, in the midst of all the blessings You send to us, help us to always remember that the greatest gift is the Giver. May we always be grateful for all Your hand brings us, but may we never be held in bondage to material possession. For Jesus' sake we pray. Amen.

Hymn for the day:
For the Beauty of the Earth

PRAYERS & REMINDERS

Question #104: For what do we pray in the fourth petition?

Answer: In the fourth petition, which is, "Give us this day our daily bread," we pray that, of God's free gift, we may receive a sufficient portion of the good things of this life, and enjoy His blessing with them.

Scripture Reading: James 2:1-20

This petition recognizes our dependence upon God. There are no other words in the Bible which express so fully and completely our utter dependence upon God. Even though we may be prosperous and secure at any given moment, yet our daily bread is a gift from God. You may be perfectly sound of mind and body with a secure position of loving family and respect of fellow man but all of these things may vanish in a moment without warning. We tend to forget in our complex technological society that our daily bread still comes from the simple processes of nature, which are under the control of our Creator God. Our dependence upon God is day by day and moment by moment.

When Israel was in the wilderness, they were given just enough manna for that day and no more. What a tremendous parable this is for our lives. God intends us to trust Him on a daily basis and not to gather to ourselves the imagined security of wealth and possession. These things are not wrong in themselves, but trusting them instead of God is a deadly sin.

One final word of reminder is in order. This prayer is in the plural. It must never be prayed as a selfish prayer. Jesus did not tell us to pray, *give me this day my daily bread*, but *give us this day our daily bread*. When we have received our requests from God for material and physical provision for our needs, and look around and see so many whose basic needs are not being met, our hearts should be filled with compassion. Furthermore it may well be that God will answer our hungry neighbor's cry for daily bread, by sending us to that one with an open heart and hand to meet the need.

PRAYERS & REMINDERS

_____

_____

_____

_____

_____

_____

_____

_____

_____

Prayer: Savior, we see in Your mercy to us, the call to be merciful. You have taught us, *Blessed are the merciful, for they shall obtain mercy.* May we believe this and act upon this truth. Help us to remember that if we give a cup of cold water in Your name, we give it to You. Amen.

Hymn for the day:
Let Your Heart be Broken For a World in Need

Question #105: For what do we pray in the fifth petition?

Answer: In the fifth petition, which is, "Forgive us our debts, as we also have forgiven our debtors," we pray that God, for Christ's sake, would freely pardon all our sins; which we are more encouraged to ask because by His grace we are enabled from the heart to forgive others.

Scripture Reading: Matthew 18:21-35

When we pray, *forgive us our debts, as we forgive our debtors*, we are touching the heart and soul of Christian doctrine and the Christian life. This petition helps us to clearly see that the Lord's Prayer is a prayer for the children of God exclusively. Only the merits of Christ's righteousness and the shedding of His blood can win for us the right to ask for forgiveness and only the person in whom the living Christ lives can offer forgiveness to others.

Years ago I heard a story that has impressed this petition on my mind. It was the story of a tombstone in a neglected old churchyard. There was no name or date on the tombstone. There was but one word, "Forgiven." Truly, this tells the story of every Christian, and this is the only epitaph that really counts. But if *Forgiven* is the watch word of our lives, then the word *Forgiving* must go hand in hand with it. For the Lord taught us to pray, *forgive us our debts, as we forgive our debtors*. In Matthew 18 the whole question of forgiveness was brought up by Peter when he asked the Lord how often he should forgive a brother who sinned against him, till seven times? The Lord's startling response was: *I do not say to you till seven times, but up to seventy times seven.* Then the Lord told the parable of the unmerciful servant for whom his king forgave him an enormous debt. In that story, the forgiven servant found one of his fellow servants who owed him a small amount of money. When the poor man asked for a little time, the ungrateful servant refused, and had him cast into debtors prison. Upon hearing this the king who had forgiven a much larger debt, canceled his previous generosity and held the ungrateful servant liable for his unpayable debt. This was a graphic way of showing us how important it is to forgive those who trespass against us.

Prayer: Dear Lord, we read of Your great mercy, yet we remain so unmerciful in our judgments of others For Your sake, and in Your name help us to be as eager to forgive as we are to be forgiven. For Your sake we pray. Amen.

Hymn for the day:
Forgive Our Sins as We Forgive

PRAYERS & REMINDERS

Question #105: For what do we pray in the fifth petition?

Answer: In the fifth petition, which is, "Forgive us our debts, as we also have forgiven our debtors," we pray, that God, for Christ's sake, would freely pardon all our sins; which we are more encouraged to ask because by His grace we are enabled from the heart to forgive others.

Scripture Reading: I John 1:1-2:2

This petition is filled with the message of the Gospel and proclaims the atonement. It focuses on the cross and what our Lord did there. Our greatest need is the need for forgiveness. Apart from this, we are truly lost souls without God and without hope. The good news of the Gospel meets this greatest need.

There is a sense in which this is a once-and-for-all prayer. There must come a time in one's life when one comes to grips with the problem of sin. The circumstances may vary but the need is the same. We may come before God as the publican in the Temple, oppressed and overborne with such guilt that we can only cry out, "God have mercy on me the sinner." Or we may come as the rich young ruler knowing something is missing and having no peace. Again, we may be as Nicodemus coming furtively, yet with a real hunger and need for relief. But sooner or later we must pray this prayer or we can never see the kingdom of God.

On the other hand, this is more than just a once-and-for-all prayer. We must pray this prayer every day and every hour in the day. The promise of the Word to believers is this: *If we confess our sins, God is faithful and just to forgive us our sins and to cleanse us from all unrighteousness.* When we come before God in prayer, we must always be aware of our need to confess sin and receive forgiveness. Sincere and honest confession of sin before the Lord is the key that opens the door to pardon and peace. How we need both!

Prayer: We stand amazed, Father, at Your incredible grace by which we are forgiven for all our sins, and cleansed from all unrighteousness. Give to us a forgiving heart that we may show our gratitude for Your amazing grace. In Jesus' name. Amen.

Hymn for the day:
Christ, Of All My Hopes the Grounds

PRAYERS & REMINDERS
_____
_____
_____
_____
_____
_____
_____
_____
_____

Question #105: For what do we pray in the fifth petition?

Answer: In the fifth petition, which is, "Forgive us our debts, as we also have forgiven our debtors," we pray that God, for Christ's sake, would freely pardon all our sins; which we are more encouraged to ask, because by His grace we are enabled from the heart to forgive others.

Scripture Reading. 2 Corinthians 2:3-11

In this petition, we confess our evil thoughts, our cruel and careless words, our every betrayal of confidence and trust, our every denial of faith. We confess our selfish motives and outlook, the deeds that displease God and hurt our fellow man. This petition also requires us to confess our sins of omission and failure. We ask forgiveness for not being kind, for not being concerned. We ask God to forgive us for not loving each other and bearing each other's burdens. I believe that we will be held even more accountable for the good we have not done, than the evil we have done. When we pray, *Forgive us our debts*, we must follow along with the words, *as we forgive our debtors.* This is the only petition the Lord took time to explain and underscore by way of illustration. If you have been forgiven by God, you must forgive. You cannot help yourself or even want to. If Christ is living in you, your heart will not be cold, hard, and unforgiving. Of course, it costs to forgive other people, but it cost God far more to forgive you that it ever cost you to forgive your brother. It cost the Lord Jesus His life, and the Father, His precious Son.

What are we to forgive? Anything and everything. How often or how much? As often as the need is there. Jesus' words to Simon Peter were *seventy times seven*, which simply means there must be an inexhaustible supply of forgiveness within your heart, a supply that is renewed daily as God forgives your sin. I often hear people say: *I cannot forgive unless the offender confesses wrong and asks me to forgive.* My answer to that is, but we must always have a forgiving spirit. Those who crucified Jesus did not ask Him to forgive them, but He asked the Father to forgive them.

Prayer: Father, grant to us, Your adopted children, kind and forgiving hearts. May Christ our Savior also be our example as we deal with offenses against us. Help us especially to forgive our brother and sister Christians, for You have surely forgiven them and us. In Jesus' name. Amen.

Hymn for the day:
Thy Loving-Kindness, Lord, Is Good and Free

PRAYERS & REMINDERS

Question #106: For what do we pray in the sixth petition?

Answer: In the sixth petition, which is, "And lead us not into temptation, but deliver us from evil," we pray that God would either keep us from being tempted to sin, or support and deliver us when we are tempted.

Scripture Reading: I Corinthians 10:12-11:1

No Christian can ever dare approach the Holy God who is our Father without praying, *Forgive us our debts.* However, no Christian should ever be content to leave it at that, but should also pray, *Lead us not into temptation but deliver us from evil.* In the former petition, we confess our sins and ask forgiveness. In the latter, we confess our weakness and ask for help and protection. These two requests naturally follow in perfect order.

If you have experienced true repentance, if you have confessed your sin to God and received forgiveness, then you have a holy dread of falling into sin again and grieving your Savior. You remember what it cost Him to forgive you and thus you wish to live a life pleasing to Him. So you pray, *Lead us not into temptation.* When we pray those words sincerely, we also must realize that we have the responsibility to avoid temptations, especially in the areas of our known weaknesses. I once was very close to a brother minister who is with the Lord now, who had been an alcoholic in his younger years. He had a special concern and compassion for others, who, like him, had fallen into that deadly trap. He learned the hard way that one does not deliberately place oneself in a situation of temptation, especially if this temptation involves a besetting sin. Though he fell again in that into that sin, God restored him, and he became a wiser man for it. So beloved ones, know what your special areas of weakness are and avoid them diligently. Someone once said, "Don't put your head into the mouth of a hungry lion, and then begin to pray, O God please don't let that lion be hungry." Wise words indeed!

PRAYERS & REMINDERS

_____

_____

_____

_____

_____

_____

_____

_____

_____

Prayer: Father, we are surrounded by many temptations of many kinds. Teach us to be wise and avoid those situations in which temptations may face us. When we are tempted, please deliver us from evil. For Jesus' sake. Amen.

Hymn for the day:
Yield Not To Temptation

Question #106: For what do we pray in the sixth petition?

Answer: In the sixth petition, which is, "And lead us not into temptation, but deliver us from evil," we pray that God would either keep us from being tempted to sin, or support and deliver us when we are tempted.

Scripture Reading: Psalm 61

This has been called a prayer for the early morning. We have so many temptations of every kind facing us every day. There are temptations of the mind as well as the body. There are so many situations filled with temptation. You have to deal with people every day who tempt you to compromise your principles and deny your Lord. Surely, every day should begin with this prayer.

This is also a prayer for the early morning years of life. Every child, every youth, should have this prayer constantly on his lips and on his heart. The older you grow the more you will understand the urgency of this request. The bird with the broken wing may fly again but not with the same freedom or to the same soaring heights. So we may be forgiven by God's grace, but sin may still weaken and lessen our freedom and our influence for good. Of course, this prayer should not be limited to the early morning hours of the day or the early morning hours of life. Even the very old have need of this prayer every day. King David was in the prime of his life and strength, maybe even a little past when he allowed himself to gaze too long upon a beautiful woman, Bathsheba, the wife of one of his most loyal soldiers, Uriah. His gaze turned to lust and his lust turned into first adultery and then to murder. This is the same man who earlier had written the twenty third Psalm, and later wrote Psalm 51. If David, "man after God's won heart" could sin to this degree, who is exempt from such temptations? The answer, of course, is no one. So our constant prayer must be: *Lead us not into temptation but deliver us from evil.* This is an urgent request and a much needed one for all ages in all places.

Prayer: Lead us in paths of righteousness for Your name's sake, O Lord. How quickly we go astray and wander far from Your paths. Guard our eyes, our ears, our minds, and our hearts, and lead us in the way everlasting. In Jesus' name. Amen.

Hymn for the day:
A Shelter in the Time of Storm

PRAYERS & REMINDERS

October 28

Question #106: For what do we pray in the sixth petition?

Answer: In the sixth petition, which is, "And lead us not into temptation, but deliver us from evil," we pray that God would either keep us from being tempted to sin, or support and deliver us when we are tempted.

Scripture Reading: James 1:12-20

This is one of the most important and urgent requests we can ever make known to God. In this prayer we ask that we may not have to face dangerous temptations. We ask our Father that we may not be led astray by our own ignorance or willingness. Far too often we wait far too late to ask for help. The time to think about the depth of the water is before we dive in and discover we cannot swim. Or again, it is foolish to put your head in the lion's mouth and then pray that he will not be hungry. So temptation should be studiously and prayerfully avoided. In this petition we ask that, when overtaken by temptation, we may not fall. God allows us great freedom, and under His providence we may be tempted. Job is a classic case in point. God did not tempt or afflict Job, but He allowed him to be tempted. There was so much at stake in Job's temptation of which he knew nothing. When we are tempted this petition asks that we may be given the wisdom to see sin for what it is and the power to resist it.

Basically, this is a prayer for a closer walk with Him who was tempted and tried at all points as we are, yet without sin. No one has ever faced the severity of temptation as Jesus faced it. No one has ever won greater victory. Because He won the victory, there is hope for us too, but certainly not in our own strength. Jesus told us in John 15, that we are to abide in Him that we may bear fruit to His glory. He said, *I am the vine, you are the branches. He who abides in Me and I in him, bears much fruit, for without Me you can do nothing.* Most certainly this applies to our ability to resist and overcome temptation.

PRAYERS & REMINDERS
_____
_____
_____
_____
_____
_____
_____
_____
_____

Prayer: Lord Jesus, we would walk with You and abide in You. We face so many overwhelming temptations that we cannot resist without Your help and power. We need You every hour. Please stay with us, abide with us. Amen.

Hymn for the day. I Need Thee Every Hour

Question #106: For what do we pray in the sixth petition?

Answer: In the sixth petition, which is, "And lead us not into temptation, but deliver us from evil," we pray that God would either keep us from being tempted to sin, or support and deliver us when we are tempted.

Scripture Reading: Matthew 26:36-46

Finally, when we pray this prayer we ask God that when we are tempted and when we do fall, that we may not be enslaved by the evil one. *Dear Lord, when I fall victim to temptation and sin, do not allow it to become a way of life with me. Do not let me, Your child, become a servant of Satan. When I am hurt, do not let me become bitter or resentful. When I see hurt and suffering all around me, do not let me become callous or careless. If I win some spiritual victory, deliver me from self-righteousness. When I am too busy to pray, don't let me think I didn't really miss very much.*

The Lord has told us through His servant James that *You have not because you ask not, and when you ask, you ask amiss that you may spend it on your desires.* How very sinful we are, even at our best. Only the indwelling Christ, through the Holy Spirit can give us grace and will power to deal with the many temptations we face almost every hour of the day. The good news is that He will do this for us if we ask in sincerity and in truth. God does allow us in the mystery of His providence to be tempted and even to fall, but in His revealed will we learn that we cannot thereby excuse ourselves, or attempt to blame God for our sins and falls. Again James tells us, *Let no one say when he is tempted, I am tempted by God. For God cannot be tempted by evil, nor does He Himself tempt anyone. But each one is tempted when he is drawn away by his own desires and enticed.* So our prayer in this petition is that we will not be drawn away from Him, or enticed by the temptations the world, the flesh and the devil place before us.

Prayer: Father, we confess before You that in our sinful natures, there is no good thing. But You have given us a new nature through the new birth. But even then we lament our weakness and sin. May all our temptations lose their power, *When Thou art nigh.* In Jesus' name we pray. Amen.

Hymn for the day:
My Anchor Holds

PRAYERS & REMINDERS

_____
_____
_____
_____
_____
_____
_____
_____
_____
_____

Question #107: What does the conclusion of the Lord's Prayer teach us?

Answer: The conclusion of the Lord's Prayer, which is, "For yours is the kingdom and the power and the glory, forever. Amen," teaches us to take our encouragement in prayer from God only, and in our prayers to praise Him, ascribing kingdom, power, and glory to Him; and in testimony of our desire and assurance to be heard, we say, "Amen."

Scripture Reading: Daniel 4:34-37.

The Lord's Prayer ends where it began, in heaven. It ends with the same concerns with which it began, the glory and the Kingdom of God. All that is said before in this prayer awaits these final words. It is incomplete without this final ascription of faith and praise. Because we can pray these last words in faith and confident hope, we are assured all the requests of this prayer are answered. If in our prayers we are always seeking the kingdom and the glory of God, there is no question about the answer. John Calvin said these words are given us that we might be reminded again our prayers are grounded altogether on the goodness and power of God and not upon ourselves. The maturity of our Christian experience may be measured not so much by the length of our prayers, but rather by the amount of praise and worship we include in our prayers.

While it is true that some ancient texts omit this ending to the Lord's prayer, others contain it. Certainly the time honored tradition of the church from the very earliest days include this final ascription of praise. Furthermore it is in perfect harmony with all that Jesus taught concerning the Kingdom of God. The great anthems of heavenly praise reported in the book of Revelation add their weight to the inclusion on these final words in the Lord's prayer. So when we pray this prayer in public or in private we may be very sure that we are being faithful to the teachings of Scripture, especially the things our Lord taught us. So do not be upset by any footnotes you may find in the margin of whatever translation of the Bible you are accustomed to reading. Be assured that you are uniting with the saints of all ages when you conclude the Lord's prayer with these familiar words of praise and affirmation.

Prayer: Father, we glory in the knowledge that Yours is an everlasting Kingdom and Yours is the power and glory forever. As we rejoice in Your Kingdom, may You grant us the joy of seeing others enter the Kingdom through our witness and love. For Jesus' sake. Amen.

Hymn for the day:
Jesus Shall Reign

PRAYERS & REMINDERS

Question #107: What does the conclusion of the Lord's Prayer teach us?

Answer: The conclusion of the Lord's Prayer, which is, "For yours is the kingdom and the power and the glory, forever. Amen," teaches us to take our encouragement in prayer from God only, and in our prayers to praise Him, ascribing kingdom, power, and glory to Him; and in testimony of our desire and assurance to be heard, we say, "Amen."

Scripture Reading: Psalm 72

At last we come to the final words of the Lord's Prayer. They form a grand finale, a capstone of faith and prayer, *for yours is the kingdom and the power and the glory forever.* What a daring thing to be able to say these words. Only the eye of faith can see it in this troubled world. Only the voice of faith can proclaim it. By these words we declare our faith in God and His Word.

When the Apostle Paul was speaking to the men on the sinking ship which was bearing him as a prisoner to Rome, He encouraged them with these words: *Sirs, be of good cheer for I believe God.* If there were a time when this testimony is needed, it is now. People are fearful and anxious. The world is in so much trouble and despair. How cheering it is to hear the voice of faith saying, *Sirs, be of good cheer for I believe God.* There is so much hopelessness all around us. People have lost faith in most institutions, even in government. Cynicism and despair are wide spread, and there are few voices of hope and cheer. God has shown us the glory of His Kingdom in His word. It is ours to believe His word, trust His grace, and submit to His everlasting Kingdom. Jesus said of believers: *You are the light of the world. A city set on a hill cannot be hidden...Let your light so shine before men that they may see your good works and glorify your Father in heaven.* If we truly believe these words, *Thine is the kingdom and the power and the glory forever,* and if we live that way, as citizens of the heavenly kingdom, then our lights will shine into the darkest and deepest recesses of doubt and fear, and people may be persuaded that there is a heavenly Kingdom, because they have met some of its citizens.

Prayer: Father, give us the faith to believe Your word as we face the storms of life. Help us to know what Daniel knew when he faced the lion's den. Help us to believe what our Savior believed when He faced the cruel cross, especially when You give us a cross to bear for His sake. Amen.

Hymn for the day:
All Glory, Laud, and Honor

PRAYERS & REMINDERS
_____
_____
_____
_____
_____
_____
_____
_____

November 1

> *Question #107: What does the conclusion of the Lord's prayer teach us?*

Answer: The conclusion of the Lord's prayer, which is, "For yours is the kingdom and the power and the glory, forever. Amen," teaches us to take our encouragement in prayer from God only, and in our prayers to praise Him, ascribing kingdom, power, and glory to Him; and, in testimony of our desire and assurance to be heard, we say, "Amen."

Scripture Reading: I Corinthians 15:20-28

In these final words, we are saying to God, *Father we are sure of you, you are trustworthy.* To the world we are saying, *God is in control and therefore we have hope.* The kingdom of God may be veiled and invisible now, but it is a real kingdom and will one day burst forth in all its glory and splendor to be seen by all. The kingdoms of this world will become the kingdoms of our Lord and of His Christ, and He shall reign for ever and ever. This prayer is an act of dedication and commitment. When we pray these words we are making a personal commitment to God and His kingdom. When we say, *Thine is the kingdom*, we have no mental reservations. We acknowledge our part in that kingdom and our responsibility to it.

Praying these words is like taking your life and placing it in the hands of your heavenly Father to use as He pleases. When you say these words in prayer you are crowning the Lord Jesus Christ as your personal King and Lord. This is an act of dedication that is final and irrevocable, yet must be renewed each day. It is also the supreme statement of true, biblical optimism. If we view life only through the spectrum of here and now, we will be overwhelmed with pessimism to the extreme. All around us we see the chaos of a fallen world, the apparent triumph of evil over good, and the inevitable victory of power over principle. It is so easy to become discouraged and even cynical. For the Christian, the truth expressed in these final words of the Lord's prayer give us grace and courage to face all the ups and downs of life. God's kingdom will prevail!

Prayer: Gratefully and joyfully we unite in affirming, *Thine is the kingdom and the power and the glory forever.* We believe Your word, and trust Your promises now and forever. Thank You, dear Lord, that You have brought us into your everlasting kingdom through Christ our Lord. Amen.

Hymn for the day:
Jerusalem the Golden

PRAYERS & REMINDERS

Question #107: What does the conclusion of the Lord's prayer teach us?

Answer: The conclusion of the Lord's prayer, which is, "For yours is the kingdom and the power and the glory, forever. Amen," teaches us to take our encouragement in prayer from God only, and in our prayers to praise Him, ascribing kingdom, power, and glory to Him; and in testimony of our desire and assurance to be heard, we say, "Amen."

Scripture Reading: Luke 16:19-31

Finally, this prayer raises life's most important question. The word *forever* implies the question, *Where will you spend that forever*? You will never face a more urgent and relevant question than this. You may say these words every day, *Thine is the kingdom and the power and the glory forever*, but it takes more than just saying the words to ensure a place in that grand forever. There is only one way, and that is the way of faith in God's Son. It is putting your faith in the Lord Jesus Christ as your personal Savior. When you have made that commitment you have entered the forever kingdom. No amount of good works, as important as they are for believers, will assure you a place in the blessed forever. Certainly there will be a judgment of rewards, based on our faithfulness and obedience to the Lord's revealed will. However, entrance into the kingdom is by faith in the Lord Jesus Christ, and His finished work of redemption. The only thing the thief on the cross had to offer was a cry for mercy. This cry for mercy implied faith in Christ to bring him into that kingdom, but that is all he had. Yet he had far more than the most zealous and pious person who ever lived who did not have that one indispensable gift…faith in Jesus Christ as Savior from sin. In our materialistic world, few ever think of *forever* in the biblical sense of the word. We are so wrapped up in our own concerns and possessions we have little time to spare for thoughts of eternity. But this last word of the Lord's Prayer brings us back to the reality we must all face.

Prayer: Lord, by the prayer You taught us to pray, our thoughts and hearts are turned towards eternity. We dare not face this somber thought in our own strength or goodness, for we have neither. You have said in Your word, *Whosoever calls upon the name of the Lord will be saved*. In faith we call upon You, dear Savior. Amen.

Hymn for the day:
Rock of Ages (Toplady tune)

PRAYERS & REMINDERS

The Prayer Life of Jesus

Scripture Reading: Mark 1:35-39; Luke 6:12-16

The Shorter Catechism ends with an explanation and exposition of the Lord's prayer. This was the prayer Jesus taught His disciples to pray. The example of His own prayer life is also an important part of His teaching on prayer. The two examples cited in the above Scripture have this in common, that before our Lord made important decisions about His own ministry on earth, He spent the long hours of the night in prayer to the Father. In Mark's account, Jesus was preparing for His first ministry in Galilee. In Luke's gospel, He prayed the night through in preparation for choosing His twelve disciples from among all those who followed Him.

There is something quite remarkable about our Lord devoting long hours to prayer. He was and is God the Son who came into the world to save sinners. He existed from all eternity and was the Father's only begotten Son. He had enjoyed full fellowship with the Father and the Holy Spirit from all eternity. When He entered the world to carry out His role as our Redeemer, He was still in perfect fellowship with the Father and the Spirit. In Him were hidden all treasures of wisdom and knowledge. He was sinless and therefore had no sin to confess. Yes He was tempted and tried in all points as we are, yet without sin. But if the Lord Jesus, the Father's beloved and only begotten Son, the sinless and perfect One felt the need to spend long hours in prayer, does this not teach us, who are weak and sinful, that we are much in need of prayer, and helpless to defeat the evil within our own hearts and face the constant temptations of Satan. We have many decisions to make for which we need God's wisdom and guidance. We have many sins to confess for which we need His abundant and constant mercy and grace. Yet so many of us act as if prayer is simply an option if we have the time. Let the example of our Lord's dependence on prayer convict us of our need, and seek the Lord constantly by never ceasing prayer.

PRAYERS & REMINDERS

Prayer: Lord Jesus, we see the perfect pattern of prayer in Your own prayer life. Help us as we search the Scriptures to discover Your example and Your teaching, that we may become true prayer warriors for Your glory. We ask this in Your perfect and powerful name. Amen.

Hymn for the day:
When My Love for God Grows Weak

The Prayer Life of Jesus

Scripture Reading: Matthew 14:13-21

Another example of our Lord praying is given in the story of the feeding of the five thousand people with only a small handful of bread and a few small fish. We are told that before He broke and distributed the food, *He looked up to heaven and blessed and broke the loaves.* Clearly He was acknowledging His dependence on the Father for the supply of food needed for the multitudes. What a lesson for us. In the Lord's prayer He taught us to say, *give us this day our daily bread.* In this example of His own asking the Father to bless the food and those receiving it, He was reinforcing His teaching by example. We, too, acknowledge that we are dependent on God for our physical needs, including the food we eat. But we are also taught to ask the Father to use the food He supplies for our good, and also for His glory. The Apostle Paul wrote that we should seek to glorify God in all we do, even in eating and drinking our food. We ask Him to strengthen us with our daily bread that we might serve and glorify Him. Having a prayer of thanksgiving for God's supply of our need reinforces the truth that we depend upon Him for all things. Little children learn this by watching and hearing their parents pray. In fact they are so impressed by this example they want to join in, even at a very early age, and we should encourage this. When Jesus was tempted by Satan in the wilderness to turn the stones into bread to feed His starving body after the long fast, both he and Jesus knew that as the Creator of all things this was within His power. But it was not within His purpose, nor would he allow Satan to tempt Him to use His power for personal gain or glory. He well knew the Father would supply His every need, and we should know that too.

Prayer: *God is great and God is good, and we thank Him for our food. By His hand we all are fed. Give us, Lord, our daily bread.* We ask this in the name, and after the example of our Lord and Savior Jesus Christ. Amen.

Hymn for the day:
God Will Take Care of You

PRAYERS & REMINDERS

The Prayer Life of Jesus

Scripture Reading: Luke 10:17-24

The prayer of our Lord recorded in the Scripture for today was a prayer of thanksgiving. I know in my own prayer life this sort of prayer is all too seldom. Maybe you have experienced the same lack in your prayer life too. I know that when I have experienced some special blessing of prayer answered, or unexpected blessing in the form of material things, or health improved, I try to express thanksgiving in my prayers, but more often than not most of my prayers are simply requests.

Here in this passage it is helpful and instructive to understand the reason for Jesus' prayer of thanksgiving. He had sent out seventy of His followers into all the places He Himself would later go. Their mission was to prepare the people for Christ's coming to their region. They were to preach the Gospel, heal the sick, and cast out demons, thereby demonstrating what the Kingdom of God was all about. He had warned these men that some would welcome them, but that many would reject them and their message. His words: *He who hears you, hears Me, and he who hates you, hates Me, and he who hates Me, hates the One(God) who sent Me,* gave them an idea of what to expect. He also warned the places to which He was sending His disciples that they would be held accountable for what they did with the message they would hear from His disciples. No doubt the Lord Himself prayed for these faithful folk who went out in His name. When they returned and reported to Jesus the results of their ministry, He rejoiced with them. Then He offered a prayer of great thanksgiving to the Father for the success of their ministry. In that prayer He also expressed great confidence in the Father's faithfulness. What causes you the greatest joy in your life? For believers, we should always be looking for the success of the Gospel, and give God great thanks when we hear of the spread of the message of salvation, and any success God gives to faithful work and workers in the Kingdom. Maybe right now would be a good time for you to thank God for His great work in this world, and for all the evidences of victories His church enjoys as we are faithful to His cause.

Prayer: Father, how thankful we are to know that the Gospel is even now reaching multitudes of people all around the world. Help us to look for, and expect great things as we are faithful to You and Your Church. In Jesus name. Amen.

Hymn for the day:
Christ Shall Have Dominion

PRAYERS & REMINDERS

_____

_____

_____

_____

_____

_____

_____

_____

_____

November 6

The Prayer Life of Jesus

Scripture Reading: Luke 18:1-8

This Scripture is not really about the prayer life of our Lord, but it does contain an interesting parable and an important lesson on prayer. This is known as the parable of the unjust judge, or more properly the persistent widow. The passage begins by saying, *And He spoke a parable unto them to this end, that men ought always to pray, and not to faint.* Right away we understand that the Lord is going to teach us an important lesson in prayer. The story itself is quite simple. In a certain city there was a judge who was not a believer in God, and so naturally he had no regard for his fellow man. In the same city was a widow who had been treated unfairly and was seeking justice from the court. The judge ignored her for a long time, but finally became impatient with her importunity, and so resolved the case in her favor, simply on the grounds he was tired of hearing her. If we want to know the lesson Christ was teaching, we have to remember He told this parable in the midst of telling His disciples about His return in power and glory. So this is not just a lesson on prayer in general, but about praying for His promised return, with confident expectation, and joyful anticipation of the blessing this will be for His faithful ones.

However, it does contain real encouragement for all prayers of believers, that we do not grow discouraged when we do not see our requests immediately answered. His reasoning is if an unjust and an ungodly judge would finally yield to the repeated requests of an unknown widow just because she annoyed him with her constant pleas, how much more will our just, holy, and loving Father keep all His promises to His elect. Once more we are directed to think especially of His promised return to reward His own and to punish those who persecute them. It is not so much that we pray for revenge on those who treat us in a cruel and ungodly way. God will take care of that. But what we pray for is the joy of receiving all the many blessings God has promised for those who love His appearing. Have you prayed lately for the Lord Jesus to come back again? Why not pray that prayer right now?

Prayer: Gracious Lord, hasten the day of Your return. We are perplexed and fainting because of all the evil in the world around us, and the unceasing battle within our own hearts. Return in all Your power and glory and fulfill our hearts' desire, and Your glorious promises. Amen.

Hymn for the day:
Lo! He Comes with Clouds Descending

PRAYERS & REMINDERS

_____

_____

_____

_____

_____

_____

_____

_____

_____

_____

The Prayer Life of Jesus

Scripture Reading: John 11:32-44

This is the prayer Jesus prayed before He called dead Lazarus from the tomb where his body had been lying for four days. You know the story of the serious, life threatening illness of Jesus' friend, Lazarus, and the frantic message his sisters sent to Jesus, asking Him to come and heal their beloved brother. While Jesus delayed His coming, Lazarus died, but instead of a failure to respond, this became an opportunity for the Lord to assure Mary, Martha, and Lazarus, that He really was the Son of God, who had power over life and death. Though neither Martha nor Mary fully understood all He said about the death of Lazarus and His power over death, still they trusted Him and believed He was the Messiah. At His request, the two sisters and their friends escorted Jesus to the tomb where they had placed the body of their beloved brother. At this point Jesus made an unthinkable demand! *Take away the stone!* The people were stunned, and Martha protested, *Lord, he has been dead four days, by this time there is an odor.* Jesus responded, *Did I not tell you, if you believed you would see the glory of God?*

After the stone had been rolled away, Jesus lifted His eyes to heaven and prayed: *Father, I thank You that You have heard me. And I know that You always hear me, but because of the people who are standing by, I said this, that they may believe that You sent Me.*

How wonderful! Even when the Lord Jesus performed His greatest miracle, He called upon the power of the Father, and gave to Him all the glory. How much less should we ever depend upon our own strength, even to perform the daily tasks we are given by the Lord. How sinful when He blesses us for us to claim any credit or glory for ourselves. Another great lesson is the confidence in which He prayed. Why pray at all, if we do not believe that God hears and answers prayer? Yes, it is true that even after our most earnest and fervent prayers, our loved ones die, yet we know the hour is coming when all who are in the grave will come forth at the word of the Lord Christ.

Prayer: Lord, You who stood at the grave of Lazarus and said, *Lazarus come forth!*, will one day raise all the dead by that same word of power. Thank You that we may live and die in that blessed hope. Amen.

Hymn for the day:
O Thou Who Hearest Every Heartfelt Prayer

PRAYERS & REMINDERS

_____

_____

_____

_____

_____

_____

_____

_____

_____

November 8

The Prayer Life of Jesus

Scripture Reading: John 12:23-33

The next time we hear Jesus at prayer was shortly after the miracle of raising Lazarus from the dead. In John 12, we read of the celebration feast held at the home of Mary, Martha and Lazarus. The next day many people were flooding into the city of Jerusalem to celebrate the Passover feast. In this context all four of the Gospels record the story of the "triumphal entry" of Jesus into the city. However, John only mentions this briefly. But John alone tells the story of the Greeks who had come to the feast and were seeking Jesus. No doubt the whole city was filled with wonder over the news of Lazarus' resuscitation, and the triumphal ride of Jesus into the city.

Jesus' response to the request was to explain the purpose of His coming into the world, and to reveal His approaching death as a part of that purpose. In verse 27 we hear Jesus saying: *Now my soul is troubled; and what shall I say? Father, save me from this hour? But for this purpose I came unto this hour. Father, glorify Thy name.* This was always the chief end, the constant prayer and purpose of Jesus, to glorify the Father. What does this teach us about prayer? Our prayer and our purpose should always be the same. In all situations we are called upon to face, in all our most fervent requests, the one controlling purpose is for God to be glorified in and through us. Instead of praying, *Father, save Me from this hour*, he prayed, *Father, glorify Thy name.* Later just before His arrest and trial and death, while praying to the Father, He prayed, *Father, if it be possible let this cup pass from me...nevertheless, not as I will, but as You will.* His prayer and purpose never changed. His passion was that the Father's will would be done, and that He would be glorified, even in the suffering and death of His Beloved Son. May this be our purpose and passion too!

Prayer: Almighty Father, our prayer also is that You might be glorified in all that happens to us either in life or death. Thank You for the example and power of our Lord's prayers. In His name we pray. Amen.

Hymn for the day:
Thy Way, Not Mine, O Lord

PRAYERS & REMINDERS

The Prayer Life of Jesus

Scripture Reading: Matthew 26:26-30

During the last Passover feast Jesus would eat with His disciples, He instituted the Lord's Supper. From that moment on the New Covenant in His blood would be inaugurated, making the old Passover no longer a sacrament of worth and efficacy. At the beginning of the feast, no doubt the customary prayers were said, and the ceremony properly observed in remembrance of the first Passover in Egypt, and the exodus from bondage. As the feast progressed, the Lord Jesus took some of the bread, and blessed it, broke it, and gave it to His disciples and said, *Take, eat; this is My body.* It is worthy of note that the first step our Lord took in transforming the sacrament of the old covenant into the most fundamental sacrament of the new covenant was that of prayer. This prayer, like so many of His prayers was a prayer of thanksgiving and consecration. This is why we always offer a prayer of thanksgiving and consecration as we begin to serve the elements of the Lord's supper. Unlike some branches of Christendom, we do not claim that our prayers have the mystic power of transforming the bread into the body of Christ, and the fruit of the vine into His blood. Nor do we believe that even when the Lord Jesus took the bread and said, *This is my body,* that the bread He gave His disciples had magically changed into His actual, physical body. No, it was a prayer of gratitude for the bread. It would be even more unthinkable for the fruit of the vine to have been transformed into His actual blood, for the Jews were forbidden to eat or drink the blood of the Passover Lamb, or any other animal. Moreover this same prohibition was even commanded to the Gentile believers at the Jerusalem council as recorded in Acts 15. What made the eating of the bread and drinking of the cup a sacramental meal, was not a magical transformation, but rather His prayer and the word of authority spoken by Christ and the command for believers to observe this until He comes again.

PRAYERS & REMINDERS

——————————
——————————
——————————
——————————
——————————
——————————
——————————
——————————
——————————

Prayer: Lord, in gratitude, we eat of the bread and drink of the cup when we come to Your blessed table. As we feed upon the physical symbols with our bodies, may we feed by faith on that which the bread and cup portray, the sacrifice and fullness of Christ our Lord. Amen.

Hymn for the day:
According to Thy Gracious Word

The Prayer Life of Jesus

Scripture Reading: Luke 22:39-46

Before these words of prayer were offered up by the Savior, He met with His disciples and went before the Father in the prayer recorded in John 17. This is known as the High Priestly prayer of our Lord. But for our purposes, we will consider His prayer to the Father while the disciples had fallen asleep and He was all alone. In many ways this was the most important prayer our Lord ever prayed, for our salvation depends on the outcome of this prayer. Of course, it was also the most difficult prayer He ever prayed and the most costly. It cost Him His life and far more. Because He knew the dreadful consequences of praying this prayer and making this decision, He agonized greatly as He prayed. By the time He had completed this prayer, He was physically, mentally, and emotionally exhausted. The writers of the Gospels, especially Matthew and Luke, record not only the words He prayed there in the garden, but also record His deep grief and the earnestness with which He offered this prayer. This is a very unique prayer in many ways, yet there is much we may learn of prayer from this poignant scene of Christ in the garden of Gethsemane.

First, we learn that prevailing prayer must involve our whole being, body, mind, and heart. We may not always fall on our faces before the Lord when we pray, but our posture in prayer may be an indication of how seriously we enter into the presence of the Lord. The sick, the aged, the invalid have no choice in their physical posture, but all others should give some consideration to this. When we are faced with situations and needs that are life shaping and future determinate, we may find that kneeling is the most appropriate posture. There may be times we need to fall on our faces before Him. If we are to pray without ceasing as we are encouraged to do, our posture will be determined by the circumstances. However, the spirit with which we pray should always be one of reverence and awe. Another great lesson we can learn from this prayer of our Lord is that when we pray, our total focus must be on the Lord. No prayer should ever be offered to God in a casual, take it or leave it attitude. We may not pray with sweat and blood dripping from our bodies, but we will need to pray at times, with tears flooding our eyes and hearts. We pray with intensity of purpose and concentration on the will of God in all our efforts to pray. Finally we learn from the Savior's prayer that above all else, we pray to the Father, *Not my will, but Thine be done.*

Prayer: Father, in all things and circumstances we pray, *Not my will, but Thine be done.* We pray in Jesus' name. Amen.

Hymn for the day:
Go to Dark Gethsemane

PRAYERS & REMINDERS

The Prayer Life of Jesus

Scripture Reading: John 17

    For the next several days we will be looking at John 17, which is truly one of the highest mountain peaks of revelation. On this first day, read through the entire prayer, and read it through at least twice. My suggestion is to read this prayer on your knees if possible and ask the Lord to open your heart to the power, the truth, and the beauty of this remarkable insight into the heart and mind of our Lord and Savior. Hear again God's admonition to Moses when he approached the burning bush : *Take your shoes from off your feet, for the ground upon which you are standing is holy ground.* In that attitude of awe and reverence read this prayer. It is obvious that the Lord Jesus prayed these words aloud so that His immediate disciples might hear Him. It is equally obvious that the Holy Spirit inspired John to record this prayer in its entirety so that we, too, might hear Him pray this prayer.

    There are a few general observations I would make about this prayer before we consider its details each following day. Though the Lord prayed this prayer to the Father, He prayed it in the presence of His disciples. When we pray in public, or even with a small group of friends, our prayers should always be directed only to God. At the same time, we do owe to those with whom and for whom we pray, to pray in such a way that they might hear what we say to God and understand what we are praying. An example of this would be when we pray with our very young children, we want them to understand what we are praying, so that they too might learn to pray to their Father in heaven in language they can understand and express. When we pray with the dying, we want our prayers in their behalf to be comforting and helpful. When we pray with the elderly, we want them to be able to hear our prayers, and thus we may have to pray with more volume than we ordinarily pray. When we pray with and for unbelievers, we will have to avoid some of the theological language we might otherwise use. Now read this prayer and then pray in Jesus' name to His Father and yours.

Prayer: Lord Jesus, You have said, *no one comes to the Father except through Me.* So we come to the Father through You and in Your Blessed name. Accept our prayers, and intercede for us, O great High Priest. Amen.

Hymn for the day:
My Jesus, I Love Thee

PRAYERS & REMINDERS

November 12

The Prayer Life of Jesus

Scripture Reading: John 17:1-5

We move now to consider this greatest of all passages in more detail. This prayer is divided into three parts. In verses 1-5, Jesus prayed for Himself. In verses 6-19, Jesus prayed for His disciples. As we shall later see, much of this part of His prayer applies to all believers. Then in verses 20-26, we hear the Lord as He prayed for the church universal and for all believers of all ages. Does it seems strange to you that the most unselfish person who ever lived began His prayer of intercession by praying for Himself? Consider two things about this. In this prayer for Himself, there was not one selfish word in it. Quite the contrary there was a complete emptying of Himself, and full surrender to the Father's will. The other consideration is that in all our prayers we come before God with a sense of our own need, even as we pray for others.

As Jesus began this prayer, His concern was for the glory of the Father, and even as He prayed for Himself, His thought and heart were ever on *"Those whom the Father had given Him.* The mission and the authority the Father had given Him were for the salvation of the elect, that they might have eternal life. This is an amazing truth, for as Jesus would later assure His disciples after His resurrection, all authority in heaven and on earth had been given Him. It was His purpose to reveal by word and His sinless life the full glory of the Father.

He began *Father, the hour has come.* The plan of the ages was about to be consummated . The blessed covenant of redemption made between the Father and the Son from before the foundation of the world was now focused on the actual sacrifice of our Lord. He was about to become the Lamb on the Altar, as well as the perfect High Priest who would offer up once and for all the final sacrifice for the saving of His people. So He said, *The hour has come.* The unthinkable was about to happen, God would provide Himself as the Lamb of substitution, even as Abraham had prophesied long before. When you bow your head in wonder and prayer even now, look up and thank God for that hour, in which your eternal salvation was secured.

Prayer: Father, even as You glorified Yourself in and by the sacrifice of our Lord Jesus Christ, so glorify Yourself in us who are saved by His work on the cross. May our highest joy and our chief end always be to glorify You. Through Christ our Lord we pray. Amen.

Hymn for the day:
The Gloria Patri

PRAYERS & REMINDERS

November 13

The Prayer Life of Jesus

Scripture Reading: John 17:1-5

Do you feel that the reading of these verses from John 17 again is unnecessary? There is more truth and more transforming power in these few words than we will ever discover. Do not grow weary in reading them over and over again, until they are deeply ingrained in your mind and heart. Jesus began His prayer with these words, *Father, the hour has come.* His earthly life was drawing towards the end. The purpose for which He had come into the world was about to be fulfilled. His death on the cross would take place the next day, and He knew all that was involved in that horror which awaited Him; the weight of the sin of the world and the agony of bearing the curse and punishment of that sin. He also knew that beyond death and the tomb, would come the resurrection, the ascension and the beginning of His reign over the church, and finally His return in triumph.

The knowledge of these events beyond the cross and the tomb and knowing the joy that awaited Him, gave Him the courage to face the cross. Yet still He dreaded it for the suffering and agony awaiting Him was indescribable and almost unbearable. A short time before this prayer with His disciples, Jesus had met with certain Greek converts who had sought Him out when they came to the Passover celebration. He revealed to these seekers the certainty of His coming death, and said to them; *The hour has come when the Son of Man should be glorified...Now is My soul troubled, and what shall I say? 'Father, save Me from this hour? But for this purpose I came to this hour. Father, glorify Your name.* Is that how we would pray if we knew some great trial of suffering lay ahead? I know I would pray, *Father, save me from this hour.* But we must always remember that we may indeed honor and glorify the Lord in and through our trials. I think our prayer in those situations should be, *Father help me to be faithful and honor you even in the midst of my pain and grief.*

PRAYERS & REMINDERS

_____

_____

_____

_____

_____

_____

_____

_____

_____

Prayer: Lord, we acknowledge that we are more concerned for our own peace, safety and well being than we are for Your glory. Forgive us and help us to look to Jesus, the author and finisher of our faith, that in joy or in pain and sorrow, we may glorify You. For Jesus' sake we pray. Amen.

Hymn for the day:
Savior, Thy Dying Love

The Prayer Life of Jesus

Scripture Reading: John 17:1-5

Jesus prayed, *Father, glorify Thy Son that Thy Son may glorify Thee.* To understand this request, we must look closely at the word *glorify*, and see that it has many shades of meaning, even as it is used in these verses. One meaning is very close to the word reveal, or show forth. I think this meaning is primarily intended in this first request Jesus made to the Father. So the essence of this request as I see it is that Jesus was asking the Father to reveal to His disciples and to the world who He (Jesus) really was. He was asking that through and by His suffering and death, people would finally realize that He really was the Lamb of God who takes away the sin of the world.

Back in my long ago days, my hobby was the cutting and polishing of gem stones. I discovered that many gem stones did not have beauty and brilliance when found in their native setting. This was especially true of opals. Something of their inner fire and beauty could be seen, but the matrix in which the opal is found had to be ground and cut away for the inner fire to be seen. That beauty was there all along, but it was my job to bring it to light, so that inner beauty might be seen. I think this helps us understand what the Lord Jesus was asking the Father. It is in the suffering of Christ that we see the greatest, clearest glimpse of God's incredible glory. That He would send His beloved Son into the world to take the sinner's place before His judgment throne reveals the depth, length, width and height of God's glory and grace, and His wondrous love for us poor sinners. So the request of Jesus, *glorify Thy Son, that Thy Son may glorify Thee,* was abundantly answered, and by that answer of grace, our sins have been taken away, and we are now the beloved children of the heavenly Father.

Prayer: Lord Jesus, You knew that because the Father would answer Your prayer You would suffer and die and bear the guilt and penalty for our sins. Yet You prayed this prayer, and because You did, we are saved from God's wrath. Thank You, dear Savior. Amen.

Hymn for the day:
Praise Him! Praise Him!

PRAYERS & REMINDERS

November 15

The Prayer Life of Jesus

Scripture Reading: John 17:1-5; Matthew 28:18-20

Jesus prayed: *As You have given Him(Your Son) authority over all flesh that He should give eternal life to as many as You have given Him.* What a remarkable statement this is! This helps us to understand more fully the meaning of John 3:16. Behind these words of our Savior lies a wonderful mystery of grace. The Father has given to the Son a vast host of people to save and to be His very own. Later in this prayer we will hear Jesus say to the Father, *They were, and You gave them to Me.* Here again we see evidences for the covenant of redemption between the Father and the Son. The Father, Son, and Holy Spirit have entered into an everlasting covenant with each other to redeem all the elect. Your salvation is forever assured and secured by this covenant.

In order to carry out this covenant, the Father has given to the Son full authority to grant eternal life to the elect, but also to pass judgment on all who refuse Him. We see this in Matthew 25, when all the peoples of the world are gathered before the Son of Man who sits upon the throne of judgment. Not only does the Lord Jesus welcome home all those who are His, but with full authority He sends all others into outer darkness and condemnation. Note too, that the gift of life eternal and all appropriate rewards are given to those whom the Father has given to the Son. Jesus went on to say: *And this is eternal life that they might know You, the only true God, and Jesus Christ whom You have sent.* Here we have not only a definition of eternal life but a strong indication of the way, and the only way by which we may inherit it. We cannot know the Father except through the Son, and we cannot know the Son unless we know that He is one with the Father. This kind of knowledge is more than mental it includes the whole being, the heart, mind and will.

Prayer: Savior, we confess that the Father has given You full authority and power to grant to eternal life unto all whom You call to Yourself. Thank You that by Your word and Holy Spirit You call us to Yourself, and gloriously save us by Your life, death and resurrection. Amen.

Hymn for the day:
Forever Here My Rest Shall Be

PRAYERS & REMINDERS

The Prayer Life of Jesus

Scripture Reading: John 17:1-5; I Corinthians 8:6

Let us explore a little further, what it means to know the only true God and Jesus Christ whom He has sent. If we understand how the word *know* is used in Scripture, this definition of eternal life takes on a fullness and richness which we may miss. So frequently when the Bible uses the word know, it means far more than just knowledge of, or awareness of certain propositional truth. When God said to Israel, *You only have I known of all the families of the earth,* He meant more than just the awareness of Israel as a people. He was speaking of a relationship of blessing and love which He had conferred upon Israel. He had chosen them and made them to be His special people. His protecting, redeeming love rested upon them. So the very essence of eternal life is to be under the blessing of God, chosen to be His people, and loved with an everlasting love. Eternal life is a relationship of love, all encompassing love. We are His covenant people, known (loved) by Him, and given the privilege of knowing (loving) Him. We know (love Him because he first knew (loved) us. The awareness of this great privilege results in joyful acknowledgement of His sovereignty over our lives and glad acceptance of His love.

Notice how the Lord Jesus carefully links this knowledge and acknowledgement to the truth. *That they might know You, the only true God, and Jesus Christ whom You have sent.* A heart knowledge of God, an intimate and saving relationship with Him is impossible apart from the truth He reveals and we accept concerning Himself, and His Son, Jesus Christ. In fact, true knowledge of God is impossible apart from His Son. Any notion that the God of the Bible, and the God of modern Judaism, and the God of Islam are the same is insulting to God, the only true God, who is only known through Jesus Christ whom he has sent. Do you know Him? Are you known by Him?

Prayer: Father, we bless You for the perfect revelation You have given us in Your Word, through Your Son. Only through Him may we know You, and only through You may we know Your Son. Help us to know (love) You blessed God, Father, Son and Holy Spirit with all our heart, mind, and strength. Amen.

Hymn for the day:
Holy, Holy, Holy

PRAYERS & REMINDERS

The Prayer Life of Jesus

Scripture Reading: John 17:4-5; 2 Timothy 4:6-8

As the Savior continued in this part of the prayer to pray for Himself, He then summed up His own earthly life in these words: *I have glorified You on the earth; I have finished the work You have given me to do.* The Lord Jesus glorified the Father during His earthly ministry in two ways. (1) He fully revealed who the Father is. He gave us the clear and perfect revelation of God. He took away the layers of "interpretations" the Rabbis had been adding to God's perfect law for hundreds of years, and took the people back to the clear revelation the Old Testament gives us of the nature and glory of God. Jesus spoke the most profound truth when He said to Thomas and the other disciples; *Whoever has seen Me, has seen the Father.* The Lord Jesus lived out all the perfections of God's nature in his life and ministry. (2) By doing this, He brought honor, glory, and praise to the Father. His greatest purpose and His greatest joy was to do the Father's will. In these two ways, He truly had glorified the Father on earth. Humanly speaking, many would say of Jesus, "but He only lived a very short life, and His ministry was only three years." Most of us feel that life has just begun at that age, and three years is a short time to accomplish all that God gives us to do. We might look at this brief ministry of Christ and wish He had stayed a much longer time. If I had been one of His disciples, I would have begged Him not to leave. I would have said to Him, *Lord, there is so much I still don't understand. There are so many hungry people. There so many lepers, so many lame, deaf, dumb and blind. Please stay with us till life is over.*

But the all knowing Son, in perfect unity with the Father's will and heart, knew He had accomplished all the Father had given Him to do . He had loved the Lord His God with all His heart, mind, and strength. He had loved His neighbor as Himself. He had therefore lived a perfect life of obedience in every way; refraining from all evil, overcoming all temptations, and doing all good. We will never be able to pray, even on our death bed, *I have accomplished all You gave me to do.* But by God's grace we may be able to say with Paul, *I have fought the good fight...I have kept the faith.* Let this be our goal and glory.

Prayer: Dear Savior, thank You that You truly glorified the Father by doing all He had given You to do. Thank You that You did all that was necessary for us to be forgiven and to have the perfect righteousness You give to us. May we glorify You always. Amen.

Hymn for the day:
O Jesus, I Have Promised

PRAYERS & REMINDERS

_____
_____
_____
_____
_____
_____
_____
_____
_____

The Prayer Life of Jesus

Scripture Reading: John 17:4-5; Hebrews 11:32-40

By His perfect life, Christ has become our righteousness before the Father. By His sacrificial and atoning death, He has become our peace with God. All this he accomplished in His all too short(from our perspective) life. Many people who have served Christ well have had ministries of many years. One example with whom we are all familiar is the long, Christ honoring ministry of Dr James Kennedy, long time pastor of Coral Ridge Presbyterian Church, with all its associated ministries. His ministry spanned over forty years, and God was glorified in him and his ministry. I think much further back in history of the amazing ministry of Pastor Heinrich Bullinger, who served the Reformed Church in Zurich Switzerland for 55 years. He had succeeded to that ministry when Ulrich Zwingli was killed in one of the battles of the Reformation era in that city. He befriended the widow and orphans of Pastor Zwingli, and raised the children as part of his own family. Many refugees from all over Europe and Great Britain, fled to Zurich to escape persecution and death. Bullinger took them in, fed, clothed and sheltered them, while still serving as Pastor of the Church , and leader of the Swiss Reformation. Time would fail me to speak of John Calvin and his tremendous influence for God and for good in so many ways. Then there was Luther, the bold pioneer of the Reformation and the champion of many downtrodden and oppressed. What a debt we owe to brave John Knox who dared to pray, *O God, give me Scotland for Christ, or I shall die!* All these and many more had very long and distinguished careers in Christ's kingdom. But compared to what our Lord accomplished in His brief life and ministry of only three years, they would all agree they had done little. What they did accomplish was by His power, and for His glory. For by His life and death, you are this moment a child of God destined for eternal joy.

Prayer: O gracious and loving Savior, You have won our salvation. Even now You are praying for us whom the Father has given You from all eternity. Help us to serve and glorify You with gratitude and joy forever. Amen.

Hymn for the day:
Praise the Savior, You Who Know Him

PRAYERS & REMINDERS

November 19

The Prayer Life of Jesus

Scripture Reading: John 17:4-5; John 6:35-40

When Jesus prayed to the Father, *I have glorified You on the earth, having accomplished the work You have given Me to do,* He went right on to pray, *And now, O Father, glorify Me together with Yourself, with the glory I had with You before the world was.* In these words we find a slight shift in the nuances of the word *glorify.* Now the Lord is praying for His humiliation to end, and His exaltation to begin. Let all heaven join in praises to Him who is alive, and was dead, and now lives forevermore. Some of the most thrilling scenes in the book of Revelation show us the Father's answer to this request. The Lion of Judah, the victorious Lamb who is at the Father's right hand, receives the homage and praise of the whole creation. His work of redemption done, His meditorial office begun, the exalted Christ has returned home to heaven and claimed His rightful crown and place.

By this request the Lord was simply claiming the promise made to Him in the covenant of redemption. Of course we cannot pray such a prayer, for we have earned naught but the Father's displeasure and wrath. We who are favored so highly through Christ our mediator, deserve only hell, for the wages of sin is death. The Lord Jesus was asking for restoration to that which was His by nature and now by the atonement. The amazing wonder is that He had been willing to give up the glory and splendor of heaven to save lost and defiled sinners like us. Can you imagine the One who had dwelt with the Father from all eternity, and ever looked upon His blessed face would this very night in which he prayed this prayer look into the evil, haughty face of the High Priest, and hear him accuse Him of blasphemy because He stated He was the Messiah, the Son of God? O the depths of His grace and love!

Prayer: Savior, from Your exalted throne of glory, look down upon us poor sinners, and claim us as Your own. We are not worthy, but You are worthy. We are sinful, but You are sinless. O, merciful and gracious High Priest, deliver us from all temptations, and plead Your blood shed for us. Amen.

Hymn for the day:
Amazing Grace

PRAYERS & REMINDERS

The Prayer Life of Jesus

Scripture Reading: John 17:6-11; Luke 22:31-34

When Jesus began His High Priestly prayer with His disciples, He first prayed for Himself, but as we have seen there was nothing selfish about His prayer. On the contrary, His one great request was that in all His suffering and death, the Father would be glorified. He also had prayed that by the resurrection and ascension, He Himself would be restored to His former glory. But even as He prayed for Himself, His mind and heart were on His beloved disciples, and now the focus of His prayer would shift to these whom the Father had given Him.

The prayer in the first part of this section begins with His acknowledging these men as those whom the Father had given Him. Earlier in His ministry, Jesus had said; *Whoever confesses Me before men, him will I confess before My Father in heaven.* Of course the primary fulfillment of that promise has to do with the final day of judgment, but even now, in this prayer, we see a partial fulfillment of the promise as Jesus confesses these men before the Father in prayer. He said: *I have manifested Your name to the men whom You gave me out of the world.* To *manifest His name* means to reveal the nature and character of God in all its fullness of truth and beauty. The word *manifest* suggests a many faceted revelation. When the light of the sun is seen through a cloud, the beautiful rainbow appears, and we get some idea of the real glory of light. When we see God through His Son, the Lord Jesus Christ, we begin to understand how glorious and wonderful He is. He is the complete and full revelation of God's nature and attributes. He alone is capable of showing us the Father, for he and the Father are one. How blessed were these fortunate men of old. But we are no less blessed, for through the written Word, we may see the living Word and through Him, the Father.

Prayer: O God, our Father in heaven, thank You that Your sent Your Son into the world to save sinners. Thank You, dear Savior, that now we may know the Father, because You have said, *whoever has seen Me has seen the Father.* Amen.

Hymn for the day:
Join All the Glorious Names

PRAYERS & REMINDERS

The Prayer Life of Jesus

Scripture Reading: John 6:43-51; John 17: 6

While praying to the Father, Jesus referred to His disciples in these words: *The men You have given Me out of the world. They were Yours, and You gave them to Me.* How are we to understand this? All believers are given to the Son by the Father in the covenant of redemption. They are given to the Son, by the Father whose they were and are from all eternity. In what sense could the Lord say of these disciples, *They were Yours?* In a general sense, this is true of all people because God is the Creator and giver of all life. But in this prayer Jesus is referring to something quite above and beyond this generality. He is referring to those whom the Father had elected for salvation from all eternity. There is a special sense in which these, and these only are intended here. In fact the word *they* is in the emphatic and exclusive sense. Don't let this trouble you. This is a truth that gives us great comfort and assurance. If you believe in the Lord Jesus Christ as the Son of God and your own dear Savior, it is because you are a gift from the Father to the Son. Listen to these comforting words of Jesus in John 10:29; *My Father who has given them to me is greater than all, and no one is able to snatch them out of My Father's hand.*

Jesus' confession of His own before the Father is based on the promises and gifts of the Father to Him. It is as if he were saying to the Father, *I am now recognizing these men as Your gift to Me. Therefore I lift them up before You for Your assurance to me and to them that You have kept Your promises to Me.* Jesus then goes another step in His confession of these men when He adds these words: *And they have kept Your word.* This was indeed an amazing thing to say about them. Remember that earlier in the evening, He had warned these men of their weakness when He said, *All of you will forsake Me.* Before this he had said to these twelve men; *O you of little faith!* But now when speaking to the Father in their behalf he says, *They have kept Your word.* The Savior sees beyond our weaknesses and our many failures and knows that one day we will indeed and forever keep His word.

PRAYERS & REMINDERS

_____

_____

_____

_____

_____

_____

_____

_____

_____

Prayer: Lord Jesus, You have confessed us before the Father, not so much for what we are now, but for who You are, and for what we will be when Your work is finished in us. Thank You for the assurance that *He who has begun a good work in you will perform it unto the day of Christ.* Amen.

Hymn for the day:
All That I Am, I Owe to Thee

The Prayer Life of Jesus

Scripture Reading: Matthew 26:37-46

How gracious is our Lord in His prayer for His disciples, as He confesses them before the Father. In light of their past failures, and with His knowledge that soon all of them would forsake Him and flee, how could He possibly say to the Father, *They have kept Your word*? This is a very crucial question for all of us, and especially for those who have doubts and fears about their salvation because they know their own weaknesses. Obviously Christ did not mean these men were sinless, or even nearly so. In fact He acknowledged that His very own would act at times as if they were not His, but of the world. The difference it seems to me is that though believers may fall, and as our Catechism says, even into grievous sins, yet they will certainly persevere unto the end, and be saved. This is not to encourage sin, but to encourage sinners like me. Do you think Jesus' disciples felt like they were saved men, and true believers in Christ as they ran in terror before the arresting officers who came to take Christ away? Do you think Peter felt like a saved man when he stumbled off into the darkness, weeping over his own weakness? But in this gracious prayer our Lord does not refer to any of their sins or weaknesses, or even their little faith. Rather, He knew that in the end they would hold on to His words as a drowning man might hold on to a life cushion, and that His word would save them, and bring them safely to shore, because they belonged to the Father. Jesus knew of them what He knows of you, that He will win the victory in your life. He knows that He who has begun a good work in you will complete it. You must believe this too, or you will sink in despair. You will never know peace if you think that your perseverance is a work of your will and will power. The Son of God is even now confessing you before the Father with these same words, *And he(she) has kept Your word.*

Prayer: Thank You, precious Savior, that you look not upon what we are now, but what we shall be by Your love and power. But please, dear Savior, work in us grace and change even now, that we may glorify you and enjoy you now and forever. Amen.

Hymn for the day:
Because I Knew Not When My Life Was Good

PRAYERS & REMINDERS

The Prayer Life of Jesus

Scripture Reading: John 17:6-8; John 6:60-71

As the Lord Jesus continued His confession of the disciples before the Father, He attests to the reality of their knowledge and faith. He said: *Now they have known that all things which You have given Me are from You. For I have given them the words which You have given Me.* What seems to us to have been a very tenuous and weak affirmation by the disciples, is accepted by Jesus as real and genuine. Before this in the upper room His disciples had said to Him, *Now we are sure that You know all things...by this we believe that You came forth from God.* Do you remember how Jesus responded to this assertion? *Do you now believe? Indeed the hour is coming and has now come that you will be scattered each to his own, and you will leave Me alone.* But in this prayer to the Father in their behalf, His words are tender towards them, and affirming

Jesus makes a three-fold assertion of those whom the Father has given Him, based on their reactions to His teachings. (1)*They have received them. (2) They have known that I came forth from You. They have believed that You sent Me.* How gracious of the Lord to say these things about them and about us who join them in confessing Christ. For three years they received His every word. When the multitudes turned away from the Lord Jesus, and walked with Him no more, He asked the faithful twelve , *Will you too, turn away from Me?* They answered for themselves and for us: *Lord to whom shall we go? You (alone) have the words of eternal life.*

Prayer: Lord Jesus, the answer of Your disciples of old is our answer too. To whom shall we go, for You alone have the words of eternal life. Amen.

Hymn for the day:
O Master, Let Me Walk with Thee

PRAYERS & REMINDERS

The Prayer Life of Jesus

Scripture Reading: John 17:9-10; Matthew 19:23-30

Jesus prayed for His disciples, and in this prayer He acknowledged them before the Father as being His true followers. Based on His testimony in their behalf, He went on to make certain requests of the Father for them. He said: *I pray for them. I do not pray for the world, but for those whom You have given Me, for they are Yours. And all mine are Yours and Yours are mine, and I am glorified in them.* Before making the specific requests on their behalf, the Lord Jesus made sure these loyal men knew that He was praying for them in a very specific sense, and in almost an exclusive sense. I will only say a few things about these words, and save a more detailed explanation for the following devotionals. The first thing to note is that the Lord's intercessory prayers are always and only for the elect. I think it is logical to assume that He prays for all the elect, even those who have yet to come to faith, but are known by Him to be among those the Father has given Him. Let this thought fill your mind as you read and hear these words. The Lord Jesus knows you and looks on you with love and favor. Is it because you are especially deserving and good that He prays for you? Not at all. He prays for you because in the grand covenant of redemption between the Father and the Son, you belong to Christ as a gift from the Father. He has chosen you in Christ from before the foundation of the world, as we learn in Ephesians 1. And because you are His as a gift from the Father, the Lord Jesus will ever mention your name and your needs in His intercession. He will confess you before the Father in His prayers, and on the day of judgment. Don't you rejoice when you know godly people are praying for you? Don't you feel a sense of relief to know that others love you enough to pray for you? How much more do we appreciate and love our Savior, who ever lives to make intercession for us, and with the perfect prayer the Father hears and answers.

Prayer: O Lord our God, how can we ever thank You enough for the never ceasing prayers of our Savior, Your Son, in our behalf. There are times we don't know how to pray, or for what. But He knows, He cares, and He prays. Thank You, Lord Jesus. Amen.

Hymn for the day:
Jesus, Lover of My Soul

PRAYERS & REMINDERS

The Prayer Life of Jesus

Scripture Reading: John 17:9-13; John 14:15-24

The time was drawing near for Jesus to leave His disciples and return to His rightful place in heaven. He has perfectly obeyed the Father and has fully instructed His disciples in the revelation of the Father. He has told them that they are His, because the Father has given them to Him. On the basis of this assured relationship, He now makes certain specific requests on their behalf. What are these requests and how are we to understand them? *Holy Father, keep through Your name those whom You have given Me.* Knowing that he was sending forth His disciples as sheep among wolves, the Master prayed for their protection. He addressed God as *Holy Father* because He wanted these men to know that God is holy and desires holiness of His people. What did the Lord mean when He asked, *Keep through Your name those whom You have given Me.?* The name of God means all the truth about God, God's revealed truth about Himself is found in the Bible alone. So this request could well mean, keep them in Your word, and later that is exactly what He did ask. God's word is the only way believers are made holy and kept holy. When we neglect God's word, we neglect the truth about God, and we neglect God Himself. When we allow the pressures of our busy lives to keep us out of the Word, we are in grave danger.

The next request the Savior makes flows out of this first one. He prayed: *That they may be one as we are one.* This takes some explanation because this is an often misused and even abused text. It is the battle cry of many who promote organic Church unions at the expense of doctrinal purity. This of course requires ignoring the context, which makes these words a pretext to promote a human agenda. What Jesus was praying for was loving respect and a spirit of oneness between all true believers. This is His agenda and our solemn duty.

PRAYERS & REMINDERS

_____

_____

_____

_____

_____

_____

_____

_____

_____

Prayer: Great and Holy God, our Father in heaven, we are grateful for Your Word. May it ever be the basis for all our relationships with other believers, that we may truly be one in the Lord. For Jesus' sake. Amen.

Hymn for the day:
We Are God's People

The Prayer Life of Jesus

Scripture Reading: John 17:12-15; Romans 8:31-39

Jesus prayed: *While I was with them in the world, I kept them in Your name. Those whom You gave me, I have kept; and none of them is lost except the son of perdition that the Scripture might be fulfilled.* All during His earthly ministry Christ had taught His disciples by word and deed the great truths concerning God and their salvation. In this way He had guarded them from error and the hatred of the world. The Good Shepherd had protected His sheep from the ravenous beasts of prey, the Devil and all His evil brood. He had also protected them from the "leaven" of the scribes and Pharisees. The Father's charge to His Son was a sacred trust, and the Son did not fail in this trust. He said, *those You gave me, I have kept, and not one of them is lost.* How could they be lost when they were given to the Good Shepherd to guard and save? But what about the mystery of Judas Iscariot? He was one of the chosen twelve. He had witnessed all the miracles of Christ, and heard every lesson and sermon He preached, yet in the end betrayed Him. How does this match with Christ's words, *of all You have given Me, I have lost none except the son of perdition?* Does this mean one can be saved, and then lost? No! Not at all. Christ was not saying, *I have saved all You have given Me, with exception of the son of perdition.* The Father did not give the Son one described as the son of perdition. How could he be a gift from the Father, when his father was the devil? The mystery of why Christ included him in the band of twelve is not explained, except to say, this too was foreseen in Scripture. On one hand Judas acted as a free moral agent and was accountable for his sin. When the word tells us, *Then Satan entered into Judas,* it was because Judas had invited him in to control his life and actions. He was not an innocent bystander. My advice to you is to leave this mystery in God's hands, and guard your heart and mind well and call upon the Savior to rebuke the Devil in your behalf.

Prayer: Father, we thank You that in Christ we have eternal security of our salvation. Help us always to resist the wiles of the Devil, and claim the promise that if we resist him, he will flee from us. In Jesus' name we ask this. Amen.

Hymn for the day:
I Know Whom I Have Believed

PRAYERS & REMINDERS

The Prayer Life of Jesus

Scripture Reading: John 17:13-19; Philippians 4:4-9

Jesus desired that His disciples might have great joy in the midst of their trials. He prayed: But now I come to You, and these things I speak in the world that they may have my joy fulfilled in themselves. Once more the Lord speaks of His immediate departure. He knew the way ahead for Himself and for the disciples would be hard, painful, and crushing. He also knew the end was sure, for He was returning to the Father. He also knew His beloved disciples would be sorely tested by what He would endure. He had promised His disciples great joy. Now He appeals to the Father to insure the fulfillment of that promise. Have you ever wondered why the Lord Jesus talked so much about joy in that upper room experience with His disciples, on the eve of His crucifixion? The joy He promised and for which He prayed was dependent on the completion of His work of redemption, which included the cross, but also the resurrection. When the disciples were at last convinced that he had truly risen from the dead, their joy was overwhelming. Assurance of Christ's victory and joy go hand in hand. No matter what may happen to us in this world as a result of the fall, including the hatred of the world, the truth of Christ's finished work of salvation produces great joy in believers. Chief among these truths is that Christ died for our sins on the cross, and this paid in full for our justification. Christ rose again from the dead in bodily form, convinced His disciples He was really alive, and ascended into heaven with the promise of His return to earth in power and glory. Whenever you feel defeated by the world, or the circumstances of your own life, remember these truths and rejoice. Joy was promised by Christ, and then He went before the Father with the request that you might know the fullness of His joy. Judas Iscariot lost joy forever when he departed from Christ in the upper room. You may have joy eternal when you come into the presence of Christ, and are embraced by His love.

PRAYERS & REMINDERS

_____

_____

_____

_____

_____

_____

_____

_____

_____

_____

Prayer: Lord Jesus, we live in a broken world, and we are a fallen people. In You alone may we have the fullness of joy everlasting. Help us to draw ever nearer to You that Your joy may become our treasured possession. Amen.

Hymn for the day:
Rejoice! The Lord is King

The Prayer Life of Jesus

Scripture Reading: John 17:15-19; John 16:25-33

I was talking with one of God's aged saints recently who had the question I so frequently hear: Why doesn't God just take me home? I'm tired of this world, and so unhappy with my lot. We know this world is not our home, we're just passing through on our way to heaven. But we cannot dismiss this life as if it were unimportant and nothing to do with our true home in God's heaven. Jesus prayed, *I do not pray that You should take them out of the world, but that You should keep them from the evil one.* In God's good time, we will be taken out of the world, but for now God has you here for His purpose, and you have the Savior's prayer that God would keep you from the evil one. The disciples had work to do, a Gospel to proclaim, and a Kingdom to offer. What a tragedy it would have been if the only witnesses to the resurrection had been taken out of the world, before they had opportunity to tell the world. Maybe God's purpose for keeping you in the world for the time being seems less spectacular to you than the opportunity given the first disciples, but it is no less important in God's sight. Maybe He wants you to demonstrate that a believer may endure the ravages of age and diseases and still show Christ to those you who have no hope. Maybe your patient endurance will open their eyes to the Savior's love so they too may go to heaven one day. I think the Savior's prayer for each of us every day we are here on earth is the same He prayed so long ago. *I do not ask that You should take them out of the world, but that You should keep them from the evil one.* God will take you home one day, but in the meanwhile ask Him to keep you from the evil one, and for Him to use you for His glory, no matter how lowly the task.

Prayer: Lord, please protect us from the evil one and help us to wait patiently for Your time to take us home to meet our Savior, and all those whom You have given Him in the great covenant of redemption. Amen.

Hymn for the day:
When All My Labors and Trials Are O'er

PRAYERS & REMINDERS

The Prayer Life of Jesus

Scripture Reading: John 17:20-26; Psalm 133

As the High Priestly prayer of our Lord draws towards its end, we hear Jesus praying in this way: *I do not pray for these alone, but for all those who will believe in Me through their word.* In this part of His prayer the Lord looks down through the ages and sees His beloved bride, the church, as it expands, grows, endures and is finally made His perfect bride for all eternity. For what shall He pray in these final words of the most powerful prayer that has ever been prayed? His requests for the church are basically two. He prays for its true unity, and for its triumph in heaven to be with Him and to behold His glory, and share in that vision glorious. The first request was contained in these words of Christ: *That they all may be one as You, Father, are in Me, and I in You; that they also my be one in Us.* Does the truth implied in that request amaze, astound, and humble you as much as it does me? We might have expected the Lord to pray, *That they might be one.* But then the Lord added these words say-ing: *As You Father are in Me and I in You, that they also may be one in Us.* These qualifying words are what gives this request such mystery and such power! What did the Lord mean by these words? The first thing we may say is that the oneness for which the Lord prayed is not primarily some outward, man made contrivance which is how so many attempt to explain these words. His prayer is that the real spiritual unity of believers resemble the inherent unity between the Father and the Son. Of course our unity with each other cannot replicate the unity within the Trinity. Why? Because the unity within the Trinity is one in essence, while our unity is one of common commitment to the Lord and His will. How is this unity best expressed so it does resemble the unity within the Trinity? The answer is simple. As we fulfill Christ's great command to love one another as He has loved us, we draw nearest to expressing the unity within the blessed Trinity, because God is love, and the Father, Son and Holy Spirit dwell together in perfect love. Their love is the foundation of our love.

Prayer: What a great and blessed God You are, O Father, Son and Holy Spirit. Fill us with Your per-fect love that we may learn to love each other. Amen.

Hymn for the day:
Blest Be the Tie That Binds

PRAYERS & REMINDERS

The Prayer Life of Jesus

Scripture Reading: John 17:20-26; Revelation 5

The grand prayer of our Lord ends with the most sublime words and concepts that eye has ever seen, ear has ever heard, or the mind of man conceived. The Savior asked that all those whom the Father has given Him may one day see His full glory. Then the Lord Jesus reinforces His request by adding these words: *And the glory which You gave Me, I have given them, that they may be one just as We are one: I in them, and You in Me; that they may be made perfect in one.* The Lord Jesus wants to make sure the Disciples really hear what He is saying, and the petition the petition He offers in their behalf. Here again, the word glory seems to revert back to the primary meaning of revelation. So this could properly read; *and the full disclosure of Yourself You gave Me, I have given to them, so that they may be made complete in their unity.* And just to make sure they understand He means more than just head knowledge, He goes on to add, *I in them, and You in Me that they might be made perfect in one.* The Apostle Paul must have already known of this prayer or maybe he even saw a copy of it. In Colossians 1:27 he wrote*; Christ in you, the hope of glory.*

How does all this work out in our experience? There is mystery and glorious truth wrapped up in these words that we dare not miss. God the Father dwells in the Son, and through the Holy Spirit, the Son dwells in believers, so that we become heirs of God, and joint heirs with Christ. Therefore, through Christ, the Father's beloved Son, we receive both pardon and peace with God, true righteousness and more. Once again I quote from Paul in 1 Corinthians 1:30: *But of Him(God), you are in Christ Jesus, who became for us wisdom from God; and righteousness, and sanctification and redemption.* This best explains what the Lord meant when He said; *I in them.* Finally, the Lord Jesus concluded His prayer with these words: *And I have declared to them Your name, and will declare it, that the love with which You loved Me may be in them, and I in them.*

Prayer: Dear Lord Jesus Christ, our Savior and our High Priest, we give You praise and thanksgiving that You prayed this prayer with Your disciples, and by the Holy Spirit, it has been preserved for us unto this very day. Thank You that You ever live to make intercession for us. Amen.

Hymn for the day:
For All the Saints

PRAYERS & REMINDERS

December 1

Hope in the Midst of Despair

Scripture Reading: Genesis 3:1-19

There is a very dark background to the glorious light of Christmas. It is the story of why Christmas was and is necessary. Let's go back to the beginning of it all in the beautiful Garden of Eden. When God created man, He created him in His own image. He created him holy, happy and undefiled. He placed him in the most perfect and beautiful surroundings possible, and provided him with every need of body, mind and soul. He gave to Adam a beautiful mate to be his companion and helper, a woman, whom Adam named Eve, the mother of all the living. He also gave to Adam and Eve another very special gift, the gift of freedom.

But with the gift of freedom there came responsibility also, the responsibility of choices to be made. And above all there was one basic choice to be made, and that choice would guide all other choices. The choice was to believe God's revealed word, trust and obey Him. The promise held out for obedience was eternal life, never-ending joy and, above all, unbroken fellowship with the Creator. At the same time, the warning against disobedience was grim and foreboding. To disobey meant death, death in all its dimensions. The immediate consequence would be separation from the Creator with physical death to follow in God's appointed time. It would seem the choice would be easily made in favor of obedience. But then enters the cunning and evil Tempter, with his very subtle temptation. He told them death would not be the consequence of disobedience, rather they would gain knowledge and with that knowledge, equality with the Creator. What a powerful temptation! Satan's first step was to cast doubt upon the truthfulness of God's word. Then he insinuated that God's purpose was suspect. That is still his approach to all of us in one form or another. First of all he casts doubts in our minds about the Bible. Then he tempts us with the question, "If God really loves you, why are bad things happening in your life?" God's answer to those doubts is what Christmas is all about.

Prayer: Dear God, thank You for Your gift of love. Thank You that You sent Your Son into the world to seek and save the lost. Thank You that He, the Good Shepherd, has found His lost sheep, of which I am one. Amen.

Hymn for the day:
Come, Thou Long-Expected Jesus

PRAYERS & REMINDERS

December 2

Hope in the Midst of Despair

Scripture Reading: Genesis 3:1-19

It seems so impossible, so unbelievable, but Satan's word was accepted over God's word, by two people who had the ability to perfectly obey God, and every reason to do so. This is especially true because, unlike us, they were still holy, and innocent of any sin. But they were subject to temptation. God did not create them as mindless puppets, but as free moral agents of whom choices were possible and required. Why God created them so has long been a subject of speculation, but the Bible never answers the "why" questions when it comes to God's actions.

So being free moral agents they had to face temptation because Satan (whose origin is wrapped in mystery) was determined to bring ruin upon God's good creation, and especially the man and his wife who were created in God's image. The story is starkly simple. They were tempted, they sinned, and they fell from their created estate of holiness and happiness. They would be expelled from Eden, and as a result of their rebellion, they who were created with the potential for everlasting life and bliss, in perfect fellowship with their Creator, came under the curse of death and the wrath of God. Never again would they be able or even willing to run eagerly to meet God in the cool of the day, or any other time. It seemed that all was lost, and that they would live out their limited days in remorse and misery over what they had lost. However, at the lowest moment, when God announced the fearful consequences of their sin, He also gave a promise of redeeming grace. And that promise would be the foundation stone upon which the story of redemption and salvation would be built. That promise was also the beginning of Christmas and all it means for us today.

Prayer: Gracious God, when all seemed lost in the tragedy of mankind's fall into sin, You let a light shine through the darkness of despair and hopelessness. Even in our own lives, often our situation seems beyond hope, but You never leave us in despair, but point us to the promised "Seed of the woman", by whom we are saved, even Christ our Lord. Amen.

Hymn for the day:
O Come, O Come, Emmanuel

PRAYERS & REMINDERS

Hope in the Midst of Despair

Scripture Reading: Genesis 3:1-19

And I will put enmity between you and the woman, and between your seed and her seed; He shall bruise your head, and you shall bruise His heel. On the surface, this may not sound like much hope in this dark picture. However, this is the very beginning of the Gospel of our Lord and Savior Jesus Christ. The woman had been won over by the serpent to his side, and away from God's side. She was the first to fall. Now God determines that in the place of obedience to Satan's charms, He will place a barrier between them that He might win her back to His way and cause. So at the very point of his triumph, Satan is frustrated by God's grace.

God went on to add, *And between your seed and her seed.* Ultimately the contest will be between the One Person in all history who could truly be called the woman's seed, and that One Person was the virgin born Son of God who became man to redeem Adam and Eve, and all the chosen seed, from the kingdom of Satan and death. By these words, God also divides the human race into two categories: the elect, whom He will save by sending His Son into the world, and the reprobate who choose to follow Satan and submit to his rule. In order to win our salvation, the Seed of the Woman must be sorely bruised and suffer much, but in so doing He will deliver the death blow to Satan by His own suffering on the cross. The Christmas message of Genesis 3:15 is that God will ultimately redeem all His precious elect from Satan's wiles and power. Not one whom the Father gave to the Son in the covenant of redemption will be lost. Jesus Christ, the true Seed of the woman said: *And I give them eternal life, and they shall never perish, neither shall anyone snatch them out of My hand.*

Prayer: We praise and exalt You, our great and gracious God. You could have left Adam and Eve and all their posterity to suffer in the darkness of despair and eternal night. But in the midst of great despair, You gave them a message of great hope, the message of a redeemer, even Christ our Lord. Amen.

Hymn for the day:
Let All Mortal Flesh Keep Silence

PRAYERS & REMINDERS

_____

_____

_____

_____

_____

_____

_____

_____

_____

December 4

A Strange but Wonderful Christmas Tree (1)

Scripture Reading: Luke 3:23-38

Where did the custom of having Christmas trees come from? I don't think anyone really knows, but lack of knowledge never seems to inhibit some people from telling you all about it. I know some folks think having a Christmas tree is a pagan practice, but they have never been able to convince me of this. They point to the practice of ancient pagans (I still don't know how they know) who were supposed to have trees in their homes to honor the gods or goddesses. So, they say, having a Christmas tree is a pagan practice. Of course, using the same logic, one might say that praying is a pagan practice since pagans pray. Therefore when we pray this is a pagan practice. Do you see how silly some lines of logic (?) run?

Having said all that, this devotional and the ones following it are not about Christmas trees as we ordinarily use that expression. No, these devotionals will focus on the family tree of our Lord Jesus Christ, whose birth we celebrate at Christmas. Some of you may be groaning about trying to read the genealogy of the Lord Jesus as we have it in both Matthew and Luke. But these genealogies tell some very interesting stories about the lineage of the Lord Jesus. Luke traces His line all the way back to Adam and Eve. One of the reasons Luke went all the way back to Adam was that he wanted to prove that Jesus was truly human (already in Luke's time, there were people who denied this) and to show that Jesus was the Savior, not just of the Jews, but of all people whom the Father would give Him. It was Adam and Eve who sinned and fell, so one of their descendents (actually Jesus was only descended from Eve by actual physical birth) must be the one to redeem the fallen race of mankind. This of course means He is your Savior, too, if you have accepted Him as your Lord and Savior.

Prayer: Father in heaven, God and Father of our Lord Jesus Christ, thank You for sending us Your Son, to be born of a woman and enter the world as we enter the world. But we are so grateful He was also God from all eternity, and then became also man by taking to Himself a true body and a reasonable soul. Amen.

Hymn for the day:
The Light of the World is Jesus

PRAYERS & REMINDERS

A Strange but Wonderful Christmas Tree (2)

Scripture Reading: Genesis 6:1-9

Noah was a just man, perfect in his generation, and Noah walked with God. Just as all people who come into this world are descended from Adam and Eve, so also are they descended from Noah. There are some striking similarities between Noah and Christ, so it is most fitting that this good man should be in the family tree of our Lord, and his. Noah was of the godly line of Seth, the son God gave Adam and Eve after wicked Cain had murdered his brother Abel. So in a sense Noah would be of "the seed of the woman". Noah's life was in sharp contrast to the people of his own generation, because by the time he came along, the world had become exceedingly wicked and was headed for a very severe judgment.

By the time our Lord Jesus was born, the nation of Israel was ruled by corrupt leaders who were hungry for power and control. One reason they hated Jesus so much was that His righteous life was a condemnation upon the apostate house of Israel. I'm sure Noah experienced the same kind of rejection and hatred. Had it not been for Noah, the entire human race would have perished from off the face of the earth. If the Lord Jesus had not come into the world, all people would be lost forever and would face the terror of an even more severe judgment. Against all human reason, Noah believed the word and warning of God and set about to ensure the safety of himself and his family by building an Ark that would endure the coming wrath. Jesus laid the foundation for the building of a spiritual temple that would be the haven of safety for all God's people forever. Yes, I'm glad Noah is in the family tree of Jesus, for as we consider him and his life, we have a better understanding of our Lord and His life, and this makes our celebration of Christmas even more meaningful.

Prayer: Thank You, Father, that good Noah was in the genealogy of our Lord Jesus. Thank that you saw in him a just man, who was perfect in his generation and a man who walked with You in a wicked world. Help us, like Noah, to find grace in Your sight that we may walk with You. In Jesus' name. Amen.

Hymn for the day:
Brightest and Best of the Sons of the Morning

PRAYERS & REMINDERS

December 6

A Strange but Wonderful Christmas Tree (3)

Scripture: Matthew 1:1-17

Guess what? For every man in the genealogy of our Lord Jesus, there is also a woman. Some of these ancestors of Jesus were great men and women of faith. Some were not. In this genealogy we find listed some very wicked kings, and we wonder why God would allow such people to be included. However, every ancestor of Jesus, man or woman, was a sinner. Some worse than others, but of each and every one we may say, "For all have sinned and come short of the glory of God."

I think three of the strangest inclusions in His genealogy were three women; Tamar, the daughter-in-law of Judah, by whom she bore a child; Rahab, the Harlot who hid the spies of Israel and saved their lives; and Bathsheba, with whom David committed his grave sin of adultery which led also to the death of her lawful husband. Uriah. She became the mother of Solomon, David's son who replaced his father on the throne of Israel. Strange isn't it? Why not just skip over these names and mention only Sarah, Abraham's wife, or maybe Ruth, though a Moabite, still a godly woman, or some of the others. I would venture to say that the inclusion of Tamar, Rahab, and Bathsheba not only reports accurate history, but is also a testimony to God's amazing grace and providence. Allowing for some questions concerning their sinful natures, actually these three women all turned out to be women of faith, who in spite of their sins, were used of the Lord to bear sons who are in the lineage of Jesus Christ. They also prepare us to understand that God in His even greater mercy and grace, includes them as spiritual descendents of our Lord Jesus. After all, the book of Romans tell us that we are heirs of God and joint heirs with Jesus Christ who was descended according to the flesh, from Tamar, Rahab, and Bathsheba.

Prayer: Dear Lord, how clearly we see Your amazing grace in the election of these three women who were ancestors of our Lord Jesus Christ. But how much more clearly do we see Your mighty grace in our election to salvation through Jesus Christ our Lord. Amen.

Hymn for the day:
How Lovely Shines the Morning Star

PRAYERS & REMINDERS

December 7

A Strange but Wonderful Christmas Tree (4)

Scripture Reading: Luke 1:26-38

Yesterday we looked at three of the women in the family tree of Jesus. Today we will look at one more woman in His family tree; the virgin Mary, the mother of Jesus. Long before in the garden of Eden, God had made a promise concerning the "Seed of the woman". He warned Satan and promised Adam and Eve, that the "Seed of the woman" would bruise the head of the serpent. In some ways, Mary is just as unexpected to play her role, as was the inclusion of the three women we looked at yesterday.

Who was this Mary? She was a young virgin girl engaged to a man named Joseph who was of the house and lineage of David. Mary was probably descended from David's line too. The usual age for young Hebrew maidens to be betrothed to a man for marriage was the early to mid-teens. We must assume she too was of this age. Beyond this we know practically nothing about her. But what we do know of the story of Mary is heart warming and wonderful. This young maiden girl was suddenly confronted with the Angel of the Lord, Gabriel, by name. She was told that she had been chosen to be the mother of the Messiah! His exact words were: ...*You will conceive in your womb, and bear a son and you shall call His name Jesus. He will be great, and will be called the Son of the Most High...* When she protested, saying, *How can this be, since I am a virgin?*, the Angel answered; *The Holy Spirit will come upon you, and the power of the Most High will overshadow you; therefore the child to be born will be called the Son of God.* Scary for a young virgin? Of course, but her answer will always rank with the most noble words of faith and submission to God's will: *Behold I am the servant of the Lord; let it be to me according to your word.* God has chosen just the right person to be the mother of the true "Seed of the Woman." May our submission to the word of the Lord be just as sincere and eager as was Mary's.

PRAYERS & REMINDERS

Prayer: Father, thank You for the lovely family tree of our Lord. How amazing, how glorious that You chose this virgin girl to be the earthly mother of our Lord. Thank You that she, too, came to saving faith in her Son who died for her and us. Amen.

Hymn for the day:
To Us a Child of Hope Is Born

December 8

We Hear The Christmas Angels!

Scripture Reading: Hebrews 1:1-14

In every story in the New Testament concerning the birth of Christ, Angels appear and have a prominent place in these narratives. Many of the Christmas hymns we sing tell us about Angels. Some of these hymns quote the words the Angels spoke or sang. Yet Angels are so remote from our own experiences and understanding, we seldom give them a thought. If we do it is a passing thought and little more. Still, it can't be denied that everywhere we turn in the Christmas story, Angels pop up! Angels were there long ago at the conception and birth of our Lord, speaking, singing, proclaiming the good news, rebuking unbelief, and bringing renewed hope to those who had lost hope.

Where are Angels today? Why don't we see or hear them at least occasionally? There is a very good reason why few if any of us ever have any real encounters with angels. The book of Hebrews tells us that the primary role of angels was to deliver God's revelation. But since the completion of the Word of God, it seems that Angels have slipped back into obscurity for the most part. What is their role if any today? The Word tells us only that they are ministering spirits sent to aid believers. Beyond that we know little of their present role.

But when Christ returns, once again angels will place a very prominent role according to the teachings of the Lord Jesus. If you ever see a real live Angel, be nice to it (him? her?). Jesus taught that the Angels will precede and accompany Him when He returns, and will gather the elect from the four winds of the earth. They will also be appointed to separate true believers from false pretenders. Some Angels will gather the reprobate and bind them and cast them into outer darkness! So they will be God's agents of mercy and judgment. The next few days we will consider the Christmas Angels in our Christmas devotionals.

Prayer: Father, we know so little of Your glorious creatures, the Holy Angels. We read of their work and at times we tremble in fear. Other times we are held spell bound and in awe as we read of the Angels who surround Your throne. Help us to understand all You would have us to understand about our fellow creatures, the Angels. In Jesus' name. Amen.

Hymn for the day:
Angels from the Realms of Glory

PRAYERS & REMINDERS

The Angel of Anticipation

Scripture Reading: Luke 1:5-25

The Story of Christmas as reported by Luke, begins with the coming of the Forerunner, John the Baptist. Right away an Angel is involved in this account. It was a dark and hopeless time in the life of God's people. They had lost their hard earned freedom bought by the blood of their valiant forebears. Their ruler was a man who had sold his soul to gain the throne. He was a grasping, greedy, bloody tyrant. Into this situation of despair, the light of Scripture falls upon two elderly people: a Priest named Zacharias who was married to the daughter of a priest. Her name was Elizabeth. "Zacharias" means The Lord remembers His covenant. Elizabeth means My God is faithful. They would soon be called upon to live up to their names! They were childless and well past the age of child bearing. They were not bitter, but they were disappointed. They are described as *righteous in the sight of God, walking blameless in all the commandments and requirements of the Lord.* Life in this fallen world may be filled with disappointments, frustrated ambitions, and empty dreams, but believers press on in God's strength.

It was Zacharias' turn to offer the incense offering in the temple. As he was fulfilling his duty, an Angel of the Lord appeared to him, with the startling message that he and his wife would soon have a son! Furthermore this son would be the forerunner promised in the book of Malachi to prepare the way for the Messiah. It seemed so impossible. In fact Zacharias expressed his doubts saying, *but I am an old man, and my wife is advanced in years.* For his unbelief he was stricken dumb until the baby was born. Then even as the Angel had instructed him, Zacharias named his new son, John. We know him as John the Baptist, but perhaps better named as John the herald, for his ministry was to announce the coming of Christ and to call upon Israel to repent, and prepare for His coming. Even today, as Christmas draws near once more, we are called upon to believe the word of God, and to repent of our sins.

Prayer: Father, may we not be as Zacharias and doubt Your word as we so often do. May we hear Your call as announced by John, to repent and prepare the way of the Lord. We ask this in Jesus' name. Amen.

Hymn for the day:
Christians, Awake, Salute the Happy Morn

PRAYERS & REMINDERS

Joseph and the Angel

Scripture Reading: Matthew 1:18-25

How much have you ever heard about Joseph, the unsung hero of Christmas? Here was a man, a carpenter by trade, who was preparing for the happiest moment of his life. He was betrothed to a young maiden named Mary, but the actual marriage had not yet taken place. Shortly before that glad event was to be consummated, Joseph received the shattering news that his beloved was pregnant, and not by him, that he knew. His heart was broken, his life was in complete chaos. His options were few. He could openly accuse her before the local Synagogue which might result in her being stoned to death. As a minimum she would be expelled from the Synagogue and forced to live in shame the rest of her life. There was a provision which allowed him to privately divorce her and give no reasons, though all would know. This was his decision, soon to be carried out. But while he was thinking, planning, and no doubt weeping over this decision, he fell into an uneasy sleep.

In that God-sent sleep, a dream began to develop that was more than a dream God sent His Angel to comfort him with a message of truth and hope that dried his tears, eased his heart, and opened his mind to a most wondrous truth. Joseph's life was in shambles. His dream of happiness destroyed, but God's message would change all that. *Joseph, son of David, do not fear to take Mary as your wife, for that which is conceived in her is from the Holy Spirit.* Mary had not been unfaithful, she had been the object of one of the greatest miracles ever since the dawn of creation. She was chosen to be the mother of the Messiah, and Joseph, His foster father! In the midst of our own chaotic lives and broken dreams God's message of Christmas speaks the same comfort and offers the same hope. Yes, life is real and can be very painful, but God has sent His only begotten Son into the world to save sinners like you and me. This gives life a depth of joy no earthly gift can possibly offer. Just as Joseph had a choice, to believe God and accept His plan for his life, so each of us face the same choice. We too, may believe God and act upon the truth of His word and experience the blessing of receiving Christ and trusting in God's wise providence.

Prayer: Father, thank You for choosing such a wise and godly man as Joseph to be the earthly father of our Lord Jesus. Thank You most of all for the gift of Your Son, by whom we have life everlasting. Amen.

Hymn for the day:
Good Christian Men Rejoice

PRAYERS & REMINDERS

The Shepherds' Angels

Scripture Reading: Luke 2:8-20

The story of the Angels appearing to lowly shepherds is the most familiar part of this familiar story of Christmas. Who doesn't know these words from heart: *Now there were in the same country shepherds living out in the fields, keeping watch over their flock by night. And behold, an angel of the Lord stood before them, and the glory of the Lord shone around them, and they were great-ly afraid.* The shepherds at the time of Jesus' birth were regarded as the lowest of the low. Why, a shepherd's testimony could not even be accepted in a court of law, they were considered to be so untrustworthy. But it was to these poor shepherds the Angel came announcing the birth of the Savior.

The announcement was not given in the King's palace or in the temple of the lordly Priests, but to the common man. Isn't that fitting? Think in what lowly state the Savior was born. He was born in a stable, wrapped in swaddling clothes and laid in a manger bed. I wonder if the shepherds were just as startled by the Angel's description of His humble birth as they were at the sight of the Angel. *Then the angel said to them, "Do not be afraid, for behold, I bring you good tidings of great joy which will be to all the people. For there is born to you this day in the city of David a Savior, who is Christ the Lord. And this will be the sign to you: You will find a Babe wrapped in swaddling cloths, lying in a manger."* It was so amazing, for them to hear that God had sent His Messiah unto them, the least of all people. And so they could believe this wonderful gift was for them; He was born where shepherds' babies might be born, and wrapped up as they would be. Then, the one great Angel was joined by a multi-tude of the heavenly hosts who were praising God and saying, *"Glory to God in the highest And on earth peace, goodwill toward men!"* The response of the shepherds? They believed the message. They went to Bethlehem as instructed, and found things just as the Angel told them. Then they went everywhere telling everyone what they had seen and heard. What a perfect way to cele-brate Christmas, then and now, for the shepherds and us!

Prayer: Glory to God in the highest, we also say and sing, dear Lord. Thank You that you sent Your Son to the meek and lowly, for such are we. Yet like the men of old we rejoice also in this won-drous story, and give You thanks that it is true, and that it was preserved for us. Amen.

Hymn for the day:
While Shepherds Watched Their Flocks by Night

PRAYERS & REMINDERS

_____

_____

_____

_____

_____

_____

_____

_____

_____

December 12

The Quest of the Magi

Scripture Reading: Matthew 2:1-12

So often people ask, who were these mysterious wise men, or Magi? Where did they come from, and how many were there? Do we really know there were three? How about the names so often ascribed to them – are these names in the Bible? So much of what many people think about the Magi has its source in legend, not in Holy Scripture or reliable history and logical deductions. And that is really a shame, because what we may know of them is so much more exciting and important than any imaginary tale you may have heard.

The Magi were from a scholarly and priestly caste which originated in ancient Babylon. They were astronomers, historians, and advisors to the King. It was said that no offering to the gods of Babylon could be made unless one of the Magi was present. Daniel and his friends who were taken captive after the fall of Jerusalem were trained in Babylon to take their places among the Magi. It is also a matter of record that many Babylonians of that day were greatly influenced by Daniel, became familiar with the Jewish Scriptures, and adopted the faith of Daniel and the Jews in Captivity. We don't know just how these Magi came to believe that a certain star would lead them to the birthplace of the coming King of the Jews, but they came seeking Him that they might do Him homage and offer Him worship. Their journey had been long, hard and dangerous, but their faith enabled them to persevere, until they came to Bethlehem, presented their gifts, and worshiped the young boy as God and King. In their homeland of Babylon, gold and costly perfumes could only be presented to royalty or as an offering to Deity. The gift they received was greater than the gifts they brought. *So, most gracious Lord, may we evermore be led to Thee.*

Prayer: Father, may we also have seeking hearts, searching out the glorious truth You have revealed in Your Son. Help us to search the Scriptures diligently, and to grow evermore in our understanding of Christ and our devotion to His kingdom. Amen.

Hymn for the day:
As With Gladness Men of Old

PRAYERS & REMINDERS

Herod's Cruel Failure

Scripture Reading: Matthew 2:13-18

What a disturbing thing it is to find a monster like Herod and his infamous cruelty as a part of the Christmas story. But how realistic to life in this fallen world is this tale of cruelty and woe. From the earliest days of the human race, when jealous Cain rose up and killed his righteous brother Abel, to this very day, hatred, murder, jealousy and inhumanity have been a constant story in the history of mankind. Herod was a special case. His rage, cruelty and killings were above and beyond even the most evil tyrants of that day. Yes he had built the imposing Temple in Jerusalem and a monumental work of design and construction it was, dwarfing the two previous Temples, and far more resplendent than even Solomon's ornate Temple. He was a very powerful man, and for the time being he had the full power of the mighty Roman Empire behind him. But he lived in constant fear and suffered from deep paranoia. He was convinced that his own sons were plotting against him, so he had several of them killed. He became suspicious of his wife and had her strangled to death, lest she bear a son who would supplant him. So when the Magi from Babylon or Persia came seeking the One who was born King of the Jews, Herod was both frightened and furious. He was not a descendent of David, he was not even a real Jew, and he knew the people longed to replace him with one from David's royal line. Upon hearing of the quest of the Magi, Herod called upon the Jewish scholars to tell him where the Christ should be born. Their reply, based on the writings of Micah, told him the King of the Jews would be born in Bethlehem. After finding he had been tricked by the Magi, he sent a squad of soldiers to kill all the male babies from two years old and under in the Bethlehem area. However, his Satan-inspired rage against the young Jesus was futile, and Jesus lived to fulfill His destiny. As we all know, that destiny was to save His people, you and me, from our sins, and take us to heaven to live with Him forever.

PRAYERS & REMINDERS

_____

_____

_____

_____

_____

_____

_____

_____

_____

Prayer: Dear Lord, as we read of that terrible atrocity of long ago, our hearts are broken. Yet all around us we see the power of Satan working through modern-day Herods to achieve their terrible goals. Help us to be faithful, resist evil, and serve the One who was born King of the Jews, and yes, of the Gentiles too, our Lord and Savior, Jesus Christ. Amen.

Hymn for the day: Thou Didst Leave Thy Throne and Thy Kingly Crown

December 14

The Hope and Joy of Anna and Simeon

Scripture Reading: Luke 2:22-38

Before the awful day when all the babies of Bethlehem were murdered, and before Joseph fled to Egypt to save the life of the child Jesus, Joseph and Mary left Bethlehem to take Jesus to the temple where two covenantal ceremonies were performed . First, at the age of eight days, He received the mark of the covenant as a sign that He belonged to the Lord. Following this, Mary would make the prescribed offering for her own purification, and then as the first male child in the family, Jesus would have been dedicated to the Lord, as the law of Moses required. While Joseph and Mary were in the Temple for these rites, they met a very old man named Simeon. He was righteous and devout, and longed for the appearing of the Messiah. The Holy Spirit had revealed to him that he would not die before Messiah came. So he waited in great hope. The same Holy Spirit led him into the Temple just as Mary and Joseph came to present their infant Son to the Lord. Simeon knew! He knew now the message of the Holy Spirit was real and true, that he would not die before Messiah came. He knew also the Spirit had led him to the temple at this precise moment. He reached out, took the baby from the surprised parents and blessed God with these now well-known words: *Lord, now You are letting Your servant depart in peace, According to Your word; For my eyes have seen Your salvation Which You have prepared before the face of all peoples, A light to bring revelation to the Gentiles, And the glory of Your people Israel.* Simeon went on to tell Mary that this child would be opposed by many, and that a sword would pierce her heart. By these words he predicted His rejection and death, even as the Prophet Isaiah had said long before.

At this same time a very elderly widow who constantly came to the temple to pray added her testimony of thanks that God had at last heard her prayers and had sent the Savior in her latter years. What a blessing for all the elderly who know the Lord Jesus. Truly we may say with Simeon and Anna, *Lord, now let Your servant depart in peace, for my eyes have seen Your salvation,* even our Lord Jesus Christ, who is our open door to the Father's house.

Prayer: Father, may all of us of old age be able to confidently say, "Lord, now let Your servant depart in peace, for our eyes have seen Your salvation." Thank You, Lord, for Christmas and all it means to us. In Jesus' blessed name. Amen.

Hymn for the day:
Once in Royal David's City

PRAYERS & REMINDERS
_____
_____
_____
_____
_____
_____
_____
_____
_____

December 15

A Promise of Peace

Scripture Reading: Micah 4:1-5; Luke 2:13-14

Many of the Ancient Prophets foretold a time of universal peace on earth. Two of the most prominent of these were Isaiah and Micah, whose lives and ministries coincided with each other. Some of the most beautiful passages in all the Bible were written by these two godly men who spoke of this coming day of peace when *They shall beat the swords into plowshares and their spears into pruning hooks; Nation shall not lift up sword against nation, neither shall they learn war anymore.* Then when Christ was born the Angels took up the theme crying out to the shepherds, **Glory to God in the highest, and on earth peace, goodwill towards men!**

In the Old Testament we have repeated promises that when Messiah comes, there will be world wide peace. When the Angels announced the birth of Messiah to the shepherds, they sang *Peace on earth, goodwill towards men.* But in a world filled with hatred, warfare, and strife, these ancient promises seem to be a mockery. With very few happy exceptions in which great nations and empires have become largely Christianized, at least outwardly, and for a short time, the long history of the world is a tale of warfare and ill will of men to men. A more careful study of Scripture will show that when Jesus came into the world to bring salvation, He laid the enduring foundation for peace by reconciling men to God and making reconciliation between men possible. But as we read what He taught, especially in Matthew 24 and 25, and John 14-16, we learn that He said many long years would pass after He went back to heaven, before He would return to establish the golden age of eternal peace. But He also promised He would make good on every promise of peace. Peter reflected the teachings of Christ when he wrote these words towards the end of his life: *We, according to His promise look for a new heaven and a new earth in which righteousness dwells.* The book of Revelation closes with a beautiful description of that renewed creation when all sin, pain, warfare, trouble and death will be no more, and all the redeemed will live at perfect peace with the Lord, with each other and with all creation. Peace on earth, goodwill towards men? Just wait, it is coming and it will exceed your best and wildest dreams.

Prayer: Praise we offer You, dear Savior, Prince of peace, for the promises which You will fulfill, and there will be peace on earth forever and ever. Amen.

Hymn for the day:
It Came Upon a Midnight Clear

PRAYERS & REMINDERS

December 16

Could We Be Wrong About Christmas?

Scripture Reading: Matthew 11:1-19

John the Baptist, perhaps better called, John the Forerunner, was described by Jesus in these words: *Assuredly I say unto you, among those born of women, there has nor risen one greater than John the Baptist.* It is very interesting to know this description of John was given after John sent two of his followers to Jesus with the question, *Are You the coming One or do we look for another?* You know what had happened to John just before this. He was standing up for God's truth, denouncing evil, and was thrown into prison because he had challenged the reigning Herod for his sinful life style.

After the record of the miraculous birth of John to his aged parents, we hear nothing of him until he suddenly came on the scene preaching repentance and preparation for the coming of the Messiah. John announced that He was at hand, and soon His work of purifying Israel would begin. John's preaching, though resented by the rulers of the people, was widely accepted by the masses, and countless thousands went out into the Jordan River wilderness to hear his preaching. They were deeply moved and convicted, and accepted John's challenge to receive the baptism of repentance and cleansing which God had promised through Ezekiel long ago.(Read Ezekiel 36:24-27). It seemed as if the whole nation was on the verge of a great spiritual revival. But then John denounced the sins of Herod, and was thrown into Herod's infamous dungeon to await his fate. It was from there he sent his followers to Jesus to ask the question: *Are You the coming One, or do we look for another.* Was John discouraged, or did he fear for his disciples? Did John follow the teachings of some Rabbis who taught there would be two Messiahs? Had the long months in the dark prison sapped his faith? That is hardly possible since Jesus referred to John in glowing words of praise. The answer Jesus gave apparently satisfied John and his disciples. Jesus simply pointed out that His own ministry proved He was the true Messiah, for His works perfectly fulfilled what the Prophets had foretold of the Messiah. His answer to John is also His answer to us. He is the One true Messiah!

Prayer: Lord Jesus, You are our Messiah, our Savior and our true King. Heal us from our doubts and fears. Amen.

Hymn for the day:
Tell Me the Story of Jesus

PRAYERS & REMINDERS

_____

_____

_____

_____

_____

_____

_____

_____

_____

_____

Could We Be Wrong About Christmas?

Scripture Reading: Matthew 11:1-19

Yesterday we looked at this passage from Matthew that tells the story of how John the Baptist sent two of his disciples to Jesus with the question; *Are You the Coming One, or do we look for another?* Remember that question was asked by John after he had been cast into Herod's dungeon for standing up for the truth. We don't understand all the implications of this question, or just what John had in mind, but it was certainly a time of discouragement for this godly man whose ministry was so powerful and so greatly used of God to prepare the way for Christ's ministry. It is even possible that John was dealing with a certain degree of disillusionment about his own ministry and the apparent failure of Jesus to take over control of God's people as their true King and heir of David's throne. The point of all this is to say that very often we may feel something of the same let down feeling when it comes to Christmas. We may be tempted to think deep down inside, if Jesus truly was and is the Messiah, why are things in such a mess in this world and in my own private world? If the Angel's song, *Peace on earth, good will towards man* is true, where is that peace and good will we still sing about every Christmas season, but see so little of the rest of the year? The answer Jesus sent back to John was a reminder that He was doing exactly what the Prophets of old had foretold of His ministry. Then he added this gentle rebuke: *And blessed is he who is not offended because of Me.* We need to hear those words and consider them carefully. Why would we be disappointed and questioning about the reality of the Christmas message. Did not Jesus fulfill all that the Prophets had spoken of old? Did He not live that perfect life of obedient righteousness which would be credited to our account by God the Father? Did He not die on the cross as the sin offering for us, and the perfect sacrifice to atone for all our sins? Was He not raised again from the dead for our justification? What more can God to demonstrate His great love for us while we were still sinners? How dare we doubt the message of Christmas. *Do you, too, want to go away?* Jesus asked His twelve disciples when the vast multitudes turned away from Him. Let their answer be ours this Christmas season. *Lord, to whom shall we go? You alone have the words of eternal life....and we believe and know that You are the Christ, the Son of the living God.*

Prayer: Indeed, Lord, to whom could we go if we turn away from You in disappointment or disillusionment? You alone are the Christ, and You alone have the words of eternal life and joy. **Amen.**

Hymn for the day:
To Us A Child of Hope Is Born

PRAYERS & REMINDERS

December 18

Christmas Imperatives

Scripture Reading: Luke 2:8-20

About this time of year, and hopefully even much sooner, people are frantically checking their list of things which must be done before Christmas. (Like finishing this month's devotionals!) How about your must list? People you want to see, like shut-ins, folks in nursing homes or hospitals? There are so many pressures on us all at Christmas time.

In this Scripture from Luke, we are reminded again of the right kind of Christmas imperatives. And for the right reasons. The message of the Angels to the shepherds placed on thee simple men some very heavy pressures. First of all they were commanded to believe the incredible. To these despised and looked down upon men, God's Angel came telling them *For unto you is born this day...a Savior who is Christ the Lord!* The promised King had at last come but not in the expected way. *You will find the baby wrapped in swaddling clothes(rags) lying in a manger.* Believe the incredible! This was and still is the first imperative of Christmas. Can you hear and see what they saw? Can your mind and heart believe what they believed? To believe the message that God was in Christ, reconciling the world unto Himself is the grand imperative for those who would celebrate Christmas, the birthday of our Lord. The next imperative grows out the first. *Let us now go even unto Bethlehem and see this thing which has come to pass, which the Lord has made known unto us.* They were ready for the next which was to have the message confirmed, and that required the step of faith, going to Bethlehem to actually see what they professed to believe. Faith took them on a journey and it always does. Faith in the message leads to a valid experience of receiving Christ as your Lord and Savior. Faith rests upon Him alone for salvation. Faith becomes the dynamic power within your life changing you and how you live. How is it with you? Has your assent to the propositional truth of Scripture penetrated your heart and life to the extent that others see what Christ has done for you? The final imperative is seen so clearly in these words: *Now when they had seen Him, they made widely known the saying which was told them concerning this child.* Come and see is followed by go and tell. Where do you stand on that imperative?

Prayer: Thank You, Lord Jesus! We believe Your word. We have experienced Your grace. We too, would tell others of You. Amen.

Hymn for the day:
Go Tell It on the Mountain

PRAYERS & REMINDERS

December 19

Conceived by the Holy Ghost

Scripture Reading: Isaiah 7:14; Matthew 1:18-25

The doctrine of the virgin birth of our Lord Jesus is one of the most important doctrines in the bible. However, there is one which precedes it and is just as important and which really gives to the doctrine of the virgin birth its true meaning. This doctrine is found in these words from the Apostles' Creed; *Conceived by the Holy Ghost.* But what exactly do we mean by this? We are all familiar with the process of human conception and birth. We know that God uses the physical union between husband and wife, man and woman , to bring forth children. This has been so from the very beginning of the human race, following the creation of mankind, male and female in God's image. After the fall, God did say words to Eve, which were the first indication that there would be one great exception to the normal process of pro-creation. He referred to "the seed of the woman". This was not a grammatical error and a careless use of words. It was and is a precise statement which laid the foundation for the fact and the doctrine of the "immaculate conception" that is the conception of Jesus in the womb of the virgin Mary apart from the physical union of male and female. I know the expression "Immaculate Conception" is sadly misused by one major branch of Christendom, but the only correct way to use this expression is in reference to the conception of our Lord's earthly body by the power of the Holy Spirit. To use this expression as some do in reference to Mary's birth dilutes and denigrates this great doctrine of Christ. The language used in both Matthew and Luke, concerning the activity of the Holy Spirit in the conception of Christ is remarkably similar to the description of the Holy Spirit's role in the creation of the world as given in Genesis 1. There we read; *And the Spirit of God was hovering(brooding) over the face of the waters.* When Gabriel announced to Mary that she would conceive and bear a Son, he explained to her that this conception would come about by a creative act of the Holy Spirit, so that which would be born of her would be called the Son of God. Therefore we sing, and rightly so, *Veiled in flesh, the God-head see, Hail incarnate Deity!*

Prayer: O Holy Spirit, by Your mighty, creative power our Lord Jesus, God's eternal begotten Son became also a man, bone of our bone, and flesh of our flesh. Glory to God in the highest. Amen.

Hymn for the day:
Hark! The Herald Angels Sing

PRAYERS & REMINDERS

Born of the Virgin Mary

Scripture Reading: Matthew 2:18-25

One of the great towering peaks of revelation is the Virgin Birth of our Lord Jesus Christ. It is also one of the great stumbling stones of Christian doctrine which offends many and is used as an excuse to reject the whole message of Christ and Christmas. Even more lamentable and even pathetic is the effort on the part of many so-called theologians to explain away and thus deny this vital and necessary doctrine of Christ. Some argue that since neither John, Mark, nor the Apostle Paul mention the virgin birth in their writings, therefore it must not be true; and if true then totally unimportant. What a ridiculous argument! In the first place, how many times must God reveal so explicitly one of His great truths before we condescend to believe it? The same people who reject this doctrine on that flimsy excuse would not accept it if it were written on every line of God's revelation, the bible. As for saying John made no reference to the Virgin Birth is not an accurate statement. He may not have been as explicit as Matthew or Luke, but consider these words from John 1:12-14. *But as many as received Him, to them He gave the right to become the children of God...who were born not of blood nor of the will of man, but of God. And the Word became flesh and dwelt among us, and we beheld His glory; glory as the only Begotten of the Father.* By deduction if the new birth of believers is an act of God, the implication strongly suggests it follows the pattern of the birth of Christ. The Word who came and dwelt among us was *begotten of the Father.* And the instrument the Father chose to use was the same Holy Spirit who was involved when God created the earth. So acceptance of the biblical account of the Virgin Birth is an essential item of faith, for by accepting the written word, we accept the living Word. And likewise, by rejecting the written word, and we reject the living Word.

Prayer: Father, we offer all praise and adoration to You for Your glorious truth and mighty power. We accept with joy and wonder the great truth of the Virgin Birth. Even more we accept by faith and with unbounded joy Your Son, our Savior, born of the Virgin Mary. Amen.

Hymn for the day:
What Child is This?

PRAYERS & REMINDERS

December 21

God's Sovereign Providence

Scripture Reading: Luke 2:1-7

These familiar words, *And it came to pass in those days that a decree went out from Caesar Augustus that all the world should be registered,* tell us a marvelous truth that God is not only in control of people and nations, but that in the wisdom of His marvelous providence, He is working out His plan of salvation through all of the events and human factors involved in the entire history of the world. Caesar had no idea that he was a mere pawn in the hands of the Emperor of the universe. Cyrus the Persian Potentate centuries before this, had no thought that in decreeing the Jews could return to Jerusalem and re-build the temple he was merely carrying out a promise God had made to the Jews through Jeremiah 70 years before his time. He did not even know that one of God's Prophets, Isaiah, had called him by name at least two hundred years before he was born, and called him God's servant, whom He had anointed for this task of restoring Israel to their home land.

Nevertheless, that is the mighty God we serve. There is a grand plan of redemption, and that is what Christmas is all about. But sometimes we forget how grand and all inclusive this plan of God is. *The decrees of God are His eternal purpose, according to the counsel of His will; whereby, for His own glory, He has foreordained whatsoever comes to pass.* The far reaching implications of this are mind boggling. If Caesar's selfish and autocratic decree was ordained of God that Jesus might be born in Bethlehem, then everything about the history and fortunes of the Roman Empire was also ordained of God, including the eventual defeat of Hannibal and the Carthaginians, and the fall of all other kingdoms which made up the Roman Empire. And what does all this have to do with Christmas. Namely this: God is in control, and God's plan of redemption including the birth of Christ in Bethlehem and all other events as they unfold will be for His glory, and for our salvation.

Prayer: Great and sovereign God, we praise You and worship you, for You are King of kings, and Lord of Lords.

Hymn for the day:
All Praise to Thee, Eternal Lord

PRAYERS & REMINDERS

December 22

Mary, the Mother of Jesus

Scripture Reading: Luke 1:26-38

Christmas is God's gift to the world, and in a very real sense it is also woman's gift to the world. God had promised that the "Seed of the woman" would finally conquer Satan who had deceived our first parents and led them into the disastrous fall. Satan had sorely wounded the human race, but his final fall and destruction were assured by God's promise to Eve so long ago. For Christ was born of Mary, a pure virgin, in whose body God wrought a miracles of creation apart from the ordinary means of pro-creation, the union of male and female.

Could it be that this is why women, and especially mothers, play such a prominent role in our celebration of Christmas? My own Father was a godly man but it is mother I remember most clearly at Christmas time. I guess this may be because father was so busy earning a living for his wife and five little children, that he had to leave most Christmas preparation to mother. My two older sisters followed in their mother's footsteps and even before they left to start families of their own, they helped to make sure that baby brother(me!) had a very merry Christmas. There was another woman who played a very important part in my early Christmas memories, a childhood friend of mother, who never married and had no children of her own. But she loved mother and always sent wonderful Christmas presents to all of he children. Some years she made the difference between having Christmas presents or not. We called her Aunt Dobby, and I never knew her real name till much later. Many years ago I wrote about Aunt Dobby, and unknown to me at the time, she was still living, and in a nursing home. Some one who knew her sent her my article, and I was told she felt like all her generosity to us was amply rewarded. It is so unfortunate that the real Mary of Scripture has been obscured by the Mariolatry cult and legend taught by one major branch of the Christian Church. The real Mary of Scripture is such a splendid person and a great example to all, women and men, of what it means to be a servant of Christ. We do not worship , but we admire and respect her and give God glory that such a woman was found to be the earthly mother of the Lord Jesus.

Prayer: Dear Lord, thank You so much for the godly example the virgin Mary is to all believers. Thank You for her submission to Your will and calling. We thank You also for our mothers, wives, sisters and all women who have enriched our lives. In Jesus' name. Amen.

Hymn for the day:
Gentle Mary Laid Her Child

PRAYERS & REMINDERS

Triumph Over Tragedy

Scripture Reading: Luke 2:22-38

There is so much suffering in this world. So many of you are dealing with very serious health problems, employment difficulties, grief that will not go away, and a host of other things which are very trying. Our own nation is once more engaged in warfare. Young men and women are dying far from home. There are deep divisions in this country which threaten to tear us apart . The once widely accepted Judeo-Christian consensus which was once our foundation seems to have been abandoned. Yet in the midst of all this, Christmas rushes down upon us again. There is a feeling of the unreal, that we are taking a brief respite from harsh and painful reality for a day or two, and then its back to normal. And we really don't much like what normal is.

Let's go back to the first Christmas, the time when Christ was born. Things weren't much better back then, and maybe a lot worse. God's people were in bondage to the Romans. The influence of Greco-Roman culture had eroded the once pure and noble religion of the Jews. The country was in turmoil, and no one was safe. A young man named Joseph and his pregnant wife had to make a long trip right aft the time her baby was due. She had that baby in a barn because there was no room in the Inn for them. Here is a young woman, probably in her teens, having her first baby in a barn unattended except for her frightened husband. Not too long after His birth, King Herod ordered all the male babies born in the area of Bethlehem killed. When Jesus' parents took Him to the temple for the required rites of the covenant, they were told their baby would be the occasion for great division among the people, and as a result, Mary's heart would be broken. But in the midst of all this suffering and tragedy God was working out the greatest triumph over evil and suffering the world had ever experienced. He is still at work doing the same thing in countless lives, and promises that one day all tragedy will end, and the victory will be complete and glorious beyond all thought. The tiny sip of joy we receive at Christmas will give way to a banquet of love and joy which will never end. Merry Christmas, and may God bless us, every one.

Prayer: Great and loving God, in the midst of the tragedy of sin and all its hideous consequences, You have won the great victory and so we live in hope through Christ our Lord. Amen.

Hymn for the day:
Good Christian Men, Rejoice!

PRAYERS & REMINDERS

_____

_____

_____

_____

_____

_____

_____

_____

_____

_____

December 24

A Devotional for Christmas Eve

Scripture Reading: Luke 2:1-20

The weary travelers were streaming into Bethlehem by the hundreds and maybe the thousands. It was the same in all the villages, towns and cities in Judea, Galilee, Samaria, and all over the Roman world, in the conquered provinces and countries. Mighty Caesar Augustus had decreed a census for the purpose of taxation. The decree required that all people return to their ancestral homes for this census. Nine months before this, a young virgin girl named Mary and been visited by God's Angel who brought the most unlikely news imaginable. At first frightened, and confused, still Mary had accepted her role as the mother of the Messiah, without fully understanding how this could possibly be since she was not yet married and was still a virgin. The Angel had explained it all to her, telling her that by the power of the Holy Spirit, she would conceive and bear a Son, to whom the Lord God would give the throne of David. Knowing what this could mean for her, the loss of her betrothed, the loss of respect, and maybe the loss of her life, Mary simply said, *Behold the handmaid of My Lord. Be it unto me according to your word.*

But what about her intended husband Joseph the carpenter, would he believe and accept her still? Not at first, of course. He was planning to privately divorce her, but once again God's Angel came and told him the same story Mary heard. So together they committed their lives to the Lord and rejoiced in their chosen roles. Then came the decree, and Joseph had no choice but to go to Bethlehem, and of course take Mary with him, for who could he trust to care for her and help with the baby when it came? Who indeed believed their amazing story? So to Bethlehem they came and while they were there, *the days were accomplished that she should be delivered. And she brought forth her firstborn Son, and wrapped Him in swaddling clothes and laid Him in a Manger, because there was no room for them in the inn.*

Now here it is Christmas Eve again, and the old, old story which is ever new, brings joy to our hearts and tears to our eyes, and so many memories to our minds and hearts. God grant you his peace, love and joy this Christmas Eve.

Prayer: Savior of the world, renew our faith and love this holy night. Calm our hearts from all fears, wipe away all our tears. Lift up Your countenance upon us and grant us Your peace. Amen.

Hymns for Christmas Eve:
Silent Night; Away in a Manger

PRAYERS & REMINDERS

_____

_____

_____

_____

_____

_____

_____

_____

_____

_____

A Devotional for Christmas Day

Scripture Readings: John 1:1-18; Galatians 4:1-7

But when the fullness of time had come, God sent forth His Son, born of a woman, born under the law, to redeem those who were under the law, that we might receive the adoption as sons. Our understanding of the truth and beauty of Christmas with all its joy, wonder and love, must begin with an understanding of the glory of our Savior before His birth in Bethlehem's lowly manger. To know the meaning of the Christian faith in its entirety, it is essential to know that the Son of Mary, was also the Son of God from all eternity; that He was with God and was God from the very beginning. Knowing this, the wonder of His birth increases until neither heart nor mind can contain the mystery and the joy. It was from heaven's highest throne He came to the manger stall. From the from the constantly thrilling chorus of Angelic hosts, singing His praises day and night, He came to hear His young virgin mother crooning her Jewish lullabies accompanied by the bleating of lambs, and the lowing of cattle. Thus He, mighty Prince of heaven, came to earth, only to be rejected by those to whom He came with salvation and grace. *He came unto His own, and His own received Him not.* He, the Lord of creation, came in such humility and loving condescension, yet there was no room in the Inn of Bethlehem for His mother to birth Him. It is customary for us to berate the Inn-Keeper who turned away Joseph and Mary when the need for shelter was so obvious. We wonder why more people did not recognize and accept Him, for He did works no mere man could do, and spoke words of truth and authority. The leaders of the Jews were frightened at the thought they might lose their power and position. The Romans for the most part simply ignored or scorned Him. But isn't it true that we also have our own ways of rejecting or ignoring Him? The Jews refused to crown Him as their King, and modern folk in His church deny the crown over their lives too. This Christmas day may the mighty Prince of heaven who came to earth for our salvation receive the honor and homage due Him from those He came to save. May God bless us, everyone.

Prayer: Thank You, O Son of God, for entering this sin-cursed world to redeem those the Father had given You from before the foundation of the earth. Take the throne of Your Church and of each one of us Your children, and reign over us now and forever. Amen.

Hymn for the day:
Joy to the World

PRAYERS & REMINDERS

_____

_____

_____

_____

_____

_____

_____

_____

_____

December 26

Christmas After the Angels Leave

Scripture Reading: Luke 2:15-20

And it came to pass, after the Angels had gone away from them into heaven... There is something almost sad about these words. This reminds me of the feelings I used to have when I was a little boy, the day after Christmas. Can you believe Christmas is already over? The calendar of events leading up to Christmas was so crowded; the demands of shopping , wrapping, and mailing were so overwhelming. The gathering of family and dear friends are so sweet, but now its all over for another year. Many people have already taken down their beautifully decorated Christmas trees. Some of you plan to go to the mall or department store to exchange or return gifts that were the wrong size or color. It may be an ugly scene at the store with people vying for the reduced price items they all want. There will not be very much peace or good will then. The "post Christmas" blues leave a bad taste and a let down feeling. Shame on us, for allowing the world's understanding of Scripture to define who we are in our celebration of the dear Lord's birth!

So what did the shepherds say and do after the Angels had gone back to heaven? *Let us go, even unto Bethlehem and see this thing which has come to pass. Which the Lord has made known unto us.* The one thing which was so overwhelming to the shepherds was not that they had seen and heard Angels, but rather what the Lord had made known unto them through the Angels. Angels may come and go, but the word of God abides forever. The celebrations of Christmas come and go with each year, but the message of Christmas is timeless. The shepherds did not allow the beauty of the Angels, nor the stark simplicity of the manger scene to obscure the glory of the message: *Unto you is born this day, in the city of David a Savior, who is Christ the Lord.* Let us make very sure that in all our celebrations of Christmas, we do nothing to obscure that message the Angels brought to the shepherds. Let the Apostle Paul sum it up in these well known words from 2 Corinthians: *God was in Christ, reconciling the world unto Himself, not imputing their trespasses unto them, and has committed unto us the ministry of reconciliation.*

Prayer: Gracious Father, on this first day after Christmas may we not lose the wonder of the what You have given to Your precious elect; *A Savior who is Christ the Lord.* May we ever celebrate and rejoice in Your gift to us every day so long as we live. In Jesus' name. Amen.

Hymn for the day:
God Rest You Merry, Gentlemen

PRAYERS & REMINDERS

The Good Bad News

Scripture Reading: Matthew 2:13-23

If you read the above Scripture, you have probably already guessed what the "good bad news" is all about. If you have not already found this out, let me quote these words from Matthew 2:20: *Those who sought the young child's life are dead.* Herod the Great, king of Judea was dead at last. But oh the suffering, pain, and sorrow He had inflicted upon so many people. He was the almost evil incarnate. Certainly he had given himself over to his anger, fears, suspicions, ungodly ambitions until he was a blight and a curse to the whole nation of Israel, and to all its people. We are first introduced to this madman in the story of the visit of the Magi to Jerusalem, *seeking Him who as born King of the Jews.* Those honest words of the seeking Magi enraged Herod and filled his heart with anger and fear. Truly he was troubled and all Jerusalem with him. Herod knew the Jews had never really accepted him as the true king, for he was not a Jew by birth nor by faith, though he had built the magnificent Temple in an attempt to win over the Jewish people to his side and cause. Then came these travelers from the east with what Herod saw as a message of doom for him. So he attempted to disguise his evil intentions by charging the Magi: *God and search diligently for the young child, and when you have found him, bring me word that I may come and worship him also.* The Magi may have been suspicious, but when they left Jerusalem for Bethlehem, they probably had all good intentions to return to Herod and bring him word. But you know the story well of how these good men were warned by God in a dream not to return to Herod, so they departed for their own country by another way. Soon Herod knew that he had been tricked, so in order to carry out his evil scheme, he sent his death squad to Bethlehem with orders to kill all the male children from two years old and under just to make sure the child sought by the Magi as the King of the Jews, would never live to claim that crown. Herod had not counted on an Angel warning good Joseph in a dream which led to the escape of him and his family, including the child Jesus. After a few years another Angel informed Joseph that he might return home, *For they are dead who sought the young child's life.* In God's good time all evil will fail, and all evil men will be judged, but those for whom *The young Child died,* will be safe in heaven forever.

Prayer: Father, thank You for this reminder that You have won, and will win the victory over Satan and all his followers, and that Your people will be rescued from all evil in Your good time, through Christ. Amen.

Hymn for the day:
I Heard the Bells on Christmas Day

PRAYERS & REMINDERS
_____
_____
_____
_____
_____
_____
_____
_____
_____
_____

December 28

The Greatness of Christ

Scripture Reading: Micah 5:2-5; Luke 1:26-33

If there is one over-worked word in the English Language, it is the word *great*. I realize that for many in this present generation (Is it X, Y, or Z?) the word *great* has been largely replaced by the word *awesome*, but let's remember that the word *great* is still much over used. Most of the time we use this word it is probably an exaggeration, especially as it applies to people. However there is One whose birthday we have just celebrated who was and is truly great in every sense of the word. His name is Jesus. When Gabriel made his amazing announcement to Mary, he said of the coming child she would bear, *He shall be great, and shall be called the Son of the Highest; and the Lord God will give Him the throne of His father, David; and he shall reign over the house of Israel forever; and of His kingdom there shall be no end.* These words alone would earn Him the right to be called great, but there is more to His greatness then even these exalted words tell. First of all, He was great in His origins. This was no ordinary men who was born in an ordinary way; He was Spirit conceived and virgin born. But even before His earthly birth and life, He was recognized in heaven as the great Prince who would one day redeem the Father's lost children. The Prophet Micah had said of the Coming One, *His goings forth are from old, even from everlasting.* What a clear teaching of the dual nature and exalted personage of our Lord. A Baby born in Bethlehem had been from all eternity? Surely we must say of Him, *He shall be great!* Later the Apostle John in looking back on the birth, life, ministry, death and resurrection of the Lord Jesus said of Him, *In the beginning was the Word. And the Word was with God, and the Word was God. All things were made through Him...*But he was not only great in His origins, but also in His status. *The Lord God will give Him the throne of His father David, and He shall reign...forever...and of His kingdom, there shall be no end.* Finally, He was great in His accomplishments, for He won salvation for all the father had given Him, a great multitude that no one may number from every kindred, tribe and language on earth. Call Him great, for he is truly the greatest of all.

Prayer: Gracious and giving God, our heavenly Father, thank You that You have given the throne to Your Son, our Savior, the Lord Jesus Christ. What a thrill to know that He is our eternal King. Amen.

Hymn for the day:
Angels We Have Heard on High

PRAYERS & REMINDERS

_____

_____

_____

_____

_____

_____

_____

_____

_____

God's Good Gifts to the Wise Men

Scripture Reading: Matthew 2:1-12

Who has not attended or taken part in a traditional Christmas play? When I was a wee lad, the best I could ever hope for was to be one of the little shepherds who kept watch over their flock by night. Only the big boys could be wise men, and they got to dress up in resplendent garments, and carry beautifully wrapped gifts down the church aisle, while singing the verses of *We Three Kings.* My first assignment as a wise man was at the age of about 15. Fortunately my voice had already changed from boy soprano to a low baritone, and I sang the verse about the gift of myrrh. That was one of the few times I ever sang a solo outside a shower, for which all who have heard me sing within or without the shower are very thankful.

The gifts of the Magi were symbolic of greater things, but they were also , and even more so symbolic of the gifts God gave the wise men and us. The gift of gold was a symbol of royalty, and so we sing, *Born a King on Bethlehem's plain, gold I bring to crown Him again, King forever...*Yes, the Magi found Him who was *born King of the Jews.* God's gift to them and us in His Son is a King who conquers all His and our enemies. The next gift was Frankincense. In the homeland of the Magi, the incense of Frankincense was offered to the gods as an oblation. The Magi offered their incense to the One true God. The Savior God gave so long ago was also God the Son in human flesh, and we still worship Him as such, and bring Him the incense of our prayers and devotion. Myrrh, third gift they brought Him, was frequently used for embalming the dead, and its strong and bitter order overwhelmed the unpleasant order of the dead. Though they did not fully understand the significance of their gift, still it was appropriate, for when the Savior's body was laid in Joseph's tomb, His friends planned to come after the Sabbath and anoint His dead body with spices and perfumes, perhaps even myrrh. The Savior suffered and died on the cross as our sin offering and substitute. These gifts God gave to the Magi of old and to us.

Prayer: Lord, all gifts we would give Thee, pale into insignificance compared to Your gift of salvation through Your Son, whom You gave for our salvation. Thank You so much for Him. Amen.

Hymn for the day:
We Three Kings

PRAYERS & REMINDERS

December 30

Christ Rejected by His Own

Scripture Reading: John 1:1-13

    The magnificent prologue of John's Gospel contain some of the most majestic words to be found in all of holy writ. *In the beginning was the Word; and the Word was with God, and the Word was God. All thing were created through Him and without Him nothing was created that was created. In Him was life, and the life was the Light of men.* How much clearer could the inspired writer possibly be? A few lines later, the announcement is made, *And the Word was made flesh and dwelt among us, and we beheld His glory, the glory of the only begotten of the Father, full of grace and truth.* From these words we learn that the Lord Jesus who was born in Bethlehem was none less than the great Creator God, who shared equally with the Father His nature and His glory. Yet this mighty Creator became man, and lived among us as a man, but also as God.

    Between the words in the first five verses of this chapter, and verse 14, there is a terribly dissonant note inject. *He was in the world, and the world was made through Him, and the world did not know Him. He came to His own, but His own did not receive Him.* In these words we find the great tragedy of the long history of mankind. In the very beginning, Adam and Eve refused to accept God's word and authority over them, and miserably fell into sin. Then when the plan of redemption, first announced to fallen mankind in the spoiled garden of Eden, was revealed to chosen Israel, the redeemer was rejected and refused. It seems so incomprehensible, until we examine our own hearts and lives and see to our shame the many ways we refuse Christ's authority over our lives. May it not be said of us who confess Him anew this Christmas time, *He came unto His own, and His own did not receive Him*!

Prayer: Gracious Lord, as we look beyond the celebration of Your holy birth and face the coming year, may we ever receive, trust and obey Him who came to save us from our Sins, the incarnate Word of God. May our celebration and our praise gladden Your great heart and please You. Amen.

Hymn for the day:
O Little Town of Bethlehem

PRAYERS & REMINDERS

Christ Received

Scripture Reading: John 1:1-18

But as many as received Him, to then He gave the right to become children of God, to those who believe in His name...and of His fullness we have all received, and grace for grace. The sad story of *He came unto His own, and His own did not receive Him,* is met and overcome by the joyful news that those who did receive Him received the incredible gift of becoming children of the heavenly Father. What greater gift could ever be given or received than this? In my childhood years, the aftermath of the great depression still lay heavily on most people in this country and around the world. By today's standards, most of us lived in poverty. Christmas presents were far fewer than even those who live in poverty today. There were no "toys for tots" or any other benevolent attempts to give Christmas toys to little children. Still we were happy and thrilled to get the things we did receive. When I was about eight years old, the impossible dream came true for me one Christmas. I got TWO wonderful presents, a big red wagon, and a wind up train(No batteries needed). I could hardly believe my good fortune, and the generosity of my parents and my aunt Dobby! All the presents of my many years since then have been measured by those two special gifts of long ago.

Here in this passage from John we are told of the most wonderful gift possible, adoption into God's family, for those who receive His Son. This is God's greatest gift. John also makes it very clear that those who receive His Son are those *who were born not of blood, nor of the will of the flesh, nor of the will of man, but of God.* I love the balance we find in these words between God's sovereignty in salvation and human responsibility and accountability. As we come to the end of this advent season, and stand on the threshold of a new year, let our gratitude and our resolution blend in with our determination that we will live as those who have truly received the Lord Jesus Christ as our Savior from sin, and the Lord of our lives. May the world know that we ar children of the heavenly Father who may be known because: *Of His fullness we have all received, and grace for grace.*

Prayer: Dear Heavenly Father, thank You for Christ and for Christmas. Help us to always celebrate the Birth of Your Son, our Savior with great joy and gratitude, and in a way that will honor Him and glorify You. We ask this in His name, for His sake. Amen.

Hymn for the day:
O Come All Ye Faithful

PRAYERS & REMINDERS

_____
_____
_____
_____
_____
_____
_____
_____
_____

Date

Printed in the United States
132099LV00002B/2/P